Sixth
Cartesian
Meditation

Studies in Continental Thought

John Sallis, general editor

EUGEN FINK

Sixth Cartesian Meditation

THE IDEA OF A
TRANSCENDENTAL THEORY
OF METHOD

WITH TEXTUAL NOTATIONS BY
EDMUND HUSSERL

TRANSLATED WITH AN INTRODUCTION BY
Ronald Bruzina

INDIANA UNIVERSITY PRESS
BLOOMINGTON & INDIANAPOLIS

Published in German as Eugen Fink, *VI. Cartesianische Meditation*.Teil 1.

Die Idee Einer Transzendentalen Methodenlehre, edited by Hans Ebeling, Jann Holl, and Guy van Kerckhoven.

Manufactured in the United States of America

Library of Congress Cataloging-in-Publication Data
Fink, Eugen.
[Idee einer transzendentalen Methodenlehre. English]
Sixth Cartesian meditation : the idea of a transcendental theory of method / Eugen Fink ; with the complete textual notations by Edmund Husserl ; translated with an introduction by Ronald Bruzina.
p. cm. — (Studies in Continental thought)
Translation of: VI. cartesianische Meditation. T. 1.
Includes bibliographical references and index.
ISBN 0–253–32273–1 (alk. paper)
1. Husserl, Edmund, 1859–1938. Cartesianische Meditationen.
2. Phenomenology. I. Husserl, Edmund, 1859–1938. II. Title.
III. Title: 6th Cartesian meditation. IV. Title: Idea of a transcendental theory of method. V. Series.
B3279.H94F4913 1995
193—dc20 94–34

1 2 3 4 5 00 99 98 97 96 95

Contents

TRANSLATOR'S INTRODUCTION   vii

                                      ❧

[DRAFT OF A FOREWORD]   1

PREFATORY NOTE [TO THE HABILITATION TEXT]. DECEMBER, 1945   2

SIXTH [CARTESIAN] MEDITATION
The Idea of a Transcendental Theory of Method

§1.   The methodological limitation of the previous Meditations   3
§2.   The theme of the transcendental theory of method   10
§3.   The "self-reference" of phenomenology   13
§4.   The problem and articulation of the transcendental theory
       of method   19
§5.   Phenomenologizing as the action of reduction   29
§6.   Phenomenologizing as a process of regressive analysis   48
§7.   Phenomenologizing in "constructive" phenomenology   54
§8.   Phenomenologizing as theoretical experience   66
§9.   Phenomenologizing as an action of ideation   77
§10.   Phenomenologizing as predication   84
§11.   Phenomenologizing as "making into a science"   100
       A) The problem of the scientificity of phenomenologizing   101
       B) The enworlding of phenomenologizing   106
       C) The concept of "science"   133
§12.   "Phenomenology" as transcendental idealism   152

APPENDICES
Texts by Edmund Husserl relating to Eugen Fink's
Draft of a Sixth Meditation

A. Appended pages and insertions *(from Summer 1933 to January 1934)*   163
    Appendix I   163
    Appendix II   163
    Appendix III   165
    Appendix IV   165
    Appendix V   166
    Appendix VI   167
    Appendix VII   168
    Appendix VIII   170
    Appendix IX   171
B. Comments and research notes   174
    Appendix X   174
    Appendix XI   178
    Appendix XII   181
C. Unassigned pages   188
    Appendix XIII   188
    Appendix XIV   190
    Appendix XV   191

TRANSLATOR'S NOTES   193

INDEX   201

TRANSLATOR'S INTRODUCTION

Eugen Fink's "Sixth Cartesian Meditation" is one of those famous unknown works in philosophy that haunt the margins of established texts while seldom if ever coming to light themselves, at least in any form other than scant fragments. Occasionally, however, one of these missing writings does become accessible in full and is at last itself known, and this is the case with the present publication. For a whole generation of philosophers in phenomenology—which is a long time in the modern age of rapid and extensive communication and scholarship—the Sixth Meditation was a work known to have been written, yet one that very few had ever seen, one that could easily be presumed not to have survived the descent of fascism and war upon Europe. Those who had read the Sixth Meditation were individuals who had maintained a close connection with Edmund Husserl even as the times darkened after 1933, and as acknowledgment of Husserl's accomplishments and of his very name came to be suppressed in Germany. Published mention of the Sixth Meditation first occurred in 1941 in France, in Gaston Berger's *Le cogito dans la philosophie de Husserl*,[1] to be followed only after the end of the war by reference to it in Maurice Merleau-Ponty's *Phénoménologie de la perception*.[2]

It was most natural, then, that, when the editing of Husserl's Cartesian Meditations was under way for the first volume of the Husserliana edition, interest would again turn to this text of Fink's. Stephan Strasser spoke of it in his editor's introduction to the *Cartesianische Meditationen*,[3] expressing the hope that, while the Sixth Meditation did not figure into the edition he was preparing, it would nevertheless be itself published as part of the whole set of revision texts that Fink had produced for Husserl for the Cartesian Meditations in that earlier decade. The texts in question—the Sixth Meditation itself and these revision texts for Husserl's earlier five Cartesian Meditations—were and are not, however, part of the Husserl *Nachlass* in the Archives in Louvain.[4]

Apart from the period when Fink resided and lectured at Louvain (from the spring of 1939 to the autumn of 1940),[5] these texts were not available even there; and not until 1971 were copies finally provided for the Husserl Archives. Arrangements for their publication got under way only after Fink's death in 1975 and after the opening of the adjunct series, Husserliana Dokumente, in 1977. It is in this series, now, that the texts have finally appeared in a two-volume edition, Eugen Fink, *VI. Cartesianische Meditation,* Part I: *Die Idee einer Transzendentalen Methodenlehre,* ed. Hans Ebeling, Jann Holl, and Guy van Kerckhoven; Part II: *Ergänzungsband,* ed. Guy van Kerckhoven.[6] It is the text of the first of these two volumes that is integrally translated here.

The question of how and why these texts were preserved and yet kept private is directly bound up with the history of their origin, which includes naturally the nature of their content. They are the product of an intimate collaborative effort on the part of two philosophers, one an established and world-renowned master, the other a youthful scholar who had just finished his doctoral work. Each had an independent mind, each highly valued the other's work, and both were deeply involved in a shared project of philosophic investigation and reflection. Yet they were different individuals in this common project; and so the project acquired from the one differing emphases and a differing character than it did from the other. Both were beginners, but differently: one was a beginner in the final stage of a lifelong thinking,[7] the other a beginner in the first realization of what would be a similar dedication. It will not be possible in this introduction to treat in any great detail the identities and differences between these two linked endeavors; and yet something of this will have to be covered, for the nature of the documents given here in English is such that the primary thing is precisely the interplay of the two thinkings. When one considers what this final period of Husserl's thinking is taken to represent, namely, the culmination of an originally Cartesian impetus that is being at the same time transcended, then the documented record of the direct interplay, the dialogue, of these two minds deep within transcendental phenomenology takes on special importance.

When we look at the title of the main text of the present translated volume, we should notice two things. First, we have here the *sixth* of a series of "Cartesian" meditations; second, the subtitle of this sixth "Cartesian" meditation, "The Idea of a Transcendental Theory of Method," is frankly Kantian. We must understand, then, what the fuller context and principal orientation of this piece are in order to interpret it properly.

In the first place, it must be recognized that Fink's Sixth Meditation was meant to follow not upon Husserl's Cartesian Meditations as they have become familiar to us up until now,[8] but upon an extensively reworked version that was produced three years after Husserl's first full revision in 1929. Fink himself described this new context in 1946 in a letter to H. L. Van Breda, then in the midst of planning the first publication of materials from the *Nachlass*, namely, the German text of Husserl's Cartesian Meditations. Fink writes:

> The glad news about the work of the Husserl Archives and its forthcoming publications is most welcome. Above all the editing of the German text of the Méditations Cartésiennes is urgently needed. As you perhaps know, Husserl was not ready to publish the German text, because he saw major shortcomings in its presentation. In the years 1932–33, when Husserl was preoccupied with the idea of this project, producing a German edition, I had to draft for him a reworking of the Cartesian Meditations.

Fink goes on to describe briefly his revision texts (all of which are now in the *Ergänzungsband*), and then goes on to say:

> After the appearance of the German text, I shall perhaps publish these revision proposals of mine for the Cartesian Meditations, proposals that Husserl had accepted. . . . As a complement to the Louvain edition of the Meditations this may have a certain historical significance, for it shows those points on which Husserl was open to a reshaping of his text. Husserl had adopted my proposals so fully that, at the time, he proposed to me that my revisions of his text and my entirely new "Sixth Meditation" (on the idea of a transcendental theory of method) be included in the planned German edition and published under joint authorship. Political developments after 1933 made it impossible to proceed with this plan.[9]

What we shall be primarily interested in is the substance of the revisions Fink had drafted for Husserl, including their culmination in the new Sixth Meditation, and the implications they held for Husserl's further work in this final period of his life; for what comes clear in them is that they contribute positively and directly to the displacement of a Cartesian-based exposition of phenomenology. To understand what these revisions represent, however, we have to know more both about the place Fink had in the enterprise of thinking that embraced both Husserl and him, and as well about the resources and concerns that Fink himself brought to his work in that enterprise. We shall therefore first review in some detail the history of the revision work on the Cartesian Meditations as it involved both Husserl and Fink, and then look more closely at the special role Fink played in Husserl's work and thinking during this final period. That done, we shall be able to focus on the texts themselves. In the course of looking at the texts it will become clear what special philosophic resources Fink was contributing to the rethinking of tran-

scendental phenomenology that is so prominent in Husserl's final efforts and
that has so strongly marked phenomenological work since.

I. Husserl's Cartesian Meditations and their revision[10]

Much is familiar regarding Husserl's preparation of an introduction to phenomenology under the title "Cartesian Meditations." The occasion was a joint
invitation from the Institut d'Études germaniques and the Société française de
Philosophie to give a set of lectures on the "Introduction to Transcendental
Phenomenology."[11] Husserl gave his lectures in two presentations of two each
on February 23 and 25, 1929, appropriately in the Amphithéâtre Descartes in
the Sorbonne. The success of his lecturing in France, which included four eminently successful days in Strasbourg, led to an arrangement for translating
into French and then publishing a more fully worked out version of his Cartesian Meditations; thus, upon his return to Freiburg (March 12), Husserl set to
work upon a revision of his Paris lectures. This revision took from the middle
of March until the middle of May, and resulted in the text that has since become familiar under that title. With the revision done and the text sent off to
the translators in Strasbourg, Husserl felt the revision could also be published
in German before the end of the year.[12]

Within a few short months, however, Husserl was confronted with reason
to think that the Cartesian Meditations as they then were would not do as an
adequate statement of his phenomenology, especially for a German audience.
The cause for this was quite simply——Heidegger. The months from September 1928 to the summer of 1929 had been a time of feverish activity for
Husserl, involving intense productivity.[13] Once the first revision of the Cartesian Meditations was finished, Husserl had to correct the proofs for his *Formale und Transzendentale Logik* (to appear that year in his *Jahrbuch*, Vol. X); he had
written that masterful text from November 1928 to January 1929, in the three
months prior to beginning work on the lectures for Paris. And other things
were happening. In the spring of 1929 Husserl had received the first part of
Georg Misch's book *Lebensphilosophie und Phänomenologie*, which was appearing in
serial form in the journal *Philosophischer Anzeiger*.[14] Misch had dedicated this
work to Husserl "on his 70th birthday," which Husserl had celebrated on April
8. In a letter written to Misch on June 27, 1929, Husserl explained that despite the press of other work he had found some time to read Misch's essay,
and had done so with great interest.[15] Although Husserl was to give Misch's
work a really close reading only a year later, nevertheless this publicly appearing treatment of Heidegger as the representative of phenomenology most

compatible with the thought of Wilhelm Dilthey now prompted Husserl to undertake a much more serious study of Heidegger's work than he had thus far made. Once the proofreading of *Formal and Transcendental Logic* was finished (July 1), Husserl therefore turned to a careful reading of *Being and Time* and *Kant and the Problem of Metaphysics*.[16] No doubt Husserl found the need for this study reinforced by what he heard when Heidegger gave his official inaugural lecture, "Was ist Metaphysik?" (July 24). It must have clearly shown Husserl the vast differences between his own and Heidegger's conception of how philosophy was to be done and what its main themes were.

The result of Husserl's long-overdue close study of Heidegger's thought was that, barely a year after Heidegger arrived in Freiburg as Husserl's successor, and only a few months after Heidegger's last expression of praise for him at the celebration of his seventieth birthday, Husserl came to the conclusion, as he expressed it to Roman Ingarden in a letter written toward the end of 1929, that "I cannot include [his] work within the framework of my phenomenology, . . . that I must reject it entirely as to its method and in the essentials of its content."[17] That this was a sudden and harsh realization is indicated in the fact that immediately before this study of Heidegger, in checking the proofs for his *Formale und Transzendentale Logik*, Husserl had left intact a reference to the coming publication ("in autumn" he even says!) of the Cartesian Meditations in their then existing form.[18] Under the impact of his newly gained awareness, however, he could no longer deem these Meditations to be adequate.

At first Husserl thought that, in order to explain the character of his phenomenology in the context of the ascendant Heideggerian enterprise, he might add an additional, lengthy introduction to what was then to be his next book, the Cartesian Meditations, which, as already revised, were virtually ready for publication.[19] But in the course of working out the topics and points that would be needed for the explanation he envisioned, he was soon led to the conviction that more than an "introduction" was needed: the Cartesian Meditations had to be given a new, more extensive revision. In December of that year, 1929, he indicated to Ingarden that a wholesale reworking of his Cartesian Meditations into a fuller systematic treatment of his phenomenology was under way, to be ready, he hoped, by the end of the next year.[20]

Work on this new, larger-scale revision of the Meditations, however, had to face interruptions by other tasks and obligations. For example, Husserl had to go over the manuscript work that Ludwig Landgrebe was doing to prepare what would become *Erfahrung und Urteil*. That was going to take time. On March 19, 1930, Husserl wrote to Ingarden that he could not really afford just then to give it that time:

I saw that I would still need 4–6 months of work, and I simply *must not* postpone the German edition of the Cartesian Meditations that long. For this will be the main work of my life, an outline of the philosophy that has come to fruition for me, a fundamental work on methods and on the problematic of philosophy. At least *for me* [it will be] the conclusion and final clarity whose cause I can champion, with which I can die in peace. (But what is more important is that I feel called upon to intervene decisively in this way in the critical situation in which German philosophy now stands.) The little French text, appearing at Easter (about 100 pages) will *not* be a mere translation of the German, because for the German public—in its present situation (the faddish swing to a philosophy of "existence," the abandonment of "philosophy as rigorous science")—what is needed is a more extensive exposition and further elaboration right up to the highest "metaphysical" problematic. I'm working full of vigor and with extreme concentration, [but] I won't be finished with the book before autumn.[21]

The motivation for Husserl's work on an elaboration of the Cartesian Meditations beyond the form of their first revision—and the form in which alone they are still known—was clearly the need he saw for a statement of his phenomenology that would explain and assert itself in the then-current philosophical climate in Germany. He saw phenomenology being rapidly eclipsed by other movements which not only subverted the principles for which phenomenology stood but also, in his eyes, grossly misrepresented what phenomenology was really about. He had to react, hoping to be listened to. (Little did he know that he had but three more years in which his voice would even be permitted to be heard.) What happened now, as the year 1930 proceeded, can only be understood in terms of this driving motivation on Husserl's part to represent his phenomenology in an effective, comprehensive statement.

In the spring, or at the latest the early summer, of 1930 Husserl finally turned to a fuller reading of Misch's treatment of life-philosophy and phenomenology, *Lebensphilosophie und Phänomenologie*. By now Husserl had the second installment as well as the first, which in their serialization carried the subtitle "A Debate with Heidegger";[22] and what Husserl now read caused him to change his plans more radically. For Misch's treatment showed that the misunderstanding and critique of Husserl's phenomenology went beyond what Heidegger said of it. In treating Dilthey's philosophy of life as standing in stark contrast to Husserl's philosophy, Misch touched upon matters at the core of Husserl's thinking. Misch emphasized in Dilthey's program the theme of living historical movement in human existence and thought, as against what he took to be the strongly logic-centered intellectualism of Husserl's works.[23] Equally distressing on top of this was surely Misch's linking of Heidegger's analysis of "Dasein" with this positive feature of Dilthey's position, and therefore the ascription to Heidegger's work of a value beyond Husserl's. It was a far broader apologia that Husserl had to provide, if his philosophy was to be properly understood, one that would show his thinking to be at grips precisely with what was most deeply and fundamentally concrete and originative in human life. For this, something more than the Cartesian Meditations was needed.

Nor was it enough simply to produce individual studies of aspects of human beings as they were treated in Husserl's transcendental phenomenology.[24] What was needed was a *framework*, a comprehensive *plan* in terms of which one could systematically link the highest principles of phenomenological method and explanation with the most manifest and preoccupying features of real existence, so that one could show clearly and rigorously how the latter were given their true and full meaning in terms of the former. Thus was conceived the monumental project of the "System of Phenomenological Philosophy," into which Husserl now threw his efforts. And with this we begin to see the place of Eugen Fink in the economy of Husserl's final period of productivity.

The *Ergänzungsband*, which as Part 2 accompanies the volume in which the texts here translated are published, opens with the plan for this new work that Fink prepared for Husserl that very summer, the "Layout for Edmund Husserl's 'System of Phenomenological Philosophy.' "[25] Dated August 13, 1930, it was ready for Husserl to take with him on a long working holiday planned for Chiavari, on the eastern half of the Italian Riviera, where he indeed studied and annotated it.[26] It is a remarkable document, both for its scope and in its detail, especially if one compares it to the much briefer sketch of Husserl's own for the same System.[27] Both the agreements and the differences between the two conceptions merit study; but for that a more extensive treatment would be needed to make clear how each, Husserl and Fink, would actually work out the plans thus envisioned. And here is where the two volumes of the *VI. Cartesianische Meditation* take on their value; for in addition to the fact that they contain important components of *Fink's* working out of the plan for a new, full systematic statement of transcendental phenomenology, the inclusion in both volumes of all of Husserl's marginal notations, additions, and modifications to the drafts in question enables us to see in the very same text something of the way Husserl agrees with or differs from Fink's conception.

For example, one signal difference is that the whole first section of the first book in Fink's "Layout," entitled "On the Beginning and the Principle of Philosophy,"[28] is not given in Husserl's outline. What is important about this section is that it gives a place of prominence to the topic "world"—specifically, the pregivenness of the world relative to any incipient philosophical reflection—as the issue by which phenomenology opens, and to which it remains bound, in the whole idea of reduction. Furthermore, it is this very section, and it alone of his whole plan, which Fink worked out in full typescript form in December 1930 and January 1931. This is the second text published in the *Ergänzungsband*, "Draft for the opening section of an Introduction to Phenomenology,"[29] where one sees as well the numerous notations Husserl made to it—he had read it closely. This is something, again, that we shall return to later.

Fink produced this 120-page typescript after his and Husserl's return from Chiavari on November 4, 1930. The sojourn in Chiavari had been a disaster for Husserl; before the first month was out, he had contracted a serious case of bronchitis and was virtually incapacitated for the rest of his stay. Fink had to work for the most part more or less alone, on their joint projects as well as on his own research tasks.[30] But on their return, Husserl again threw himself into his work. He had now pretty well adopted the overall plan of Fink's "Layout." In the middle of the weeks during which Fink was at work on his typescript, Husserl showed his altogether positive disposition toward Fink's plan in a letter to Ingarden written December 21. In giving a brief description of "the systematic work on fundamentals in phenomenology" which he now meant to produce, Husserl follows this very conception that Fink had provided him; and after it he adds, "my most talented Fink is the vigilant helper in this, without him I would be lost."[31] (We shall return later to this kind of testimony on Husserl's part regarding Fink's role in the work of this period.)

From the spring of 1930 to the spring of 1931 Husserl produced a rich variety of *Forschungsmanuskripten* on topics such as the world of human life and history,[32] the "flowing live present" as having ultimate constitutive function,[33] and the problem of intersubjectivity, which, in contrast to the treatment in his Cartesian Meditations, was analyzed here as having a primordiality with the reflecting monadic "I."[34] One context for these studies was, of course, the philosophic situation that turned Husserl to the idea of the new comprehensive systematic presentation of phenomenology; but this was not the only task that he and Fink were laboring over. Another important project, to which we have here given no mention yet, was to bring Husserl's 1917–1918 Bernau time-consciousness studies to coherent and intelligible form, a task which Husserl had given entirely over to Fink, even while he, Husserl, was producing new materials on the question of temporality.

The extent of the work which the "System of Phenomenological Philosophy" alone would demand, however, was beginning to weigh heavily. On February 16, 1931, Husserl wrote to Ingarden:

> I'm working furiously. [But] unfortunately the new work will not be ready for
> *Jahrbuch* XI, despite the breathless efforts of the whole last year, which thank
> God! have brought a great deal of internal clarity and self-corroboration, but
> as well demanded a lot of refashioning, more precise defining, etc. I'm putting
> into the *Jahrbuch* the Cartesian Meditations (expanded by Fink and if need be
> by myself) and the Bernau manuscripts on time, which Fink by himself has al-
> ready made into a unified text (and a rather comprehensive one).[35]

Here, in telling Ingarden that, even while working on the "new work," he will
get the Cartesian Meditations out anyway, Husserl realizes he is faced with a
dilemma. On the one hand, what was really needed, and what his own rich
investigations really led to, was something broader in conception than the
Meditations; but to bring that something—embodied in the systematic plan
Fink had worked out for him—to satisfactory completion was an enormous
task. There were serious grounds for doubt that it could actually be done,
given the demands it would make upon him, especially in view of his age—
he was now in his seventy-second year—and the illnesses he seemed too often to fall prey to. On the other hand, the Cartesian Meditations were
basically finished, and thus were far closer to readiness for publication. But if
they were to be brought up to the level and comprehensiveness of Husserl's
new realizations, they would need extensive reworking; and the effort at reworking them in turn would reveal the basic limitations under which the overall conception of the Meditations suffered.

For the next three years Husserl tried to find a way through this dilemma
by in effect choosing both horns, at times with one or the other more promi-
nently featured;[36] but the way to choose both was to have Fink do the major
part of revision on one of them. So it was that Fink was to work on revamp-
ing the Cartesian Meditations, with Husserl himself joining in directly at different times, and with the two of them talking everything over as the work
advanced. For example, in the summer of 1931, after Husserl's lecture tour
to Frankfurt, Berlin, and Halle,[37] Fink produced his first revision texts for
Husserl's First Meditation, texts contained, again, in the *Ergänzungsband*.[38] The
plan for the Meditations that Fink was following, in which they would be expanded quite a bit more than in the version translated into French, had already
been sketched out earlier, in 1929 in one such sketch and in 1930 in another,
before the turn to the idea of the new systematic work. In particular, in addition to modifications in the first five Meditations, there were now to be two
entirely new Meditations.[39]

Malvine Husserl wrote to Ingarden on June 14, 1931, first to explain how
valuable Husserl had found the critical remarks Ingarden had made on the
Méditations (in the French translation), and then briefly to describe the further
work that was now to be done on them:

The German edition is in any case to be expanded and enlarged by two Meditations. Dr. Fink is working on this together with my husband, there are
still more manuscripts brought in, and everything is thoroughly discussed in
their daily walks. You know, of course, how well Fink is able to enter into
these intentions and how far his training in Husserlian phenomenology has
developed.[40]

Mrs. Husserl does not mention what the new Meditations were to be; but
Fink's own notes from the period do make clear at least Fink's ideas on this.
One of these Meditations, the Sixth, was to be a "critique of phenomenological experience and cognition," while the Seventh would be a "prospectus on
the future metaphysics of phenomenology."[41]

At this point, Husserl was once again of a mind to focus on the Meditations
rather than on the new System.[42] Yet by November Husserl reverted once
more to the prior decision: he would turn the editing of the Meditations over
to Fink entirely, and he himself would work on the System.[43]

It must be kept in mind that Husserl's repeated change of plans did not represent a shift in philosophic views. On the contrary, the constancy of the objective he had set for himself and the coherence of the insights he was gaining
in pursuit of it were precisely what provoked the oscillation between the two
alternatives. In the context of philosophies claiming to be more concrete than
transcendental phenomenology, and therefore claiming to displace it, he
wanted to compose a clear and comprehensive statement of that phenomenology that would be adequate to the situation. It is in Husserl's letters that
one sees this again and again—for example, in this one, to his oldest and closest friend, Gustav Albrecht, from December 30, 1930:

So this year I've thought and thought, written and written, having always before my eyes these times inimical to me, the younger generation deluded by
the collapse, how by what I would say I might make them gain the ears that
hear and the eyes that see. What is tragic in the situation is that, while I'm absolutely certain that in the last decade I've brought my phenomenological philosophy to a maturity, to clarity and purity, to a breadth of problems and
methods encompassed that traces out the genuine meaning and path for philosophy for all the future—a new generation has come on the scene that misinterprets my published fragments and incomplete beginnings in their deepest
sense, that propagates a presumably improved phenomenology and reveres
me as the old man who is now passed by. So I am once again alone philosophically, the way I was when I began; and yet how fulfilled, how sure the
future! In the last year, in minute reflections, in the most careful final fashioning and filling out, everything has been shiningly confirmed, but I am still not

> finished with the preparations, I still have some difficulties facing me, and es-
> pecially what is now the hardest of all, systematic presentation.[44]

We saw earlier how this last difficulty continued to plague Husserl. As he told
Albrecht in another letter a year later (December 22, 1931), what was not
coming for him was that blaze of synthesizing creativity by which he could
compose a fully rounded book in one sustained drive, as he had done with
Ideas and the *Formal and Transcendental Logic*.[45] But this time it was much harder
to get everything together "in his head" beforehand, so that the writing could
come, as it were, in a flow and a rush. The work was much more extensive and
difficult than expected, and thus Fink was now given the task of expanding
and readying the Cartesian Meditations for immediate publication, with the
System to follow as soon as Husserl could manage it. (When Husserl finally
did get everything together in his head and begin to compose a coherent
whole, circumstances and the occasion would lead to something oriented
somewhat differently than the present project; what would result would be
the Crisis writings.)

Here, then, is the situation finally in which the second and last set of Fink's
revision texts for the Meditations was written,[46] and in which the Sixth Meditation itself was produced. In the summer of 1932 Fink wrote revisions for the
first five of Husserl's Meditations, though the work on the revision of the Fifth
was broken off before being completed.[47] At this point he turned to composing the Sixth. As indicated by Husserl's notes recording the dates on which
he received this text as it was being written, the Sixth Meditation was produced over the course of the next several months, from at least part of July until August 15 (note 1 below), from then until September 8 (note 169, below),
from that date until October 5 or 8 (note 307, below), and finally from then
until October 21 (note 517, below). This whole set of compositions is itself a
noteworthy productive effort on Fink's part—over three hundred pages of
text as printed in the two-volume edition, in a six-month period; but, as
we shall see (in section IV), it was something for which Fink had been preparing in his own mind for some time. The end result was to have been a publication of Husserl's original Meditations with Fink's revisions, including the
Sixth Meditation. What is not clear is whether in such a joint publication
Fink's revisions would actually replace the portions of Husserl's texts that they
were meant to replace, or whether they would be added rather as supplementary alternatives.[48]

Husserl's reading of this set of Fink's writings for the Meditations was one
factor contributing to the dominant tenor of Husserl's mind during much of
1932. The other was the fact that early in the year the intense labors Husserl

had devoted himself to, without achieving the breakthrough to productive synthesizing and composition on his own part, led to a severe depression.[49] The passing of months and years seemed ever more pitiless and unforgiving for someone at his advanced age, and the task that was so urgent remained still undone. Returning to a more positive outlook, Husserl began thinking that it was his *Nachlass* that would ensure the eventual appreciation of his message, even if he remained unable to produce the still needed large systematic work. In any case, his perspective now extended quite beyond the work on the Meditations. Contributing to that, however, was the very work being done on the Meditations, Fink's work in the summer and fall of 1932.

Husserl, of course, was well-acquainted with the thinking that guided Fink's conception of the revision to be done on the Meditations. Their daily conversations ensured that. Even as Fink was beginning the composition of the second set of revision texts, Husserl knew that it would be "quite different" from the Meditations as he had done them in his own version of 1929.[50] And what Husserl actually read when Fink handed him the revision texts was indeed just that, a very different, no longer very "Cartesian" Cartesian Meditations! The revision Fink was producing corresponded closely to the approach Husserl described to Ingarden in a letter from June 11, 1932, i.e., that what was needed was a "total turning around of philosophy," "a really concrete explication that moved from the natural having of the world and of being to ascend to the 'transcendental'-phenomenological stance, a concrete grounding of the method and universal problematic of transcendental phenomenology."[51] Husserl's reading of Fink's revisions for the first five Meditations[52] was soon displaced, however, by his much closer attention to the Sixth Meditation. Indeed, over the next two years Husserl would restudy the Sixth Meditation several times, with annotations stemming from at least two of these readings.[53] Undoubtedly too, it had to be during or after one of these readings on Husserl's part that Fink wrote the "Foreword" to his text (see below), signaling certain basic differences between his thinking and Husserl's.

The first reading, of course, was the one done as Husserl received the text from Fink. The second came in the summer of 1933—in the first of what were to be many evil seasons; for on January 30, 1933, Hitler had been named Chancellor, and the National Socialists had taken power. The political situation had a deeply disturbing effect on Husserl and placed Fink in a hopeless situation, in both cases because of the anti-Jewish racism of Nazi doctrine. The first instance officially affecting Husserl came on April 14 in a move by the Gauleiter of Baden, Robert Wagner, to comply with the government's decree to purge all state offices of "non-Aryans." Despite being retired, Husserl, because of his Jewish origins,[54] was formally dismissed from the university, an act which, while it could not affect any official responsibilities—Husserl had none—was seen as a shocking statement of intent.[55] This action was soon after rescinded by virtue of an exception in the national law for those, among others, whose sons had fallen in World War I; yet there was no doubt in anyone's mind about what was meant despite the exemptions: those who were not "Aryan" were no longer to be considered "German." It would be two years before the Nuremberg Laws on Citizenship and Race would annul all such exemptions (September 1935),[56] yet Husserl (correctly) took the present measure to mean, in effect, unqualified exclusion, for himself and his family and for anyone like them.

> Since the autumn of last year I have been on the way to one of my old states of depression, and increasingly so since political developments have taken their oppressive effect on my mind. Finally, in my old age, I had to experience something I had not deemed possible: the erection of a spiritual ghetto, into which I and my children . . . are to be driven. By a state law to take effect hereafter and forevermore, we are no longer to have the right to call ourselves German, the work of our minds [*Geisteswerke*] is no longer to be included in German cultural history [*Geistesgeschichte*]. . . . I have had much that was difficult to overcome in my long, perhaps all too long life. . .; but here it touches my philosophical development, which for me, in my uncertainty, in my unclarity, was a struggle over the life and death of the mind [*um geistiges Leben und geistigen Tod*].[57]

To make matters worse, on April 21 Heidegger was chosen *Rektor* of the university, and began his public involvement with Nazi policies, such as was in evidence in his highly publicized entry into the party on May 1 and his *Rektoratsrede* on May 27.[58] Then on May 10 came the evening of the burning of books in university cities around Germany, although apparently rainy weather in Freiburg discouraged it there.[59] On July 1, during an effort to recover by vacationing on the Schluchsee, in the Black Forest, Husserl wrote to his friend Albrecht concerning, among other things, the dismissal of his son, Gerhart, from his position at the university in Kiel:

> Unfortunately the months since the New Year are nearly lost for my work. . . . How can you bring about the inner quiet, the pure turn inward, the retreat from the world, that belongs to philosophy? I naturally put every effort into trying. I struggle for every good hour. I think the high air, the coun-

try solitude will help. It is awful for me to meet with other people, and then
to talk again and again about the same things, which is totally pointless.[60]

As it turned out, the weeks in the mountains were the most fruitful period of
work for Husserl that year.[61]

It was during these same months of upheaval in 1933 that Fink, because of
his work and close association with Husserl, suffered his first setback as well,
namely, the preclusion of any possibility of proceeding to the *Habilitation*.[62] As
Fink recounted it after the war,[63] in 1933 Husserl had recommended that Fink
offer his "Meditation on the 'Idea of a Transcendental Theory of Method' " as
a *Habilitationsschrift*. This attempt failed "for political reasons," as the course of
events after January 30 easily explain. Nevertheless, Fink reworked the Sixth
Meditation as an article defending Husserl against Neo-Kantian misinterpretation and criticism, giving it the title "The Phenomenological Philosophy of
Edmund Husserl and Contemporary Criticism."[64]

Husserl read through this adaptation of the Sixth Meditation in May, and
wrote a brief foreword to it for its publication in *Kantstudien*. The closing lines
of this foreword are a remarkable public subscription to Fink's treatment, and
bear reading: "At the request of the distinguished editorship of *Kantstudien* I
have carefully gone through this essay, and I am happy to be able to say that
there is no statement in it that I could not make fully my own, that I could not
explicitly acknowledge as my own conviction."[65] We shall return in the next
section to the character of testimony like this on Husserl's part. At this point,
however, it is worth noting the situational context for this particular public
statement by Husserl.

In Husserl's eyes, especially given the direction that was taken by the man
who had succeeded him in the chair at Freiburg, there was no one in Germany
whom Husserl could recognize as authentically representing his transcendental phenomenology. In addition, he, Husserl, belonged to a class of person that had now been declared undesirable in, or, more accurately, inimical
to, the kind of life that Germany was being driven to adopt—with astonishing efficiency and relentlessness. Husserl clearly wanted to authenticate Fink's
representation of his phenomenology, and he was doing so out of thorough
familiarity with the thinking that went into the article in question. He also
wanted to support Fink's voice as being equivalent to his own, despite the fact
that to do so was certain to reinforce the official disrepute in which Fink already stood because of his close association with Husserl. There was courage,
defiance, and despair at play together here, and both Husserl and Fink surely
knew it. Fink in fact knew well what Husserl was doing in writing the foreword; among his notes from the period there is a scrap of paper with two brief

paragraphs that are obviously a draft for precisely the foreword that Husserl wrote. But Fink's brief statement is far less assertive and unconditional than the one Husserl himself provided,[66] and Fink later recounted his surprise at Husserl's forceful subscription to his essay.[67] Husserl clearly had said more than Fink expected or thought necessary.

This second reading of the Sixth Meditation, in mid-1933, apparently both indirect (in the form of the *Kantstudien* article) and direct, occasioned at least one of the Appendixes given here.[68] A third reading came later, at the end of the year, when Husserl, needing to stir his philosophic interest, turned once more to Fink's manuscript, apparently with the idea of proceeding with the publication of the revised Cartesian Meditations.[69] This was the period when Husserl wrote most of the manuscript reflections that are included in the present volume as Appendixes to the main text.[70]

This is the time, too, when those in Husserl's circle of philosophic colleagues had the opportunity themselves to read Fink's Sixth Meditation.[71] Fink had sent his carbon copy of the text to Felix Kaufmann in Vienna, who shared it with Alfred Schutz during the Christmas holidays, 1933–34. Kaufmann returned it to Fink prior to his writing Fink on July 20, 1934. In mid-August Gaston Berger, then president of the Marseille-based Société d'Études Philosophiques, came to Freiburg to visit Fink and Husserl.[72] This was the first time Berger and Husserl (and Fink) had met, and Husserl was quite impressed.[73] Berger must have struck an equally sympathetic note with Fink, because he returned to Marseille with Fink's own carbon copy of the Sixth Meditation—for some reason without the last section, §12. It was via Berger's possession of this copy that various French philosophers were subsequently able to read Fink's text, in particular Maurice Merleau-Ponty and Tran-Duc-Thao.[74] The account of the character and extent of the influence of Fink's treatment of transcendental phenomenology upon the French interpretation of Husserl—especially with its focus on the final period work—has yet to be given.

The year 1934 was a turning point for Husserl, when existing projects would begin to yield to a new and final undertaking. The dilemma Husserl had faced out of the urgency he felt to bring out a statement of his position that would be faithful to the true deeper insights of his thinking in both comprehensiveness and concreteness, and in that way would be effective in the context of the times, this dilemma had not been resolved. Husserl could not feel confident that the Cartesian Meditations would do the job, and the massive System was not getting written. Yet in a situation where "in these times of revolution turmoil becomes the normal thing," as Husserl describes it,[75] he had to get on with his life's work—he was now seventy-five years old. This meant two things now: helping with Fink's work on editing the manuscripts on time, and then preparing his *Nachlass* for the future. Already in the latter part of 1933 these had become matters of high importance, especially the latter.[76] The book on time that Fink was working on Husserl hoped to see finished in the next year; but progress was extremely slow, and Husserl had repeatedly to write in the course of 1934 that it was still not ready.[77] Of the problems involved here, one certainly was that Husserl's thinking on time was still in progress. That Fink's work would be taking this new thinking into account—and indeed Fink's work was part of the very instigation for this further development in Husserl's thinking—was certainly a central complicating factor.[78] Also, given the state of affairs in the country and his age and frequent infirmity, Husserl's concern for the condition and fate of his massive and ever-increasing collection of manuscripts was growing.[79]

Here is where a breakthrough finally came—and it would be Husserl's final achievement. Around the beginning of August 1934, Husserl received an invitation to send a letter-address to the International Philosophical Congress being held in Prague on September 2–7, on "the present task of philosophy."[80] The thoughts that Husserl developed for this occasion eventually, through several stages—most particularly the lectures in Vienna and Prague in 1935—led to the set of writings known as the Crisis texts. But equally important in Husserl's eyes was the fact that within the next year serious discussions got under way on the idea of establishing a place for his *Nachlass* in Prague, where his vast manuscript studies could be preserved and worked on in the interest of eventual publication. What would become the final surge of integrative writing on Husserl's part, something that eluded him in the tasks both of adequately revising the Cartesian Meditations and of producing the vast new System, was now in its first glimmering.[81] At the same time, serious, full-scale effort would now be put into organizing Husserl's manuscripts and unpublished texts into systematic order. For this latter purpose, Ludwig Landgrebe, in commission from and with the financial support of the Cercle Philosophique de Prague, spent three weeks in Freiburg with Fink doing just this.[82]

We shall later see some of the linkage that exists between the Crisis writings and the two projects we have been following here, revision of the Cartesian Meditations and the new "System of Phenomenological Philosophy." For the present, a first purpose has been fulfilled, namely, to give a historical, descriptive account of the place of the present translated text in the productivity of Husserl's final period. A second preliminary task, however, still remains, namely, to portray more fully the character of the role Fink played in this productivity, and to show how his own background prepared him for the special contribution he made to this development in Husserl's phenomenology.

II. Eugen Fink as Husserl's co-worker

It was always well known that Fink had been Husserl's assistant during the final ten years of Husserl's life, but the view many took of the career Fink followed after the war, from 1945 on, led to a disinclination to take that work with Husserl prior to the war into account to any important extent in interpreting Husserl's transcendental phenomenology. The reasons for this tendency, and for the independence Fink showed when he finally began his own career, are too complex to take up here;[83] but this attribution of nonorthodoxy to Fink with respect to Husserl suggests the angle along which to set the line of sight through the next portion of our treatment here. We have seen how during the very period in question Husserl made a public statement precisely guaranteeing, and without the least qualification, Fink's "orthodoxy" with respect to Husserl's thinking. Husserl's foreword for Fink's article in *Kantstudien* was no mere public gesture of polite patronal support for a young protégé made in a period of Husserl's own severe personal disappointment and growing isolation. He meant it to be taken for what it plainly said, and he affirmed as much privately in his letters.[84] And as we have seen, Husserl was speaking out of thorough familiarity with the article both in its origination from the Sixth Meditation and as a separate essay.

There is more to this than meets the eye, however, and Husserl himself gives us a pattern for distinguishing important elements of this larger complex of factors in a letter to Albrecht written May 19, 1934.

> The Fink paper [i.e., the *Kantstudien* article] is of course excellent. I worked over it a bit before publication, but in regard more to the intelligibility of the presentation. He has come so far that everything is good throughout, and I can really agree to every word. Yet he is an exceptional person, and he doesn't even want to take the *Habilitation* (in his intractable desire for independence he of course cannot be a cipher in a mass) in order to be able to live entirely for phenomenology, for the completion of my manuscripts.[85]

There are four issues that emerge from this remark (and from others like it that one could cite from Husserl's correspondence): 1) the way Husserl and Fink worked together, as the context for both the agreements and differences that are to be found in the thinking each respectively does; 2) Fink's choosing to stay with Husserl during this trying period of Husserl's last years; 3) the character of the dedication Fink had to Husserl and to the philosophy contained in the vast body of Husserl's writings; and 4) the character of the judgment Husserl makes about Fink, the last of his many research assistants. We can best approach these matters by returning to the historical account just given and filling it out with more detail about the situation in which the Sixth Meditation was produced. This will give us the material needed for reaching some clarification in the four issues raised.

To see how Fink worked with Husserl, for example, let us look at the way Fink came into the position he held with Husserl, beginning with his entry into philosophy in the first place. Fink came to Freiburg for the winter semester of 1925–26, after a first semester of study at Münster. Except for one summer semester taken in Berlin in 1926, he followed all of Husserl's courses until the latter's retirement in 1928[86]—six semesters in all at Freiburg. When Heidegger arrived in 1928 to begin his lecturing in the winter semester, 1928–29, Fink followed his courses as well.[87] In 1929 Fink received his doctorate with a dissertation on the imagination,[88] which in its briefer initial essay form two years earlier had received a university writing prize. The defense of the dissertation took place on December 13, 1929, in the presence of both Husserl and Heidegger as, respectively, *Referent* and *Korreferent*—the only time these two participated jointly in a degree conferral, the symbolism of which has many sides to it. For the expansion of his prize essay into a dissertation, Fink had been under the direct guidance of Husserl, who made available to him both personal copies of published works and sets of unpublished manuscript material. In late 1928, in great part on the basis of the same prize-winning essay, Husserl selected Fink, now twenty-three years old, to take over the post that Ludwig Landgrebe had held as Husserl's assistant since 1923. Landgrebe had received his doctorate in 1927, and Husserl had to find a replacement for him. Though Landgrebe would continue to work with Husserl until 1930, through the support of the Notgemeinschaft der Deutschen Wissenschaft,[89] Fink began now too with Husserl in the position of assistant—the last one Husserl would have.

Initially Fink's assistantship was financed by research support Husserl had received as a university professor, but that ended in 1930.[90] From then on, when Fink's position was no longer that of a university stipulated assistantship, securing funds for Fink to continue working with him became a constant struggle. At first Husserl obtained government support through the help of a former Göttingen student now in the education ministry, Adolf Grimme. Then, with the repressions of 1933, more exceptional sources had to be sought, namely, from private organizations and individuals both in Germany and abroad.[91]

It is in Husserl's letter of thanks to the same Adolf Grimme in March 1930 that we find one of the many statements to be brought into consideration in

determining more accurately the place of Fink in Husserl's productivity during the period in question. Husserl writes:

> Thanks to your kindness, I have secured for one more year the assistant with-
> out whom at my age I would not have the prospect of bringing the main re-
> sults of my scientific life to literary achievement. Indeed, the largest and, as I
> also believe, the most important part of my life's work still lies in my manu-
> scripts, which can hardly still be managed because of their quantity.
>
> Sparked and gladdened by this support, I am working with a freshness
> and concentration as if I were twenty years younger. A special piece of good
> fortune is that I was able for the last time to train yet another brilliantly tal-
> ented student and assistant (Dr. Eugen Fink), who has a command of the
> whole breadth and depth of phenomenological philosophy in all its complex
> difficulties; for he has studied all my sketches and drafts and now works un-
> der my direction.[92]

It was in the final stages of Fink's completion of his own first major project,
the dissertation of 1929, that contacts with Husserl became regular and extensive. By January 1930 Fink was coming daily to the Husserl home for work
with Husserl, including the regular walks in the nearby forest and hill envi-
rons of Freiburg during which so many of their conversations together were
held.[93] Everything they were working on was thoroughly discussed.[94] Fink
was not simply someone who helped in wording and typing, collation and organization. Husserl's family saw this clearly; no previous assistant had had
such a full part in Husserl's actual work.[95] In March 1933—during a period the
distressing significance of which for Husserl (and for Fink) we have already
briefly seen—Husserl asserts this with great earnestness in a letter to another
former student of his:

> For five years now [Fink] has been in almost daily contact with me. All the
> sketches and drafts (old and new) and horizons of my thinking I have talked
> through with him, and we think together: we are like two communicating ves-
> sels. He has been trained to take over my vast *Nachlass* and get it into finished
> literary shape. He also of course attended Professor Heidegger's lectures sev-
> eral semesters, and was therefore his student academically, but never in a
> philosophical sense. And he was just as little ever an "Hegelian." It would be
> completely wrong to think that new intellectual motifs that are alien to the
> consistent thrust of my earlier development have taken effect on me through
> him. From its first breakthrough to pure self-awareness with respect to its
> methodological meaning (in 1905, with the phenomenological reduction),
> constitutive phenomenology has had a consistency that is absolutely its own,
> similarly to the way modern exact physics since Galileo does.

What Dr. Fink, and only he, says, therefore, is absolutely authentic, and when (on the basis of my writings and manuscripts) he speaks of the stages of development of phenomenology, that has unconditional precedence over everything that my earlier listeners are able to say. . . . In addition, a genuine elucidation of the historical development of a philosophy (in the philosopher) can only be given on the basis of the way its meaning takes shape in its full maturity; only then can one understand the structure of the dynamic in each lower stage.[96]

We shall see as we proceed how Husserl's view here has to be modulated, but for now let us review just a little more of the testimony Husserl gives on Fink, so as to have all the more important aspects of the latter's work with him in hand as Husserl himself viewed them.

Perhaps the strongest expression of Husserl's dependence on and appreciation of Fink is a statement he makes to Fink directly, in one of the rare occasions when they communicated by mail owing to different plans for the summer of 1934, which Husserl was spending in Kappel, a town up in the Black Forest:

You have been for years now no longer my "assistant," you are not my secretary, not my intellectual servant. You are my co-worker, and, in addition, my seminar, my teachership [*Lehrtätigkeit*].[97]

Husserl here clearly acknowledges Fink's status as a mind with a contribution of its own to make in the work they were both involved in—and he wants Fink to know that. But there is another side to this now mature intellectual relationship between the older Husserl and the younger Fink, and Husserl gives voice to it succinctly in another letter from a few months later. Writing to Albrecht on October 7, 1934, he says:

Fink is extraordinary as a collaborator, useless as an assistant, and very labile in his psychological structure. This is where there is deep and serious worry. On him depends the future of phenomenology—namely, he is the only one who has an exhaustive knowledge of my manuscripts, who can really understand and work them out, and doing that means having not just a schoolboy's mind but one that productively thinks with you, that fills in gaps and understands how a development is going, etc.[98]

It was surely not always easy for Fink to work so intimately with Husserl, given not only the vast difference in age and professional status but differences as well in outlook with regard to phenomenology; and the strains surely accentuated whatever psychological limitations Fink had. But these limitations, worrisome as they may have been, were far outweighed in Husserl's eyes by Fink's outstanding intellectual abilities and the indispensable, special part he played in Husserl's ongoing work.[99]

Fink himself wrote a description of his role in Husserl's philosophical projects during those intense years, and his account is worth reading:

> Husserl, far from training me to be for him a march-in-step disciple, valued my work with him above all for its strongly critical tendency. In these seven years I critically worked over numerous manuscripts, made draft sketches for our compositions and proposals for revisons of already published works, as well as edition plans. Deferring my own philosophic work to collaboration in a philosophy that had already reached world significance was not for me a problem of ambition. That kind of thing had no import in the atmosphere of work around Husserl. Husserl acknowledged my intellectual independence precisely by always seeking my productive contradiction and my criticism, which he needed as a stimulus to objectivate his creative thinking. Thus arose in precisely those years his most important research manuscripts. In this period, when Husserl sought to bring in the harvest of his long life of investigation, I acted, as it were, as an intellectual catalyst for him.[100]

There is clear concordance between Fink's representation and Husserl's, for example, when we see the latter speaking of Fink as providing him a "resonance,"[101] as being a "co-thinker" with him[102] and not a "mere mouthpiece."[103] But it is time now to qualify and nuance this concordance in terms of the realities that show both in the texts from documents just cited and in the translated materials that lie before us in this edition. In other words, we can now offer some clarification on the first of the four issues raised earlier.

For one thing, all indications are that the relationship which developed between Husserl and Fink went beyond that which Husserl had had with his other assistants. Fink entered into the economy of productive thinking and writing that Husserl maintained during his retirement years more intimately than previous assistants had—the testimony from the correspondence by Husserl and others in his family is unequivocal on this. One reason for this lay in the circumstances of the time. Husserl had retired: the lecture hall was no longer the forum for him to develop his thinking in the company of others (even if Husserl's lecturing was not dialogue but virtually uninterrupted monologue). Apart from the still usual visitors to the Husserl home, both colleagues and friends, the only regular contact with a listener or a questioner was in the person of his assistant, Fink. In the regimen of Husserl's daily work, as the retirement deepened—and especially after 1933—this contact quickly came to be a fact of paramount need; Fink became Husserl's "seminar" and "teachership" (see Husserl's letter to Fink, quoted above, from the summer of 1934).

As Fink's contact with Husserl became more intense, it underwent a transformation in kind. From an initial stage of "subordinate assistant activity," Fink's work became that of "independent productive cooperation," and then finally a "unique intellectual symbiosis."[104] What happened was that Fink's special abilities and intellectual resources had begun to show. We saw earlier Husserl's attesting to Fink's "intractable desire for independence" and his characterization of their work together as that of "two communicating vessels." With this we perhaps touch upon the essential feature of the situation, namely, Fink's independence; for what can independence be without difference, and with difference there is non-uniformity. Yet when the independence is a non-uniformity *in the same philosophical enterprise*, when two distinct thinkers join in a single philosophic endeavor, then the philosophy in question can begin to be, and has to be viewed as, more than the individual contingent thinking of a contingent human individual. In addition to the fact that the philosophy becomes more than a contingent product of some individual human mind, and can begin to attain the status of trans-contingent validity that allows for it a measure of genuine truth,[105] the philosophy has to be seen as a *joint product*; its identity is not linked to a single thinker. What this means here is that, documented in the texts translated in the present book, and in the larger collection of materials that give them their context and from which the present introduction is drawn, Husserl's phenomenology, at least as it reached its maturity in his last years, *was not just Husserl's*—it was Husserl's *and Fink's.*

The question of agreement and difference in the same philosophical enterprise—the question therefore also of its *identity*—is not one that can be exhausted here; the purpose has been rather to show how it is raised in regard to the collection of texts given here when they are set in their essential context. Seeing the texts in this context also shows that there is a larger question that embraces all four of the issues raised earlier.

Although there are specific things that need to be said to each of those issues, in the end they all come down to the question of how it is that different thinkers participate in—or do *not* participate in—a same philosophical endeavor, and how that endeavor is to be identified as a distinct, specific *philosophy*. Answering the question *what* phenomenology is involves in part answering the question *who* phenomenology is, or, rather, who *are* phenomenology! Once again, the issue is being raised, rather than resolved, here; and it is being raised as a primary issue fundamental to the very character of the texts assembled in the two-volume set of the *VI. Cartesianische Meditation*. These texts—together with their context, which this introduction is furnishing—not only present the issue, but are a pivotal contribution to the attempt to resolve it.

Let us now turn to the second of the four issues: why did Fink choose to stay with Husserl? The basic elements of the answer have already been given. We have seen how Fink, owing to the circumstances of the time, had no possibility of an academic career if he stayed with Husserl. At the same time Husserl himself tells us that the alternative facing Fink, to concede to the demands of the "coordination" of the universities in conformity with Nazism, was one he could not accept: "in his intractable desire for independence he of course cannot be a cipher in a mass." One central reason, therefore, why Fink stayed with Husserl was that that was where he could do philosophy, free of ideological constraint. Fink himself attests to the model seriousness of Husserl's dedication to philosophy. He describes "the essential virtues of this kind of work-dedicated philosophy, the passionate honesty and conscientiousness, the tenacious and constant perseverance in questioning and searching, and the unconditioned ruthlessness against all one's own already gained 'positions.' "[106] Despite the fact that to stay with Husserl involved constant difficulties with the authorities, for Fink the grace of these years with Husserl was "the luckiest thing in my life."[107]

This, however, did not mean quite the same thing for Fink as it did for Husserl, which brings us to the third of the four issues posed by the joint texts we have before us, namely, the character of Fink's dedication to Husserl's philosophy. Husserl's hope quite clearly was that Fink would work in their common philosophical endeavor by primarily laboring over Husserl's manuscripts, so that, as we saw, Husserl speaks of Fink's dedication to phenomenology as being for the sake of "completing my manuscripts." But the way Fink would "complete" Husserl's manuscripts was to produce something with a fair degree of originality in it, not in contravention to Husserl's phenomenology but not in literal orthodoxy to it either. It was rather the product of thinking through phenomenology with that essential measure of critical independence that was the hallmark of Fink's work with Husserl. To act otherwise would be for Fink no longer to act in the philosophic dedication which was the whole point of Husserl's work.[108] In a note from early in his work with Husserl Fink writes:

> A philosophy only speaks and freely gives itself to someone who has an innermost kinship to it. Inner kinship, however, means *to be other*. Only as an Other, and not as a mimicking ape, can the one who asks a question expect an answer. Interpretation of a philosophy is always more than that which is

present in the text. A philosophy is never a fixed fact. *Texts are the corpses of the living spirit.*[109]

It is clear that Husserl realized this side of Fink's independence, as the passage from Husserl's letter to Albrecht from October 7, 1934, shows; but the *extent* of difference that "productively thinking" and "filling in gaps" allow is the difficult question. Equally difficult too is the question of the extent of difference that *Husserl* might allow while still acknowledging the position that results to be "his own conviction," as he put it in his foreword to Fink's *Kantstudien* article. In other words, the kind of dedication Fink had to Husserl's thought and writings can only be determined by understanding the character and extent of the differences between them in their understanding of phenomenology. That is, the resolution of the third issue lies in the way we settle the fourth.

The fourth issue poses the following question: what are we to make of Husserl's judgment about Fink, in subscribing so wholeheartedly to Fink's representation of phenomenology as he, Husserl, was familiar with it in the many examples of Fink's work before him? When Husserl says, for example, "What Dr. Fink, and only he, says, therefore, is absolutely authentic,"[110] to what extent can or does this "authorize" Fink's treatment, say, here in the Sixth Meditation, where, reading it with the Husserlian notations, we actually *see differences* between what Fink says and Husserl's views?

Let us first take care of one suspicion that might easily arise from reading the statements of Husserl's that we have already seen. When one compares these remarks on Fink to the ready self-giving in trust and identification that Husserl had shown in an earlier decade for *Heidegger*,[111] and when one sees how mistaken Husserl really was in that instance, as he finally himself realized, then one might wonder if Husserl's judgment could be just as mistaken in the case of Fink. The two situations, however, are quite different. While Heidegger had for a number of years had frequent conversations with Husserl, for example on Husserl's regular walks on the Lorettoberg near his home, and even though Husserl often talked about doing joint work with him, Heidegger never actually entered into the regular regime of Husserl's work the way Fink did.[112] Despite the fact that Heidegger was given as the editor of Husserl's "Vorlesungen zur Phänomenologie des inneren Zeitbewusstseins," in Husserl's *Jahrbuch* in 1928, he had in fact done very little editing, and the text was virtually that which Edith Stein had produced ten years earlier.[113] In contrast, Fink worked through all of Husserl's manuscripts, and was doing direct manuscript revision, the results of which Husserl was familiar with. Finally, the products of Fink's writing on phenomenology were closely read and annotated by Husserl, not to mention extensively discussed between the two men, such as in the case of the present Sixth Meditation. Again in contrast, the one effort at collaboration between Husserl and Heidegger, on the article for the *Encyclopaedia Britannica,* came late, after Heidegger's own contrasting position was already well formulated. The effort resulted in little concordance between them, and ended in an impasse.[114]

No, Husserl was acquainted with Fink's work with a directness and detail that simply were not true for Heidegger's work.[115] The question remains, however, to what extent, despite the unrivaled extensive contact between himself and Fink, Husserl really grasped the differences that might lie in Fink's treatment of phenomenology in contrast to his own. The question becomes more acute when one sees the difference in explicitness with regard to core philosophical ideas between the drafts Fink produced and Husserl read, and the notes which Fink wrote for himself during this period of work with Husserl.[116] Moreover, Fink explicitly attests to reservations and disagreements between Husserl and himself in regard to the Sixth Meditation.[117] Finally, Cairns's *Conversations* as well give clear and sometimes detailed indication of such differences. Could this be another case of Husserl's not knowing where the philosophical mind of his assistant really lay?

The question goes to the heart of the texts in the present translation, and we must approach it on the basis of the documentation available. One important portion of this documentation has already been represented by the many references drawn here from Husserl's correspondence; another, the collection of Fink's notes, will be referred to in the fourth section of this introduction when we finally address the texts themselves. At this point, however, certain main members of an overall framework can be set in place.

First of all, Husserl did indeed know there were differences; this shows in his notes to the Sixth Meditation. But the essential point is that Husserl saw these differences as differences that had their identity and their force *within a larger encompassing whole of common agreement.* Secondly, that larger encompassing whole was transcendental phenomenology *in its mature stage of both self-conception and self-criticism.* The elaboration of this final stage was precisely the work of Husserl's last ten years, and accordingly of Fink's participation in it—and that is precisely the objective of the Sixth Meditation. As we have seen, the "Layout," Fink's outline for the new systematic work Husserl envisaged as replacement for the Cartesian Meditations, embodied that same character of fully mature self-conception and self-criticism. In fact, Fink's strength lay precisely in formulating comprehensive self-conception and self-criticism, rather than in producing the painstaking detail work that was Husserl's special genius. The differences from Husserl that emerge in Fink's compositions result precisely from this work of comprehensive self-interpretation and reconception under the impact of critical reflection on principles. These differences, therefore, are perhaps far more like differences between levels or phases of self-development than differences between rival positions. And this kind of difference is not only endemic to philosophy as such, it is eminently typical of Husserl's own philosophical growth.[118] Thus when one sees Husserl's alterations and comments on Fink's text, what is clear is that these refinements are made out of deep appreciation of, on the one hand, Fink's grasp of the *issues*, and, on the other, his mastery of the *principles* whereby to formulate the issues in transcendental phenomenology and thus to move toward their resolution.

In other words, the differences from Husserl that emerged in Fink's thinking were *genuine problems for and within transcendental phenomenology*, genuine problems that developed intrinsically within it rather than antagonistically confronting or undercutting it from the outside. That problems of this order were raised was as things should be. Paradoxically, then, Husserl could subscribe in principle to what Fink was writing, even though Husserl himself might not grasp the depth of implication it might have, or the radicality with which, within phenomenology itself and out of its intrinsic dynamic, fundamentals were being challenged and needed critical reconceiving—or, to put the point more strongly, even though he might dispute to Fink himself (and did) some of the content of Fink's assertions.[119] Paradoxically, Husserl could state that Fink understood phenomenology as no other did, he could accept the plausibility of Fink's points, and yet he could miss the wider implications or even argue with Fink to reject them. Husserl had been doing something like this for himself with himself for his entire career. Now, however, the "himself" with whom Husserl was in debate was a very decidedly *other* "himself"—Fink.

Here, then, in general lines, is how one should read Husserl's statements about Fink—such as the one quoted above from the March 1933 letter to Feuling—and how one can reconcile such statements with the manifest fact that there are differences between Husserl and Fink in the texts here before us. This, however, leaves untouched the question of what happens in Fink's thinking *after* the period of his work with Husserl, when he quite clearly does not take up the work of producing studies in phenomenology based on Husserl's manuscripts, as Husserl intended him to do.[120] That matter would quite clearly take us too far beyond the present context and will have to be left aside here. It is, nevertheless, pertinent to the context of the texts given here to know something of their fate after Husserl's death and up to their editing in Husserliana Dokumente.

III. The Sixth Meditation and Louvain

With the turn in Husserl's thinking, chronicled above at the end of section I, the body of work already done on the Cartesian Meditations was set aside. This did not mean that the thinking that had gone into it went dormant; far from it! Indeed, its vigorous continuation was precisely what made for the strength of the writings that became the Crisis texts. The Cartesian Meditation drafts themselves, however, became submerged in the ever-increasing *Nachlass* that would mark the long event of Husserlian phenomenology.

Fink, however, always considered the Sixth Meditation to be his own composition. The issue came up within a year after Fink's emigration to Louvain in the spring of 1939, on the heels of the transfer of Husserl's *Nachlass* out of Germany to the University of Louvain (see above, note 5). Fink had left Germany in order to pursue the career he could not have under Nazi rule; and in Louvain he finally began university lecturing. This respite, however, did not last long. Upon the invasion of Holland by the German army, May 10, 1940, Fink was arrested as a "fifth columnist" together with Ludwig Landgrebe, who had also moved to Louvain from Prague. They and others were shipped in cattle cars to the south of France, where they remained until the Germans in turn occupied that country. Being then freed, Fink was able to return to Louvain (July 10), where he again took possession of the original typescripts of both the Sixth Meditation and his revisions for the other Cartesian Meditations. Van Breda, now the central figure in the preservation of Husserl's legacy, had to acknowledge Fink's claim of authorship:

> Before leaving Louvain in 1940, Fink had asked me to return to him the only copy of this "Sixth Meditation" that we possessed in Louvain. He told me he considered it his own property, given that he no longer had any other copy of that article. I acceded to his rationale. The result is that we no longer possess the text in question.[121]

Under the German occupation, however, Louvain was not a place where Fink could remain, and before winter both he and Landgrebe returned to Germany: Fink to Freiburg, and Landgrebe to Hamburg.

What followed for Fink in Freiburg were not years for doing philosophy academically.[122] Within three weeks of his return there, during which he was repeatedly interrogated by the Gestapo, he was ordered to report for military service. Refusing to enter officer training, the normal course for someone with advanced academic status, he was assigned as a simple recruit to the area around Freiburg, where he could be kept under surveillance. He spent the war serving in air attack observation posts in the hills around the city and up in the Black Forest.[123]

With the collapse of the German Third Reich, however, in the slow restitution of academic institutions and personnel under Allied occupation, Fink was given the chance to return to the university. Here the Sixth Meditation appears again, for Fink chose to submit it as the text for his *Habilitation.* The reasons Fink gave for doing so are indicative of the way his work with transcendental phenomenology was evolving, and of the kind of continuity he saw that work to have with Husserl.

> My *Habilitation* was put forward by the university senate as a case of "political reparation" and conceived as the restitution of the Husserl tradition. I chose for the work [to submit] the "6th Meditation," with its highest of authorizations, from Husserl himself, even though I have more important works at hand. This way I have given symbolic expression to the fact that I want to take up the tradition of Husserl, not in orthodox following, but in the continuation of the intellectual impulses received from Husserl.[124]

In a letter to Gerhart Husserl, Husserl's only surviving son, Fink says substantially the same thing, adding two additional points, however. The first is that he, Fink, had submitted "the same work that in 1933 at Husserl's advice I had worked out for a *Habilitation,* namely, a meditation on the 'Idea of a Transcendental Theory of Method.' " He goes on to say: "It was for me an act of piety to take the *Habilitation* as Husserl's student with precisely that work which he had acknowledged as altogether to his mind and as a creative continuation of his thinking."[125]

As we saw, Fink's relationship to Husserl in the very years of closest work with him was a conflicting combination of identification and sharp critical difference. Testimony of the sort just cited shows very much the same elements. Fink felt an immensely strong fidelity to Husserl at the same time that he had to depart from many of Husserl's own formulations and characteristic philosophical tendencies in order to follow what he, Fink, took to be the continuing dynamic that Husserl's own thinking had launched. This same duality characterized as well production of the Sixth Meditation and he felt the critical element was quite strong there.[126] Critique, therefore, is intrinsic to his position in phenomenology. In his personal notes is to be found a continuing, radical critique of tenets central to Husserl's thinking, precisely on the basis of phenomenology's own objectives. And thus it was that Fink remained hesitant that his Sixth Meditation be made widely available; it needed a carefully prepared context to be understood for what it was and as he had meant it.

Despite the conflictual elements in Fink's own place in phenomenology, the consolidation of the Husserl tradition began to take shape, among other ways, in the form of the establishment of additional Husserl Archives first in Freiburg, under Fink's direction, and then in Cologne, under Landgrebe, in each case as a branch of the central deposit at Louvain. However, when the Cartesian Meditations were under preparation at Louvain, it was clear to Fink that the Sixth Meditation was not to be conceived as properly belonging to the text of the Meditations as it stood in Husserl's first complete revision of 1929.[127] As Fink explained to Strasser, in reply to the latter's inquiries during the editing work on the *Cartesianische Meditationen*, Husserl had decided "to rework the 'Meditations' radically for the German edition" and that Fink's revision proposals were to be part of a thus *new* "Cartesian Meditations." What is of interest in his revisions, Fink goes on to say, is that, especially in the case of the Sixth Meditation, Husserl's handwritten notations to the text show "the most fundamental points that Husserl advanced on the methodology and systematic coherence of phenomenology."[128] The revision texts that Fink had written and kept in his possession, in other words, belonged in a context in which Husserl was moving beyond the texts that Strasser was editing. That context, of course, is what this introduction has been attempting to reconstitute.

We have now reached the point in our background account with which we began, namely, the point at which Fink's revision texts for the Cartesian Meditations became available at Louvain, ultimately to appear in print in the two-volume edition in Husserliana Dokumente. It is time as well to turn to these documents themselves and to explore in overview what it was during that distant decade that they so importantly for transcendental phenomenology, and problematically, put into words.

IV. The Sixth Meditation: issues and resolutions

From the account that has been given here of the setting for the Sixth Meditation in the work of Husserl and Fink in the early 1930s, one key lesson emerges. Just as Husserl's own writings do not have the character of final statements, but rather mark important stations in a process of continual probing, reconception, and self-criticism, so Fink's text here is itself provisional. Gaston Berger, who received a copy of the Sixth Meditation from Fink himself, was already aware of this, describing it as a "working document" that "presents none of its ideas as definitive," but rather "constitutes a concrete moment in the investigation."[129] The work represented in the text, therefore, was work that *carried on further*, both in the remaining few years of Husserl's life, and in the career that Fink pursued after Husserl's death. The value of the document, therefore, lies in the dynamic of philosophic thinking in phenomenology that it forces us to rekindle from that distant period and to reanimate and carry on in our own minds; it does not consist in some kind of "doctrine" that might be derived from the text (e.g., "Fink's position" as against "Husserl's," "as it was then").

Of course, the fuller movement of investigation in which the "moment" of the Sixth Meditation is born is precisely what is represented by the second volume of the set comprising Husserliana Dokumente II, namely, *VI. Carte-sianische Meditation, Teil 2: Ergänzungsband.* Therefore, despite the fact that the present translation is only of the first of these volumes, our introductory treatment of the investigation in question has to include consideration of elements from the texts of this *Ergänzungsband.*[130]

In our review of the historical context for the Sixth Meditation, we have already seen the way two main projects were under way and were interrelated in the period represented by the texts given in the two volumes of documents. These two projects were 1) the effort to produce a revision of the Cartesian Meditations that would confront the issues prominent in the philosophic community in Germany at the time, and 2) the plan to produce an entirely new comprehensive systematic presentation of transcendental phenomenology. As we have also seen, between these two programs something of a tension and incompatibility existed, so that the doing of one meant the diminishing of need for the other. To show how this situation is illuminated by the texts of the *Ergänzungsband* is the first step to take now.

A) Countering the Cartesianism of phenomenology

The two texts that open the *Ergänzungsband* are the "Layout for Edmund Husserl's 'System of Phenomenological Philosophy' " and the "Draft for the opening section of an Introduction to Phenomenology," the latter being Fink's working out of the first section of the first book of the overall plan detailed in the "Layout." With these texts one sees immediately one of the main elements of difference from the Cartesian Meditations, namely, in the way the *starting situation* is determined for phenomenological reflection to begin, that is, the way the stage is set for performing the phenomenological reduction. What makes this point crucial is that adequately and critically explicating the nature of the reductive move directly depends upon how one conceives this starting situation.

Fink's "Draft" takes the Cartesian theme of the idea of science and explicitly sets it back into the situation of life in the world; cognition as such, and therefore science, is an operation oriented in and to the world. The structural condition needing to be thematized and elucidated in order to explicate the significance of the enterprises of scientific reason is therefore that of the *world as pregiven* (chapter 1 of the "Draft"). The move of reduction, then, is to be the effort to reach an understanding of the essential all-embracing role of the world not only for the mundane life of psycho-physical humanity, but also precisely for the total range of the functioning of subjectivity (chapter 2). In contrast, the 1929 text in the published *Cartesian Meditations*, starting off from the idea of science as enjoining the aim for absolute grounding, seems to move *away from* the world to an apparent self-sufficient, self-present ego. Correspondingly the phenomenological reduction seems to function to safeguard absolute self-sufficiency on the part of the reflecting ego and absolute purity and independence *from* and *against* the world.

When, now, Fink tries to work the explication of the reduction as it is sketched in the "Draft"[131] into the text of the Cartesian Meditations, especially as this is done in his second revision,[132] he must in effect replace the whole previous text of the opening First Meditation as Husserl's version has it. Clarification of the reasons for this comes out gradually in the course of Fink's virtually new "Meditation I," particularly via the penetrating critique made of presuppositions that remain unnoticed in the concept of the "ego" that the Cartesian turn supposes itself to reach. In summation Fink writes:

> Up until now our meditation has taken a course that in developing the motivation of philosophical questioning into the universal questioning of the obviousness with which the world holds good [*Weltgeltung*] did so by way of restoring the idea of science as the grounding of knowledge of the world in regress to the apodicticity of the "I am." This whole path now seems to have been the wrong way to go.* The first serious entry upon it has raised some serious doubts, which set tottering the whole aim of the "Meditations."[133]

And Husserl underscores the correctness of Fink's claim in his remark to this passage at the point marked by the asterisk: "So it was! A sheer muddle, and wrongheaded as a course of reflection."[134]

This extraordinary assertion by Fink, and Husserl's concurrence with it, needs to be seen in relation to what it leads up to in Fink's text. It comes at the point where he is about to discuss the *reduction*. And his discussion of it is precisely oriented to the whole question of what all is implied by the "world," naive belief in which it is the function of the reduction to transcend. The section on the reduction[135] that immediately follows the section from which the above text is taken gives, then, an analysis of the extraordinarily deep-reaching structures of the world which turn out to have been overlooked and naively presupposed in the explication of the ego as it is presumed to be so dramatically found in the Cartesian turn, the Cartesian "discovery" of a secure "I am, I exist."

What is so provocative about Fink's analysis is that he argues that this naive presupposition has to be acknowledged even when in phenomenology a transcendental character is claimed for that ego. This leads, then, to the exigency for a far greater radicality in the reduction, an exigency that would require an analysis of belief in the world [*Weltglaube*] that would not itself be subject to conditions of world-inherence, that would therefore require a "subjectivity" to perform it that would also itself not be inherent in the world, and which, in the reduction, would become reflective upon itself precisely as non-world-inherent. Finally, this radical step counter to world-inherence is ultimately to be taken as the move that *reintegrates* the world in the economy of transcendental life itself.

> In the natural attitude [belief in the world] can never become thematic. We can indeed as human subjects reflect upon our beliefs, upon individual acts of believing, but never upon belief in the world itself. This belief in the world, as the universal medium in which we live, is in principle *not a psychological fact* (as individual acts of believing are psychological facts). It is not we as humans that perform belief in the world in our psychic life; for as humans we are already something believed in within belief in the world. In other words, it is not man that is the real performer of belief in the world, but rather *transcendental experiencing life,* which is laid bare by the method of the phenomenological epoche, to which the correlate is the correlation of man-to-object. World-belief is thus a *transcendental fact* (not a psychological fact): the *primal happening of our transcendental existence.* With the phenomenological epoche our transcendental existence splits into the phenomenological onlooker removed from world-belief and the transcendental experiencing life that puts world-belief into action. Thus split, transcendental life turns upon itself, becomes objective to itself, and comes back to itself in thematic self-elucidation.[136]

Here, then, in this tight and explicit reintegration of belief in the world into the total economy of transcendental life, we find one basic component of the whole process that is in evidence in Fink's revisions for the Cartesian Meditations, the process, namely, of divesting those Meditations of at least some elements that characterize them as "Cartesian," the process of *de-Cartesianizing* them. That process then continues through the rest of Fink's revision texts precisely via the centering of the course of the Meditations upon this theme of the world. For example, the first section in Husserl's 1929 text for Meditation II is entirely replaced in Fink's revision. This section, §12: "The idea of a transcendental grounding of knowledge," reflects both the Cartesian ideal of science and Cartesian egoic autonomy. Having dropped this section, Fink then composes a whole new beginning for the following section, §13, in place of its first three paragraphs, in order to recast the way one would approach the topic of the fourth paragraph, namely, "the second stage of phenomenological research," "the criticism of transcendental experience and then the criticism of all transcendental cognition"[137]—which is precisely the topic of the Sixth Meditation itself.

What Fink puts in place of these removed portions of Husserl's text is a long treatment, in six subsections, of the two elements revealed by the reduction, viz., the world as such and transcendental subjectivity.

> *The double action of the phenomenological reduction* consists in this: first, that it is the move leading back to an always hidden, itself non-worldly subject-for-the-world, that it presents the world-transcending discovery of transcendental subjectivity; but, second, that with it there first comes about the discovery of the *genuine sense of being that the world has.*[138]

Here is where the ground is laid for posing the deepest issue of the Sixth Meditation, namely, the question of the nature of transcendental subjectivity precisely in its function of thematizing phenomenological principles and procedures for the sake of critically explicating and validating them. For it is in the present sections that, corresponding to the "double action" of the phenomenological reduction, there is a double thesis on being. The first component runs thus:

> Plainly "worldliness," when we reflect more carefully, is the most fundamental *basic and primal characteristic of everything accessible to us in the natural attitude:* every being, however it may be different from all other beings, is still *in the world.* The idea of being is congruent to and coincides with the idea of world-inherent being.[139]

From this there results this corollary regarding that subjectivity which to be properly transcendental must also be world-transcending:

> In no way is the characterizing of transcendental life as "non-worldly" a directive to construe this non-worldliness in the light of the religious or metaphysico-speculative relationship of transcendence that is believed (and perhaps only believable) *in the natural attitude.* In other words, the non-worldli-

ness of transcendental subjectivity *transcends each and every form of non-worldliness that belongs to the natural attitude and is possible within it.* . . . Transcendental subjectivity is *neither a being in the world nor is it not in the world,* in any way whatsoever that the latter is conceivable with the means of comprehension belonging to the natural attitude.[140]

Finally, Fink takes pains to make clear that the world as an all-comprehensive structure must be seen as itself having two main moments:

the phenomenon of the world (which is for the non-participant onlooker the bracketed deposit of what is taken as holding [*der eingeklammerte Geltungsbestand*] has the *intrinsic structure of a correlation,* namely, between human experiencing and the totality of (*genuinely and mediately) experienced objectness in that experiencing. The phenomenon of the world is **human existence [*Existenz*] and its surrounding world as made a phenomenon by the epoche.[141]

That Fink's explication here has implications in the Sixth Meditation has already been mentioned and is to be expected; but it is important to signal one other place where resonance from the present texts should be noted, namely, in Husserl's Crisis-texts. Apart from the anticipations of the concept of the "life-world" as an element in the starting point for phenomenology,[142] §43 of the *Crisis* has Husserl explicitly both endorsing the approach to the reduction "by asking after the *how* of the world's pregivenness," and criticizing the Cartesian approach as seriously disadvantaged.[143] However, these two important points regarding the methodology of phenomenology do not occur fortuitously in that section of the *Crisis* or only as a last-minute realization on Husserl's part. If we take the work that Fink was doing on revising the Cartesian Meditations as a line of focus for the criticism that was being pursued in the project of revision *as a joint endeavor,* and one that was under constant review by both Husserl and Fink, then the course of development in Husserl's transcendental phenomenology through the 1930s gains considerably in focus and intelligibility.

It must be recognized that what Fink, alongside Husserl, was working on here in these revisions was no mere experiment or tentative possible option about how phenomenology *might* be represented. It was in fact taken by them as the way it *had* to be understood. This comes out clearly in other documents from the time, in particular the exchanges by letter carried on by Husserl and Fink with Husserl's colleagues and former students. For example, we have already seen Husserl's remark to Ingarden from the time when Fink was at work on the second revision texts (in the summer of 1932), the very ones just represented. Husserl's description of "a really concrete explication that moved from the natural having of the world and of being to ascend to the 'transcendental'-phenomenological stance"[144] very much corresponds to the orientation of Fink's revisions here. Later in the year this same critical clarification of phenomenology was given clear representation on two occasions. Alfred Schutz had written a review of the *Méditations cartésiennes* and had sent it to Husserl for comment before submitting it for publication.[145] It was Fink who replied, at Husserl's request and after thorough discussion with him of the points to be made regarding Schutz's review.

Fink explains to Schutz[146] that the Cartesian Meditations do not really state explicitly just what they are meant to be, namely, "the systematic unfolding of the phenomenological reduction." This only implicit objective, however, is accomplished not through "actual concrete constitutive analysis" but rather by laying out in summary "the full breadth of transcendental subjectivity." The result of these limitations is not only misunderstanding of the role of the explications of meditation V (on empathy and intersubjectivity), but also other misinterpretations such as were to be found in the draft Schutz had sent Husserl. In particular, one is easily led to suppose that the Meditations were advocating a "withdrawal into the apodictic self-certainty of the 'I am'," as if it were only *transcendent objects* that were "bracketed" rather than the whole double-sided phenomenon of the world, i.e., "innerworldly objects and innerworldly 'subjects' " together, the latter including "human immanence together with the mundane apodictic evidentness that belongs to it (the 'I am')."[147]

The problem, it turns out, is that Husserl's *Ideas I*, despite its groundbreaking value, is dangerously misleading. And when it is used to set the perspective of interpretation for later writings, deep misunderstanding occurs. This, now, is what Fink explains in writing to Felix Kaufmann, toward the end of this same year, 1932. Kaufmann had prepared reviews of Husserl's *Méditations cartésiennes* and his *Formale und transzendentale Logik*[148] and had sent them to Freiburg for comment. Again it was Fink who was charged with taking care of this.[149] In his letter to Kaufmann, Fink explains that the difficulty here is very much the same as that which the Cartesian Meditations give rise to, namely, that it looks as if "bracketing" applies only to entities that are transcendent to human consciousness, that is, those of outward-directed experience. Concurrently what seems to be clearly enjoined is an "absolutizing of the 'immanent' being of the apodictic egological existence of the I." Instead of this one-sided representation of "bracketing of the world," the epoche has to be seen as having a double inclusion, namely, of both "transcendent and immanent being." In this way the natural attitude has to be more correctly conceived not as some kind of human psychological stance toward outwardly experienced entities, but rather as human being itself, i.e., "the being of the subject within an already existent surrounding world."[150]

The formulations here, of course, are Fink's; but at least the direction of the interpretation they embody has to be seen as concordant with Husserl's own views. And this criticism of *Ideas I* will be repeated in the Sixth Meditation, where Husserl's comments show no disagreement.[151] Once again, this is one of the important elements of continuity with the later *Crisis* work.[152] Here, however, we must return to Fink's revisions for the *Cartesian Meditations*, to touch upon at least one more topic there. Beyond other topics raised by the *Meditations*, the one that causes particular difficulty for most readers is the question of *intersubjectivity*, the theme of the last and longest of the five Meditations in the 1929 version.

Fink's orientation here follows consistently from the overall recasting he works out for the entire work, namely, by way of centering issues in the question of the world as all-embracing framework of continual reference for reductive movement to transcendental reflection. He prepares for it in a text proposed for the end of Meditation IV,[153] in which the question of genetic analysis is set within its proper matrix, namely, immanent temporality. Analysis of immanent temporality in transcendental subjectivity can only be done through constant reference to the immanent temporality of *human* (i.e., worldly) subjectivity—not only by way of there having to be a radical *difference* between the two, but also in terms of the question of their *identity*.

> In its first stage of its explication now [the transcendental ego] shows a certain pregivenness, namely, that of the articulation of its intentional life and of immanent time as the form of its life. Transcendental pregivenness has a parallel corresponding to it in the pregivenness of human immanence. The two coincide, or rather are identical, except that the self-apperceptions of humanity fall away by the epoche.[154]

One sees, therefore, that while human immanent time has definite limits— birth and death—and thereby displays a wholeness structure, transcendental immanence seems to show no such limits and no such definability as a discriminable whole. "Rather we have [here] the peculiarity that the totality of transcendental immanent time is wholly hidden, and thereby also the temporal range of the ego."[155] In order to try to determine the context of being for transcendental time—which at this point is quite *un*determined—the whole issue of the relationship of the transcendental ego to the human ego has to be more closely examined. For

> what is immediately clear from the reduction is that man is a unitary something-that-holds [*Geltungseinheit*] set within transcendental life, a correlate of the life of belief of the ego. Thus it is plain that all consolidations of meaning

that make up the sense "man" are references to corresponding transcendental systems of the giving of meaning. This, now, belongs to the full sense of "man": that a human stands in generative linkage to other humans, that he is dependent in being upon "others," that he originates from them.[156]

With this consideration Fink enters into the question of others and the Other, the primary issue of Meditation V. He proposes a series of insertions[157] that offer a clear counter-movement to the focus of analysis in Husserl's existing version. Rather than beginning with the place of others as set in the object-constituting performance of the ego as autonomous monadic center, Fink proposes to enter the presentation of intersubjectivity on the transcendental level by setting out the problem of the constitution of the ego itself, namely, *in terms of its own limits within the larger context of transcendental time* (and therefore in terms of both its ontological wholeness and its ontological dependency). Such an approach is "an *intrinsic consequence* of the phenomenological reduction. If the transcendental sphere of being reaches altogether beyond the ego, then this reaching beyond can only occur in the form of a transcendental intersubjectivity."[158] The problem, of course, is that here one is attempting to explicate trans-egoic structuring on the transcendental level using as clues the phenomena of trans-individual complexity and multiplicity on the human level. To do this legitimately, however, requires resolution of the larger question of the relationship of identity and difference between the worldly—of which the human is a prime case—and the transcendental, which is one of the principle issues of the "Transcendental Theory of Method," i.e., the Sixth Meditation.

One of the interesting results of Fink's approach here is the way Husserl's ego-centrality is retained as important but is nevertheless *circumscribed* in a radical way.[159] As he proceeds[160] Fink makes clear that if it is only with transcendental subjectivity that the world can be constituted in its full objectivity, and if the transcendental Other is simply not effectively encompassed by the action of a monadic ego's own self-reflectively mastered constitutional processes, then there appears to be some kind of necessary *supposition*—not a clear disclosure—of a constitutional process beyond the (or, better, my) ego's own life precisely as egoic.[161] Such a supposition of another action complementary to one's own, however, has to be somehow demonstratively indicated in one's own course of living experience, and this is precisely the function of *empathy*.[162] Empathy has the effect of setting a limit to the efficacy of unmediated egoic self-intuiting right in the question of the most basic constitution of all, that of the world as the universal pregiven horizon for any and all subjective life whatsoever. The countermovement of the anti-Cartesian element to the Cartesian is nowhere stronger than here, where a portion of Husserl's own text itself is integrated to make the point.[163] It should be noted that this will not be the only place where Fink underscores the challenge to the intuitive evidential immediacy basic to Husserl's phenomenology which arises from the intractability of certain issues, issues that need to be resolved in order for phenomenology to be philosophically coherent and defensible.[164]

Before concluding this survey of the writing projects Fink prepared prior to composing the Sixth Meditation and presupposed by it, we have to make one or two remarks. The first is that we can see how Fink's recasting of the Cartesian Meditations turned out to be indeed "quite different," as Cairns reports Husserl to have said of it.[165] It was a difference, however, with which Husserl was familiar from the time of Fink's producing the "Layout for the System of Phenomenological Philosophy," for that approach was consistently put forward by Fink in his work for Husserl. That Husserl would consider a different approach than Fink's specific way of casting the situation from within which one can best move to phenomenology seems clear from other remarks Cairns reports;[166] but the alternatives in Husserl's mind do not seem to take issue at all with regard to the main lines of Fink's program, namely, the interpretation of the reduction in terms of the thematic centrality of the question of the world as pregiven, on the one hand, and, on the other, a clear and critically deepened treatment of the world as *encompassing* human immanence rather than "bracketed off" from it to leave it in some kind of supposed untouched autonomy. Here, then, we have one of the basic "framework" agreements between Husserl and Fink that undergird Husserl's subscription to Fink's treatment of phenomenology.[167]

The second remark in order here regards the intriguing parallel to the very points Fink develops on intersubjectivity that lie in this whole operation of producing a new text for the Cartesian Meditations. At a level lower than that of world-constitution but directly analogous to it, the cooperative philosophizing that was going on is precisely an example of an activity in which the limitations of one individual's intellectual powers are transcended by the actions of an Other linking up and cooperating with the first to give rise to a piece of work that cannot be identified as exclusively the product of either taken singly. This is obviously true in Fink's case, but the point here is that it must also be true for Husserl! Clearly a great part of the final period rethinking of Husserl's transcendental phenomenology is simply not the work exclusively of Husserl. The deposit of working manuscripts that Husserl wrote during this retirement years, the years of Fink's work with him, is but one component of the full documentary material. If Fink was a co-thinker with Husserl, then his own manuscript materials from the period are the second main component; and indeed a complete collection of Fink's notes from the period of his work with Husserl are preserved in the Fink *Nachlass* in Freiburg. But the relationship between such documents and the texts before us has to be correctly construed.

The *Nachlass* manuscripts and notes of both Husserl and Fink, rather than being finished statements, are explorations, sudden insights carried on so as to assess their worth, reactions of the moment, renewed considerations of recurrent themes, etc. The drafts before us in the two volumes of the *VI. Cartesianische Meditation*, on the other hand, represent the effort to refashion these preliminary stirrings of thought into a finished, coherent statement.[168] Here Fink, though he was working on *Husserl's* phenomenology, was not simply *repeating* what was contained in Husserl's working manuscripts, but—similarly to the way Husserl would himself handle his own writings—rather *refashioning* it into more achieved realizations, realizations which would embody something of his own thinking too. The texts before us, therefore, are not "pure" Husserl—and they are not "pure" Fink either. And this is as it should be. For in these documents we have the demonstration of *intersubjectivity at work in transcendental phenomenology itself*, and as an *essential element* of its accomplishment precisely as philosophy, i.e., as something that goes beyond individual biographical identity.

But then if Fink's work during the period in question cannot be understood without Husserl, then Husserl's work during these years cannot be understood without Fink's. While in Fink's notes there is constant reference to Husserlian issues, it must correspondingly be supposed in principle that Husserl's manuscripts will reflect the issues and queries through which Fink focuses his work for Husserl. That this is the case is shown to a limited extent by the selection of Husserlian texts that accompany the Sixth Meditation in the present translation; but the connection between Husserl's manuscripts and Fink's work with him must go far beyond this, given the integral and omnipresent role in Husserl's regimen that Fink held. There is important work here yet to be done.[169]

B) A transcendental theory of method for phenomenology

The task undertaken in the Sixth Meditation was something long called for in Husserl's phenomenology and anticipated by Fink early in his work with Husserl. Toward the end of his *Formal and Transcendental Logic*,[170] Husserl mentioned "transcendental self-criticism" as the root-critique of all others in phenomenology, and Fink referred to that mention in his dissertation.[171] But the proposing of it that really counts is Husserl's call for such self-criticism in the

Cartesian Meditations itself, in the version he produced in 1929. Early in the text, in §13 of Meditation II, Husserl explains that the first stage of phenomenology, namely that represented by the Meditations under way, "is *not yet philosophical in the full sense.*" What is yet necessary is the *second stage,* namely, "the *criticism of transcendental experience* and then the criticism of *all transcendental cognition.*"[172] As he points out later in §63, in the "Conclusion" of the work, this stage of self-criticism is where "the ultimate problems of phenomenology"[173] get addressed. This is precisely the task Fink's Sixth Meditation takes up, as can be clearly seen from these lines in its first section:

> It is the proper task of the *transcendental theory of method* to make phenomenologically understandable the whole systematic enterprise of phenomenological inquiry, the structure of methodological procedure, the rank and style of *transcendental cognition* and "science." Its task, therefore, is to submit the phenomenologizing thought and theory-formation that functions anonymously in phenomenological labors to a proper transcendental analytic, and thus to complete phenomenology in ultimate *transcendental self-understanding about itself.* In other words, the transcendental theory of method intends nothing other than a *phenomenology of phenomenology.*[174]

It takes only a brief scanning of the table of contents of the Sixth Meditation to see some of the major themes which this phenomenology of phenomenology, this transcendental theory of method would cover. The mere listing one sees there, however, belies the depth to which the methodological reflection reaches into main practices and elements of phenomenology. For in the conception of methodology outlined in the text, and in accord with Husserl's own prescription in his Meditations, the methodology had to be a work of *criticism:* not a mere description of methods employed, but transcendental reflection on the very basics of the whole enterprise of doing phenomenology, certain of which turn out to be more problematic than originally seemed. All in all, the influence of the greatest of all transcendental critics, Kant, is felt here.[175]

There is an organizational clarity to Fink's Sixth Meditation that makes a summary here redundant. From the beginning the text clearly states the goals to be reached and the steps needed to reach them. Connections and transitions are quite explicit, and resumés are provided at pivotal points. The reader is led systematically through the vast field of Husserl's phenomenology with the deft hand of one familiar with its intricacies. But the Sixth Meditation itself as it stands has a provisional character to it, being not the fully carried-out project of a "transcendental theory of method," but rather, as Fink actually calls it on the title page of the original text, a *draft for* that project, a working draft detailing the questions to be addressed and setting the terms for addressing them. In this way it is a draft working up "the *idea* of a transcendental theory of method,"[176] rather than its final worked-out realization. And it is no beginner's manual; it is, once again, the sixth of a set of studies, and one must be familiar with the first five before being able to engage in the issues which this sixth defines.

All this Fink himself explains in the first four sections, where two things become clear. First of all, there are specific formal methodological issues that need to be raised. The hitherto most elusive of these—elusive precisely because the Sixth Meditation had been so long inaccessible—is the question of a *constructive* phenomenology, namely, of the necessity of a non-intuitional dimension in order for phenomenology actually to fulfill its objectives. But as with all issues in phenomenology—and this is the second major point here—methodological matters depend for their resolution precisely upon radical explication of the central phenomenological procedure, the reduction. To explicate the reduction in its radical sense, however, is to raise not just formal methodological issues, but substantive issues of profound and all-encompassing import, involving, for example, the distinction between the transcendental and the mundane, or between appearance and being. And these substantive issues lodge centrally as well in the highest of questions for a transcendental theory of method, namely, the explication of *transcendental reflection* as such. For in phenomenology an explication of transcendental reflection must also be an explication of *the subjectivity that transcendentally reflects*, or, as Fink puts it, of the transcendental "onlooker."

In order, therefore, to highlight the philosophical import of the Sixth Meditation, we must try to see the way these substantive issues are presented in that document. As might be expected, the treatment of them here will be in continuity with the revision texts for the previous five Meditations, which we have just reviewed in their basic orientation; and the reason simply is that transcendental phenomenology in general is governed throughout by the implications of the reduction. We can gain an effective angle of approach upon the real thrust of the Sixth Meditation from two kinds of documents, one from Husserl, the other from Fink.

In 1933, in the turbulent early months of the Nazi seizure of power, Husserl wrote a letter to Dietrich Mahnke, a former student of his with whom he had been in regular correspondence over the years. The letter gives Husserl's long reply to some questions Mahnke had asked Husserl about the Cartesian Meditations (in the 1929 version in the French translation), particularly the Fifth.

Mahnke, because of his work on Leibniz,[177] was particularly interested in the way Husserl, in the Fifth Meditation, opened up his concept of the monad in an intermonadic dimension. Addressing Mahnke's questions, Husserl writes:

> You are the first to have understood the immense significance of my studies on transcendental intersubjectivity, the true, transcendental theory of "empathy," and to have recognized the great seriousness of the little French "*Méditations*" as that of a new *discours sur la méthode*, as one could also call it. All its questions go to the center. The question of the meaning of the implication of monads, therefore of all monads in me, the philosophically reflecting ego. They are precisely mere "meditations," mere inauguration of the move a radical reflection on method is to make. The implication is to be understood quite seriously, quite literally, an intentional implication that does not have a "real" implication in addition to itself. The whole disjunctive antithesis between "mutually inclusive" and "mutually exclusive" falls away, when the transcendental attitude is reached, when an absolute all-inclusive intentionalism is carried through (or, when the world is thoroughly treated as that which it is, [viz.,] meant, intentional world on the basis of intentional harmony in holding good [*aus intentionaler Geltungseinstimmigkeit*]). . . .

After discussing several main phenomenological concepts (e.g., recollection, sympathy, constitutive analysis, historicity), he continues:

> What comes before all else is the radical self-reflection *à la méditation cartésienne* that makes possible a fundamental and ongoing labor, an all-inclusive reflection on method, leading back to the beginning, to the in itself first beginning which nothing else can precede in any meaningful sense.
>
> From the beginning, what is immensely difficult is the doubleness of the sense of being in I, we, subjectivity 1) as subjectivity for the world, in whose functioning world gains sense (the world only makes sense as meaning being for subjects that intend the world); and 2) as subjectivity that itself belongs to the world. Both belong essentially together. How, why, in what form, in what possibilities and necessities subjectivity, although creative of the world, must nevertheless objectivate itself as human and animal—to make that explicitly understandable is the great, endless theme; but the specific path along which to proceed is found and has been trod.[178]

Husserl's words here clearly acknowledge and reflect the four years of work on his Cartesian Meditations that had in the immediately preceding twelve-month period culminated in Fink's revision texts and the Sixth Meditation; as Husserl says, "the specific path along which to proceed is found and has been trod." What Husserl writes clearly shows that the methodological question in phenomenology, in the "radical self-reflection" that phenomenology puts into practice, the question of the nature of the move back to the *beginning* beyond which questioning cannot go, is ultimately going to involve the central substantive difficulty of the nature of the difference and identity between human and transcendental subjectivity, between the subjectivity that lives and subsists within the world and the subjectivity that constitutes the world and all in it. And that is precisely the pivotal question that we find highlighted in the documents we draw upon here on Fink's side, namely, in his two notices to the Sixth Meditation, the earlier "Foreword" and the "Prefatory Note" from ten years later.[179] It is in these two notices that not only the concordance between Fink and Husserl is asserted—here specifically in the context of revision of the Cartesian Meditations—but the character of the basic difference between them is explained. The clarification of that concordance and that difference, in terms of the ideas that Fink acknowledges are the guiding concepts of his work, is what we shall be seeing in the remaining treatment here.

Here are the main assertions made by Fink in these notices to take as rubrics for our study:

> The exposition of the problem of a transcendental theory of method, adhering in all closeness to Husserl's philosophy, is determined here by an anticipatory look at a meontic philosophy of absolute spirit.
>
> —Foreword

> The phenomenological inquiry developed here presupposes "Méditations Cartésiennes," . . . [but] it also goes further inasmuch as it expressly puts into question the methodological naiveté found throughout the "Méditations Cartésiennes," . . . [T]he essential thing [is] the aporia whether and how the horizon from which "being" is finally to be understood is itself "existent," whether and how the *being* of the *temporalization* of what is existent is determinable.
>
> —Prefatory Note

The straightforward way of stating the concordance and difference at play here is to say that for Fink the form of self-critique that phenomenology makes in a transcendental theory of method is governed by explicitly raising the question of being within it, whereas for Husserl there is no real need in transcendental phenomenology to make a special issue of the question of being. We shall shortly see that for Husserl this is not a *dismissal* of the question of being, but rather a basic difference in judgment about how it is adequately handled. This difference, however, is accompanied by further differences in how the explication of the identity and difference between transcendental and human subjectivity is worked out by each of the two philosophers. In

Fink's case this leads to being guided by the preliminary idea of a "meontic of absolute spirit," whereas for Husserl there is no corresponding theoretical position. Apart from specific objections or qualifications to what Fink develops in the "Sixth Meditation," there is on Husserl's part only the explicit assertion of the programmatic place for an eventual explicit phenomenological "metaphysics," where something corresponding to Fink's "meontic" might find a place.[180]

Following the indications from Fink's own two notices, and in keeping with the exposition given earlier of the context of his reworking of the Cartesian *Meditations*, we shall focus our treatment of the Sixth Meditation upon four topics:

    1) the question of being;
    2) the problem of the world in its pregivenness;
    3) the meontic;
    4) corollary issues.

1) The question of being

There is no doubt that Fink was indebted to Heidegger for his appreciation of the importance of the question of being for philosophy. As early as his work on his dissertation Fink explicitly acknowledges this in his personal notes;[181] and the issue to which it directly gives rise is the question of the kind of being to determine for the subjectivity that one reaches in the reflective move of the phenomenological reduction.[182] This, of course, was the question at the center of the dispute between Husserl and Heidegger on the article for the *Encyclopaedia Britannica*.[183] Coming after several years of working over the question in his own notes, what Fink does in the Sixth Meditation is something Heidegger could not do, namely, raise the issue in such a way as to make it both accessible to Husserl and appreciated by him (even if he might not agree entirely with Fink's way of treating it). For Fink, introducing the question of being into phenomenology radicalizes and clarifies the issue of the "doubleness" of subjectivity, a) as transcendentally constituting, and b) as transcendentally constituted, i.e., a) as transcendental and not in the world, though wholly and teleologically for the sake of the world, and b) as human and precisely *in* the world. The question that now arises is this: If the transcendental and the human differ radically in *kind of being*, how could they yet be in any legitimate sense *identical?* The concept that enables Husserl to agree thus with Fink on the validity and centrality of the problem (which is what shows in Husserl's May 1933 letter to Mahnke, cited above),[184] even while not fully agreeing with him on the further elaboration of steps to resolve it (which is what Husserl's notes to the Sixth Meditation demonstrate), is the concept of "enworlding" [*Verweltlichung*].

Here is an issue that is directly involved in one-half of the whole text of the Sixth Meditation: in §10, Phenomenologizing as predication, and in §11, Phenomenologizing as "the action of making into a science." Husserl introduces detailed marginal comments and changes throughout these sections. Many of his longest comments and reflections and a large proportion of the additional manuscript materials he wrote in connection with the Sixth Meditation deal with aspects of enworlding. In fact, one finds in this body of materials a long systematic treatment of one of the principal ideas for which Husserl's Crisis texts have generated so much interest, namely, the role of experiential life-in-the-world for the very exercise of cognition (particularly of scientific cognition); and yet the published Crisis texts give only summary indication of the theoretical concept, enworlding, that gives that idea a firm place within phenomenology.[185]

How that place is established in the Sixth Meditation, however, should be carefully noted. Enworlding is not dealt with here primarily to explain human being, i.e., as a finding before the analytic gaze of reflection, but in order to elucidate the conditions for the possibility of that reflective "gaze" itself, as governed by the strictures of the phenomenological reduction. The Sixth Meditation is not a treatise on human experience but a transcendental theory of method, a phenomenology of phenomenology.[186] Nevertheless, in it one finds that features of life in the world such as corporality, sociality, history, "existence," all matters that many take to escape any authentic handling in *transcendental* phenomenology, or to stand in irreducible challenge to it, are the very features that a specifically transcendental inquiry is *obliged* to explore, precisely in order to explicate its own program. We shall return later to the way one or another of these matters is accordingly treated.

What is pivotal in Fink's handling of the question of being, however, is the specific way the concept of being is set within reduction-governed phenomenology. Here, just as our first understanding of the world arises in the natural attitude, so we first gain an idea of being in the natural attitude. But in inverse order to our natural way of taking things, the natural attitude idea of world and of being is not the *concrete* idea to which a philosophically developed idea would stand in contrast as *abstract*; rather, for phenomenology *the natural attitude idea is abstract*, and the idea of the world and that of being first gain their concreteness when they are related back to constituting subjectivity. The world, then, and the being of that which is to be found in the world, are concretely understood when they are understood as *constituted*.[187]

Correspondingly, however, the constituting "agency" must not be understood abstractly either, i.e., as if it had a being of its own apart from its constitutive effect. This is the particular danger of representing the constituting
"agency" in the guise of human immanence absolutized into a region set apart
from the world—the very deficiency *Ideas I* labored under. Concretely considered, constituting "subjectivity" "is" exclusively *in* this process of constitution. Here is Fink's formulation of this point, together with Husserl's additions,
here in angle brackets ⟨ ⟩, and his marginal comment to it, marked [Mg:]:

> Constitutive genesis, however, is not something that *goes on merely* ⟨on occa-
> sion, accidentally⟩ *"attributively"* in transcendental subjectivity, as if that sub-
> jectivity first already were (as substance, as it were) and then would in addition
> engage in constitution. Rather subjectivity is nothing other than ⟨the where
> and, in conformity with its I-centering (polarization)⟩ the *wherefrom of this gen-
> esis*, it is not there *before* the process ⟨but⟩ simply and solely *in the process*.

> [Mg: World and transcendentality—not coexisting or not-coexisting, not in
> accord or in strife, not regions that are together or not together in a total re-
> gion, not correlation in a more comprehensive universe of being—transfor-
> mation of all natural concepts.][188]

This, of course, is the proper context too for determining the sense of *human being*. Here is where Fink goes further than Husserl had in two ways: 1) in
identifying human being with "the natural attitude," and 2) in therefore wishing
to replace the term "natural attitude" with one that would accordingly be more
fitting. This is another telling point in the recasting of phenomenology to
cleanse it of deficiencies found in earlier presentations. Already in 1930 Fink
was speaking for Husserl, at Husserl's authorization, to explain how not to
take the expression "natural attitude." In a letter written July 13, 1930, to a
French correspondent named Monsieur Gary, Fink explains that the term does
not mean any kind of factual behavior-setting orientation or contingent psychological stance, but rather the "condition of the possibility of all factual attitudes; all factual attitudes remain *within* the natural attitude."[189] Even before
that, in his dissertation, Fink had made clear that the "natural attitude" was
the "attitude that made up human being itself, the setting up of man as a being in the whole of the world."[190] Accordingly, because "natural attitude" was
too ambiguous a term,[191] Fink replaced it in his own thinking with the
one used regularly in the Sixth Meditation: "captivation in/by/to the world"
[*Weltbefangenheit*]. In this Fink knowingly diverged from Husserl, who continued to use "natural attitude" despite its ambiguities.[192]

Two final points linked to Fink's weaving of the question of being into transcendental phenomenology need to be mentioned. On the one hand, since it

is as an operation of human subjectivity in the world that all cognition takes place, the lineaments of cognition originate and are determined in linkage to the world. On the other hand, since being and knowing "are the two inseparable components of the cognitive relation," since "every cognition only has its truth insofar as it measures up to the existent itself, 'accords' with it," that is, since "there can in principle be no other object of cognition than what is existent" (below, page 71), then the realm of knowing and being is simply the realm of the world. This straightforward Kantian thesis was already explicitly asserted by Fink in his revisions for the Second Meditation, as we have seen, and it is no less explicitly stated in the Sixth Meditation: "The *world* as the total unity of the really existent [*des real Seienden*], boundlessly open in space and time, . . . : in a word, *being [das Sein]—is only a moment of the Absolute*" (below, pages 143–144). The argument at this point in the text has to do with the way "the Absolute" cannot be, as such, "a being," or, in any explicable way, within the realm of being, thus dramatically reinforcing the equivalence of "the world" and "being." And Husserl makes not one dissenting comment whatsoever on this equation![193] We shall return to the question of "the Absolute" in the section on the meontic.

The fact remains, however, that in the Sixth Meditation Fink's thinking on the matter of being and the world lies more just below the surface rather than in plain sight in the text. It is in his personal notes that one finds the explicit formulations that directly and clearly state the point. There, for example, Fink calls the world "the universal horizon of being," and correlatively speaks of "captivation in the world (the natural attitude) as the horizon of all being," and even as "bewitchment in the idea of being."[194] For Fink it is Kant who is to be credited with raising the question of the limits of the idea of being, and of identifying those limits with the world. Once again, this is not something that is expressed in the Sixth Meditation, but it is unambiguously and repeatedly asserted in Fink's personal notes. Fink puts the idea succinctly thus in a note from 1934: "Kant's philosophy as the first exhibiting of the *cosmological horizon of the idea of being*."[195] We are thus led to the second of our topics for focusing the reading of the Sixth Meditation, namely, the world as the all-encompassing horizon of being within which human being and any activity taken by human being are in principle set.

2) *The problem of the world in its pregivenness*

The problem here can be stated rather simply. To human being functioning in the world, the world is always already there. As thus always pregiven, the world as the realm of existents has to be accounted for in transcendental

phenomenology in terms of constitution. But if the world is the horizon of being, i.e., is the framework of the realm of being as such, within which any particular existent must be set in order to be, then it is not by any kind of origin
in the activity of some kind of existent that this constitution of the world in
its pregivenness can be explained. The only thing to which such constitution
could be ascribed is *that which lies antecedent to being!* And how can sense be made
of "that which lies antecedent to being"?[196]

The sense that antecedency to being on the part of constitutive process
could have is precisely what Fink sees the transcendental theory of method,
driven by the exigencies of the phenomenological reduction, to have to explicate; and a great part of the Sixth Meditation is devoted to formulating this
issue in its main elements and ramifications. Here is where the import of the
critique of *Ideas I* begins to play out most radically. For if the proper understanding of the reduction exorcizes the false idea that the epoche absolutizes
human immanence, that the world and transcendental subjectivity are two
spheres of being somehow set side by side with the second "causing" the
first,[197] then the likeness to human immanence that transcendental subjectivity inevitably has in the phenomenological analysis of constitutive agency has
to be taken critically as the inadequate dressing of the trans-mundane in the
guise of the mundane, the clothing of the trans-existent in the representa-
tional garb of the existent. Simply put, the pregivenness of the world cannot
really be accounted for in terms of something that can only have validity
within that pregiven world.

The result is that not only must the adequacy of concepts that represent
constituting agency in terms of human egoic immanence be questioned, so
also must the recourse to a *multiplying* of such egoic immanences, albeit in communication, i.e., recourse to intersubjectivity. Precisely to the extent that constituting agency has to be taken as antecedent to being, it has to be taken as
not adequately representable in the conceptuality appropriate for being. That
leads, then, to Fink's use of the term for the whole dimension of constituting
agency, "pre-being," for which he mounts an explicit argument.[198] In understanding this term one has to be careful not to fall into precisely the error that
Fink takes pains to correct, namely, that of thinking that "pre-being" is a realm
of being *before* being! as if the "pre-" were the adverbial usage, meaning "antecedently." One must rather take "pre-" in the prepositional sense, meaning
"antecedent to." The term "pre-being" (and its adjectival forms, such as, here
in the translation, "pre-existent") therefore means, not "being in an antecedent
way" i.e., being that is antecendent (to some other kind of being), but "antecedent to being altogether as such"!

Here too is where Fink urges that a specific exercise of the reduction of the
idea of being is needed (pages 74–75 below). Husserl, on the other hand, does

not see this to be necessary; however much he agrees with Fink that the meaning of being is transformed in properly transcendental phenomenology, he does not see a thematic treatment of that transformation to be necessary. (More will be said on this a little later.)

The question of the pregivenness of the world, however, does not simply raise the question of the *inadequacy* of mundane cognitive conceptuality with respect to transcendental constituting operations, it also requires us to recognize the inescapable *necessity* of it, precisely in regard to those transcendental matters. For if philosophic reflection in general, and phenomenological analysis in particular, is always done in human operations, if "human immanence is nothing other than transcendental constituting subjectivity enveloped by enworlding self-apperceptions and 'stationed' in the world" (page 47 below), then if that human philosophizing (or phenomenologizing) aims to conceive and reflect upon transcendentally constituting operations it must do so by conceiving them after the manner of some kind of operation *in the framework of the world.* Here we reach the problem that a transcendental theory of method must specifically address, and which is central to the Sixth Meditation, namely, that of clarifying the condition for the possibility for phenomenological cognition from the point of view of the *horizon of meaningfulness* for its cognitive explications. This all comes out clearly at the end of §8 in the interwoven combination of Fink's text and Husserl's additions and changes. There, as Fink explains, "the theme of the theoretical experience of the phenomenologizing I," i.e., "world-constitution," is the uppermost stratum of a complex structure of operations and the only stratum that holds what is actually in being, viz., the constituted world as the totality of existents. All other strata in the underlying structure of operations "can become thematic in a mode of experience *that only forms an analogy* to an experience of what is existent." To thematize the "pre-existent," in other words, one has to represent it as *something like* the existent, one has to "ontify" it.[199] It is Husserl, now, who makes explicit in his reformulation of Fink's sentences and in comment to them that this means producing a "thematic universe" that is a *world,* wherein transcendental structures can be conceptualized so as to make sense.[200] This, of course, in turn raises the whole question of the semantic character of language as transcendentally employed, to which we shall turn shortly. Right now, however, we must note that we have at this point the main elements for what Fink calls the "meontic," and some brief explanation of that is needed next.

3) *The meontic*

Though mentioned only in the "Foreword" and nowhere in the text of the Sixth Meditation itself,[201] the "meontic" is one of the notions most often and continually recurring in Fink's personal notes during the period of his labors with Husserl.[202] A full explication of what is involved in it would go far beyond what can be presented here, yet a few points must be at least discussed in connection with the themes of the present text.

In fact, though only in three instances, Fink uses terms in the Sixth Meditation that are clearly equivalent to "meontic" but without the formal terminological identity that the latter term has in his notes. For example, "non-ontic" is used twice in regard to the transcendentally "pre-existent," and "non-ontological" once.[203] More important than the terms, however, are the issues and the lines of their resolution that Fink proposes. Two issues in particular are 1) how "pre-/non-existent" transcendental subjectivity relates to mundane/ human subjectivity, forming a unity of identity in difference, and 2) how that same transcendental agency as absolute constitutive source relates to the world that is its constitutive end-product, forming with it a unity in bipolar differentiation.

The solutions anticipated by Fink to these two issues are clearly indicated. 1) If enworlding in the form of human consciousness is a constitutive necessity for all levels of transcendental subjectivity—i.e., in particular for transcendental subjectivity a) as *intending* the world (and thus transcendentally constituting it), and b) as *reflecting upon* that intentional achievement (and thus phenomenologizing, especially in a transcendental theory of method)—then the "full-sided subject" at issue in phenomenology is neither the transcendental subject taken purely in its transcendentality nor human being taken as uninvolved with the transcendental, but is rather "transcendental subjectivity 'appearing' in the world."[204] 2) It comes out clearly in the Sixth Meditation that the whole function of the transcendental is to constitute the world as its telos, rather than first happily subsisting in splendid uniqueness and then subsequently getting to work producing the world. The "Absolute" in the phenomenological sense, then, is this whole of the world-constituting operation, "the comprehensive unity of *the existent as such and the pre-existent* (of *mundane and* 'transcendental' being), of *world and world-origin*" (below, page 143).

The crucial point, however, is that in each case the "unity" is a "*unity of antithetic determinations*" (below, page 134). The antithesis here, however, is not an antithesis of elements that stand opposed or in contradiction to each other within a common framework of reference, but rather an antithesis *with respect to the framework of reference itself.* The opposites in question are not set within the horizon of being or of the world, but precisely stand one *within* and the other *outside* that very framework.[205] As a result, any concept attempting to represent the "pre-existent," the transcendental properly taken, will be a concept a) that "protests" against this transcendental usage and b) that can only have sense when explicitly taken and interpreted *with* the meaning native to it in its non-transcendental home, that is, with the meaning against which it "protests" (see below, page 89). These are basic elements of Fink's notion of the "meontic."[206] Not only must the dimension of the "meontic" not be characterized in terms of the opposition between being and non-being as an opposition *necessarily set within the framework of the world,* but the two terms of the "meontic" antithesis *must be kept integrated,* else the true meaning of each will be missed.[207] In effect, then, what Fink proposes at the heart of phenomenology's transcendental theory of method is a philosophy of the meontic!—or, as he himself put it in his "Foreword," "a meontic philosophy of absolute spirit."

It is at this point that we can move to some final remarks on corollary issues.

4) Corollary issues

There are two issues that most merit our attention here, both relating directly to the meontic thrust of Fink's proposals, and both matters of principal interest to students of Husserl's phenomenology in what is taken to be its preeminent final development, i.e., the Crisis texts. The issues are those of *language* and *intersubjectivity.*

In §§10 and 11, readers of the *Crisis* will find a fuller development of ideas with which they are already familiar from Husserl's essay on the origin of geometry.[208] The main questions Fink addresses are 1) how does the language used for transcendental assertions relate to language as a phenomenon intrinsically of mundane origin and character?—§10; and 2) what makes it necessary for transcendental reflection to embody itself in language (i.e., enworld itself) in the first place?—§11. In both cases, the answer has to take account of the radical nature of the transcendental properly conceived, i.e., as the "preexistent" or, if one were to read into the text Fink's real thinking, the "meontic" precisely in its "protested" but nonetheless necessary self-enworlding articulation in the conceptual representation of a human thinker. Here too one finds significant differences between Husserl and Fink on what steps are necessary in order to ensure the proper understanding of the transcendental, despite clear agreement on the radical difference of the latter with respect to the worldly.

For Fink it is necessary not simply to acknowledge that the sense of words used for the transcendental must be radically changed; one has to set in motion a specific procedure to ensure it. Because for Fink the question of being is so fundamentally and explicitly important, he takes it to be specifically necessary for reflection to focus thematically on the meaning of being in relation to the transcendental. Thus he argues for a specific reduction of the idea of being—which means a critique of the supposed legitimacy of the *language* of being (see below, pages 93–94). For Husserl, on the other hand, this kind of explicit focus on the meaning of being is simply not thought to be a necessary operation. That a radical transformation of sense take place is not in question; but for Husserl, that transformation in sense will be achieved gradually as phenomenology proceeds. For Husserl the terms and concepts brought into use are bound to have their meaning determined from phenomena in accord with the grasp of evidentness in which they are held, and not via specific attention to those terms and concepts as such.

Yet Fink's whole argument leads to the conclusion that it is not possible for the transcendental as properly taken to appear properly *as* transcendental, i.e., as "pre-existent"—*as meontic;* for in itself, not belonging within the realm of being (though in principle relating necessarily to it in constituting action), it "is" not something that *can* "appear" at all, much less in evidentness![209] It can only "appear" in an *enworlded* appearance, that is, in a "protesting" self-manifestation, that is, one that can only be understood by a step of discernment beyond the moment of intuitional presence.[210] Thus it is that Fink, too, in effect sees the explication of being to be one of those topics that requires a dimension of reflective analysis in phenomenology that works beyond the strict limits of the intuitional giving of something in its very self [*Selbstgebung*]. In fact, his explication of the structural relationship that binds being with "pre-being" is redolent of the supple speculative terminologies of the great German Idealists, Kant, Fichte, and Hegel.[211]

On intersubjectivity, now, the question is not whether transcendence of singular subjectivity is fundamental to the constitution of objectivity and actuality in the world; that is already established by the work and reworking of Meditation V. Moreover, §11 of the Sixth Meditation explicitly asserts intersubjective enworlding as a necessary condition in order for phenomenological reflection upon its own doings to be achieved as science, as rational knowing. The root question is rather whether the "intersubjectivity" in question is to be characterized in terms of, and parallel to, the individuality and multiplicity of *human* subjectivity. And that amounts to asking whether intersubjectivity, conceived in its proper transcendental sense—once again, as "pre-existent" (or *meontic*)—should ultimately be spoken of as built up of individuals (see below, pages 125 and 144–145). Here, of course, we touch upon an issue whose ultimate resolution awaits work that never was really brought to completion by either Husserl or Fink, despite the labor of both on it: the analysis of primordial temporality and the metaphysics of individuation. This was a project that punctuated Husserl's entire career, from the early lectures on time-consciousness of 1905, through the Bernau studies of 1917–1918, to the renewed efforts of the early 1930s, when Fink was charged as well with the reworking of Husserl's manuscript studies even as new ones were being produced.

That, however, is another whole story that is largely unknown and that remains to be resurrected from the notes and drafts that these same two philosophers left behind. For the present the text before us now has to be read. And it has to be read as the work of the two precisely as two—in dialogue, in joint commitment, and in difference. Indeed, once one is made aware of the way it is the question of being that accentuates the difference that there must be if each is a genuine thinker, then one has to ask about the effect of this difference within phenomenology. Does the difference result from development from within phenomenology, or must it be accountable to importation from outside it? Emerging from the stage of self-criticism, does it corrode and negate, or does it consolidate and reestablish? It is not a simple matter, for, as we saw in section II above, it involves the whole issue of what constitutes one particular philosophy as against another, as well as against something we might call "philosophy as such."[212] But in addition, the question of *a* philosophy and philosophy "*as such*" also involves the matter of how philosophic work is to be identified with a *particular* philosopher—which of course is one of the very issues of the Sixth Meditation as a transcendental theory of method. Nevertheless, to the degree that actual interplay in thinking between individual human philosophers is intrinsic to the realization of philosophy, to that degree genuine philosophy is under way in this text. To that same extent also it can be said that the program of phenomenology is being carried out. While, therefore, these documents are witness to the failure of one particular project to come to completion, they testify as much to the thinking that continued on into another beginning.

V. On the translation

Some word of explanation is needed now about the texts assembled in the present volume, and about the translation. In the first place, what is translated here corresponds exactly to the textual contents of Volume I of the German edition in Husserliana Dokumente. The only things left out are the text-critical description and notes. The aim is to make it possible to check the original wording of both Fink and Husserl despite the complexity of connection between Fink's text and Husserl's notations. Some unavoidable exceptions to exact correspondence will be explained shortly. To aid in checking the original German, the runningheads on each page of the translation here give the pagination of the corresponding text in the German edition.

In addition to the information already given in earlier sections on the principal text translated here, something needs to be said further about the two
other components, the two one-page prefatory notes by Fink, and the manuscript materials by Husserl given here as Appendices. Full detail can, of course,
be found in the respective text-critical explanation in the Husserliana Dokumente edition. In a departure from the arrangement of the German edition,
the two prefatory notes have here been placed *before* the main text rather than
after it.

The first note, entitled "Draft of a Foreword" in the Husserliana Dokumente edition, is a sheet of typed text by Fink obviously from a time soon after one of Husserl's close readings of the Sixth Meditation, but which carries
no date. It was found in Fink's *Nachlass* attached to a copy of §12 of the text
with the handwritten description: "Prefatory page removed from the 'Transcendental Theory of Method'." On the envelope holding these papers Fink
had also written: "Professor Berger took §§1–11 with him to France, where
they were cited in several publications."[213]

The second single-page text, "Prefatory Note [to the Habilitation Text],"
is a statement Fink wrote in December 1945 (a date given on the page itself)
as he was preparing to present the Sixth Meditation to serve as a *Habilitationsschrift*, as recounted above.[214] There is an apparent inconsistency between the
way the Sixth Meditation is described in this "Prefatory Note" and the actual
sequence of events involved in its writing. All extant documents and texts
show that the Sixth Meditation was in fact first written in 1932 *as* the "Sixth
Meditation," following directly Fink's work on revision texts for the first
five in that same year. All documents and texts also show that Fink, with
Husserl's consent and recommendation, also had in mind to submit the same
material for his *Habilitation*. The present "Prefatory Note," however, in referring to an "initial essay form," is the only document that suggests that this material may have existed earlier in some form other than the present *Sixth
Cartesian Meditation*. However, no such earlier form of any kind is to be found.
There are plenty of indications in Fink's notes of preoccupation with the *themes*
of the Sixth Meditation in the years before its actual composition, but none
that he wrote up a "Transcendental Theory of Method" in any kind of earlier
draft. We can read Fink's speaking of "initial essay form," therefore, as indicating that he had at least conceived the *idea* of a transcendental theory of
method independently of its becoming an explicit sequel to Husserl's existing
five Cartesian Meditations.[215] In this way it may well have been intended all
along precisely as a possible *Habilitationsschrift*.

Fink indeed considered the Sixth Meditation to be his own production—
within Husserlian transcendental phenomenology—and it was put forward

three times *as* his own. The first time was its figuring in the endeavor in early 1933 to proceed with the *Habilitation,* which, as we have seen, came to naught. The second was its incorporation into the *Kantstudien* article of 1933 (appearing in early 1934); and the third was its being used—successfully—for the *Habilitation* in late 1945 and early 1946. Indeed, the *Kantstudien* article is the only variant "draft"—precisely in "essay form"—of the Sixth Meditation.²¹⁶

The Appendices are all manuscripts by Husserl that stand in explicitly documented connection to the Sixth Meditation. This connection was made either on the manuscripts themselves, or by their having been assembled in a folder on which was written by Husserl the designation "Ad VI. Meditation" (Appendices II–X and XIII–XV were all contained in this folder). As one would expect, there are material connections between Fink's text and many other Husserlian manuscripts, but this involves a much broader principle of selection and interpretation.²¹⁷

This English translation faithfully follows the editorial layout of the Husserliana Dokumente edition; but the disposition of the Husserlian notations in relation to the main text should be explained. In the first place, Husserl wrote his notes on the page (all in Gabelsberg shorthand) wherever the kind of notation he was making (alteration of one or several words, general comment, etc.) best fit. The amount of this notational material on any one page varies widely, some pages showing none, others carrying numerous individual entries, still others having all or nearly all of the free margins filled. In a few instances Husserl's remarks continue on the reverse side of the sheet. An editorial decision was made to differentiate these various notations not by way of physical location on a page, which would have required incredibly cumbrous textual machinery, but in terms of function; and in most instances function corresponds nicely with location. As a result, the notations are all placed at the bottom of the pages to which they belong and are designated by one of four categories, as indicated by an abbreviation in square brackets at the beginning of each note entry. While the general plan in the German edition has been followed, two small deviations have been introduced.

In the first place, since Husserl's notations do not really represent an element *subordinate* to Fink's text, that is, since they represent thinking that is at least *co-equal* to Fink's—a point essential to the nature of the present text as a whole as well as to the interpretation which this introduction is pursuing— these notations cannot really be considered *footnotes.* Accordingly, despite the fact that a footnote mechanism is used, Husserl's notations are given here in a print close in size to that of Fink's text. What is Husserl's, however, is in all cases marked off by angle brackets: ⟨ ⟩. Secondly, in the translation here the placement in Fink's text of the numerals referring to Husserl's notations is meant to indicate as consistently as possible the nature of the remark the reader can expect to find in these notations. The following table explains the system being used:

—[Alt.] = Alteration. Footnote numerals are placed immediately before the word or phrase affected. Frequently several alterations occur in an extended passage. In this case, the note number may be placed immediately before the first word of a portion of the text which precedes the actual alterations but which has been carried into the footnote for the sake of greater coherence or readability. The passage thus included may continue on past the actual alterations until some natural break, once again in the interest of intelligibility. In all cases, then, the angle brackets make clear which portions of the wording are Husserl's actual alterations.

—[Ins.] = Insertion. Notation numerals are placed at the point of insertion, after a preceding word or before a following word, depending upon whether the insertion continues the preceding thought or adds an initial point to the one that follows (see notations 15, 16, and 45 for the first case, and 46 and 51 for the second). Also, when for the sake of greater intelligibility a portion of the text is carried into the notation itself (e.g., note 269), as just explained for Alterations, then the numeral is placed immediately before the first word thus carried into that notational material. As with Alterations, Husserl's insertions are indicated precisely by the angle brackets.

—[Sup.] = Supplementary addition. Footnote numerals are placed immediately after the word which forms the point at which the supplementary remark is meant to carry on the thought. (Examples are notes 347 and 365.)

—[Mg.] = Marginal comment. The footnote numeral is placed after the word ending the passage to which the comment pertains.

The arrangement is not perfect, and there are exceptions to the general scheme described above as required by the particular notational situation. There are also instances here of divergence from the numbering in the German edition, owing to the fact that the sequence of words in the English text will not always be sufficiently close to that in the German. These instances are few, however, and amount only to a reversal of the order between a pair of numbers. They are the pairs 376–377 and 427–428. In one further case (the pair 263–264) the reversal is necessary because of the way a principle of differentiation has been adopted here for placement in the text of the numerals for Husserl's notations.

There have been several kinds of interpolation made by the Husserliana Dokumente editors as well as by the translator. Within the texts any such interpolated words or phrases which, for the sake of clarity, are to be read as a continuous part of the text are put in square brackets: [ ]. Also in square brackets are explanatory insertions by the translator put in for various reasons, e.g., giving the original German terms, or making up for absent contextual reference in quotations, etc. In the Husserlian notations, various details of information by the editors or translator are placed in square brackets and the respective source indicated by either "Ed." or "Tr." At two points the translator has added a brief marginal remark of Husserl's that is given in the text-critical section of the German edition rather than as a numbered notation to the passage where it originally occurs. These two remarks, notes 8 and 34, are both marked [TK: 226], which indicates the page number where they occur in the Textkritische Anmerkungen of the German edition.

There is a supplementary footnote series (in the proper sense of the term "footnotes") added by the translator both in the main text and in the Appendices. Designated by letters of the alphabet instead of numbers, these footnotes contain in general two sorts of items. One kind gives explanations which the translator thought would be helpful to the understanding of the text particularly in translation. The other consists of notes of various kinds. For example, some give a few more internal cross-references which, worked out by Guy van Kerckhoven but not included in the notes in the edition as published, are helpful for keeping track of the development of the exposition.

With the number of Husserl's writings appearing in English translation, something of a community of English terminology for Husserlian terminology has been built up. Some explanation of how the present translation shares in or departs from that community is therefore in order as a final discussion in this introduction.

There is an additional element of complication in the present work in that it is not just a Husserlian vocabulary that it displays. Fink has a style of conceptualization and wording of his own, distinguishable from Husserl's in important matters, even if those matters are ones that Husserl thinks out along with Fink. One finds, therefore, that terms not of the usual usage in Husserlian texts become central and prominent here. In general, then, the translation must accordingly preserve something of a stylistic and/or terminological singularity by virtue of its dual authorship.

Regarding actual renderings, there are a number of terminological points in the translator's footnotes that need not be repeated here. Brief explanation, however, is needed regarding, first, certain general practices that were followed, and then the reasons why certain especially difficult terms are rendered as they are in divergence from the dominant practice in Husserlian translations.

A. General practices

The set of terms that it is most trying to have to render into English are the "being"-words, given the way etymologically different terms available in German on the one side and in English on the other can have different subtle and shifting connotations. Several considerations had to be kept in mind in searching for a way of handling the situation:

1) In the texts comprising the present work, there is little if any material distinction between *Sein* or *sein*, on the one side, and *Existenz* or *existieren* on the other. Heidegger's sensitizing of philosophical perception so as to see a basic distinction between these terms, *Sein* and *Existenz*, is not followed by either Fink or Husserl here. Given the strength and popularity of that sensitization, however, there seemed some merit in allowing the English to show that lack of differentiation in the German by giving at least some indication regarding which terms are in fact used in the German in particular instances, rather than freely varying the English with no concern for reflecting the actual usage in the German. In other words, any misplaced emphasis on a distinction might be countered not by obscuring the largely interchangeable German usage, but by displaying it at least to some extent, while not controverting acceptable English usage.

2) The usages of the English participle "being" are far more restricted than those of the German *seiend*. Some usages of *seiend* in German just do not have an equivalent in a usage of "being" in English. Instead, the equivalent in English can be "existent." This means that the English "existent," or "existing," usually shares with "being" much the same sort of interchangeability as holds between the corresponding German terms. These and several other complicating circumstances (e.g., the use of *Dasein*, which similarly is used with no Heideggerian connotations here) seemed best resolved by resorting to the following scheme of translation practices with respect to "being"-words:

German	English
Existenz, existieren	Existence, Exist [*existieren*] (always capitalized or with the original German word in brackets)
existentiell	existential (always)

Sein	being (never "existence")
seiend	existent, existing, in being (never "existential" or "ontic" or "ontological")
Seiendes	something existent, [the] existent, [a] being
das Seiende	the existent, that which exists, that which is existent (occasionally "beings")
Dasein	being, existence (but not capitalized)
ontisch	ontic
ontologisch	ontological

The practice of capitalizing an English term in order to reflect the situation in which of two largely synonymous words one may be of Germanic origin and the other a Latin derivative has been followed in this translation in other instances as well. The rule adopted here, however, is that if *no other way* of distinguishing the two is available, then the term of Latin derivation is capitalized in English: [218]

	German	*English*
1)	*Idee*	Idea
	Vorstellung	idea (sometimes)
2)	*Objekt*	Object
	Gegenstand	object

Two examples of frequent usage in which the different German terms are easily indicated without capitalization are:

	German	*English*
1)	*Vergegenständlichung*	objectification
	Objektivation or *Objektivierung*	objectivation
2)	*Ego*	ego
	Ich	I

B. Some particularly difficult terms

One could discuss at great length how to render in English any number of German terms, especially as they are used in Husserl's or Fink's German; but here only three perhaps merit brief, more specific explanation:

1) There are a number of frequently used terms formed around the noun *Geltung* and the verb *gelten*. While no such thing as a "general meaning" ever figures into actual discourse, the many senses a particular expression of this sort

can have in actual usage are all contextually concretized ways of asserting the quality or status of something by which it "holds good." For Husserl, one of the biggest questions for phenomenology to resolve is how things confronting us on any of several experiential levels (e.g., the intellectual, or the perceptual) confront us as *solidly* "holding good," i.e., as having validity we cannot reject or existence we cannot deny. Since the first move of phenomenology is to try to see any such status of "holding good" as the effect of the subjective action of constitutive intentionality, *Geltung* is "that by virtue of which something is taken as holding good," or, as one of Cairns's recommendations has it, *Geltung* is the "acceptedness" of something.[219] The present translation, then, in the main adopts two solutions, to use either Cairns's term "acceptedness" or variants of the circumlocution "taken as holding good." (Occasionally, though, I have permitted myself to vary this by straightforwardly using "validity," e.g., in notation 84 below.)

2) Another term of special Husserlian usage is *aktuell*. In the present text, apart from the occasional instance where it means "actual" as contrasted mainly with "potential" (and even there as well), it usually has to be given the sense of "the actual precisely in the exercise or occurrence *right now* of an act of constitutive realization." In other words, the term fuses actuality as a "state" with actuality as a temporal dimension, as "now." (See below, translator's note "cc.") In the translation, then, such usages of *aktuell* are rendered in a variety of ways that include the temporal qualification: e.g., "as a present actuality," "of the actual moment," "present-moment" (or "actual-moment").

3) The last term to discuss is one for which one particular rendering in English has begun to have a certain general acceptability. That term is *Evidenz*, and the more frequent rendering is "self-evidence." The trouble with this expression is that it usually carries a heavily *logical* connotation. That is, the dominant technical usage of the term implies the possession of a logical and semantic character on the part of an asserted proposition such that that proposition is immediately convincing by a mere moment of reflection on it in its logical and semantic character. For Husserl, however—and Fink follows Husserl totally in the way he too uses the term—*Evidenz* is the ultimate condition of ascertainment precisely in the *experiential* condition of being the object for a subject. *Evidenz* is the "evident-ness" of self-manifestation to an *experiential* cognitive agent, that is, it is the culminating correlational term of a process of intentional action on the part of subjectivity by which the item in question comes to be given *in its native self,* and not merely in a mediating anticipation, indication, or representation. Accordingly, inelegant as it may be, the rendering chosen here for *Evidenz* is "evidentness," and for *evident* simply "evident."

The present translation is not a perfect representation of the original texts. Nor is it a substitute. It is meant rather as a *mediator*, as an aid to enable someone to begin approaching the originals with a comprehension that can grow the closer one comes to them precisely by way of this transfer into English. The question of the translatability of philosophical thinking as expressed in language is itself a philosophical issue, which, once again, in the very discussion carried on in the Sixth Meditation regarding "transcendental language," is one of the themes of the work, at least by close implication.

Several organizations are responsible for the support that was indispensable to the completion of the present translation. First of all, the National Endowment for the Humanities made it financially possible for me to take leave from my home university to complete the translation. For the actual expenses of the stay in Freiburg in Breisgau during which I did that work and began a study of the background to the text, particularly regarding Eugen Fink as both a thinker and a person, I am indebted to the generosity of the Fritz Thyssen Foundation, as well as to the University of Kentucky Research Committee. The major part of the cost of producing the first computer-processed typescript was also covered by the Fritz Thyssen Foundation, with again the University of Kentucky Research Committee contributing, particularly in the use of equipment. Finally, I wish to thank the Pädagogische Hochschule Freiburg, where the Eugen-Fink-Archiv is located, for having so graciously made space and facilities available during the period of my work in Freiburg.

Several years intervened between the work of translation and its publication, during which time my study of the context and content of these texts has been immeasurably deepened by extensive study of the Fink *Nachlass* in Freiburg. The extended periods of that study, indispensable for preparing the present introduction, were supported by the Alexander von Humboldt Foundation and the National Endowment for the Humanities. Special assistance for briefer but indispensable follow-up research visits to Louvain was generously provided by the Southern Regional Education Board.

A more personal debt of gratitude, however, is owed to a number of others with whom I have been in contact all during this task. The Husserl Archives in Louvain and its staff, and Samuel IJsseling in particular, have been most helpful and supportive. Indeed, I must especially thank the Husserl Archives for permission to quote from the Husserl correspondence in this introduction. In Freiburg the numerous and fruitful discussions with Jann Holl and Franz-Anton Schwarz, who were both students of Fink's in their university years, were greatly appreciated. And the hospitality and solicitousness of Ferdinand Graf, also one of Fink's former students and Director of the Eugen-Fink-Archiv there, made the routines of work at a desk less burdensome. Back in Lexington, Ted Fiedler, of the German Department at the University of Kentucky, gave considerable time to helping me catch the nuances of the original wording, and lastly I wish to thank Shannon Price for the superb job of computer-typing the text, with all its typographic and notational complexities.

The warmest thanks, however, go to two people, each major influences in my work at Freiburg in different ways. Guy van Kerckhoven, final editor for the two Husserliana Dokumente volumes, has been an utterly selfless collaborator, a boundless resource, and an excellent colleague in the work, beyond translating, of *understanding* the Sixth Meditation and the Husserlian stream of accomplishment within which it is lodged. His exhaustive assembling of documentary material in the Husserl Archives, together with his initial sketch of highlights from the Fink *Nachlass* in Frieburg, formed the indispensable initial basis for my understanding of the historical context of the texts here. For example, the identification of the letters in the Husserl correspondence relevant to Fink's work with Husserl that I have been drawing from in this introduction I owe directly to Guy van Kerckhoven. Finally, the extraordinary graciousness and unreserved generosity of Mrs. Susanne Fink have been the sustaining element for this project (and others). For taking care of innumerable practical necessities both great and small, and, more than that, for helping me to see something of the living reality of Freiburg not only now but in the ambit of undertakings that comprised her husband's life, I am deeply grateful.

NOTES

Where a published English translation is not explicitly indicated, translations of German texts are by the present translator.

1. (Paris: Aubier, 1941), p. 115 note 1; English translation by Kathleen McLaughlin, *The Cogito in Husserl's Philosophy*, Northwestern University Studies in Phenomenology and Existential Philosophy (Evanston: Northwestern University Press, 1972), p. 92. While in Berger's book there is only one direct reference to the Sixth Meditation, Berger draws extensively from the several essays that Fink had published in the 1930s, and more than any other from Fink's 1933 *Kantstudien* article. (Altogether there are 36 footnoted references to Fink in the book.) As will be explained later, that *Kantstudien* article is based directly on the Sixth Meditation.

2. (Paris: Gallimard, 1945), pp. i and xv; English translation by Colin Smith, *Phenomenology of Perception*, International Library of Philosophy and Scientific Method (London: Routledge & Kegan Paul, 1962), pp. vii and xx.

3. Edmund Husserl, *Cartesianische Meditationen und Pariser Vorträge*, ed. Stephan Strasser, Husserliana I (Den Haag: Martinus Nijhoff, 1950), p. XXVIII.

4. They are catalogued in the designation P II, i.e., as not an official part of the deposit of Husserl's literary legacy, since they are considered Fink's work, rather than Husserl's.

5. That is, from the period of Fink's emigration to Belgium (March 16, 1939), following the transfer of Husserl's *Nachlass* to the Institut Supérieur de Philosophie, until his repatriation to Germany (autumn 1940) after the German occupation of Belgium. On the intricate and perilous process of secretly removing Husserl's *Nachlass* from Freiburg to Louvain, one must read H. L. Van Breda, "Le sauvetage de l'héritage husserlien et la fondation des Archives-Husserl," in *Husserl et la pensée moderne,* Actes du deuxième Colloque International de Phénoménologie, Krefeld, 1–3 Novembre 1956, ed. H. L. Van Breda and J. Taminiaux, Phaenomenologica 2 (La Haye: Martinus Nijhoff, 1959), pp. 1–42. See also below, section III of this introduction.

6. Husserliana Dokumente II/1 and II/2, Dordrecht: Kluwer Academic Publishers, 1988. Part I carries the subtitled description "Texte aus dem Nachlass Eugen Finks (1932) mit Anmerkungen und Beilagen aus dem Nachlass Edmund Husserls (1933–1934)." Unfortunately, in the production of Part II the subtitled description of Part I was mistakenly repeated in place of the correct one for Part II, given in the final typescript as follows: "Texte aus dem Nachlass Eugen Finks (1930–1932) mit Anmerkungen und Beilagen aus dem Nachlass Edmund Husserls (1930–1932/33)."

7. Husserl's sentiments about his own status as finally, in his last years, a true beginner are most forcefully expressed in his "Nachwort zu meinen 'Ideen zu einer reinen Phänomenologie und phänomenologischen Philosophie,'" first published in his *Jahrbuch für Philosophie und phänomenologische Forschung,* 11, 1930. The text is reprinted in Husserliana V, pp. 138–162, and the passage relevant here is on p. 161 in that edition. A new English translation is now available in Edmund Husserl, *Ideas Pertaining to a Pure Phenomenology and to a Phenomenological Philosophy,* Second Book: *Studies in the Phenomenology of Constitution,* trans. Richard Rojcewicz and André Schuwer, Edmund Husserl Collected Works III (Dordrecht: Kluwer Academic Publishers, 1989), "Epilogue," pp. 407–430.

8. That is, as they are known in the following versions:

1) *Méditations cartésiennes, Introduction à la phénoménologie,* tr. Gabrielle Pfeiffer and Emmanuel Levinas, Bibliothèque de la Société Française de Philosophie (Paris: Armand Colin, 1931). This translation was made from an expanded version of the original Paris lectures—expanded in particular by a Fifth Meditation that went way beyond the few sketchy remarks on intersubjectivity in the original set. On May 17, 1929, at Husserl's direction, Fink sent this version to the translators, who were working under the general direction of Alexandre Koyré.

2) "Cartesianische Meditationen, Eine Einleitung in die Phänomenologie," in Edmund Husserl, *Cartesianische Meditationen und Pariser Vorträge,* ed. Stephan Strasser, Husserliana I (Den Haag: Martinus Nijhoff, 1950). Despite some differences and variations, the Husserliana text is basically the same as the one Husserl provided for the translation into French, namely, the first revision of the original lectures that was completed by early May 1929.

3) *Cartesian Meditations, An Introduction to Phenomenology*, tr. Dorion Cairns (The Hague: Martinus Nijhoff, 1960). Cairns's translation is based, once again, on the same basic text as in 1) and 2); however, Cairns also made use of a copy of the text ("Typescript C") that differs in some passages from the version used for the edition in 2), and which conforms more closely to the French translation, 1). On the whole matter of these texts and their variations, see the treatment in the second edition of Husserliana I (1973), "Zur Textgestaltung," pp. 221–228, and especially the "Einleitung" by Elisabeth Ströker in the Philosophische Bibliothek: *Cartesianische Meditationen*, Hamburg: Meiner, 1987.

9. This letter from Fink to Van Breda, written from Freiburg on October 26, 1946, is in the Husserl Archives in Louvain (and a copy of it is in the Fink *Nachlass* in Freiburg). A letter of Fink's written on November 1, 1946, to Stephan Strasser, in reply to a series of questions Strasser has asked about certain details regarding the composition of the Meditations, again indicates the nature of Fink's own revisions and of the place of the Sixth Meditation, and of his interest in publishing them as a complement to the Louvain edition. Fink explains that for both the Cartesian Meditations and Husserl's *The Crisis of European Sciences and Transcendental Phenomenology* (English translation by David Carr, Evanston: Northwestern University Press, 1970), it was he, Fink, who had introduced the section divisions and their titles into Husserl's original text (which the latter had written without explicit breaks). He then remarks in regard to the revision texts he had written for Husserl's Cartesian Meditations: "These drafts are quite interesting above all by reason of the fact that Husserl had occupied himself with them so intensively and had added extensive notations in shorthand. These notations, especially in the case of the Sixth Meditation, contain the most fundamental points expressed by Husserl on the methodology and systematic coherence [*die Methodik und Systematik*] of phenomenology." This passage is quoted in the "Vorwort" to *VI. Meditation*, Husserliana II/1, pp. XI–XII; the letter is preserved in the Fink *Nachlass* in Freiburg (and a copy is in Louvain).

10. The full account and chronology of Husserl's preparation and delivery of the Cartesian Meditations, of his revision of them, and of his vacillation between alternate projects for giving a definitive statement of his phenomenology for the German philosophic public is provided by the following studies: 1) Stephan Strasser, "Einleitung" to *Cartesianische Meditationen*, Husserliana I, pp. XXI–XXX (an English translation by Thomas Attig has been published in the *Journal of the British Society for Phenomenology*, 7 (1976), pp. 12–17); 2) Iso Kern, "Einleitung" to Edmund Husserl, *Zur Phänomenologie der Intersubjektivität*, Part III, Husserliana XV (Den Haag: Martinus Nijhoff, 1973), pp. XVI–LXV; 3) Karl Schuhmann, *Husserl-Chronik, Denk- und Lebensweg Edmund Husserls*, Husserliana Dokumente I (Den Haag: Martinus Nijhoff, 1977), pp. 340–441.

11. The occasion is described in the *Avertissement* to the French translation, p. V. In the introductory remarks made by Xavier Léon to open the sessions (included in the same *Avertissement*), Husserl is lauded as "le maître le plus éminent de la pensée allemande." Such encomia would soon ring hollow as academic and political events unfolded in Husserl's own country, Germany.

12. Letter to Ingarden, May 26, 1929, in Edmund Husserl, *Briefe an Roman Ingarden,*
ed. Roman Ingarden (Den Haag: Martinus Nijhoff, 1968), pp. 54–55. Ingarden,
whom Husserl called "the dearest and truest of my older students" (letter to Ingarden,
December 2, 1929), had studied with him in both Göttingen and Freiburg, and remained in contact through both letters and visits until Husserl's death in 1938.

13. The description is Husserl's: "in a fever of work," as he puts it in a letter to
Georg Misch from June 27, 1929, published in the "Nachwort" to the third edition of
Misch's *Lebensphilosophie und Phänomenologie, Eine Auseinandersetzung der Diltheyschen Richtung
mit Heidegger und Husserl* (Stuttgart: B. G. Teubner, 1967), pp. 327–328. This letter
(along with others that Husserl wrote to Misch) is now included in the ten-volume
edition of Husserl's entire correspondence, Edmund Husserl, *Briefwechsel,* Bd. VII,
Husserliana Dokumente III/7 (Dordrecht: Kluwer, 1994), pp. 274–276.

14. Misch's book (see note 13) appeared in *Philosophischer Anzeiger* in three installments. The second and third installments appeared in the spring of 1930 and in November 1930 respectively.

15. This is in the letter of June 27, 1929, mentioned in note 13 above.

16. Husserl's copies of these two texts, both with handwritten dedications by Heidegger and both in the Husserl Archives at Louvain, carry remarks and markings that
indicate what Husserl found to be either of interest, not clear to him, or objection-
able. A study of Husserl's reading of *Being and Time* via his notes in the text is given in
D. Souche-Dagues, "La lecture husserlienne de *Sein und Zeit,*" *Philosophie,* 21 (1989),
pp. 7–36.

17. The letter was written December 2, 1929, *Briefe an Ingarden,* pp. 55–56. (The
correspondence between Husserl and Ingarden is now included in Husserl, *Briefwechsel,* III, pp. 175–335, but it will be cited here in its first publication.) An even stronger
rejection of Heidegger is expressed in a letter to Alexander Pfänder written a year
later, January 6, 1931, cited in Kern's "Einleitung" (Husserliana XV, p. XXII), and published in Herbert Spiegelberg and Everhard Avé-Lallemant, *Pfänder-Studien,* Phaenomenologica 84 (Den Haag: Martinus Nijhoff, 1982), pp. 345–349. Indeed, there he says
that he himself finally came to realize what everyone else had already known, that
Heidegger was doing something completely opposed to his, Husserl's, own philosophic commitment. (This letter to Pfänder is also now in Husserl, *Briefwechsel,* II, pp.
180–184.) See also Husserl's letter to Dietrich Mahnke, January 8, 1931, *Briefwechsel,*
III, p. 476.

18. Husserliana XVII, p. 11 note 1. (*Formal and Transcendental Logic,* tr. Dorion
Cairns, The Hague: Martinus Nijhoff, 1969, p. 7.)

19. "Author's Preface to the English Edition," in Edmund Husserl, *Ideas: General Introduction to Pure Phenomenology,* tr. W. R. Boyce-Gibson (London: George Allen & Un-
win, 1931), p. 30. See Kern's explanation of the differences between the English
version and the German of this text, owing to Husserl's rapid shifting of plans regarding the Cartesian Meditations in the years 1929–1930; Husserliana XV, p. XXV
note 3. One of the things left out in the German was the paragraph with this an-
nouncement.

20. *Briefe an Ingarden* p. 56—the very next passage in the December 2, 1929, letter cited above in note 17.

21. *Briefe an Ingarden*, p. 59.

22. The last part, published in November 1930, was termed "A Debate with Heidegger and Husserl." In a letter to Misch dated November 16, 1930 (published in Alwin Diemer, *Edmund Husserl, Versuch einer systematischen Darstellung seiner Phänomenologie,* Meisenheim: Anton Hain, 1956, pp. 393–394; *Briefwechsel,* VI, pp. 282–283), Husserl tells him that he finally received the last part of the work. See Kern's "Einleitung," Husserliana XV, pp. XLII–XLVIII, for fuller treatment of the way Misch's book affected Husserl's thinking at this time. Kern's thesis there about the cause of Husserl's further change of plans is being followed here.

23. In the letter to Misch of November 16, 1930 (see above, note 22), Husserl discusses Misch's misunderstanding of the real thrust of transcendental phenomenology, which had been worked out beyond the stage of concentration on logic which Misch in his study seemed to have taken as characteristic of phenomenology as a whole. Husserl says: "For with the 'transcendental reduction' I was convinced I had gained ultimate actual, concrete subjectivity in the entire fullness of its being and life, in its not merely theoretically operative but all-inclusive functioning life: absolute subjectivity in its historicity." He then alludes to the new systematic work in preparation.

24. Kern indicates the nature and extent of some of these studies at this time; "Einleitung," Husserliana XV, pp. XXXI–XXXIII.

25. "Disposition zu 'System der phänomenologischen Philosophie' von Edmund Husserl," *Ergänzungsband,* pp. 3–9.

26. Husserl writes to Cairns, September 23, 1930: "I'm working with my excellent assistant, Dr. Fink, on a new systematic outline of transcendental phenomenology (the problematic reaching all the way to ethico-religious, to the 'metaphysical' problems). Hopefully it will appear in 1931." *Briefwechsel,* IV, p. 25.

27. Husserl's outline is not published in the *Ergänzungsband,* but is included in Kern's "Einleitung," Husserliana XV, p. XXXVI, along with Fink's. Kern discusses the two plans on pp. XXXV and XL–XLI.

28. *Ergänzungsband,* pp. 4–6.

29. *Ergänzungsband,* pp. 10–105. Entitled, "On the Beginning of Philosophy," the draft is of Section I of the projected Book I: The Stages of Pure Phenomenology.

30. There is one packet of notes specifically from Fink's Chiavari working holiday with Husserl, Eugen-Fink-Archiv Z-VII XVII/1–32. One sees in this set, for example, notes on the proposed large systematic work (Z-VII XVII/10a–11b, 32b), on the continuation of his doctoral dissertation (Z-VII XVII/1a–2b, 5a, 7a, 24a–b), and on the phenomenological analysis of temporality (Z-VII XVII/4a–b, 8a, 12a, 14a, 15a–b, 18a, 29a, 30a–b).

31. *Briefe an Ingarden,* p. 64. The description in question is on pp. 63–64. Kern draws particular attention to the significance of this description of Husserl's to Ingarden ("Einleitung," Husserliana XV, p. XLI).

32. See Kern, "Einleitung," pp. XLIV–XLV, and especially the long listing of MSS titles in note 1 on p. XLV.

33. Kern, "Einleitung," p. XLVI and note 2.

34. Kern, "Einleitung," p. XLVIII, and especially the long text quoted on p. XLVIII–L.

35. *Briefe an Ingarden*, p. 67. Ingarden's discussion of the situation regarding the Bernau "time" MSS in his note 52 to this letter (pp. 167–173, but in particular pp. 171–173) is helpful to the reader, who otherwise has little information available.

36. For a detailed account of the back-and-forth movement on Husserl's part, see Kern, "Einleitung," pp. L–LXV.

37. Husserl gave the same lecture, "Phänomenologie und Anthropologie," in all three places. (*Husserl-Chronik*, pp. 381–382; Kern, "Einleitung," Husserliana XV, p. LII.) That lecture is now published in Edmund Husserl, *Aufätze und Vorträge (1922–1937)*, ed. Thomas Nenon and Hans Rainer Sepp, Husserliana XXVII (Dordrecht: Kluwer Academic Publishers, 1989), pp. 164–181.

38. The texts designated "Nr. 1" and "Nr. 2," pp. 106–133.

39. Fink's notes for revising the Cartesian Meditations have been edited in Ronald Bruzina, "Die Notizen Eugen Finks zur Umarbeitung von Edmund Husserls 'Cartesianischen Meditationen'," *Husserl Studies*, 6 (1989), pp. 97–128. As one would expect, the themes of these two new Meditations were in fact to have an integral place as well in the project of the new, larger systematic work that was the on-again/off-again alternative to the Cartesian Meditations. See the explanatory notes in the article just mentioned.

40. *Briefe an Ingarden*, p. 68.

41. These phrases are from Eugen-Fink-Archiv Z-VI LXVI/4a and /6b, from sometime in 1930. For further explanation see the article by Bruzina referred to in note 39.

42. See Kern, "Einleitung," Husserliana XV, p. LII–LIV, especially the letter to Ingarden from August 31, 1931 (*Briefe an Ingarden*, p. 71).

43. See Kern, "Einleitung," Husserliana XV, p. LIV, where Cairns's report on a conversation from November 9 (*Conversations*, pp. 37–38) is cited, together with a passage from a letter of December 22, 1931, to Gustav Albrecht.

44. Husserl, *Briefwechsel*, IX, pp. 75–76.

45. Husserl mentions how *Ideas* was written in this way in six to eight weeks, and *Formal and Transcendental Logic* in two months, and that this is what he was expecting to happen for the System. This important letter to Albrecht from December 22, 1931 (*Briefwechsel*, IX, pp. 77–81), is one we shall return to again. In the letter to Stephan Strasser from November 1946 that was quoted earlier (above, note 9), Fink also speaks of this characteristic of Husserl's, that he composed his works for publication, in this instance the revised Cartesian Meditations of 1929, "in a continuous stretch, without an outline in front of him or a plan previously worked out. This was a most astonishing phenomenon, and never ceased to amaze me: he wrote as if in a trance."

46. *Ergänzungsband*, pp. 134–275. In a letter to Van Breda, October 26, 1946 (copy in the Husserl Archives), Fink himself summarizes the extent of these revisions, all of which, of course, can be seen in the now published edition: 1) a whole new First Meditation (*Ergänzungsband*, Text No. 3, pp. 134–191); 2) a series of new sections for the Second Meditation, viz, on "the double operation of the phenomenological reduction"; on "transcendental subjectivity as not a being in the world"; on "the phenome-

non of the world: the pregivenness of the world"; on "the questionableness of transcendental subjectivity"; on "the indeterminateness of transcendental subjectivity"; on
"the transcendental ego" (*Ergänzungsband*, Text No. 4, pp. 192–219); 3) several new
sections for the Third Meditation, such as on "the correlate of the systems of transcendental evidentness: world-actuality" and "the full scope of the egological problem of world-constitution" (*Ergänzungsband*, Texts Nos. 5–6, pp. 220–231); 4) new
passages for existing sections and several new sections, e.g., on "the situation of the
essence and the constitution of the essence," and "transition to the transcendental
problem of intersubjectivity" (*Ergänzungsband*, Texts Nos. 7–13, pp. 232–243); 5) new
passages for existing sections and a pair of new sections, e.g., on "the higher-level
problem of the transcendental theory of the experience of the other" (*Ergänzungsband*,
Texts Nos. 14–17, pp. 244–275).

47. See the "Textkritische Anmerkungen" in *Ergänzungsband*, pp. 305–307. According to Guy van Kerckhoven, in his unpublished "Vorwort" to the two-volume edition, it is possible that Husserl's wish to send his original 1929 version of the Cartesian
Meditations to Alfred Schutz in Vienna, for the purpose of producing several copies
of it, is what occasioned Fink's having to cut short his revision of the Fifth Meditation
("Vorwort," pp. XXIII and XXIV, in note 3 to p. VIII). The fact of being thus prema-
turely broken off should in no way be taken to indicate lesser importance for the Fifth
Meditation, for in fact Husserl put fundamental importance on the Fifth, as he stated
to Ingarden: "Real understanding has to come only after [reading] the Fifth, and the
urgent need to begin over again from the First." (*Briefe an Ingarden*, p. 73, letter of November 13, 1931.) Ingarden's note to this passage (pp. 175–176) is a helpful statement
of what an adequate reading of the Cartesian Meditations requires.

48. Both possibilities are allowed by indications in the texts themselves. For example, they are termed both "drafts for refashioning E. Husserl's 'Méditations
Cartésiennes'" and "supplements [or addenda] to Edmund Husserl's 'Méditations
Cartésiennes.'" (See *Ergänzungsband*, "Textkritische Anmerkungen," p. 305. The
"Draft of a Foreword"—see below—gives them the latter designation.) One may
suppose that a definitive formula was never settled upon, since Husserl never finally
brought them to actual publication.

49. See Kern, "Einleitung," Husserliana XV, pp. LX–LXII.

50. Cairns, *Conversations*, p. 71, the entry from May 4, 1932.

51. *Briefe an Ingarden*, p. 78. Husserl goes on to speak of the difficulties the readers
of his published writings have in grasping the deeper sense of his philosophy, even
those with the best intentions and interest, such as Ingarden himself.

52. Only the texts for the first two Meditations were extensively annotated by
Husserl, *Ergänzungsband*, Texts Nos. 3–4, pp. 134–220.

53. Van Kerckhoven has traced the three different readings by Husserl here described: the first as it was produced, the second in July 1933, when Fink was preparing it as an article for *Kantstudien*, and the third in December 1933 to January 1934.
See the "Textkritische Anmerkungen," *VI. Cartesianische Meditation*, Teil 1, pp. 225–226;
also van Kerckhoven's unpublished "Vorwort," p. XXXIII, note 30 to p. XIV.

54. Though born into a liberal Jewish family, Husserl converted to Protestantism when he was twenty-seven, and lived as a Protestant the rest of his life. Cf. *Husserl-Chronik*, pp. 1 and 15.

55. See Husserl's letter to Albrecht from July 1, 1933, *Briefwechsel*, IX, p. 92.

56. On these decrees, see Louis L. Snyder, ed., *Hitler's Third Reich, A Documentary History* (Chicago: Nelson-Hall, 1981), pp. 111–112 and 211–214.

57. Letter to Dietrich Mahnke, May 4, 1933 (*Briefwechsel*, III, pp. 491–492). Mahnke, who had studied under Husserl at Göttingen, was now professor of philosophy at Marburg. This letter is a most important one for revealing Husserl's mind on the whole philosophical, political, and personal state of affairs in which, in 1933, he finds himself.

58. On the relations between Husserl and Heidegger during this period, see Hugo Ott, *Martin Heidegger, Unterwegs zu seiner Biographie* (Frankfurt: Campus Verlag, 1988), the chapter entitled "Edmund Husserl und Martin Heidegger," pp. 167–179. Husserl speaks of Heidegger and his involvement in the letter to Mahnke of May 4, 1933, (*Briefwechsel*, III, pp. 492–493).

59. See Ott, *Martin Heidegger*, p. 182. Ott briefly discusses the contradictions in the evidence that the book burning actually occurred. Another account of the incident flatly states it was announced, but did not take place on May 10. It was then planned for June, but was prevented by rain (*1933, Machtergreifung in Freiburg und Südbaden*, Stadt und Geschichte, Neue Reihe des Stadtarchivs Freiburg i. Br. Heft 4, Freiburg; Karl Schillinger, 1983, p. 49).

60. *Briefwechsel*, IX, p. 94.

61. See Husserl's letter to Gustav Albrecht, December 30, 1933, *Briefwechsel*, IX, pp. 97–99.

62. Fink was not himself Jewish, being from an old Alemannic family in Konstanz, and therefore corresponding to what for the Nazis was Germanically "pure."

63. The account here is based primarily on a letter Fink wrote to Husserl's son, Gerhart, October 25, 1946 (copy in the Fink *Nachlass* in Freiburg). (An alternate draft of the letter was not sent, and gives substantially the same account.) Two other documents support this statement, with less detail: 1) the document written by Fink and dated June 1, 1945, "Politische Geschichte meiner wissenschaftlichen Laufbahn": "*Habilitation* and thereby a career in higher education was no longer conceivable for me in Nazi Germany—as long at least as I compromised myself by maintaining the relationship to my Jewish teacher." (P. 3; copy in the Fink *Nachlass*.) 2) A second, briefer statement of the same sort, a "Lebenslauf," from August 2, 1945, in which Fink says: "In January 1930 I followed Professor Husserl's request and as his Assistant assumed the work of elaborating and preparing for publication a large manuscript on the constitution of time, and in addition worked on a piece planned as an *Habilitationsschrift*, which was essentially ready by the end of 1932. With the National Socialist upheaval of 1933 all hope [of this] was quickly brought to an end for me. A *Habilitation* was out of the question, so long as work with the philosopher proscribed because of his Jewish origin, and therefore work that was deemed a political scandal, was not broken

off." (P. 1; copy in the *Personalakten,* Universitätsarchiv Freiburg.) An apparent inconsistency between this account and the indication given in the "Prefatory Note" of December 1945 (see below), will be dealt with in section V below.

64. "Die phänomenologische Philosophie Edmund Husserls in der gegenwärtigen Kritik I," *Kantstudien,* 38 (1933), pp. 321–383. In his "Politische Geschichte" Fink mentions that this article actually appeared in 1934; if so, it must have been very early in 1934, for Alfred Schutz wrote to Fink on January 4, 1934, about the article, which he had just carefully read (copy in the Fink *Nachlass*). Possibly Fink really had in mind its separate publication by Pan Verlag in 1934. In a letter to Cairns, November 15, 1933, Husserl mentions that the issue with this article—a "major, excellent essay"—had not yet appeared; and the reason he gives for it was the fact that *Kantstudien* was undergoing *"Gleichschaltung,"* the process of "coordination" that was turning all intellectual institutions into entities in harmony with Nazi policies (*Briefwechsel,* IV, pp. 33–34). (Husserl's recommendation to Ingarden on December 13, 1933, to catch the new *Kantstudien* issue in order to read Fink's essay is ambiguous; it can mean the issue was actually out, or that it soon would be—*Briefe an Ingarden,* p. 87.) Fink's essay is reprinted in Eugen Fink, *Studien zur Phänomenologie, 1930–1939,* Phaenomenologica, 21 (Den Haag: Martinus Nijhoff, 1966), pp. 79–156; English translation in R. O. Elveton, *The Phenomenology of Husserl, Selected Critical Readings* (Chicago: Quadrangle Books, 1970), pp. 73–147. The article is published with roman numeral "I" in the title, which suggests that it was meant to be followed by at least a second part. It was thus understood by Dietrich Mahnke at Marburg, as he asked Fink precisely about this point in a letter to him from January 13, 1934, acknowledging his receipt of a copy of the article (letter in the Fink *Nachlass*). Indeed, there are clear indications in Fink's notes from 1933 that he had a second part precisely in mind, and specifically, "Lebensphilosophie und Phänomenologie. (Edmund Husserls phänomenologische Philosophie in der gegenwärtigen Kritik II)" (Eugen-Fink-Archiv Z-XI 25b). More detailed mention is given a year later in a list of projects for the fall, 1934 (Eugen-Fink-Archiv Z-XIV II/1b). It is conceivable that, in developing the idea of adapting the Sixth Meditation as a *Habilitationsschrift* in 1933, Fink thought of expanding it in just this way. Perhaps then with the *Habilitation* blocked, the next best idea might have been to publish this material as a set of two articles. As yet, however, there is insufficient documentary evidence to establish that this is what actually happened.

65. "Vorwort von Edmund Husserl," *Kantstudien,* 38 (1933), p. 320; reprinted in *Studien zur Phänomenologie,* p. VIII. The foreword is dated June 1933. In a letter to Ingarden from December 13, 1933, Husserl says the same thing much more succinctly: "Watch for the new issue of Kantstudien with Dr. Fink's article—everything just as if I had said it." (*Briefe an Ingarden,* pp. 86–87.)

66. The note (Eugen-Fink-Archiv Z-XI 48a–b) carries the date June 27, 1933, and runs as follows:

"The following article opens a series of arguments that, on the basis of the philosophy of E. Husserl, deal with critical objections brought against it. The intention from the outset is to characterize not the opposing positions themselves in their relationship to the phenomenological philosophy of E. Husserl, but rather the objections they raise against phenomenology.

"In accord with the wish of the directors of *Kantstudien*, I declare that I completely agree with Dr. Fink's treatment."

67. According to Herbert Spiegelberg, Fink later recounted his amazement at Husserl's approval of the article, seeming to miss the critical intent it carried. (In the next section we shall be treating the radically critical dimension of Fink's exposition of Husserl. Suffice it to say here that Fink's critique is one he attempts to develop on the basis of the internal dynamic of transcendental phenomenology, and that therefore the critical thrust directly depends upon the correctness that his understanding of its principles achieves. It is at least to this understanding that Husserl subscribes.) The remark is recorded in Spiegelberg's *Scrapbook*, as Schuhmann quotes it in an entry added in the revised edition of the *Husserl-Chronik* presently in preparation (an entry to be added to page 430 in the first edition).

68. Appendix X below.

69. In the letter to Albrecht from December 30, 1933, Husserl describes the deep anxieties and partial successes of the year. He mentions the offer of a position in Los Angeles, which he was seriously considering, and speaks of the possibility once more of bringing out the Cartesian Meditations, again, in revised form as representing his whole philosophical position. *Briefwechsel*, IX, pp. 97–99.

In a letter to Felix Kaufmann from January 5, 1934, Husserl says: "I have plunged into work, and to enkindle my interest I am going over the valuable draft of the 'Sixth Meditation,' which I had already studied earlier—with it I am having intense discussions with Dr. Fink. This year I really hope to get something into publication." *Briefwechsel*, IV, p. 201.

70. It goes without saying that the manuscripts included here are not the only ones which Husserl was stimulated to write by his reading of Fink's texts, or by discussions with him on issues formulated in them. The strict restriction in the selection of texts is explained in *VI. Cartesianische Meditation*, "Textkritische Anhang," pp. 221–222. More will be said about this later.

71. This part of the account as well is drawn from van Kerckhoven's research, again from his unpublished "Vorwort," pp. XXXIII–XXXIV, note 31 to p. XIV.

72. Berger had written to Fink in connection with an offprint of an article that Fink had sent him, "Was Will die Phänomenologie Edmund Husserls?" which had just been published in the journal *Die Tatwelt* (10, pp. 13–32; subsequently reprinted in *Studien zur Phänomenologie*, pp. 157–178). Berger wanted to discuss with Fink "positions and solutions taken by phenomenology on certain problems in the theory of knowledge." At the same time, he asked if it were possible to meet with Husserl. (Letter from June 25, 1934, in the Fink *Nachlass*.) Soon after, Berger wrote a brief review of Fink's article in *Les Études Philosophiques* (8, 1934, pp. 44–45).

73. In a letter to Albrecht, October 7, 1934, Husserl describes his pleasure at this meeting: "He has been studying my difficult writings for ten years, and showed himself to be so settled, so deeply perceptive—I wished I had in Germany but a half dozen

like him, who understood and worked with me! Yet I knew nothing about him, he had
never been among my listeners." *Briefwechsel*, IX, pp. 105–106.

74. Merleau-Ponty's account of his reading is cited on pp. 421–422 in H. L. Van
Breda, "Maurice Merleau-Ponty et les Archives-Husserl à Louvain," *Revue de Méta-
physique et de Morale*, 67 (1962), pp. 410–430. Tran-Duc-Thao speaks of his reading in
a letter to Van Breda from September 27, 1943 (quoted in van Kerckhoven, unpublished "Vorwort," p. XXXIV). In a letter to Herbert Spiegelberg, June 4, 1973, Van
Breda explains that no trace of this copy of the Sixth Meditation has been found
among Berger's papers (quoted in van Kerckhoven, ibid.).

75. Letter to Albrecht, May 19, 1934, *Briefwechsel*, IX, p. 100. Husserl's son, Gerhart, for example, no longer had any hope for finding a position in the university.
Husserl writes, "at least he is not prevented in Germany from working in his study"
(p. 101).

76. See his letter to Ingarden, October 11, 1933 (*Briefe an Ingarden*, pp. 83–84).

77. See the letter to Cairns, May 18, 1934, *Briefwechsel*, IV, p. 43.

78. The new studies in question comprise in the main the C-series of manuscripts.
In a letter to Cairns, November 15, 1933, Husserl describes the overall structure of
the two-volume work that was to result from Fink's work: a first volume on "the theory of temporal process [*Zeitigung*]," and a second on "the recent investigations on time
since 1930." (*Briefwechsel*, IV, p. 33.) One can see the same structure for Fink's work on
time in the two reports he wrote in applying to the organization called the "Notgemeinschaft der Deutschen Wissenschaft," one for mid-1933, the other for mid-1934.
(Copies are in the Fink *Nachlass*.) The support he had got for the work from this organization was maintained until his continued identification with Husserl became too
great an obstacle. The publication of his essay in *Kantstudien* proved too scandalous to
ignore, according to his own account in his 1945 "Politische Geschichte . . . ," p. 3,
and in late 1934 funding was cut off. This organization too had been "coordinated"
(see above, note 64) (Husserl's letter to Albrecht, October 7, 1934, *Briefwechsel*, IX,
pp. 103–106). Klaus Held, in his *Lebendige Gegenwart*, Phaenomenologica 23 (Den
Haag: Martinus Nijhoff, 1966), treats Husserl's new studies on temporality—the C-
manuscripts—in some detail; but the whole project of which they form a part has remained unconsidered. However, that will be one of the pivotal matters treated in a
monograph presently under preparation by the translator and dealing with the whole
Husserl-Fink collaborative thinking, specifically with respect of Fink's contribution.

79. Letters to Ingarden from October 11 and November 2, 1933 (*Briefe an Ingarden*,
pp. 83–85), and that to Albrecht, October 7, 1934, *Briefwechsel*, IX, pp. 103–106.

80. This letter is now published in *Aufsätze und Vorträge* (*1922–1936*), Husserliana
XXVII, pp. 240–244. See the editors' "Einleitung," pp. XV–XXIX, for an account of
the circumstances.

81. The course of this whole development is now clearer with the publication of
the new volume edited by Reinhold Smid in the Husserliana series, *Ergänzungsband zur
"Krisis"* (Dordrecht: Kluwer Academic Publishers, 1993). For a briefer treatment Kern's
"Einleitung" is helpful, (Husserliana XV, pp. LXV–LXVI, including in particular his

notes 2 and 4 on p. LXVI). The account by Kern in his *Husserl und Kant*, Phaenomeno-logica 16 (Den Haag: Martinus Nijhoff, 1964), pp. 46–50, is also worth consulting.

82. See *Husserl-Chronik*, the entry for March 1935, p. 458.

83. Herbert Spiegelberg's account in *The Phenomenological Movement, an Historical Introduction* not only represents but contributes to this view of Fink (Phaenomenologica 5/6, 3rd revised and enlarged edition, The Hague: Martinus Nijhoff, 1982, pp. 242–248).

84. See above the quote in note 65. In a postscript to a letter to Cairns, May 18, 1934, Husserl writes: "We're waiting for your reaction to Dr. Fink's new essay—I have thought it over with him, it is of course 'authentic'." *Briefwechsel*, IV, pp. 44.

85. *Briefwechsel*, IX, p. 100.

86. Actually, according to Fink's academic course record (*Anmeldungsbuch*), Husserl began a course in the winter semester, 1928–29, "Phänomenologie der Einfühlung" (see *Husserl-Chronik*, p. 338), which, however, he did not finish.

87. Fink continued to follow Heidegger's courses after his doctorate and well into the first years of his work with Husserl. All in all, Fink attended Heidegger's courses in Freiburg from 1928 at least through 1931, with nearly complete handwritten notes from seven of them. After 1931 Fink seemed to have had less time to give to it, although it is clear he continued to follow what Heidegger was doing.

88. The original dissertation title is "Beiträge zu einer phänomenologischen Analyse der psychischen Phänomene, die unter den vieldeutigen Titeln 'Sich denken, als ob', 'Sich nur etwas vorstellen', 'Phantasieren' befasst werden" (Halle: Karras, Kröber & Nietschmann, 1930). Published at the same time in Husserl's *Jahrbuch* XI, it was given the title "Vergegenwärtigung und Bild, Beiträge zur Phänomenologie der Unwirklichkeit (I. Teil)," which is also the title in its reprint in Fink's *Studien zur Phänomenologie*. The projected second part was never published.

89. *Husserl-Chronik*, pp. 337 and 361. Landgrebe moved to Prague, where he completed his *Habilitation* in 1934 under Oskar Kraus with a study of the philosophy of language of Anton Marty.

90. See Husserl's letter to Heidegger, May 9, 1928 (*Briefwechsel*, IV, p. 154), where, before having chosen a new candidate for the position, he mentions that he has received an extension of support for a student assistantship for two years, until April 1, 1930. See also *Husserl-Chronik*, p. 332.

91. Fink himself, in his "Politische Geschichte," mentions the Moses Mendelssohn Gesellschaft (1933–35), the London School of Economics (1936–37), and then American sources, one of which Husserl indicates is apparently the Rockefeller Foundation (letter to Albrecht, December 30, 1933, *Briefwechsel*, IX, p. 98). Another source of support was the private means offered by an American, Dorothy Ott, who was studying with Husserl and Fink in 1936–37 (letter from Malvine Husserl to Elisabeth Rosenberg-Husserl, September 15, 1937, *Briefwechsel*, IX, p. 494). There were also contributions from the Japanese who came to study in Freiburg (Husserl's letters to Fink, July 21, 1934, *Briefwechsel*, IV, p. 94, and to Albrecht, October 7, 1934, *Briefwechsel*, IX, p. 105).

92. Letter from March 3, 1931, *Briefwechsel*, III, p. 90. See also Husserl's letter to Mahnke, January 8, 1931, where Husserl's delight in Fink's abilities and promise contrasts with his disappointment with Heidegger, *Briefwechsel*, III, pp. 474 and 476.

93. On the daily contact, see Husserl's letters to Boyce Gibson (July 16, 1930, January 7, 1932, *Briefwechsel*, VI, pp. 140, 142), and to Dietrich Mahnke (December 31, 1933, where Husserl says that he has been working "daily for almost two years" with Fink, *Briefwechsel*, III, p. 512). Fink's regular presence is attested in the frequent letters to Elisabeth Rosenberg-Husserl (see January 16 and May 31, 1930, *Briefwechsel*, IX, pp. 374, 375–376). For the later years, 1931 and 1932, Cairns's *Conversations* is a clear record of the same thing. On the regular walks, see both Husserl's and Malvine's letters to Ingarden, March 19, 1930, and May 15, 1931 (*Briefe an Ingarden*, pp. 60 and 68), and to Elisabeth Rosenberg-Husserl (letter of February 3, 1932, *Briefwechsel*, IX, p. 401).

94. As Husserl put it to Ingarden, March 19, 1930, "in daily walks I talk over with him all my work, experiments, and plans" (*Briefe an Ingarden*, p. 60).

95. See Malvine Husserl's letter to Elisabeth Rosenberg-Husserl, March 24, 1935, *Briefwechsel*, IX, p. 453.

96. Letter to Father Daniel Feuling, March 30, 1933, *Briefwechsel*, VII, p. 89. The occasion was Husserl's reading of the published proceedings of a conference of the Société Thomiste which Feuling had sent him and in which Husserl's phenomenology was the center of discussion—*La Phénoménologie*, Juvisy, 12 Septembre 1932, Journées d'Étude de la Société Thomiste, Les Éditions du Cerf. Prior to the conference, which had been attended by Alexandre Koyré and Edith Stein, representing Husserlian phenomenology, Feuling during a pair of visits had spent several hours with Fink in which the latter had explained to him "the final development of transcendental phenomenology." Feuling had especially valued these sessions in that Koyré and Stein had "represented and stressed the earlier form of phenomenology" (letter from Feuling to Fink, September 27, 1932, in the Fink *Nachlass*).

97. Letter from July 21, 1934, *Briefwechsel*, IV, p. 93. In the letter Husserl was trying to lift Fink's discouragement over his work on the "time" book he was trying to finish on the basis of Husserl's manuscript. Husserl earnestly invited Fink to join him at Kappel for rest and reinvigoration—and to afford Husserl once more the opportunity "to hold stimulating discussions with you, as it has become a need for me to do in order to keep regularly going." Immediately after this comes the passage just quoted.

In the "Lebenslauf" of August 2, 1945, Fink writes: "Already in 1932 Husserl had converted the assistant relationship to one of co-worker, in recognition of the independent and productive work I was doing in the elaboration and in part redoing of his manuscripts." While the terms "assistant" (*Assistent*) and "co-worker" (*Mitarbeiter*) are technical terms for a position in the academic hierarchy of assignments and work, it is clear that Husserl and Fink, in describing their relationship, also take the terms in their differing characterization of the work they respectively name.

98. This letter in the Husserl Archives has been cited here several times (above, notes 73, 78, and 79). In it, among other things, Husserl was telling Albrecht about

his letter to the congress in Prague, which marks the beginning of Husserl's turn to the Crisis texts project.

99. The strain that working in Husserl's phenomenology put upon Fink—among other things, in view of the situation of uncertainty and blockage after January 1933—and which thus disclosed the limits of Fink's particular psychological constitution is one of the main concerns Husserl speaks of in the only two letters (of any length) written by Husserl to him (March 6, 1933, and July 21, 1934, *Briefwechsel*, IV, pp. 90–94). The second of these letters is the source of the quote given just before the last one; Husserl is trying to encourage Fink by underscoring both Fink's importance to him and Husserl's confidence in him.

100. "Politische Geschichte meiner wissenschaftlichen Laufbahn," June 1, 1945, p. 2. The length of time Fink mentions is calculated as the period during which Fink was mainly working on Husserl's manuscripts to prepare particular sets of them for publication, most notably the Bernau manuscripts on time and time-consciousness, and the Cartesian Meditations. He counts it as the period 1930–1937. After 1937, in the first months of 1938, the last of Husserl's life, illness made Husserl incapable of further work.

101. "I am most grateful for your concern and support for Dr. Fink. Without him nothing can come of my manuscripts, and I can no longer productively work without the resonance that I find so fully with him." Letter to Felix Kaufmann, September 11, 1933, *Briefwechsel*, IV, p. 197. Husserl then recommends to Kaufmann the *Kantstudien* article and the then still anticipated book on time.

102. In a letter to Felix Kaufmann, October 29, 1931, he mentions how "the daily conversations with Dr. Fink, an incomparably intense co-thinker, keep me fresh and productive." *Briefwechsel*, IV, p. 184.

103. In a letter to Rudolf Pannwitz, May 17, 1934, Husserl writes in the margin: "Dr. Fink is a wonderful man—no mere mouthpiece!" but this remark is not given in *Briefwechsel*, VII, pp. 218–219, where the letter is published. As in so many letters from these first years of Nazism, Husserl also tells Pannwitz of how he has had to spend so much of his energy in struggling for the "possibility of living in the realm of transcendental intellectuality." In the flood of "all too human humanity" swirling around him in the events of that period what he is striving for is, "in the *tranqu[illitate] animi* of the 'non-participant observer,' to be as a functionary of the Absolute."

104. These are Fink's expressions from his description of his years with Husserl in his "Politische Geschichte meiner wissenschaftlichen Laufbahn," of June 1, 1945. See also note 97 above.

105. The argument indicated here needs to be laid out much more fully, for example, along the following lines. As set specifically within the framework of phenomenology: the analysis of the validity that a specific item of philosophical knowledge—i.e., an assertion expressing some specific insight—would claim beyond contingent factuality has to clarify both the thematic object side (noema) and the thematizing, experiencing subject side (noesis). A condition of transcendence over contingent, individual factuality is needed on both sides. Here the way the subject side

gets beyond contingent, individual factuality is being alluded to. This is in fact in parallel to the considerations Fink develops in §11 A) in the Sixth Meditation (see below). For a preliminary and complementary treatment of this issue, see Ronald Bruzina, "Solitude and Community in the Work of Philosophy: Husserl and Fink, 1928–1938," *Man and World*, 22 (1989), pp. 287–314.

106. "Politische Geschichte," p. 2.

107. In the "Lebenslauf" from August 2, 1945.

108. In a note from 1936, Fink writes: "The caricature of the 'philosopher': the 'good disciple,' who lives in the illusion of a notion of service, and passes over his life. (Example: Husserl's conception of a good successor, a role that is intended for me!)" Eugen-Fink-Archiv OH-VII A/5a.

109. This note (Eugen-Fink-Archiv Z-V VI/13b, emphasis Fink's), written in 1929, is actually speaking of the problem of reading Hegel; *mutatis mutandis* it can also apply to Husserl. (The packet of notes among which it is placed shows Fink confronting Husserl and Heidegger together and undoubtedly reflects Fink's attendance in the latter's lectures in 1929.)

110. Letter to Feuling, March 30, 1933, quoted above (see above, note 96).

111. Some of this shows in Ott's treatment of the relations between the two, *Martin Heidegger*, pp. 104, 126, 174–175. See also Karl Schuhmann, "Zu Heideggers Spiegel-Gespräch über Husserl," *Zeitschrift für Philosophische Forschung*, 32 (1978), pp. 591–612.

112. See Husserl's letter to Pfänder from January 6, 1931 (in *Pfänder-Studien*, ed. Spiegelberg and Avé-Lallemant, pp. 345–349). There Husserl retrospectively admits that Heidegger had in fact never really disclosed his own thinking at all!

113. Cf. Rudolf Boehm, "Einleitung des Herausgebers," in Edmund Husserl, *Zur Phänomenologie des inneren Zeitbewusstseins (1893–1917)*, Husserliana X (Den Haag: Martinus Nijhoff, 1966), pp. XIX–XXIV.

114. See Walter Biemel, "Husserl's *Encyclopaedia Britannica* Article and Heidegger's Remarks Thereon," in Frederick Elliston and Peter McCormick, eds., *Husserl, Expositions and Appraisals* (Notre Dame: University of Notre Dame Press, 1977), pp. 286–303.

115. One should mention as well that in his letters to friends Husserl never spoke of Heidegger with a characterization like that he gave of Fink, regarding mastery of phenomenology and intimate collaborative involvement.

116. The complete sets of these notes from the Fink *Nachlass* are housed in transcription in the Eugen-Fink-Archiv at the Pädagogische Hochschule Freiburg.

117. See Fink's "Foreword" and "Prefatory Note," below.

118. The remarks Richard Zaner makes in his Foreword to Cairns, *Conversations*, are well taken here: "Hardly any insight or result is regarded by Husserl, even at this late date in his career, as definitively established: He . . . finds it necessary continually to re-examine, research again and again, terrain which most of his followers and critics would like to regard as 'Husserl's established views,' but which Husserl himself is never wont to accept as established and closed to further discussion. . . . The present *Conversations* give ample evidence that Husserl meant precisely what he said: every

effort, and claim, to know inherently require phenomenological explicative criticism, and that itself necessitates continuous *transcendental* self-criticism" (p. XI). Needless to say, this is precisely what Fink was doing for and with Husserl.

119. It should be mentioned, too, that, as Cairns's *Conversations* routinely imply, Fink showed an understandable deference toward Husserl; after all, Fink was a young man working with a distinguished emeritus professor. The deference, however, must have included also a measure of reticence on Fink's part, for much the same reason. Fink's notes for himself were bound to be more explicit about his own thinking than were his conversations with the eminent Master, in which nonetheless there is every indication that he did express his own thinking, even if modestly and diplomatically. The few of his personal notes that record actual conversations with Husserl suggest precisely this (e.g., Z-XII 4c; OH-VI 15; OH-VII 36). It is reasonable to think, therefore, that Husserl was not *fully* acquainted with the ideas Fink was working over in his own mind, so that, just as Husserl adopted a measure of over-optimism regarding Fink's dedication to his (Husserl's) manuscripts, so also he was not acquainted with the details of Fink's critical position in its more vigorous expression.

An interesting comment pertinent here is made by Van Breda to Merleau-Ponty, in a letter from December 17, 1945: "I have just read your fine book on the Phenomenology of Perception. . . . It seems to me that it is too strongly under the influence of the 'Sixth Meditation,' which is a text by Fink, not Husserl. This text, as well as the article by Fink in *Kantstudien*, is basically a critique of the very bases of Husserl's thought, although the author has indeed hidden his opposition, and Husserl himself in his splendid naiveté did not notice it—at least as concerns the article in *Kantstudien*." The argument I am presenting is meant to accord with this assertion of Van Breda's, and with others he made on the basis of close acquaintance with Fink, though with some lessening of the sharpness of formulation. For example, in Van Breda's letter to the French publishing house Aubier, December 17, 1945, speaking of the "Sixth Meditation" he writes: "Fink did not like to have his draft widely known, because his critique is basically quite severe. . . . At the time he wrote these pages it would have been very difficult for him to express his thinking in a more straightforward way." (Letter in the Husserl Archive.)

120. Another issue that needs to be addressed in detailing the work Fink did with Husserl is that Fink developed a conception of *philosophy* that differed from Husserl's —or rather, one should say, that inverted the relative emphasis to be placed on the different functions essential to philosophy, namely a) the search for *findings* able to be asserted and justified with precision and clarity in statements, and b) the radicalizing and renewal of the *questions*, especially in the form of the engagement of one's being and not just the preoccupation of one's theoretical mind. Needless to say, once again, that must remain unexplored here.

121. Letter to Aubier, December 17, 1945, in the Husserl Archive (see above, note 119). As explained earlier, Fink had given his own copy, the carbon copy of the typescript, to Berger in 1934 and had never got it back.

122. Notwithstanding, in the Fink *Nachlass* is a collection of notes Fink made during the war, "Eremetie (Aphorismen aus einem Kriegstagebuch, 1940–1944)." The reflections figure on Nietzsche more than anybody, both meditatively and critically.

123. The main testimony here is the letter Fink wrote to Gerhart Husserl, October 25, 1946, but did not actually send (in the Fink *Nachlass*). (See above, note 63.) In addition, his letter to Husserl's daughter, Elisabeth Rosenberg-Husserl, February 4, 1947, contains significant particulars (copy in the Fink *Nachlass*). Mrs. Susanne Fink as well recounts much of the detail of these war years.

124. Letter to Van Breda, October 26, 1946, in the Husserl Archives. It should be mentioned that documents in the *Personalakten* in the Universitätsarchiv, Freiburg, confirm Fink's account here.

125. Letter of October 25, 1946 (in the Fink *Nachlass*), the draft that actually was sent. See above, note 63. The term *Pietät* that Fink uses here was one that, according to Mrs. Susanne Fink, he used frequently in his later life in reference to the relationship he felt toward Husserl. In his letter to Husserl's son, Fink was trying to clear up a misunderstanding on Gerhart's part stemming from indication he had received that Fink had taken his *Habilitation* under Heidegger, whose role in the events of the 1930s had made him anathema to Husserl's family. In fact it was a professor Robert Heiss who wrote the evaluation recommending acceptance of "The Idea of a Transcendental Theory of Method" as the required *Habilitationsschrift*. (*Gutachten* from February 16, 1946, in the Philosophische Fakultät-Sekretariat, Freiburg.) Fink recounts that Heidegger had also been asked by the faculty for an attestation, but had restricted himself in replying that—as Fink reports it—"having been fully authorized by Husserl, the work needed no further attestation." Whatever document Heidegger may have written to this effect has not yet been located in Freiburg.

126. See the remarks of Van Breda quoted above in note 119.

127. See above, note 8.

128. Letter from November 1, 1946. See above, note 9.

129. Berger, *Le cogito dans la philosophie de Husserl*, p. 115 note 1 (*The Cogito in Husserl's Philosophy*, p. 92). This characterization is surely drawn from the discussions Berger held with Fink during his visit with him.

130. One compelling reason, of course, as was explained earlier is that the Sixth Meditation itself is meant to follow the first five *in the version that would result from the adoption of Fink's revisions.* One has to include some consideration of those revisions, therefore, to understand what the Sixth Meditation presupposes.

131. In fact Fink's treatment of the reduction in the "Draft" recalls his way of representing it in his dissertation of 1929. See "Vergegenwärtigung und Bild," §4, *Studien Zur Phänomenologie*, pp. 10–14.

132. In the *Ergänzungsband*, Texts Nos. 1–2 are Fink's first effort at revising the *Cartesian Meditations* and Texts Nos. 3–17 are those in his second revision.

133. Text No. 3, section e, "Schwierigkeiten einer Erkenntnisbegründung vom Ich aus," *Ergänzungsband*, pp. 155–156. (Another, more technical way of rendering the

phrase *die Selbstverständlichkeit der Weltgeltung* would be "the obviousness of the validity of the world.")

134. *Ergänzungsband,* p. 155, note 111.

135. *Ergänzungsband,* Text No. 3, section f, "Die Phänomenologische Reduktion," pp. 158–191.

136. *Ergänzungsband,* pp. 186–187. (Emphasis Fink's.)

137. *Cartesian Meditations,* tr. Cairns, p. 29.

138. *Ergänzungsband,* p. 192. (Emphasis Fink's.)

139. *Ergänzungsband,* p. 199. (Emphasis Fink's.)

140. *Ergänzungsband,* p. 200. (Emphasis Fink's.)

141. *Ergänzungsband,* Text No. 4, section c, "Das Weltphenomenon: die Vorgegebenheit der Welt," p. 202. Two phrases are marked in the translation here to indicate Husserl's alterations, as follows:

* for "genuinely" Husserl writes "directly" (note 307);

** for "human existence and its surrounding world" Husserl writes "human existence [*Dasein*] as consciously having the world and consciously living out in the world thus had" (note 308).

142. Examples of this can be found in *Ergänzungsband,* Text No. 4, from which the quotes immediately above were drawn, as well as No. 17, together with §5 from the "Draft": "Die vorläufig bestimmte Aufgabe einer Auslegung des natürlichen Weltlebens."

143. Edmund Husserl, *The Crisis of European Sciences and Transcendental Phenomenology,* trans. David Carr (Evanston: Northwestern University Press, 1970), p. 154.

144. Letter from June 11, 1932, *Briefe an Ingarden,* p. 78.

145. The review appeared in the *Deutsche Literaturzeitung,* 51 (18 December 1932), col. 2404–2416. It should be noted that on July 7 in that same year, 1932, Fink, at Husserl's request, had sent Schutz the master typescript of Husserl's 1929 text of the Cartesian Meditations in order for Schutz to have copies made of it for Husserl to provide to a number of people most interested in studying it in the German (e.g., Cairns and Ingarden). This very likely was one reason for Fink's more sketchy treatment of the revision for Meditation V. The master typescript was returned by mid-September. (The full details of the identity and relationship of both master typescript and copies are given in van Kerckhoven's unpublished "Vorwort," note 3 to p. VIII.)

146. The phrases in the lines that follow are all drawn from Fink's letter to Schutz from September 25, 1932, in the Fink *Nachlass* in Freiburg.

147. In Fink's first set of revisions, in the course of the text proposed to replace §§7–11 of Meditation I, he pursues the question whether there is a world-bound character to the concept of apodicticity, i.e., of that whose non-existence is not conceivable (*Ergänzungsband,* Text No. 2, section a, pp. 109–114). This is also the approach implied in Fink's second revision (Text No. 3, section c, pp. 148–150).

148. The review of the *Méditations cartésiennes* appeared in the *Zeitschrift für Nationalökonomie,* 5 (1934), 428–430, and that of the *Formale und transzendentale Logik* in the *Göttingische Gelehrte Anzeigen,* No. 11/12 (1933), 432–448.

149. It is clear from Kaufmann's letters to Husserl (November 27 and December 19, 1932, *Briefwechsel*, IV, pp. 188–190) that, though he sent the review drafts to Fink, this was as Husserl wished it.

150. Letter from December 17, 1932; copy in the Fink *Nachlass*.

151. See pp. 43–44 below.

152. The last paragraph of §43 (*The Crisis of European Sciences and Transcendental Phenomenology*, trans. Carr, p. 155) is the most concise confirmation of this.

153. This is Text No. 12 in the *Ergänzungsband*: "General exposition of the constitutive problems of genesis" (pp. 239–242), to be added to the end of §39. Then Fink replaces §40 and §41 with Text No. 13 (*Ergänzungsband*, pp. 242–243); §40 and §41 are dropped because they treat of transcendental idealism, which, as Fink notes, comes into discussion in the Sixth Meditation (*Ergänzungsband*, p. 242, note 381).

154. *Ergänzungsband*, p. 241.

155. Ibid.

156. This quote is from the opening lines of Text No. 13, p. 242, in the *Ergänzungsband*, which is to make the transition to the newly written opening for the Fifth Meditation itself (Text No. 14, pp. 244–250).

157. *Ergänzungsband*, Texts Nos. 14–17, pp. 244–275.

158. *Ergänzungsband*, p. 246.

159. Already in 1929, in his dissertation, this was an important point for Fink: "possibilities of apodictic insight such as we can express them in egological explication may perhaps undergo transformation or even cancellation in moving into the transcendental problematic of intersubjectivity" (*Studien zur Phänomenologie*, p. 16). Husserl urges a similar caution to Ingarden in a letter from November 13, 1931, in connection with the latter's having had to break off comment on the Cartesian Meditations after having dealt only with the first four: "Plainly you take it to be not so important to work through to the end and think that after 1–4 you already understand what is meant there. But only after the Fifth is real understanding going to come, and [with it] the urgent need to begin over again from the First." *Briefe an Ingarden*, p. 73, bracketed insertion mine.

160. *Ergänzungsband*, Text No. 16, pp. 251–255, which were meant to be inserted between §48 and §49.

161. *Ergänzungsband*, pp. 259–262.

162. *Ergänzungsband*, p. 262.

163. In Text No. 17 (*Ergänzungsband*, pp. 256–275) Husserl's own words are cited (pp. 256–257) to underscore the *mediated* character of the demonstrative showing [*Ausweisung*] of the constitutional contribution provided by the transcendental Other.

164. See in particular §7 in the Sixth Meditation.

165. *Conversations*, p. 71, in the entry for May 4, 1932.

166. *Conversations*, pp. 75 (May 11, 1932), 80–82 (June 2, 1932). This difference shows as well in Husserl's notes to the very beginning of Fink's "Layout," *Ergänzungsband*, p. 4, note 2.

167. See the discussion above, pages xxxi–xxxii.

168. A number of Husserl's working manuscripts are included in each volume, such as those below in the Appendixes; these working manuscripts, in their often telegraphic style (see, for example, Appendix IX below), illustrate the contrast between such early thinking and the finished drafts (even if these later drafts are still somewhat preliminary). In the texts included here one also sees the difference in writing and thinking style between Husserl and Fink, a difference that comes clear as well in the typed-out resumé notes Fink made of Husserl's courses as a student: "Grundprobleme der Logik," WS 1925/26 (in the Husserl Archives, Louvain); and "Natur und Geist," SS 1927 (in the Fink *Nachlass*, Freiburg).

169. In preparing the two-volume edition Guy van Kerckhoven restricted the selection of Husserlian manuscripts to those with clear direct reference to the Sixth Meditation. (See the explanation in "Zur Textgestaltung," *VI. Cartesianische Meditation, Teil 1: Die Idee einer Transzendentalen Methodenlehre*, pp. 221–222.) Nevertheless, in searching through the entire deposit in Louvain van Kerckhoven prepared notes on both certain and probable connections between particular Husserlian manuscripts and the themes of the drafts Fink wrote for him. It is to be hoped that he will be able in the future to return to work on this.

170. Edmund Husserl, *Formal and Transcendental Logic*, trans. Dorion Cairns (The Hague: Martinus Nijhoff, 1969), §107 c, p. 289.

171. "Vergegenwärtigung und Bild," *Studien zur Phänomenologie*, p. 16.

172. *Cartesian Meditations*, trans. Cairns, p. 29. Emphasis Husserl's.

173. *Cartesian Meditations*, p. 151.

174. See below, §1, "The methodological limitation of the previous Meditations."

175. As becomes clear from Fink's personal notes, Kant is one of the two or three most dominant influences on Fink's thinking after Husserl and Heidegger, Hegel and Nietzsche being the others. The profound way in which Kant's thinking has affected Fink's work, however, is too much to go into here.

176. As explained in the "Textkritische Anmerkungen" (*VI. Cartesianische Meditation, Teil I*, p. 224), the title page carried the following:

> Eugen Fink
> The idea of a transcendental theory of method.
> (Draft for a Sixth Meditation for E. Husserl's "Méditations cartésiennes." August–October, 1932)

177. *Eine Neue Monadologie* (Berlin: Reuther & Reichard, 1917). Mahnke was preparing a new edition of this work, as he explains in his letter to Husserl, March 15, 1933 (*Briefwechsel*,. III, pp. 487–491).

178. Letter of May 4, 1933, *Briefwechsel*, III, pp. 495–496 and 498. See above, p. xix at note 57, where Husserl's remarks on the political situation are quoted. The point Husserl makes as the first passage quoted here continues is worth noting: "In the world the inner and the outer exclude each other, in the natural attitude. In the phenomenological attitude they are compatible, indeed, more than that, they mutually require each other as necessary correlates." One should not overlook the stunning contrast between Husserl's views on community, in terms of "monadic intersubjectivity," and

those of the political and social policy—*"Gleichschaltung,"* coordination into homo-
geneity under a supreme leader—that was at this very time being implemented in
Germany, including in the universities, and nowhere with more dedication than in
Freiburg under Heidegger's rectorship. Indeed, Husserl remarks sardonically that
Heidegger's "theatrical" entry into the Nazi party on May 1 was a "splendid conclu-
sion to this supposed philosophic friendship of minds."

179. See below, "Draft of a Foreword" and "Prefatory Note." Husserl also underscores this issue in several places in the *Crisis* (trans. Carr), §§53,54, and 57 (esp. pp.
201–202).

180. In the *Cartesian Meditations* itself Husserl calls for treatment of the "supreme
and ultimate questions" (§64, p. 156); and in a letter to Gustav Albrecht, June 3, 1932,
he spells these out in more detail: "The highest of all questions . . . are the 'metaphysical': they concern birth and death, the ultimate being of the 'I' and of the 'we'
objectivated as humanity, the teleology that ultimately leads back to transcendental
subjectivity and transcendental historicity, and naturally as highest item the being of
God as the principle of this teleology, and the meaning of this being in contrast
to the being of the first Absolute, the being of my transcendental I and the all-
encompassing subjectivity that discloses itself in me—which together with the 'constitution' of the world as 'ours' pertain to the true locus of divine 'working'—speaking
from God's viewpoint, the constant creation of the world in us, in our transcendental
ultimately true being." *Briefwechsel*, IX, pp. 83–84. These are clearly issues that Fink's
treatment touches on, and there is no doubt that Fink had definite ideas about how a
metaphysics for phenomenology might work out—in terms precisely of his *meontic*.
But the question of the extent to which Husserl wanted him to proceed with it, or
might have subscribed to some of it, is too large to pursue here. (Treatment of this
whole topic will be given in the monograph on the Husserl-Fink collaboration.) Min-
imally one should recall that the full scope of revision for the Cartesian Meditations
included the idea of a *Seventh* Meditation, which would work out specifically the way
metaphysical issues get treated in phenomenology.

181. In the course of a note on the redaction of §2 of "Vergegenwärtigung und
Bild"—precisely on the question of "the kind of being, the basic ontological character of the 'psyche' "—Fink remarks parenthetically: "Recently learned through Heidegger to understand the problematic of ontology" (Eugen-Fink-Archiv, Z-IV 15a).
The note is from the period 1928–1929, but cannot be dated more precisely than that.
Although Fink had acquired and read *Being and Time* in the summer of 1927, he only
began following Heidegger's courses after the latter arrived in Freiburg for the winter semester of 1928.

182. For example, in another note, probably from 1929, Fink writes about reor-
ganizing the dissertation so as to delay all discussion of "the kind of being of 'egological subjectivity' " until the projected third section, on "temporal analysis," so that
there it would be clarified "on the basis of the *horizon of the kind of being* possessed by absolute transcendental subjectivity" (Eugen-Fink-Archiv Z-I 89a). While there is a

large number of notes on Fink's completion and reworking of his dissertation, no full-scale draft of its revision survives.

183. See Walter Biemel, "Husserl's *Encyclopaedia Britannica* Article and Heidegger's Remarks Thereon," in Frederick Elliston and Peter McCormick, eds., *Husserl, Expositions and Appraisals* (Notre Dame: University of Notre Dame Press, 1977), pp. 286–303.

184. Here, too, we have another element of "framework" agreement with Fink on Husserl's part, and that undergirds his strong public subscription to Fink's *Kantstudien* article.

185. See *Crisis*, trans. Carr, pp. 113 (§29), 186 (§54b), 210 (§59), 262, 264 (§72), and 340 (Appendix IV, which is §73 in the Husserliana edition).

186. This distinction corresponds to Fink's division of phenomenology into a) the theory of elements [*Elementarlehre*] and b) the theory of method [*Methodenlehre*], this latter being the analysis and criticism of the principles of operation for the theory of elements. See §2 below, "The theme of the transcendental theory of method." The organizational concepts here come directly from Kant, who divides his *Critique of Pure Reason* in exactly this way: I—Transcendental Doctrine of Elements [*Elementarlehre*], II—Transcendental Doctrine of Method [*Methodenlehre*] (trans. Norman Kemp Smith, London: Macmillan & Co., 1958).

187. These remarks are all drawn from §5, pp. 42–43, below.

188. Below, p. 45, including notes 132 and 133.

189. Copy in the Fink *Nachlass*. At the beginning of the letter Fink explains to M. Gary that Husserl, being quite taken up with a "large new publication"—which can only mean the "System of Phenomenological Philosophy" then in the stage of early conception—regretfully has to ask Fink to reply for him. He then states that "the present answers to your eleven questions were put before Professor Husserl and authorized by him." The letter is most helpful for its treatment of the way phenomenological terms have to be interpreted. The identity of M. Gary remains obscure.

190. *Studien zur Phänomenologie*, §4, p. 11. In this same "Introduction," which comprises §§1–7 of "Vergegenwärtigung und Bild," Fink also sketches out the problem of the doubleness of subjectivity, viz., as transcendental and as human, and of the "mundanizing" or "finitizing" of the former as the latter (pp. 9, 11, and 14).

191. From a period soon after the writing of the Sixth Meditation, Fink writes: "Terminologically, instead of 'natural attitude' *'captivation in the world.'* The Husserlian expression, natural attitude, is open to misunderstanding and is used, and by him [Husserl] himself, in two ways: 1) the immediate attitude of life, the pretheoretical, in contrast to the theoretical reflective; 2) counterconcept to the transcendental attitude." Eugen-Fink-Archiv Z-XI III/5a; my addition in brackets.

192. Cairns, in his *Conversations*, September 23, 1932 (p. 95), reports Fink's comment on his own preference in distinction from Husserl's. And Fink describes his explicit introduction of the expression as "distancing itself from Husserl" in a set of pages from 1933 or early 1934 that is the longest discussion of the term in his personal notes (Eugen-Fink-Archiv Z-XIII XVIII/2a). It is worth remarking that Maurice Merleau-

Ponty's replacement of Husserl's expression with "*préjugé du monde*" is quite possibly an adoption of Fink's term; for *préjugé du monde*, although an expression that retains too strong a possible connotation of psychological behavior, does indeed translate *Welt-befangenheit*, in one of its possible readings. The basis for the equivalence *Weltbefangenheit* = *préjugé du monde*, can be seen in the text below, on p. 72.

193. In fact, he phrases things himself in that same vein in one of the manuscript studies written to the Sixth Meditation. In Appendix XII, in the course of reflecting on the "horizons," he speaks of "the horizon of that which is already accepted as existent—the horizon of being." While the context may not really allow the unqualified interpretation that would accord with Fink's thesis, nonetheless, given Husserl's reticence to focus on the question of being at all, as well as his well-known basing of the concept of world upon the horizonal structure in general, it could be a significant indication.

194. The first two quoted phrases, written in the latter half of 1931, come from Eugen-Fink-Archiv Z-IX XVII/6a and XVII/7a respectively, while the third is from Z-XI 13a, written some time in 1933.

195. Eugen-Fink-Archiv Z-XX 7a. As one might expect, there is a development in Fink's realization of this, but the principle is already clearly established in 1929 (clearly with some stimulus to Fink's thinking from Heidegger) as we can see for example in Eugen-Fink-Archiv Z-V III/2a–b, which deals primarily with the question of the temporality and the constitution of the world. Two notebooks from 1935 (Eugen-Fink-Archiv OH-III and OH-IV) have long discussions on Kant and this thesis, and both Fink's Dessau lecture of 1935, "Die Idee der Transcendentalphilosophie bei Kant und in der Phänomenologie," which Husserl had read (published posthumously in Eugen Fink, *Nähe und Distanz, Phänomenologische Vorträge und Aufsätze*, ed. Franz-Anton Schwarz, Freiburg: Karl Alber Verlag, 1976, pp. 7–44), and his notes in preparation for it (Eugen-Fink-Archiv Z-XVI) reflect this idea. Here we see that Kant is important not only for the formal structure of a transcendental theory of method, but also as the initiator of a philosophy of the limits of cognition, in particular, a philosophy that asserts the limits of the world to be the limits of intutition-based cognition.

196. For passages that show this problem, see the following examples: on the pregivenness of both the world and beings in the world with respect to human being (itself in the world), see pp. 37ff. and 94f.; on this same pregivenness with respect to the cognition performed by human beings, see p. 81ff. (In these same passages the contrast is also made to the condition of antecedency that the transcendental constituting agency must have.) Finally, Husserl's reflections on the problem can be seen in Appendixes IV and XIV below. Once again, Husserl's alterations and remarks to Fink's text in passages like the above are additional indications of his thinking.

197. See above p. lii, and the text below on pp. 43–48. Husserl's additions in notes 125 and 133 are to be particularly noted.

198. The use of this term is explained in §§8 and 9.

199. These snatches of phrases are all from p. 76 below.

200. Notes 254 and 257, to p. 76.

201. Indeed, it nowhere occurs in any of the texts Fink published during this period either, those collected in *Studien zur Phänomenologie.*

202. Reflections on meontic issues occur in Fink's earliest as well as his latest notes from the period. It would seem that Fink got his ideas about it from the Neoplatonic current in Western philosophy, to which his first exposure was his early reading of Giordano Bruno. This is one of several influences independent of either Husserl or Heidegger.

203. Below, pp. 90 and 142. Any difference between "non-*ontic*" and "non-*ontological*" is unimportant here inasmuch as both, having to do with being, are basically world-bound, whereas the "pre-existent" is not at all.

204. See below, p. 116. In this passage Fink is actually talking only about the subject performing transcendental reflection, and not about subjectivity as constituting. Nevertheless, the point remains a fortiori applicable to the latter, as is clearly implied throughout the texts of revision for the Cartesian Meditations.

205. See in particular p. 142ff. below.

206. The "protest" as discussed here is explicitly identified as belonging to the "meontic" in several of Fink's notes from 1929 and 1930, i.e., long before writing the Sixth Meditation. It characterizes his thinking prior to and while sketching out the plan for the "System of Phenomenological Philosophy." (Eugen-Fink-Archiv Z-V VI/18a–23a and Z-VII XXI/15a.)

207. This is one of the main points of the passage below on pp. 134–135. In Fink's personal notes, from a folder containing materials from 1930–1931, one finds the following more succinct statement of it: "If we thus put forward the thesis that the correspondence of world and absolute subjectivity is not that of abstract and 'concrete,' because this kind of relationship is already oriented on the lead provided by the mundane relationships in being, then we find ourselves in no antithesis to Husserl's statements when he characterizes this questionable relationship in the above sense. It is instead obvious for Husserl that *constituting subjectivity* is not 'existent' in any sense belonging to the pregiven world, but has a 'being' of a kind primordially proper to it [*ein 'Sein' ureigener Art*]. Absolute subjectivity is ontologically 'opaque'; i.e., positively taken it is not an ontological problem at all. It is to be explicated only in a careful, necessarily 'false' conceptuality. The relationship of ontic-ontological concepts to meontic concepts is a remarkable one. They do not stand alongside each other, each relating to different realms, but rather are in mutual transposition." Eugen-Fink-Archiv Z-XV 31a–b.

208. *Crisis*, trans. Carr, Appendix VI, pp. 353–378.

209. On this whole difference between Fink and Husserl, see below, p. 71ff., especially Husserl's comments in notes 236 and 241. Here too is the further implication of Fink's raising the question of the framework of evidentness as necessarily the framework of the world (see above, p. xli).

210. See below, pp. 131–135. Husserl's objection here (e.g., in note 489) has to do more with the way Fink is formulating things than with the point being made.

211. Indeed, here we find the basis, in the period of Fink's work with Husserl, for the critical assertions Fink later makes on the need in phenomenology for a specula-

tive component. See Eugen Fink, "Die intentionale Analyse und das Problem des spekulativen Denkens," in *Nähe und Distanz,* ed. Franz-Anton Schwarz (Freiburg: Karl Alber Verlag, 1976), pp. 139–157.

212. One should notice in connection with this question the usage in Fink's text of the term *ein Philosophem* as distinguished from *die Philosophie.* The first refers to a particular instance or element in philosophy, the second to philosophy as such. (See herein the translator's note kk to p. 101, below.)

213. On Berger's visit, see above, page xxi.

214. See above, pp. xx and xxxiv.

215. It is always possible that Fink actually did write out some kind of initial sketch of a "Transcendental Theory of Method," and then destroyed it when he proceeded to compose the Sixth Meditation. There is no trace of such a draft if it ever existed; and there are no indications in Fink's personal notes of some such initial draft.

216. In a letter to Cairns quoted earlier (above, note 84), Husserl in fact refers to this article using the same term that Fink gives in the problematic phrase from the "Prefatory Note": "essay," "treatise," or "paper" [*Abhandlung*].

217. See p. xlv and note 169 above.

218. This general manner of reflecting the original wording in German is suggested by Dorion Cairns in his *Guide for Translating Husserl,* Phaenomenological 55 (The Hague: Martinus Nijhoff, 1973). The present translation follows this idea only to a certain extent.

219. See Cairns, *Guide for Translating Husserl,* p. 61.

Sixth Cartesian Meditation

THE IDEA OF A
TRANSCENDENTAL THEORY
OF METHOD

[DRAFT OF A FOREWORD]

The following text originated in connection with the assignment the author had received as assistant to Edmund Husserl to sketch out addenda[a] to
the "Méditations Cartésiennes." It was planned as a new Sixth Meditation.

The author attempted to formulate a series of problems that remained latent in Husserl's philosophy. Indeed in Husserl's phenomenology the idea of
a phenomenology of phenomenology, a reflection on phenomenologizing, is
an essential moment of the systematic conception. The exposition of the
problem of a transcendental theory of method, adhering in all closeness to
Husserl's philosophy, is determined here by an anticipatory look at a meontic philosophy of absolute spirit.

This is documented in the restriction that Husserl's judgment sets on this
work, though assenting to it. Husserl finds the antithesis between the constituting and the phenomenologizing I to be too strongly emphasized, and finds
the difficulties of transcendental predication exaggerated. He defends the
concept of the philosophizing subject as individual against its reduction from
the philosophizing subject that begins as individual spirit to the deeper life of
absolute spirit that lies prior to all individuation—a reduction made in this
text but certainly not explicitly. Husserl disputes the idea that man philosophizes only "seemingly" ["*scheinbar*"], since the transcendental ego is indeed itself "man" (by self-apperceptive constitution, of course). That is, Husserl does
not carry the distinction between transcendental subject and man over into
the dimension of individuation.

PREFATORY NOTE
[TO THE *HABILITATION* TEXT].
December, 1945

The manuscript presented here, "Idea of a Transcendental Theory of Method," has the form of a "Sixth Meditation." An explanation is needed.

The initial essay form was rewritten at Edmund Husserl's request, for he wanted to attach this manuscript as a sixth Meditation to his planned German edition of his "Méditations Cartésiennes." The aim was to express our collaboration through a shared publication.

The phenomenological inquiry developed here presupposes the "Méditations Cartésiennes," and originates on the basis and within the limits of the problematic inaugurated there. However, it also goes further inasmuch as it expressly puts into question the methodological naiveté found throughout the "Méditations Cartésiennes," a naiveté which consists in uncritically transferring the mode of cognition that relates to something *existent [Seiendes]* into the phenomenological cognition of the *forming* (constitution) of the existent. It is not the iteration of philosophical reflection into a phenomenology of phenomenology that is thereby the essential thing, but the aporia whether and how the horizon from which "being" ["*Sein*"] is finally to be understood is itself "existent" ["*seiend*"], whether and how the *being* of the *temporalization* of what is existent [*das Sein der Zeitigung des Seienden*] is determinable.

The "transcendental theory of method" that is guided by this aporia is not given full thematic development here, but is only outlined in a formal and preliminary way in its Idea, i.e., it is set out as a problem.

2

Sixth
Cartesian
Meditation[1]

THE IDEA OF A
TRANSCENDENTAL THEORY
OF METHOD

§1. The methodological limitation of the previous Meditations

Originating in the radicality of utmost self-reflection, our meditative thinking, in performing the phenomenological reduction, brought us into the dimension in which we *stand before* the problem-field of philosophy. Instead of

---

1. [Mg.] ⟨[Pp. 3–54] gone through August 15, 1932, [pp. 54–88] September 8,
1932; to [p. 101] October 8; to the end on October 21. Dr. Fink's draft.⟩

[2]inquiring into the being of the *world*, as does traditional "philosophy" dominated by the dogmatism of the natural attitude, or, where inquiry is not satis-
fied with that, instead of soaring up over the world "speculatively," we, [3]in a
truly "Copernican revolution," have broken through the *confinement of the natural
attitude*, as the horizon of all our human possibilities for acting and theorizing,
and have thrust forward into the *dimension of origin for all being*, into the constitutive source of the world, into the sphere of transcendental subjectivity. We
have, however, not yet exhibited the *constitutive becoming of the world* in the sense-
performances of transcendental life, both those that are presently actual and
those that are sedimented; we have not yet entered into constitutive disciplines and theories. What we have first done, rather, is to sketch out the *Idea*
of constitutive clarification as the Idea of the analytical inquiry that moves
back from the "phenomenon of the world" (from the acceptedness-construct
[*Geltungsgebilde*][b] in reductively disclosed transcendental life) into the construction of the acceptedness, into the processes of world-actualization. But
this predelineation did not itself go beyond a quite *preliminary and general characterization*. And the reason is principally this: there can be no adequate characterization of phenomenological cognitive actions *before* concrete analyses
are carried out; the method and system of these cognitive actions *cannot be anticipated*, nor can the essentially new kind of thing which in phenomenological cognition transcends the style of knowing found in worldly knowledge be
comprehended on the basis of the "philosophical" tradition of *world-bound* philosophizing and cognizing. The preliminariness and indeterminateness of the
indications we gave regarding *inquiry back to world-constitution* arose from our
wanting to be careful that from the outset we not encumber or even conceal
genuine philosophical comprehension in the phenomenological sense, viz., *constitutive understanding*, by a preset "characterization." In the context of our Meditations, reference to constitutive regressive inquiry was only meant to
indicate the *task* of philosophical cognition, a task which is not yet achieved
as such by the phenomenological reduction, but which the reduction first
makes it possible to set. Keeping within the objectives of our Meditations we
are not able to take up this task. To do so requires lengthy and comprehensive development. These Meditations aim to be only "prolegomena" for future
phenomenological investigations into constitution that would specialize in
the problems here set out; they are prolegomena, however, in the sense that
no constitutive reflection is at all possible without them. What is therefore
first sought in these Meditations is the *whole of basic philosophical reflection*

---

2. [Alt.] ⟨asking what the world is,⟩
3. [Alt.] ⟨in the first⟩ truly "Copernican revolution"

through which the dimension of philosophical inquiry as such is opened and philosophy thereby introduced. An *introduction to philosophy*, as *laying the foundation for the possibility of philosophizing*, i.e., of comprehending the world and what is existent in it on the basis of its ultimate transcendental origins in constituting subjectivity, is nothing other than the *carrying out of the phenomenological reduction*. It is a process whose *beginning* was the *"egological"* reduction, which is the production of the transcendental onlooker and of the reductive return to "ultimate" transcendentally positable life, to the life that experiences the world and has it (but which is concealed by the enworlding self-apperception of human being [*des Mensch-Seins*]); and it is *completed* in the *"intersubjective"* reduction, that is, in the full unfolding of co-constituting *intersubjectivity*, which is *implied* in the transcendental ego (and which displays its legitimacy also transcendentally by a first constitutive interrogation of "empathy intentionality"). The complete drawing forth of "being," as it falls to our charge by the primal philosophical act of the reduction, the survey of its most general structures, the appropriation and preliminary description of the *reductive givenness* of transcendental life were the *theme and methodological horizon* of the previous Meditations. We have not thereby advanced into the properly constitutive strata of transcendental life, but remained in the general explication of reductive givenness as the *field of action for starting the regressive inquiry that will disclose constitution*, which inquiry we were only able to indicate in its most general Idea. The basic general considerations that *make possible* proper philosophizing are at an end. Having overcome *world naiveté*, we stand now in a new naiveté, a *transcendental naiveté*. It consists in our unfolding and explicating transcendental life only in the *presentness [Gegenwärtigkeit]* in which it is given us by the reduction, without entering by analysis into the "inner horizon" of this life, into the performances of constitution. Yet this first stage, in the *generality* of its treatment, is not a mere "program" for the philosophical undertaking that would do the actual work. It is the *first real step of the work* itself, it is the presupposition for beginning the special constitutive investigations. Only when one explicitly makes one's own that accession to the transcendental positing of being which is actually gained in performing the reduction, only when transcendental life has become visible to the full extent of its givenness, can one begin the move back into the depths where constitution takes place.

All our preceding explications, seen methodologically, remain at the *first stage* of regressive phenomenology.[4] c Of course this stage itself already shows

---

4. [See the revision sections Fink wrote for the Third Meditation, *Ergänzungsband*, Text No. 5, pp. 223–224, and for the Fourth Meditation, Texts No. 8 and No. 10, pp. 233, 236–238.]

a multiplicity of steps and articulations, and is itself not an exploration that as it were proceeds on one level in its inquiry into the new land of transcendental being won by the reduction; it is rather one that unfolds methodologically in a succession of steps. Thus the immediate and *first* thing given in the phenomenological reduction is the transcendental existence [*Existenz*] of the egological stream of life in the full concreteness of its living present.[d] Again, the first thing that can be laid hold of in this concreteness is the flowing life of experience in its flowing present actuality[e]; and only after this flowing life is antecedently surveyed may the habituality[f] of having the world, which belongs as a present actuality to just this flowing movement, be brought into grasp. In accord with this *double-sidedness* in egological concreteness, two directions are prescribed for the project of constitutive inquiry: a constitutive analytic of the *flowing life of experience (static phenomenology)*, and the constitutive inquiry back into the sedimented performative life that is implied in present actuality-held *habitualities (genetic phenomenology)*.

If, then, the point of breakthrough to transcendental life, the transcendental ego, is described and fully unfolded in the first stage of regressive phenomenology, we have essentially two possibilities for proceeding further. Either we actually get into the concrete disciplines of constitutive investigation, and carry out static and genetic analyses of constitution, or we first of all develop the *full* content of being as it is given us by the reduction, we disclose the hidden implications of the ego: co-existent [*koexistierend*] transcendental intersubjectivity. These two possible ways of proceeding are not at all, however, of equal standing. The methodologically correct procedure is rather to keep to the first stage of regressive phenomenology and to cover it in its *whole breadth*, to complete the *initial form* of the phenomenological reduction, egological reduction, in the *final form*, intersubjective reduction. It is only by disclosing transcendental intersubjectivity (even if only in its proto-modal form) that constitutive regressive questions, which in every instance proceed from the construct of acceptedness which is "the phenomenon of the world," achieve the rank that makes possible adequate understanding of the *intersubjective* world as the correlate of a transcendentally communicating constitution. That is, if we immediately go into constitution within the *egological restriction*, then on the basis of egological performances we shall never be able adequately to explain the intersubjective sense of being that constituted objectivity has. There are elements left over in the problematic of egological constitution that do not come clear and which compel us to *return* to the methodologically first stage of regressive phenomenology and broaden the *contracted field* within which regressive inquiry into constitution began its work.[g]

For this reason our explicative move in the preceding Meditations has kept to the first stage of regressive phenomenology, especially since for us it is primarily a matter only of *disclosing transcendental subjectivity to the extent that* it is given in and through the phenomenological reduction. What is given in the reduction is simply a universe of monads *co-existing in the present [gegenwärtig koexistierend]*: I, as transcendental ego, and the transcendental "others" that are demonstrated and attested to in my experience of someone else. But whether this universe of monads has the structure of a "universe," whether it represents an open or closed plurality, whether to the fellow humans that are given *mediately* in the "phenomenon of the world" (others in the past, those not here present in the mode of the present [*gegenwärtig-anwesenden*]) there corresponds actually transcendental "others"—we do not know any of that in this first stage.

In order here to press on to a *knowing* and to realize a constitutive comprehension, we have to step beyond the methodological horizon of the first, the preliminary explication, and, even more, we have to move beyond the *regressive style* of intentional-constitutive clarification. Simply returning to the "internal horizon of constituting life" does not do it. We do not have here in this sense an analogue to the *regression* that moves from a) the intentional experiential relationship with respect to others not present in the mode of the present, back to b) the constitution and constitutive recognition of others that is implied right in that experiential relationship. What is required here is rather a whole *movement out beyond* the *reductive givenness* of transcendental life, what is required is an examination of the *"external horizon of the reductive givenness"* of transcendental life, an examination that finds its necessary motivation in the at first unresolvable "problems at the margins" of regressive phenomenology, and which is predelineated by that motivation. An examination of this kind, however, insofar as it abandons the basis of transcendental "givenness," *no longer* exhibits things *intuitively*, but necessarily proceeds *constructively*. However, before one can outline the independent problematic of *"constructive phenomenology,"* one has first to have carried out "intuitive" regressive phenomenology in its essential parts, one has to have been stranded on the rocks, on the problems that lie at the margins of the regressive analytic, in order from that point to receive the motivating impulse for the constructive project. Whatever methodological character, or transcendental cognitive rank, or sense of "construction," the "constructive" phenomenology that follows upon fully carried out regressive phenomenology may have, we can *in no way anticipate* just now. We only mention it because we wish to advert to the *openness* of the systematic of phenomenology, the *step-like character* of phenomenological theory-formation, which just does not allow *absolutizing* some particular stage

or some particular concept of phenomenology. Alluding to the idea of a constructive phenomenology gives us further the possibility of locating the disclosure of transcendental subjectivity, as done in the preceding Meditations,
in the whole of the phenomenological systematic. Even though the latter is
not already given in the manifoldness of its stages, nevertheless the distinction indicated between regressive phenomenology (as the constitutive analytic of reductively given and "intuitively" demonstrated transcendental
subjectivity) and constructive phenomenology (as the totality of all the motivated constructions that go beyond the intuitive givenness of transcendental life) draws a fundamental line of demarcation by which the highlighting
of the methodological stage of our preceding Meditations gains relief. In that
we designate them as the first stage of regressive phenomenology, we assign
their *"methodological place"* in the system of the open problematic of phenomenology,[5] which system is for us, of course, at this point only given in an *empty
awareness*. The phenomenological system itself as the architectonic of transcendental philosophy cannot be drawn up ahead of time, but is only *to be obtained from the "matters themselves" by passing through concrete phenomenological work*. It
is the proper task of the *transcendental theory of method* to make phenomenologically understandable the whole systematic of phenomenological inquiry, the
structure of methodological procedure, the rank and style of *transcendental cognition* and "science." Its task, therefore, is to submit the phenomenologizing
thought and theory-formation that functions anonymously in phenomenological labors to a proper transcendental analytic, and thus to complete phenomenology in ultimate *transcendental self-understanding about itself*. In other
words, the transcendental theory of method intends nothing other than a *phenomenology of phenomenology*.

This now is what we wish to turn to. But can we at all form even only
a rough idea of it *before* we have *practiced* and *applied* the phenomenological method in thematic surrender to the matters themselves, in the self-
absorption of the thematizing stance in which one does not reflect upon the
method itself? But in raising this doubt, are we not led by an idea which we
have in the *natural attitude* with respect to the relationship of positive scientific
research to the so-called "theory of science," which comes after the fact and
in a way only registers methods that are already in use? In the field of transcendental phenomenology, then, is not precisely the relationship between
thematic research and reflection on method a proper concern and one that for

---

5. [On this, see the topical listing for the third section of Book I of Fink's proposal
for a "System der phänomenologischen Philosophie," in *Ergänzungsband* pp. 7–8.]

us is still *questionable?* Obviously we may not explicate this relationship by taking our lead from the more or less factually familiar relationships of mundane
theory of science. Yet within the first stage of regressive phenomenology,
with which we are now acquainted, and therefore within "thematic" phenomenology, we already have a series of "methodological reflections," beginning
with the phenomenological reduction, the primordial reduction, the intersubjective reduction, and so on. And in addition these are in no way some kind
of thematic elaboration of reflections on method that *come afterwards;* rather,
they first *open up* the dimension and stages of concrete phenomenological investigations. On the other hand, we also have to guard against determining
the relationship between the reflection on method that opens up [an area of
analysis] and the analysis it thereby makes possible, in too close an analogy
to the reflections on method in the positive sciences that perform an antecedent opening-up function. In the positive sciences the antecedent exhibiting of the a priori takes up the function of antecedently throwing light
on the engagement of research in its thematic field, of providing the "basic
concepts," of ensuring progress by giving beforehand a system of structural
laws that govern the whole thematic field. (E.g., the mathematico-geometric
projection of pure spatiality[6] as the antecedent a priori light cast upon nature
for physics!) The *basic phenomenological reflections* in the different reductions,
however, are *not the projection of an a priori* in the thematic field of phenomenological research, but are *disclosures of quite a special kind* that do not and cannot
have in principle any mundane analogue—and showing this belongs itself to
the task of the transcendental theory of method. Let us first, then, keep the
two worldly ideas of methodological theory (one that registers by hobbling
along behind, and one that casts light antecedently in an a priori way) at a distance and try to form the concept of the transcendental theory of method in
rough preview. For in the context of our general Meditations, it is not for us
to make a detailed *presentation* of it, but only an *outline of the Idea* of that kind of
theory. It is therefore not requisite that we already have gone through phenomenology in all its stages, and not even that we have a definite understanding of the stages of the phenomenological problematic and of the
horizons of work that belong to it. Rather, in order to be able to set up the
general problem and give the sense of a transcendental theory of method it is
already enough to have the explications of regressive phenomenology, but
above all an understanding of the *phenomenological reduction.*

---

6. [Mg.] ⟨or rather spatio-temporality⟩

§2. The theme of the transcendental theory of method

We gain a first approach to a preliminary characterization of the transcendental theory of method by determining its *theme;* and here of course we have
to take the concept "theme" in a broad and imprecise sense. What will
be needed at the same time is reflection on the *phenomenological reduction.* This
latter is not just the fundamental reflective realization that establishes the
possibility of philosophy; rather, along with that it contains *in nuce* the
whole systematic of phenomenological philosophy. The phenomenological reduction
is formed—as we saw[7]—in a reflective epoche possessed of an unpre-
cedented dynamic structure: [8]transforming himself through the deepest self-
reflection, man transcends himself and his natural human being in the world
[*natürlich menschliches Sein in der Welt*] by producing the transcendental onlooker, who as such does not go along with the belief in the world, with the
theses on being [*Seinsthesen*] held by the world-experiencing human I. Rather,
he takes a look at that belief in the world in such a way as to inquire back behind the "world-character" of world-believing life, behind humanness, and
thereupon to reduce that life to the transcendental constituting experience
of the world that was concealed by the apperception of the human. [9]Thus
through the reduction the *proper theme of philosophy* is revealed: the *transcendental
constitution of the world* in the syntheses and unity-formations, the habitualities
and potentialities of transcendental life, which as such displays the unity of
an intersubjectivity of monads that is communalized in the process of constitution. The *constitutive becoming,* the transcendental cosmogony, the world-

---

7. [See Fink's earlier revision texts for Meditation I: Text No. 2 d) α) (*Ergänzungsband,* pp. 125–128), and Text No. 3 f) α) (pp. 173ff.), as well as the detailed treatment
in Chapter 2 of his draft for the first part of his *Disposition* of 1930 (*Ergänzungsband,* pp.
79ff.).]

8. [Alt.] transforming ⟨myself⟩ through the deepest self-reflection ⟨I transcend my
natural self-apperception as a human I in the world⟩ by producing the transcendental
onlooker, ⟨as which I⟩ as such ⟨do⟩ not go along with the belief in the world, with the
theses on being held by the world-experiencing human I. Rather ⟨I take⟩ a look at that
belief in the world in such a way ⟨namely that I⟩ inquire back behind the "world-
character" of world-believing life, behind humanness, and thereupon ⟨reduce⟩ that life
to the transcendental constituting experience of the world that was concealed by the
apperception of the human. [To this whole correction, Mg.] ⟨in I-discourse⟩ [TK:
226]

9. [Alt.] ⟨In this way⟩

creative activity of the universe of monads, is the constant theme of the *transcendental theory of elements*.

This latter is, first of all, a *"transcendental aesthetic,"* that is, the[10] explication of the "phenomenon of the world,"[11] the explication of the *cogitata* as *cogitata* and of their universal structures, the description of acceptances that hold good and the unities they form purely as such, of structural types and of essential forms, in order thereby to secure *guidance* for the correlative description of *cogitationes*, of the many modes of consciousness in which any *cogitatum* in question is given as an identical unity.

Secondly, the transcendental theory of elements is *regressive phenomenology* (which we only developed in its first stage): inquiry back from the living unities of the transcendental experience of the world, from acts, into the deeper constituting strata of transcendental life. (We can also designate this as the "transcendental analytic.")

Thirdly, the theory of elements is *constructive phenomenology* ("transcendental dialectic"): the totality of all phenomenological theories that in motivated constructions go beyond the reductive givenness of transcendental life. If regressive phenomenology has the constitutive genesis of the world as its theme, insofar as, through the method of intentional analysis of constitution, it comes to have its *proper identity shown* as *present and past genesis* in the subsistent transcendental universe of monads given through the reduction, in contrast constructive phenomenology has to pose and answer, among other matters, transcendental questions about the *"beginning" and "end"* of world-constitution, both egological and intersubjective.

If the *object* of the transcendental theory of elements is world-constitution (as given and as constructible), then the *"subject"* of that theory is the transcendental onlooker, the *phenomenologizing I*. This I, of course, stands in a "personal union"[h] with the transcendental I-life that is thematic to it. But with the

---

10. [Ins.] ⟨correlative⟩

11. [Mg.] ⟨thus of the universal flowing concreteness of the world, and of the latter itself *as* the concretum, indeed as a synthetic unity in the how of the flowing modes of holding good and the contents accepted as holding good (presentational contents). Herewith the correlative description of *cogitationes* and *cogitata qua cogitata* concerns above all the set of structural types that remain invariant in the flow, and this set of structural types is then the constant base or horizon for the description of the *cogitationes* of single mundane realities—*cogitationes* that stand out in a particularity, that are to be activated—and for the description of these realities themselves in the what and how of their modes of holding good.⟩

performance of the phenomenological reduction a *radical split* takes place within transcendental being. The phenomenologizing I of reflection stands in *stronger contrast* to the transcendental life it thematizes in [12]its movement of world-constitution than an I of reflection in the natural attitude ever does to the egoic life that is reflectively grasped. Has not the phenomenological on-looker extricated himself from the *innermost vital tendency* of transcendental life, [13]actualization of the world, precisely by the *act of the epoche*? But does the transcendental onlooker, who does not participate in the constitution of the world, still at all *"constitute"*? And if so—*what sense* does "constitution" still have? We have gained a phenomenological understanding of world-forming transcendental subjectivity by passing through the theory of elements; but we are still not able in the light of this understanding to comprehend the "phenomenological onlooker," although the latter does not stand outside transcendental life. In the field of "transcendentality" there remains, therefore, something still *uncomprehended*, precisely the phenomenological theorizing *"onlooker." Nothing other than this very onlooker is the theme of the transcendental theory of method,* which therefore is [14]the phenomenological science of phenomenologizing, the phenomenology of phenomenology.

(Note: The present review of the phenomenological reduction gives us an insight into the basic lines of the problematic of phenomenolgy which are implied in it:
I.   Self-reflection on the part of man, radicalized into
II. The phenomenological reduction: initial seeming subject of the reduction,[15] man; in performance[16] bracketing of man, included in the bracketing of the world, transformed into the transcendental onlooker, this latter reduced to transcendental world-constitution.

---

12. [Alt.] ⟨that life's⟩
13. [Alt.] ⟨the naive achievement of the flowing-synthetic holding-good of the world in its concreteness in world-actualization⟩
14. [Alt.] the phenomenological science ⟨of the performance that takes place as phenomenologizing, the systematic science of its methodological performance, wherein the being [*Sein*] that is explicated in phenomenology is the performance that is [thus] expanding. Accordingly the transcendental theory of method can also be designated as the phenomenology of phenomenology.⟩
15. [Ins.] ⟨I⟩
16. [Ins.] ⟨of the⟩

III. Transcendental theory of elements:
    a) Regressive phenomenology
        (Transcendental aesthetic   Subject: Transcendental
        and analytic)   onlooker
    b) Constructive phenomenology   Theme: World-constitution
        (Transcendental dialectic)

                               Subject: Transcendental
                                    onlooker
IV. Transcendental theory of method   Theme: Transcendental
                                     onlooker   )

§3. The "self-reference" of phenomenology[17]

The *theme* of the transcendental theory of method is the phenomenological onlooker. At the same time the onlooker is also the *subject*, i.e., the
one doing the cognizing and theorizing in the theory of method. The theory
of method is, therefore, nothing other than the process of that subject's
self-objectification. The transcendental onlooker directs himself upon himself
cognitively, and enters into the attitude of reflection. It is not in this reflection, however, that the knowing about itself on the part of the phenomenologizing I is first formed; rather, in performing the reduction, in explicitly
setting itself up in the epoche, the phenomenologizing I is already there and
open to itself in a mode of self-consciousness (of being-for-itself). The
reflection of the transcendental theory of method makes the unthematic
self-knowing of the I treating phenomenological themes into an explicit
self-thematic study.[18] Thus from a formal point of view, the reflection of
the transcendental onlooker upon himself has a *structure analogous to human*
self-reflection. Human consciousness of the I and self is also already there
before "reflection." The "anonymity" of experiential life, of external experience turned toward things, for example, is not a failure and loss of self-
consciousness, but rather is just its *normal mode*. Reflection only objectifies the
previously unthematic [19]self-knowing of the I.

---

   17. [On this and the next section see below, Appendix XI.]

   18. [Mg.] ⟨Everything which the onlooker might discover is in this sense pregiven, unthematically already ready.⟩

   19. [Alt.] ⟨self-apperceiving⟩

In the same way, of course, the transcendental onlooker also is open and [20]clear to himself in the thematization of the processes of world-constitution. [21]But can the thematizing attitude of the phenomenoloical onlooker be at all put into comparison with the thematic unreflected attitude of the natural experience of the world? By no means, for the thematic interest of the "non-participant onlooker" is already a thematizing, an action, on the part of a re-flective I, and not on the part of an I that is straightforwardly involved in liv-ing. The observer is, after all, the proper subject of "transcendental reflection," the one properly doing the transcendental reflection! Do we therefore have in the "theory of method" the self-objectification of an already reflective I and thus *reflection "on a higher level"*? This is of course correct in a *quite formal sense*, yet we also have to keep in mind that transcendental reflection cannot be com-pared with reflection simply put, reflection as a mere change of direction in a straightforward attitude, that transcendental reflection does not represent re-flection in a *preknown and pregiven* sense, and so cannot be comprehended by means of the ways used in *worldly structural knowing* to understand reflection and its iterability. Transcendental reflection, fashioned into the phenomenologi-cal reduction, *does not objectify a knowing of itself by the transcendental I that is perhaps already there.* Rather, it *opens up and discloses* this transcendental life of the I for the very first time, it lifts it out of a hiddenness and "anonymity" that is as old [22]as the world. Obviously, then, the "anonymity" that is here removed by the reduction has a basically *different fundamental sense* than in unthematic human self-openness prior to reflection on oneself. "Anonymity" is a *transcendental con-cept* here and designates the way in which transcendental world-constitution proceeds precisely in the mode of *self-concealment and self-forgetfulness*, in the tran-scendental mode: natural attitude. In the phenomenological reduction there occurs the "awakening" of the transcendental constitution of the world, and the process of coming to transcendental self-consciousness is accomplished. In and by the thematizing of the phenomenological onlooker constitutive cosmogony comes to itself, steps out of darkness and *"being-outside-itself"* into the luminosity of transcendental *"being-for-itself."* Thus the transcendental *theory of elements* is the *movement of "coming-to-itself"* on the part of transcendental

---

20. [Alt.] ⟨apperceptively given⟩

21. [Alt.] But ⟨despite this⟩ the thematizing attitude of the phenomenological on-looker ⟨cannot⟩ be ⟨placed on the same level⟩ with the thematic unreflected attitude of the natural experience of the world; for the thematic interest [etc.]

22. [Ins.] as the world ⟨of naive pregivenness, the world of men as men who know themselves naively in it.⟩

subjectivity, carried out by the phenomenologizing onlooker in his theoretical activity; and this is so *inasmuch as and to the very extent that* transcendental subjectivity is the *constituting source of the world* as the universe of all that is existent. In the transcendental *theory of method*, now, it is the *uncovering* of this coming-to-itself of constituting subjectivity that for its part is to come to self-consciousness; or, otherwise put, transcendental subjectivity as that subjectivity that *lays bare and takes sight of* transcendental world-constitution[23] comes itself to self-consciousness. Reduced to an abstract formulation, the transcendental theory of method is [24]*transcendental becoming-for-itself on the part of transcendental becoming-for-itself.*

Granted that transcendental reflection on the phenomenological onlooker, the thematizing of phenomenological thematizing, does not represent simple reflection "at a higher level," because the phenomenological reduction cannot of course be taken in analogy to a reflection that is given in a worldly way, we can still pose the question: Is there really, with this Idea of the transcendental theory of method, an *independent problem* of its own here, viz., that *after the theory of elements* as the thematizing of transcendental life—including the acts of cognizing, theorizing, and *reflecting*, etc.—we still have explicitly to analyze the transcendental act of phenomenological *self-thematization*? Is reflection upon phenomenologizing *more* than a mere *instance of reflection as such* (differing only by its new object), which must already then have found an explication and constitutive analytic in the theory of elements? Is not what we have here a *"self-reference"* in phenomenology, a structure that we already are acquainted with from other sciences, from *worldly* sciences? Do not these kinds of self-reference and the "problems" that accompany them (e.g., the danger of "infinite regress") often turn out upon closer scrutiny to be harmless and relatively easy to clear up?

Let us recall some cases of self-referential sciences in the natural attitude. To begin with we can distinguish *three types* which we shall consider in three particular sciences. Let us take the *theory of historical science [Historik]* as the first case. This has historical change as its theme, but not just as the course of events (political happenings in the broadest sense), but change, development, and decline in *human culture*, and therefore including human knowledge, forms of science, human worldviews, the change in the ideals normative for the human desire to know, etc. The theory of historical science, then, has at the

---

23. [Mg.] ⟨in addition judgmental expression and theory itself!⟩

24. [Alt.] *transcendental becoming-for-itself ⟨and becoming-theoretical-for-itself⟩ on the part of transcendental becoming-for-itself.*

same time as its theme the *factors that condition human knowledge* a) in the *historical situation* and b) in the *relationship to history [Geschichte] then obtaining*.ⁱ This means that the theory of historical science thematizes, among other things, first, the *history done in historiography [die Historie der Historiographie]* and, second, the *conditioning of any particular writing of history* by the historical tendencies in the life of a particular historical era. Indeed, even the normative ideal for recent historical writing, the ideal of an "objective writing of history," is regarded as *relative* to the era of the general cultural ideal, "objective science." However this extreme "historicism" may be a falsification and distortion of true theory of historical science, still what is very clear in it is the peculiar *"self-reference"* of the science of history. *Historicizing cognition takes itself as "historical,"* it relativizes itself. The theory of historical science refers back to itself, not primarily because it includes its own tradition (*past* historical writing) in its theme, but *inasmuch as it inserts itself into the context of historical becoming*, it construes itself as a *future theme* for future historiography. Precisely inasmuch as it takes itself *sub specie futuri*, it has knowledge of its own historicity [*Historizität*]. It cannot, of course, cognize itself in its episodic conditioning; as a *present* historicizing action it cannot take itself "historically," i.e., as *past*. That is, it cannot *actualize* its own "self-reference"; its "self-reference" consists only in this, that the life that pursues the theory of historical science moves in an *apprehension of itself in present actuality* as a potential theme for a future historiography.

Distinguished from this self-reference as self-relativizing (through apperceptive self-articulation in the projected historical process) is the *self-reference of logic*, or, more precisely formulated, the self-reference *of the logician*. Does not logic as a science, as the theoretical activity of the logician and the result of this activity, refer to itself in that the judgments and sentences in which the logician sets forth and predicatively preserves his logical cognitions are themselves in turn subject to the laws of logic?²⁵ Is not logic-producing thinking itself in a prior way already ²⁶governed by the system of laws that it discovers? ²⁷ To be sure, the thinking of the logician, e.g., categorial intuition, is simply an *"example" of thinking*, is, as this determinate, individual thinking, structured normatively from the beginning by the universal logical laws of *all thinking whatsoever*. The self-reference of the logician, like that of the historian, is

---

25. [Mg.] ⟨Not too many questions!⟩

26. [Here Husserl adds quotation marks around "governed"]

27. [Alt.] To be sure, the thinking of the logician ⟨has from the first the apperceptive character of logicity, thus that of⟩ an *"example" of thinking*; as determinate, ⟨de facto⟩ individual thinking it is from the beginning ⟨co-⟩structured normatively [etc.]

characterized by a procedure that *subsumes the thematizing action itself into the complex which is its theme*, except that the subsumption has a different form in each case. In the earlier instance, it is a self-relativizing through anticipation of *its becoming a theme in the future;* here it is a thematization that takes itself as a mere *exemplary applied case* of the overall logical normatizing of thought and predication which is expounded in universality in the theme study itself. In neither do we have an "infinite regress."j It is only with the third case of self-reference, in[28] *psychology*, that the danger of an infinite regress appears. Here is a science that refers to itself in that psychological cognition is itself something psychologically given, a psychological fact, and *as such* falls within the thematic domain of psychology. The theory of historical science and logic are sciences of the *straightforward attitude*, whereas the thematic domain for[29] psychology is from the first only given in a[30] *reflective* attitude. That also conditions the character of the self-reference proper to it. Its self-reference has the structure of a *reflection on a higher level*. In the thematic research of the psychologist the living research activity remains in the *anonymity of an ongoing function;* only by a return in reflection can the previously functioning I (and its cognitive life) become thematic—but it does so once again *for a functioning I*. Must we not disclose this I, now, on a new level of reflection, and so on *in infinitum*, if we really wish to know the totality of psychic being?[31] Is *"regressus in infinitum"* thus really unavoidable? Careful consideration will show us, however, that we need not fear an "endless regress" in psychology. For a regress of that kind only holds for

---

28. [Ins.] ⟨pure intentional⟩

29. [Ins.] ⟨pure intentional⟩

30. [Ins.] ⟨continually⟩

31. [Mg.] ⟨The iteration of reflection would have to be produced and thematized and in endlessly multifarious forms of modification, if the psychologist, or psychology, would set himself, or itself, the task of bringing the individual being [*Sein*] of psyches [*Seelen*] to exhaustive cognition. But that is a task which is senseless from the start. No psyche, neither my own nor another's, is in this sense fully knowable, in its full individuality—as on the whole nothing mundane is knowable in this sense of fullness. To know me objectively as psychologist, to know me according to my temporospatially localized, abiding existence [*Dasein*], as someone likewise knowable by anyone, that belongs to the theme of psychology. But this task of an objective cognition, of a cognition in principle producible universally for anyone at any time, does not include but rather excludes the task of displaying the totality of what is psychic in me, of my self-reflection and of reflection on others. But the "universal validity" of objective cognition of an individual psyche and again of empirical groups of psyches is only feasible at all along the path toward a universal psychology as the science of the physical in the world.⟩

the iteration of reflection if the particular functioning I is to be cognized in precisely that *specific actual moment* of its functioning. This sort of aim, however, is not that of psychology; for psychology is a science, i.e., it seeks *universal* knowledge. Already in its first thematic area, in the attitude of reflection upon human psychic life, it never reflects upon this or that momentary act, e.g., the act of perceiving together with its contingent content, but upon that which is *typical of or even common by essence* to all factual individual acts of perception; it reflects upon the perceptual act *as such*, upon presentification [*Vergegenwärti-gung*] in the *universality* of its intentional essence, etc., etc. In this attitude turned toward universality on the part of its knowledge, it also reflects upon the anonymity of the functioning cognitive life that is doing the psychology. In just this "universal" way, it apprehends also the open iterability[32] of reflection. It has no need to follow a regress to infinity really in an actual instance; rather, it understands this regress in its *universal structure*, and comprehends it in such a way that no level of the open iteration chain of reflections could lead to a previously anonymous psychic act of cognition that might have an *essentially new kind* of structure, one not encompassed as such in the horizonal understanding of the "and so on" of the iteration process. It is not *de facto* iterations of reflection that psychology ever makes its theme, but the *iterability of reflection*. Thus the *theme* of psychology already includes reflection and the possibilities therein implied of folding back upon itself to envelop itself [*Schachtelung*]. There is accordingly no essential difference between reflection as thematized in psychology and the reflective activity of the psychological study itself; they have one and *the same intentional essence*, except that the second has set science as its special goal: it aims for universality in its cognition. Ordinary self-reflection and that of "psychology" not only have an essential intentional constitution in common, but they also show themselves to be in accord in having the same *internal style of cognizing*. The thematizing that is performed upon the thematizing activity of psychology does *not have to modify* the cognitive style of psychological reflection; it is, after all, only a "reflection on a higher level." The possibility, then, of referring back to itself causes *no special problem*. The self-reference of psychology does not require an *epipsychology* that would have to undertake a specific investigation of, say, the basic special character of psychological cognition and psychological experience—as something in principle different in kind from the other psychic self-reflection

---

32. [Mg. at the top of the MSS page] ⟨This will also probably still have to be incorporated into the revision.⟩ [Husserl is presumably referring to Fink's revision of Husserl's five Cartesian Meditations.]

under investigation in psychological research. For the cognition at work in psychology is only a *particular case* of psychic reflection as a whole, which for the most part is performed and practiced prior to and outside theoretical activity. If we have carried out a psychological explication of reflection in general and, furthermore, thought about the scope of the evidentness of "inner experience," as well as conducted a systematic critique of it, then we have *at the very same time* already grounded the possibility of the reflection at work in psychology, we have already performed the *self-critique of psychology.*

The *absence of distinction* between ordinary reflection (that which is thematized in psychology) and the reflection of psychological thematization itself, with respect to their intentional essence and the internal style of their cognition, is based ultimately upon the fact that both are experiences of "something immanently *existent.*" They move on the same object-plane, that of immanent *being.*[33]

What kind of "self-reference," now, is that of *phenomenology?* Our look at the theory of historical science and at logic enabled us to see without more ado that phenomenological self-reference has another kind of structure. [34]Obviously the same as psychology! Is there not here again confirmation of the "parallel" between transcendental phenomenology and psychology? Is not a special reflective consideration of phenomenologizing cognition here too *unnecessary*, since a transcendental explication of reflection and even a constitutive analytic are already accomplished in the theme of phenomenology? Or is what we have here something *quite different?*

§4. The problem and articulation of the transcendental theory of method

We have rejected *mundane* ideas about a theory of method, whether as a reflection that, following upon a science practiced, thinks over the methodological procedure therein exercised, or as the a priori projection antecedent

---

33. [Sup.] ⟨The concept of being here is the natural-worldly one, the immanence that of the pure psychic.⟩

34. [Alt.] ⟨And at first it might seem to be⟩ the same as [that of] psychology. ⟨And that there is⟩ here again confirmation of the parallel between transcendental phenomenology and psychology. ⟨Therefore one might deem⟩ a special reflective consideration of phenomenologizing cognition here too *unnecessary*, since a transcendental explication of reflection and even a constitutive analytic are already accomplished in the theme of phenomenology. ⟨But careful reflection shows things here to be quite different.⟩ [To this alteration, Mg.] ⟨Getting rid of the questions!⟩ [TK: 226]

to the start of scientific research. We have designated the phenomenologizing onlooker as the "theme" of the transcendental theory of method, in
contrast to the theme of the transcendental theory of elements, world-
constitution. Inasmuch, then, as phenomenology in the theory of method is
directed to its own activity[35], therefore making itself thematic, the obvious
presumption is that it can be considered a science that refers to itself. But in
that very construal there are *fatal mistakes* if phenomenological self-reference is
taken as *analogous* to the self-referential structure of a mundane science. The
self-reference of phenomenology is *radically different* even from that of *psychology*; [36]it may not and cannot in any way be comprehended by taking one's lead
from psychological self-reference. In what, now, does the *difference in principle*
consist? Psychological thematizing is psychic being in exactly the way its thematized object is; it has the very same *nature in respect to being [Seinsnatur].* The
self-reference of psychology consists precisely in the fact that the doing of
psychology is a psychic process. In an analogous sense one could say that phenomenologizing activity is transcendental being in exactly the same way as
the being [*Sein*] thematized by it. And yet things are *altogether different* here from
what they are in psychology. Transcendental being is not only *"discovered"* and
disclosed by the performance of the phenomenological reduction, it is also
extended by a transcendental being [*Sein*] that has no homogeneity in kind of
being [*Seinsnatur*] with the being [*Sein*] that is reductively disclosed. In other
words, performing the phenomenological reduction breaks open a *cleft* in the
field of transcendental subjectivity and sets up a *separation of transcendental being*
into two heterogeneous regions. The transcendental theory of elements has
to do with one of these regions, transcendental constitution (the formation of
the world and being). The life of the phenomenologizing onlooker, *"non-
participant"* in world-constitution and *distancing itself* from it by the epoche, is
the object of the theory of method. The distinguishing of the theory of elements from the theory of method is thus not a "scientifico-technical" one
(e.g., antecedent or after-the-fact theory of method), but one between
"regions," and is grounded as such in a *dualism in transcendental life.*[k] We have to
make this dualism still clearer. Let us draw a contrast once more with psychology. To do psychological study is to exist psychically in exactly the
same way as that to which such study addresses itself cognitively. The self-
reference of psychology has its basis in a *monism of being*: theme and thematizing activity are identical in their being-structure.

---

35. [Ins.] ⟨in the phenomenologizing I⟩
36. [Ins.] [The insertion Husserl makes here merely adds a grammatically needed
pronoun; the English rendering already supplies it. —Tr.]

To what extent is this *not* the case with phenomenology? Phenomenologizing has world-constitution as its theme. Put more precisely, it has as its
first theme the transcendental experience of and having of the world and as
correlate to these the "bracketed" phenomenon of the world. The transcendental experience of the world is—as we of course know from the phenomenological reduction—nothing other ³⁷than human immanence divested of
human apperception. We find in it now all sorts of acts: acts of outer and inner experience, reflections and possible iterabilities of reflection. All these
acts are experiences of *that which is existent*, of things given in outer or inner experience—except that now, because of the phenomenological onlooker upon
this life, that which is experienced in this experience, the "existent," has been
bracketed and transformed into *phenomenon*³⁸. ³⁹The phenomenological onlooker, however, does not remain thematically focused upon the transcendental experience of the world (the experience of the existent, including
reflection upon the immanently existent), but *inquires back* from *experience* of the
world to *constitution* of the world, inquires back from *finished and ready* ways-of-
taking-things-as-holding-in-being [*Seinsgeltungen*] to the *processes of the formation*
of those ways of accepting things in being and thus also to the *deep constitutive
strata of acts of reflection*. The transcendental onlooker uncovers the *teleological tendency* of all constituting life, the *tendency aimed at being*. What he basically comprehends in this regressive move is that *the existent is only the result of a constitution*,
and that *constitution* is *always constitution of the existent*.

But is this *uncovering* of the being-tendency (enworlding) of all constituting
life itself caught up *in* the being-tendency⁴⁰? Does phenomenologizing un-

---

37. [Alt.] than human immanence ⟨changed in its value (concretized) by transcendental reflection in the epoche.⟩

38. [Ins.] ⟨and has become a transcendental clue⟩

39. [Alt.] The phenomenological onlooker does not ⟨of course⟩ remain thematically focused upon the transcendental experience of the world (the experience of the
existent, including reflection upon the immanently existent), but *inquires back* from *experience* of the world to *constitution* of the world, inquires back from *finished and ready*
ways-of-taking-things-as-holding-in-being to the ⟨internal and external contexts and⟩
processes of the formation of these ways of accepting things in being and thus also to the
deep-constitutive strata of acts of reflection. The transcendental onlooker uncovers ⟨at the
same time the universal⟩ *teleological tendency* ⟨that moves through and encompasses⟩ all
constituting life, the *tendency aimed at being* ⟨in the totality of being.⟩ What he basically
comprehends in this regressive move is that *the existent is only the result of a constitution*, and
that *constitution* is *always constitution of the existent*, ⟨that is, in an all-embracing constitution of a universe of being.⟩

40. [Ins.] ⟨[the tendency] toward worldly being⟩

cover[41] "something existent"? [42]Or, rather, [does phenomenologizing un-
cover] precisely the *becoming of being* (of the world) in the processes of constitutive formation-in-being, which are themselves not "existent," at least *not*
"existent in the sense of worldly being," for worldly being is in principle the *end-*
product of processes of constitutive performance? Is the reflective thematizing
of constitutive becoming something *different in principle*, something different in
its intentional experiential sense, from the reflective thematizing of "immanent being"? [43]The reflection that is *constitutively clarified* in the transcendental
theory of elements is human self-experience (experience of "immanent being")—only precisely transcendentally reduced. This reflection, having lost
its humanness by the epoche, stands *in the being-tendency;* the constitutive interrogation of that very tendency brings into light the implied realm of hidden constituting life.

But is the activity of *constitutive interrogation* and *clarification*, the uncovering
of constitution, itself a "constituting" act? And is *reflection upon this activity* a reflection upon "something existent" or upon the sort of something that at least
stands in the constituting tendency toward being, in the *finality of world-*
actualization? Does reflectively turning back upon phenomenologizing have
the same act-intentional structure and the same "constitutive essence" as reflection that is clarified thematically in the transcendental theory of elements
(as an occurrence in the transcendentally reduced stream of experience
[*Erlebnisstrom*])?

In these questions is found formulated the *problem* of the transcendental theory of method. In the *dualism* of transcendental life (i.e., transcendentally constituting life and phenomenologizing life!) lies the basis for the problematic
of transcendental self-reference—and not, as with psychology, in the *monism*
of psychic being. [44]It is precisely because the subjective performance of phenomenologizing is *different* from the transcendental performance of constitution, precisely because the uncovering of constitutive becoming itself is not

---

41. [Ins.] ⟨once again⟩

42. [Alt.] ⟨The answer will have to sound negative, what is shown is⟩ the *becoming*
of ⟨worldly⟩ being in the processes of constitutive formation-in-being, which are
themselves not "existent," ⟨namely,⟩ not *"existent in the* ⟨natural⟩ *sense of worldly being"*;

43. [Ins.] ⟨Let us consider:⟩

44. [Alt.] It is precisely because the subjective performance of phenomenologizing is *different* from the transcendental performance of ⟨world-⟩ constitution, precisely
because the uncovering of [the] constitutive becoming ⟨of the world⟩ itself is not ⟨it-
self⟩ "constituting," ⟨namely, in the sense of world-constitution,⟩ that the *problem* [etc.]

"constituting," that the *problem,* the *question* of the transcendental "being" of phenomenologizing exists in the first place. Because the constitutive explication and clarification of human self-reflection (in its reduced form!) upon "immanent being" does not yet yield understanding of the transcendental structure of phenomenologizing, the latter remains an uncomprehended *residue* in the self-clarification of transcendental subjectivity, a self-clarification that strives toward universality; and it is what motivates the *project of outlining the Idea* of a transcendental theory of method.

But if phenomenologizing is not a "constituting"[45]—in the way its theme is—, if we have therefore come to see precisely the problem of the transcendental theory of method, are we then perhaps allowed to harbor the thought that phenomenology is not a "self-referential" science at all? An idea like that would surely have its *motive* in the recognition of the difference and internal division in transcendental being, in the insight reached regarding the difference in "mode of being" between the phenomenological theme and phenomenological thematizing. [46]Is not phenomenologizing as such the object of a science entirely different from the world-constitution disclosed by it? Perhaps in formal analogy to a worldly non-self-referential science, e.g., botany as the science of plants? After all, theme and thematization are here too entirely heterogeneous in kind of being. That phenomenology is neither self-referential nor non-self-referential in any kind of already recognized worldy sense is just what makes for the special difficulty in understanding the Idea of a transcendental theory of method. The heterogeneity between transcendentally constituting being and the transcendental activity of the phenomenological onlooker is no plain straightforward difference (as the doing of botany is different from the object of botany), but is an antithesis and split *in transcendental life itself,* a setting of itself against itself: *identity in difference, antithesis in self-sameness.* In the performance of the phenomenological reduction, transcendental life, in producing the "onlooker," steps *outside itself,* splits itself, divides. This dividing [*Entzweiung*], however, is the *condition of the possibility of coming-to-itself* for transcendental subjectivity. As long as transcendental life goes on in undifferentiated unity, as long as it is *only* world-constituting activity, so long is it also in principle unaware of itself; it proceeds in the mode of the natural attitude. Producing its effects in the blind, teleological tendency of constitutive orientation to the world (as to the final end-product of its constituting activity), transcendental life lives, as it were, always *out away from itself in the world,*

---

45. [Ins.] ⟨of the worldly⟩
46. [Ins.] ⟨Accordingly⟩

it achieves itself in a deep "anonymity," it stands illumined only on the plane of *constituted end-products*, i.e., in the world, as *human* I-consciousness, [47]it is "with itself" [*bei sich*] in a way that is precisely *closed off* to the genuine living depth of the transcendental subject. Now, in the reductive epoche a *countertendency* is formed in transcendental life, a countercurrent to itself, a noncompliance and nonassociation with the direction that life takes in performing the action of constitution; and there is instead a movement back *against* this direction of life, a *breaking up of the tendency of life toward the world as its finality*. With that and because of it transcendental life raises itself out of its [48]age-old hiddenness. *No longer participant* in belief in the world (in the constitution of the world), the onlooker discloses, by reduction action, the transcendental source and dimension of origin for belief in the world, he "discovers" transcendental subjectivity as constituting.

The self-dividing of transcendental life—in the phenomenological reduction—does not, however, annul its *unity*, which overarches this internal self-opposition. Here lie difficult and still obscure problems. There is indeed legitimate doubt whether the "identity-structure" of transcendental life can be at all comprehended with the "logical categories" of identity that we find already given us. *Unity in division, self-sameness in otherness of being*, and similar turns of phrase are[49] only figurative modes of expression that give no more than a mere *indication* of the persistent problem here. The thematic treatment and *transcendental-logical* clarification of these problematic relationships of self-sameness within transcendental life belong, among other things, in the transcendental theory of method. The "place" for these questions is still to be shown.

Still the problem of a transcendental theory of method has in a preliminary way become clear to us thus far, that we understand the *self-reference peculiar to* phenomenology, which is what constitutes the problem, as based a) [50]on the *self-sameness* of phenomenologically thematized and thematizing life, inasmuch as both are enclosed within the comprehensive unity of "transcendental being," and, on the other hand, b) on their *difference*, in that one is world-constituting and the other is not.

---

47. [Alt.] [Here Husserl merely adds a grammatically helpful pronoun; the English rendering already supplies it. —Tr.]

48. [Alt.] ⟨world-bound⟩ [Husserl changes *weltalten* to *welthaften*. —Tr.]

49. [Ins.] ⟨here⟩

50. [Alt.] on the ⟨flowing coinciding of self-sameness⟩ [To which Mg.] ⟨"Coinciding" [*Deckung*] of life as constituting in itself the self-sameness of the I.⟩

⁵¹The phenomenological theory of elements is the reductive disclosure and analytic of the constitution of the world. However, the understanding of transcendental life that arises in it does *not* include an insight into the transcendental being of phenomenologizing life (⁵²in contrast to psychology, which in its theme study already produces the understanding of its own activity as a reflecting). ⁵³That last matter is the theme of the transcendental theory of method. But, inasmuch as ⁵⁴phenomenologizing is nothing other than *doing the transcendental theory of elements*, the theory of method has to do with the methods exercised and put in practice in the theory of elements⁵⁵. However, in no way is it thereby a "theory of method" in a usual (mundane) sense. It neither simply follows upon the theory of elements, nor precedes it or intervenes in it as "reflection on method."

The concept "theory of method" has a certain ambiguity the basis of which lies in a diverse, multifarious use of the concept "method." For example, one understands by method in a completely superficial sense the arrangements, practices, etc. of *research technique*, which are supposed to produce the givenness conditions for the theme ([thus the] experiment). ⁵⁶Another time it means rather the *dispositional* stance of cognizing. Or by method (way, approach) one understands not a "how" of cognizing, but a "what," viz., the *most general basic insights* into the thematic region (whether these disclosings be a priori projections or of some other nature).⁵⁷ Corresponding to the three concepts of method are three views of the theory of method, that is, as normative

---

51. [Ins.] ⟨It has become clear to us:⟩

52. [Alt.] (in contrast to psychology, which ⟨just as it understands all psychic activity⟩ in its theme study, ⟨so⟩ already ⟨contains⟩ the understanding of its own activity as a ⟨psychological⟩ reflection ⟨and theorizing⟩).

53. [Alt.] ⟨Phenomenologizing⟩ is the theme [etc.]

54. [Alt.] ⟨it⟩

55. [Sup.] ⟨(the experiencing reflections and the theorizings based on them)⟩

56. [Alt.] Another time it means rather the ⟨activity⟩ of cognition ⟨as actually exercised and as⟩ *dispositional*. Or by method (way, approach) one understands ⟨not that which one finds by directing one's look at⟩ cognizing but ⟨at its⟩ "what," viz., [etc.]

57. [Mg.] ⟨The paths of scientific activity whose course lies in acquired theoretical propositions, along which paths end-constructs intended by the I are gained through these series of intermediate constructs. So particularly in generalization as typical paths of grounding from theoretical grounds to theoretical consequences (e.g., as general theories). Perhaps the expression theore*matic* methods would be clearer here, methods for theorems, for reaching theorems from theorems as grounds, whereby noetic thought itself functions anonymously, remains unthematic.⟩

disciplines, as in each case a theory of the right or appropriate method. (We are leaving out of consideration the theory of method which, in renunciation of norm-setting altogether, simply records them; this is nothing more than a mere historiography of methods.)

The *transcendental* concept of method of course designates primarily a "what" of cognition ([58]not an arrangement of cognitive practices!). But methodic reflections, i.e., the most general theme-disclosing insights, [59]belong in the transcendental *theory of elements*, and precisely *not* in the "theory of method." This latter refers to the methods of the former only insofar as what it wishes to make the object of a transcendental clarification is precisely the life that is *functioning* in the methodic reflections of the theory of elements, that is, the activity of phenomenologizing. It at no time has to decide whether phenomenological theorizing is "suited" to its object, world-constitution, whether it is true so far as its self-explication goes, whether it proceeds in the right method; and therefore it does not have to conduct, in this sense, a critique of method. But it is "critique of method" in another, more fundamental sense. What it does is put in question something that within the theory of elements is not to be put in question at all, [60]the *intuitional character* of phenomenological cognition itself, it inquires into the *evidentness* given there, it makes its specific problem the *predicative explication* of this evidentness, etc.—in a word, the *methodic functioning* in the transcendental theory of elements that is turned away from its own self and toward phenomenological "things themselves" becomes as such the theme of a transcendental [61]analytic.

But do we not here unwittingly get into an *"infinite regress"*? If we make the functioning onlooker an object, do we not have a functioning I that does the objectifying? Of course—but that does not create a further problem, at least not a "crux." For the onlooker upon the phenomenologizing onlooker is not an I with a different transcendental "mode of being," there is *no cleft* between these two as there is between the constituting I and the "non-participant" onlooker. We have no need at all to take the regress to infinity, since the higher levels of intentionality can bring in nothing further that would be *in principle* new; they can only objectify the *de facto thematizing that was just functioning*. But the theory of method, as a *science* aiming for *universal* cognitions, has no inter-

58. [Alt.] (⟨and⟩ not an arrangement of ⟨merely⟩ cognitive practices)

59. [Ins.] ⟨still⟩ belong ⟨themselves⟩

60. [Alt.] ⟨in the first place⟩ the *intuitional character*, ⟨the evidentness character as such of⟩ phenomenological cognition itself. ⟨It⟩ inquires ⟨further⟩ into the ⟨immediate and mediate⟩ *evidentness* given there, [etc.]

61. [Alt.] ⟨dialectic.⟩

est in the functioning found in some de facto moment.62 (Indeed, we ought only use the expression "universal" with *extreme* caution here; for what the "universality of cognition" can here mean is still altogether a problem.)

The whole characterization so far of the Idea of the transcendental theory of method *has been developed out of the structure of the phenomenological reduction.* But not in such a way that we lived *in* its performance *in actu.* It has been done rather in this way: we—already standing in the transcendental attitude—reflected on the reduction, more precisely put, on the *act of reducing;* our movement was one of explicating the activity of reductive phenomenologizing. In other words, we were acting—if in very primitive fashion—already in the *transcendental theory of method* in that we were outlining the *Idea* of that kind of project. This means the transcendental theory of method *presupposes itself;* we can only gain the concept of it if we already, in a certain sense, practice it. It therefore shares in the fundamental structure of phenomenology as such: the *self-conditioning* of all phenomenological understanding. (This is, once again, a problem for the theory of method.)

We were able to extract the *Idea and problem* of the transcendental theory of method from the phenomenological reduction, 63even if only by way of an aim-setting general conception. 64But the *most general articulation* of the problematic itself is already contained in a structural understanding of the phenomenological reduction, inasmuch as precisely that understanding involves insight into the *stages* of the phenomenological theory of elements.

We can divide the whole problematic of the transcendental theory of method into *two groups* of questions:

A. The thematization of the life that phenomenologizes in the transcendental theory of elements as performing
    1) 65the reduction,
    2) regressive analysis,
    3) "constructive phenomenology."

---

62. [Mg.] ⟨And the universal that lies in the ascertainment done in an individual functioning as something to be always re-identified by memory?⟩

63. [Alt.] even if only by way of an ⟨anticipatory, indeterminately⟩ aim-setting general conception ⟨and preliminary certainty.⟩

64. [Alt.] But the *most general articulation* of the problematic itself is already contained in a ⟨horizonal⟩ structural ⟨anticipation⟩ of the phenomenological reduction, inasmuch as precisely that understanding ⟨produces⟩ insight into the ⟨movement through stages taken in the theory of elements⟩.

65. [Alt.] [Husserl merely adds to these three items grammatically useful definite articles; the sense is not materially altered, especially for an English rendering. —Tr.]

B. The thematization of phenomenologizing life, *without regard* to the always
   specific "how" of its functioning, and taking it in its *most general* functional
   modes as the activities of theoretical experience, of ideation, of explication,
   of the doing of science.[66]

Within the goal of our Meditations, which are supposed to give only an
orientational overview on philosophy, we naturally cannot bring the theory
of method concretely to full elaboration. [67]How are we at all to objectify the
phenomenological activity that functions in the theory of elements if we have
not yet lived in this activity? Can an idea of methodic functioning be in some
way "anticipated"? As long as we stand in the natural attitude, phenomenologizing activity is not given in some prior way even in its wholly *empty possibility*, nor can it be devised by "scientific" imagination however inventive. It only
exists at all *as a possibility* by the performance of the reduction, in which the
world is "transcended" not only as actually given but also in the style of its
possibilities. We have indeed performed the phenomenological reduction,
and are thereby in a position to [68]set in motion the regressive constitutive inquiry that starts out from the initially given transcendental egological experience of and having of the world (and from the present transcendental
intersubjective experience of the world given by performing the intersubjective reduction). [69]Up until now we have not yet actualized this possibility. We
are still in the explication of the first stage of regressive phenomenology. [70]But

---

66. [Mg.] ⟨This paragraph is unclear by virtue of an ambiguity. There are here not
two strata of "problems," for that would mean two strata of *theoretical tasks* . . . The first
performance is the pretheoretical task of uncovering actual and habitualized life as
the theory of elements; as this *life* [it] ought to be brought above all to the intuition
that gives it in its very self; the second and founded performance is the theorizing
done on the basis of this intuition. Namely, first of all as eidetically universal theorizing and theory, which makes up the eidetically universal science, transcendental
theory of method (*phenomenology* of constitution-*phenomenology*). By it theoretical determination of the de facto life of my phenomenologizing activity in its lower stages first
has a definite sense, which to be sure becomes itself problematic in its scope.⟩

67. [Alt.] How are we at all to objectify the phenomenological activity ⟨which is
mine as phenomenologist,⟩ [and] that functions in the ⟨development of the⟩ theory
of elements if we [etc.]

68. [Alt.] ⟨bring⟩

69. [Alt.] ⟨But⟩ we have ⟨nevertheless⟩ not ⟨explicitly⟩ actualized this possibility.

70. [Alt.] But to just this stage itself there already belongs ⟨the guiding horizonal
predelineation of the⟩ *problem dimension*⟨s⟩ of constitutive regressive inquiry ⟨which
build up in stages in it; how else could we have comprehensively delineated in systematic indications⟩ the most universal constitutive disciplines and theories⟨?⟩

to just this stage itself there already belongs *explicit knowledge of the problem di-mension* of constitutive regressive inquiry, inasmuch as we were able to indicate precisely the most universal constitutive disciplines and theories. Although we cannot reflectively objectify the specific phenomenologically theorizing activity that goes on in the transcendental theory of elements before we have gone all the way through the[71] theory of elements, [72]still the first stage of regressive phenomenology which we have carried through would already offer a whole series of questions for explication; and it is by explicating them that we could gain entry into the transcendental theory of method itself and present it in a first, introductory way. We are making do, however, with a few quite preliminary remarks that will serve to make clearer the *outlines of the prob-lematic* of the transcendental theory of method.

§5. Phenomenologizing as the action of reduction

The phenomenology of the phenomenological reduction is the *first problem* of the transcendental theory of method—"first" indeed not only as the problem that necessarily introduces things, but also as the *fundamental problem*. The phenomenological reduction is not an arrangement of cognitive practices that one simply has to execute in order to enter into the phenomenological attitude, and then can put behind oneself, but is precisely the basic philosophical act that first antecedently sets up the possibility of philosophizing, in the sense that all concretely conducted philosophizing is only a *development of the reduction itself.* In this very same way, now the phenomenology of the phenomenological reduction already implies the *whole* transcendental theory of method. All later particular methodological reflections are in principle nothing but the *unfolding and developing* of methodological consequences that are already latent as such in reflection upon the phenomenological reduction.

How are we to bring into view—in the merely *indicational* manner inaugurated—the problems that a theory of method regarding the phenomenological reduction must pose? Forgoing a "systematic" procedure, we pick out a few lines of inquiry that can nonetheless clear up the sense of the phenomenological reduction to the point where we shall have in hand a reply to typical misunderstandings and objections.

---

71. [Ins.] ⟨more definitely developed⟩

72. [Alt.] still the ⟨general characterization of the⟩ first stage of regressive phenomenology [etc.]

The first question we address concerns the problem of the *beginning* of phenomenology. Inasmuch as phenomenology gets its real beginning precisely in the reduction as the pregiving and opening up of the problem dimension of philosophy (in a phenomenological sense), we can first of all ask not only *how* phenomenologizing comes about as the performance of the reduction, but *why* it takes place at all. In other words, this is the *question of the motivation* of the phenomenological reduction. It is naturally not a question of the de facto motivation in the phenomenologist at any particular point, but[73] of the *grounds* upon which the cognitive effort of the philosopher, at the beginning of his philosophy, is compelled, or ought to be compelled, to give up the natural attitude and to enter upon the performance of the reduction. Do these "grounds" already lie *within* the natural attitude? Are there compelling *mundane* motives? Is there a grounds-giving configuration of cognitions, of whatever kind, that leads out of the natural attitude into the transcendental? Are there ultimate incompatible elements in the natural attitude, internal contradictions, "unresolvable problems," that require a deeper dimension of treatment? Is there in the natural attitude some stance of cognition and knowing that compels and demands the transition to the reduction? Or is it that the reduction in the end *fundamentally* does *not* arise from motivation stemming from the natural attitude? For "natural attitude" man is not the reduction, in confronting him as a piece of writing, that which is simply incomprehensible? Why in the world should I "inhibit" experiential belief? Is it not precisely by confidence in experience that I first have the world, the existents I deal with, the things that surround me, that I study, that I want to make objects of scientific investigation? Of course experience can deceive; but as a scientist I do not have blind trust in experience, I already have at my disposal a kind of critique of experience; I can distinguish between a) cognitions that are certain (e.g., the axiomatic), b) those for which the corroborating course of experience is the motive of their certainty, and c) mere scientific hypotheses, etc. Why should I now simply "bracket" *everything* that is experientially accepted[74]? Do I not then stand before "nothingness"? Are cognition and science at all still possible? Is it not paradoxical and nonsensical to renounce knowledge altogether out of fear of possible deception?

These are *typical reactions* by natural consciousness to the preposterous demand of a universal abstention from belief.[75]

---

73. [Ins.] ⟨although led at first by that de facto motivation⟩ [it is a question] of the *grounds* [etc.]

74. [Ins.] ⟨everything evident relating to worldly experience, and even all evident matters that claim to be apodictic⟩

75. [Sup.] ⟨The point is to strip this of its apparent support.⟩

But is there not a variety of ways that take us out of the natural attitude? Of course—76 and it is also a *desideratum* of the transcendental theory of method to discern and present the totality of all possible ways into transcendental philosophy. 77For example, in the Idea of a radical self-reflection there is already involved "in some way" reflective consideration of the deepest "self," of the depth of my own life that, as transcendental subjectivity, is covered over by my human being [*Menschsein*]. But does self-reflection, which of course begins as reflection on the part of a human individual coming to self-questioning about himself and his being in the world, necessarily have to *shift over into* transcendental self-cognition as self-knowledge progresses?78

If another time our worldly "philosophizing" takes its beginning from reflection on the Idea of science, then we envisage the inner teleological sense of scientific activity as an aiming for knowledge that, *being ultimately grounded*, has a *final validity*. But what does "ultimately grounded knowledge" mean—in the horizon of the natural attitude? What is the Idea of ultimate grounding and demonstration that is already guiding us here? Obviously this: 79the return to (optimal) experiences that "give something in its very self." Thus, for example, mathematics is a science which is ultimately grounded in accord with its Idea: namely, in the return to "axioms," i.e., to 80cognitions that have an uncondi-

---

76. [Alt.] and it ⟨becomes hereafter⟩ a *desideratum* [etc.]

77. [Alt.] ⟨One such way lies in starting from⟩ the Idea of a radical self-reflection. ⟨In it⟩ there is already involved "in some way" reflective consideration of the deepest "self," of the depth of my own ⟨being and⟩ life that, as transcendental subjectivity, is covered by my human being. But ⟨why⟩ does self-reflection, [etc.]

78. [Mg. marked as explicitly referring to the passage from "the depth of my own life" to the end of the paragraph.] ⟨Still it is "I" who acquires and performs the apperceptions by which I am human-I to myself [and] acquire for myself the predicates of humanness. This refers therefore to the fact that all the experiential and cognitive content in which I am for myself—but in constant change of contents at any one moment for myself—constantly who I am, presupposes me as the apperceiving I that fashions my human being-sense and has that being-sense in this acquired fashioning. The I that constitutes the mundane sense of being, and that apperceives and goes on fashioning myself in ever new forms, comes into view, becomes the central theme. It becomes a problem how it is purely and consistently to be grasped and distinguished from the human "I am," how the world as phenomenon, as correlate to constitutive performances, is to be radically and universally understood, how these performances themselves and the world that has its naive validity from them, world as performance-construct, are to become investigatable.⟩

79. [Alt.] the return to ⟨intuitions⟩ that "give something in its very self" ⟨and to the insights to be mediately grounded on them.⟩

80. [Alt.] ⟨insights⟩

tioned ultimacy, and regarding which it is basically senseless to inquire further back. Can it be at all shown in the natural attitude that the Ideas of "ultimate grounding," which guide all scientific activity, are themselves still *"presuppositions"* in a deeper sense? Does not the natural attitude consist, among other things, precisely in not recognizing these presuppositions *as* presuppositions? Does not "natural attitude" man, e.g., as scientist, already believe (with natural right) that he has fulfilled the requirement of "freedom from prejudice" there where the transcendental philosopher sees him still *afflicted* with the most elementary prejudices? "Compelling" motivation for the phenomenological reduction is not there in the natural attitude—and for reasons of principle.

Man's self-reflection[81] first becomes a way into the transcendental attitude when it is "radicalized" in a sense such as is precisely not possible in the natural attitude, radicalized, namely, to the *annulment* of the natural attitude.

[82]The Idea of prejudice-free, ultimately grounded science can never be radicalized to the *transcendental* questioning of the presuppositions of the worldly Idea of knowing and science as long as one holds precisely to the mundane Idea of science, the mundane Idea of grounding and of freedom from prejudice.

In being deeper and more radical, the self-reflection that takes place in the reduction is not different from human self-reflection by a matter of *degree*, as if both self-reflections were of a unitary type; rather, it is *qualitatively* different from the latter. The radicalization that leads to the reduction does not lie in the direction of *man's* reliance upon himself for ever more radical and deeper self-reflections. The self-reflection of the phenomenological reduction is not a radicality that is within human reach; it does not lie at all within the horizon of human possibilities. Rather, in the actualizing of the reduction a self-reflection occurs that has a wholly new kind of structure: it is not that man reflectively thinks about himself, but rather that transcendental subjectivity, concealed in self-objectivation as man, reflectively thinks about itself, beginning[83] *seemingly* as man, annulling itself as man, and taking itself down as man all the way to the ground,[1] namely, down to the innermost ground of its life.[84]

---

81. [Ins.] ⟨his path to autonomy⟩

82. [Alt.] ⟨Likewise⟩ the Idea of ⟨truly autonomous ⟩ science, ultimately grounded ⟨to infinity⟩, can never [etc.]

83. [Alt.] ⟨in self-concealment⟩

84. [Mg.] ⟨namely by this, that it directs itself to the life that puts itself into acceptedness with the flowing, continual apperceptive sense man and holds it there, and to itself as constant I of this life, but as the life in which world and human existence [*menschliches Dasein*] in the world constantly gain the sense they have at any particular

Thus it is that not even the demand for an ultimate grounding of all knowing in absolute freedom from prejudice leads to transcendental freedom from
prejudice and the transcendental concept of science. That concept too is not
simply the greatest conceivable enhancement of the mundane idea of scientific radicality. Transcendental radicalism is of a nature that is different in
principle: [85]motivated by transcendental insight, it puts into question what
can never be put into question at all in the natural attitude.

In view of this situation, is there still any sense in speaking of [86]*ways* into
the transcendental attitude? If we take ways into phenomenology to mean a
continuity in motivation that begins in the natural attitude and by inferential force
leads into the transcendental attitude, then *there are no such ways.* That does not
imply, however, that talk of "ways" into phenomenology is altogether senseless. Thus, for example, to start out from the Idea of a radical self-reflection is
one actual way; [87]for in the performance of self-reflection of this kind there
can spring up that transcendental illumination that first opens up the course
of a self-reflection that has to be radicalized in a new sense; because on the
occasion of a decisive and unwavering turn inward into oneself the dispositional possibility is created for catching sight, in a productive, anticipatory
way, of the dimension of transcendental radicality. [88]The way [into phenom-

---

moment and the value they have as holding in being [*Seinsgeltung*]. But it is not in the
natural attitude, in the continuous persistence in self-apperception as man, that one
gains precisely this constituting life, this life that brings being-sense to validity [*Geltung*] and has that being-sense in itself; one only gains it by a leap of transcendence
over one's natural self, one's human being [*Menschsein*].⟩

85. [Alt.] motivated by transcendental ⟨viewing of constitutive life⟩, it puts ⟨the-
oretically⟩ into question [etc.]

86. [Husserl puts quotation marks around "ways"]

87. [Alt.] for in the performance of self-reflection of this kind, ⟨one that is first
pursued radically in naturalness (and thereby lies in the expansion to iterative infinity), the⟩ transcendental ⟨shift of the epoche⟩ can ⟨break through and the previously
unrecognized transcendental field⟩ can spring ⟨into view, whereby⟩ the course of a
self-reflection that has to be radicalized in a new sense first opens up; because [etc.]
[In Fink's wording "opens up" (*aufbricht*) is transitive—as the English renders it here—
but Husserl gives it intransitive force, as the English of his note has it. *Aufbrechen* can
be either transitive or intransitive, but an intransitive sense is not grammatically possible in Fink's clause here. —Tr.]

88. [Alt.] The way [into phenomenology] ⟨of course⟩ only becomes compelling if
we ⟨had already acquired in the first upsurge of the epoche and reduction an—at first⟩
quite obscure—⟨viewing of the transcendental horizon.⟩

enology] only becomes compelling if we already bring a transcendental knowing with us—even if one that is quite obscure. So also the way from the Idea of an ultimately grounded, valid science becomes compelling when we are already able to look for "ultimate grounding" in the direction of transcendental foundation-laying, when we no longer keep to worldly freedom from prejudice, which, viewed transcendentally, is still a thoroughgoing captivation in prejudices.

Here too the *way from psychology*, the *way from logic*, and whatever other way we may wish to construct, all have the peculiarity that they only become ways into phenomenology in the first place [89]if a *phenomenological foreknowing* already illuminates the way. [90]All these ways are not paths that lead [into phenomenology] in the sense of a course of thought that first arises in the natural attitude, then proceeds to develop in some way as a constant, continuous cognitive process that finally has to terminate in the transcendental attitude. But they do lead to philosophy [91]in that they lead to *extreme situations* for the natural attitude; it is in these, then, that transcendental cognition can flash out. [92]For example, when being trained in pure inner psychology, which comes forward as one of the sciences related to the world, we stand in a definite basic presupposition, we stand on the *basis of the world*.[93] The thematic attitude toward what is a psychic existent is an attitude toward a *world-region*, and we are aware of it as such already at the outset. As a theme for psychology I have now, among other things, the acts of world-experience [94]in which the

---

89. [Alt.] if a *phenomenological pre*⟨consciousness has⟩ already ⟨made conscious the horizon of the way in question, as of all ways.⟩

90. [Alt.] All these ways are not paths that lead [into phenomenology] in the sense of a course of thought ⟨,whether inductive or deductive,⟩ that first arises in ⟨the constant world-consciousness of⟩ the natural attitude, ⟨as if this sort of thing would ever⟩ proceed to develop in some way as a constant, continuous cognitive process that finally ⟨had⟩ to terminate in the transcendental attitude.

91. [Alt.] in that ⟨by their iterative infinitization⟩ they lead ⟨me, the one self-reflecting,⟩ into *extreme situations* for the natural attitude;

92. [Alt.] For example, when being trained in ⟨a genuine, pure intentional⟩ inner psychology [etc.]

93. [Mg.] ⟨As psychologizing I, I am at the same time constantly in the world that is pregiven to me out of the flowing-steady achievement of the experience of the world, as man among men, among co-investigating psychologists in particular. I as well as this we stand thus continuously on [the basis of the world].⟩

94. [Alt.] in which ⟨what the world at any given time is for me⟩ first proves itself for me,

being of the world first proves itself for me, and through which the world is there for me at all.[95] Now, when I explicate my psychic being in an actual concrete way, I recognize that I have no other world than the one experienced in my experiences, the one meant in my beliefs; [96]that, among other things, the distinction between the psychic *representation of the world* and the *world itself,* on the basis of which I apprehend the theme study of psychology as abstract and as opening onto *a* world-region, is first achieved in my own psychic being. With this insight I enter an extreme situation for the natural attitude. If now it dawns on me that the *apprehension* of this experiencing, belief-meaning life (in which the world comes to givenness and supposedness for me in the first place) *as a human life in the world* is a *belief-construct [Meinungsgebilde]* which originates precisely in that life, and which that genuinely experiential life has kept quite hidden from me, then the *breakthrough to that questionability* is achieved the meditative mastery of which represents the *performance of the reduction.*[97]

Whence, then, does the motivation for phenomenologico-reductive activity ultimately come, [98]if it is not to come about through knowledge acquired in the horizon of the natural attitude? Phenomenological cognition is *never motivated by mundane* but always by *phenomenological* knowledge. The concept of

---

95. [Mg.] ⟨Every question about the world is a question already in the world that is existent for me; pervading all experience and unintuitive belief in and having of being with respect to the mundane as these are motivated by experience is the flowing-steady certainty of the world, which as the constant basis for all questions cannot become a theme for questions, except for this one: to ask *what the* world is, what is in it as steady existent and [something] to be known, [and which] thereby determines it itself at any given time in its what. Indeed the world can itself become thematic as something that exists in certainty, but not in the sense whether world is or is not. World-certainty is mine or anyone's, is itself an event in the world, as are all of us, of whose psyche it is a living moment. It may well be criticized for truth or falsity, but only in the everyday form, whether it is a correct representation of that of *the* world which it precisely and in certainty brings to representation. Every mundanely real thing stands in the disjunction, whether it is or is not, stands in the corresponding possible questionability. But not the existence [*Existenz*] of the world, the world as basis for all questions.⟩

96. [Ins.] ⟨I see, however, [also] that others and all co-acceptednesses that I take over obtain their sense and validity from out of myself. I see that,⟩ among other things, [etc.]

97. [Mg. written along the edge and referring to the passage running from "that, among other things," to the end of the paragraph:] ⟨To work over again more carefully, a little more carefully.⟩

98. [Alt.] if it ⟨can⟩not come about [etc.]

motivation too must at the same time be freed from mundane ideas and taken in a new transcendental sense. This is the problem of the proper method- ological character of the phenomenological *fore-knowledge* that first makes it possible to pose the radical questions—in a new sense of 'radical'[99]—, to pro- vide the motive for performing the phenomenological reduction. Or to put it another way: it is the *problem of the self-conditionality* of all phenomenological understanding. The phenomenological reduction *presupposes itself.* This means that we can never bracket *"all"* prejudices, were such a purpose even to occur to us in the context of worldly reflection, if we do not in some way already have the transcendental insight that the *being of the world* as a whole (including therefore my own human being) is a *"prejudice,"* i.e., an unexamined unity of acceptedness. A universal epoche is not only not feasible in the natural atti- tude, but is senseless.[100] It always has an ultimate limit in the very being of

---

99. [Ins.] ⟨and universal, infinite⟩

100. [Mg.] ⟨Nevertheless, the "epoche" means according to our considerations the thematic abstention from the certainty regarding being that at any given time I have in a straightforward fashion, in order to bring purely and exclusively into the- matic focus the respective subjective modes of consciousness (the modes of appear- ance, the I-modes of attention, of ways of acceptedness, also those of habitual onward-moving acceptedness with respect to the activity of grasping and perform- ing something in present actuality, etc.). In the natural attitude I can, in exercising intentional-psychological interest, and with every mundane-real thing that presents itself to me as existent (or in modalities of being), carry out without difficulty this epoche and the reduction to the corresponding pure investigation. Thus on my world-intentional experiences, as well as on those of other subjects that disclose themselves to me by empathy. However, not to be overlooked is the fact that at the same time, in every such single epoche and therefore in the universal progression to- ward all items occurring at some given time or possibly occurring, I maintain in their regard, in steady, unbroken action, horizonal acceptednesses, namely, that flowing- standing, but unthematic world-validity which lends to every occurring item being- sense and being-acceptedness as an existent in *the* world, or which—as it may be put—constantly holds the world in acceptedness as the universe *wherein* the existent is [and] is in certainty regarding its being for me, just as on the other side too this certainty regarding being continuously [and] constantly receives therefrom the be- ing-sense: the psychic [side] of my human existence [*meines menschlichen Daseins*] in the world. In constant progression from single epoche to single epoche I never lose the being-acceptedness of the world as the universal basis and background for all that is existent, whose unthematic certainty regarding its being accordingly belongs to me without ceasing in all my natural life, belongs to me with everything that has come and at any given time does come to particular acceptedness within it, and in all be- ing-modalities.⟩

the one posing the questions. Can the questioner place his own self and thus his own inquiry in question? Is that not *analytically* countersensical? But what thus seems to be countersensical on the basis of the natural attitude becomes all at once *"full of sense"* if we—at least in an implicit knowing—are already capable of *distinguishing* between ourselves [101](as a unity of self-acceptednesses, of self-apperceptions) and a deeper self in whose life these concealing self-acceptednesses have their origin.

If the phenomenological reduction in its full performance opens up the problem dimension of philosophy, then this anticipatory phenomenological foreknowledge first discloses the *direction and the possibility of the action of reduction*. The self-presupposition of the phenomenological reduction is thus not such that it presupposes itself as *explicitly* performed, but only in that it can only begin [102]if a transcendental knowing comes beforehand in the form of if posing a question in an extreme and radical way. The motivation for the action of reduction is the awakening of a questionableness that indeed [103]enters the scene in the natural attitude, but which in principle "transcends" the horizon of all questions that are possible within the natural attitude. The lines of transcendental questioning that are ways into phenomenology are disclosings that possess a new methodological character. We therefore have to keep them sharply *distinct*, seen purely methodologically, from a mode of disclosure that at first sight seems to show broad correspondence.

That we can only expressly make our inquiry into transcendental subjectivity if we in some way already recognize it—is that not just a particular instance of the *universal structure* of questioning as such? Does not every search for _____ already presuppose a [104]knowing of what is sought?

And yet the character peculiar to phenomenological disclosure does not allow its being comprehended on the basis of this universal structure of all[105] understanding; indeed it stands in a *fundamental antithesis* to it. All *worldly* [106]understanding is always led by a *knowing of the pregiven*, is always grounded in the antecedency of apperceptions of the most general kind over every particular experience of the individual. Prior to every question about some particular existent there is a pre-understanding of the general region of being in

---

101. [Alt.] (as an ⟨apperceptive acceptedness-unit composed of⟩ self-acceptedness, ⟨in constantly proceeding⟩ self-apperceptions) and a deeper self in whose ⟨apperceiving⟩ life these concealing self-acceptednesses have ⟨their place and⟩ their origin.

102. [Alt.] ⟨if the awakening of a transcendental fore-sight⟩ comes beforehand [etc.]

103. [Alt.] ⟨arises⟩ in the natural attitude

104. [Alt.] ⟨fore⟩knowing

105. [Ins.] ⟨natural questioning and⟩

106. [Alt.] ⟨questioning⟩

which I look for that existent. It is out of the pregiven, general horizon-understanding that I then project the question.[107] The "circle of understanding," however, is the *basic formal structure of understanding* only as long as one remains in the *natural attitude*. The pregivenness is the pregivenness of the world in and for "natural" experience. Even though in order to be carried out the transcendental reduction presupposes a pre-illuminating transcendental understanding, this *"presupposing"* is still not a preunderstanding in the sense of a *knowing of the pregiven*. Transcendental subjectivity is *neither given nor pregiven* in the natural attitude, it is in no sense [108]there.

But not only is the disclosive foreknowing of transcendental subjectivity, in taking place precisely as the "motivation" of the phenomenological reduction, *not made possible* by the pregivenness of all [109]that is existent, it is also itself, as a new kind of "disclosing," not a case of newly emergent knowledge of something pregiven. These *"breakthroughs to the transcendental dimension"* do not pregive transcendental subjectivity [110]*as* a dimension, *as* a field, they do not,

---

107. [Mg.] ⟨The relationship described between question and question-situation, however, holds only in the natural attitude. It is of course true that every question presupposes its question-horizon, into which it inquires, from which it itself also draws its sense. But only as long as the natural attitude is not broken through is this horizon that always holds ahead of time the world as that which is pregiven at any given time in changing situations. In the breakthrough of the phenomenological reduction all natural questioning, as questioning that moves into the world-horizon, is inhibited. I.e., all activity—experiencing, valuing, acting—on the [world-]basis, the striving that moves through all situationality and everything in it determining things, and which is directed to harmonious certainty of being and being-acceptedness, is put out of play. In the radically and universally altered attitude the transcendental I and its constituting life come into view, the I that ultimately has and constitutes the world and the situationally modal world as sense-of-being. But this new horizonal consciousness does not have, for instance, the universal and at each given moment particularized form of the human world with its continual familiarness-structure. It is not that [here] another world is pregiven, only [now] a transcendental world, pregiven in a sense similar to the way in which the world is pregiven in the natural sense. Obviously too the transcendental sphere is not unknown and hidden in a natural sense of the words—in which sense of course everything unknown must have its pregivenness form, its typical familiarness. In no [such] natural sense is the transcendental world in itself there, only hidden.⟩

108. [Husserl puts quotations marks around "there"]

109. [Husserl puts quotation marks around "that is existent"]

110. [Alt.] *as* ⟨an in the most general way familiar and formed⟩ dimension, *as* ⟨"world"⟩, they do not ⟨intuit,⟩ in an *a priori* way as it were, the universal structures of

in an *a priori* way as it were, recognize the universal structures of transcendental life, they do not take up the function of giving antecedent guidance to all further individualizing cognitions; rather, they only prepare the phenomenological reduction, which is the proper opening of transcendental life.

To clarify methodologically the self-presupposition of the reduction in its lines of motivation, which only seemingly belong to the natural attitude, is a wide-reaching complex of problems in the transcendental theory of method. In a certain sense even, it is the [111]*final problem* of the whole theory of method as such, inasmuch as in the complete thematization of phenomenologizing the "why" of it, i.e., the transcendental tendency of coming-to-oneself, first gets understood.

All we shall do here is indicate the *fundamental distinction* between mundane pregivenness (and the specific self-presupposition based on it that is found in mundane scientific research, i.e., the circularity in understanding!), and the *entirely different* disclosure found in the phenomenological foreknowledge of transcendental subjectivity in *transcendentally* self-radicalizing inquiry.

The theory of method of the phenomenological reduction, however, has to do not only with the "why" of the action of reducing, but also, and above all, with the "how" of phenomenologizing itself. Is it not precisely the phenomenological onlooker who does the reducing? To explicate the action of reduction in all its internal moments and to objectify it, to display the complicated dynamic relations in methodic clarity, to treat thematically the problem of the unity of the three I's that belong to the structure of the phenomenological reduction (the human I standing in the natural attitude, the transcendental constituting I, and the transcendental phenomenologizing I)—that is something we are not in a position to do in view of our aim simply to lay out clearly the project of a transcendental theory of method.

We wish simply to indicate and emphasize that the reducing I is the phenomenological onlooker. This means he is, first, the one *practicing the epoche* and then the one *who reduces*, in the strict sense. In the universal epoche, in the disconnection of all belief-positings, the phenomenological onlooker produces himself. [112]The transcendental tendency that awakens in man and drives him

---

transcendental life, they do not take up the function of giving antecedent guidance to all further individualizing cognitions ⟨as the preknown horizon for everything that is unknown⟩; [etc.]

111. [Alt.] ⟨the concluding problem⟩

112. [Alt.] The transcendental tendency that awakens in ⟨me the⟩ man and drives ⟨me to inhibit the world-certainty that constantly unifies itself in the flow of pregivenness and therewith⟩ to inhibit all ⟨natural⟩ acceptednesses ⟨thematically⟩ nulli-

to inhibit all acceptednesses nullifies man himself; man *un-humanizes [ent-menscht]* himself in performing the epoche, that is, he lays bare ᵐ the transcendental onlooker in himself, he passes into him. This onlooker, however, does not first come to be by the epoche, but is only *freed* of the shrouding cover of human being [*Menschsein*]. The transcendental tendency *awakening in man* is nothing other than the transcendental onlooker's "internal" *phenomenologizing that is already at work in the projection of motivation.* In that in his action (the universal epoche) the onlooker brings himself out into the open, he is also the *first* transcendental I (and transcendental life) that comes to itself as such. But the coming-to-himself of the phenomenological onlooker only makes possible a *more fundamental* coming-to-oneself: in the cognitive life of the phenomenologizing I transcendental subjectivity comes to itself *as constituting.* [113]In other words, the onlooker is only the *functional exponent* of transcendentally constituting life, an exponent that of course does not itself in turn perform a constituting action but precisely through its *transcendental differentness* makes self-consciousness (becoming-for-oneself) possible for constituting subjectivity. This self-consciousness develops in that the onlooker that comes to himself in the epoche *reduces "bracketed" human immanence* by explicit inquiry back behind the acceptednesses in self-apperception that hold regarding humanness, that is, regarding one's belonging to the world;[114] [115]and thus he lays bare transcendental experiential life and the transcendental having of the world.

---

fies ⟨me⟩ ⟨the⟩ man ⟨my⟩self; ⟨as⟩ man ⟨I no longer am, with my whole psyche in which I refer myself to the world, just as humans as a whole and the world as a whole simply no longer are, or the world simply no longer is as universal field of existence [*Daseinsfeld*]. So I⟩ lay bare the transcendental onlooker in ⟨me, I⟩ pass into him. This onlooker, however, does not first come to be by the epoche, but is only *freed* of the ⟨barrier of anonymity in which transcendental life proceeds as that which constitutes the world and me the man in the familiar forms of pregivenness.⟩ The transcendental tendency awakening ⟨in me as⟩ man [etc.]

113. [Alt.] In other words, the onlooker is only the *functional exponent* of transcendental [Husserl makes this an adjective instead of an adverb] ⟨world-⟩constituting life, an exponent that of course does not itself perform a ⟨world⟩-constituting action but precisely through its *transcendental differentness* makes self-consciousness (becoming-for-oneself) possible for ⟨this⟩ constituting subjectivity.

114. [Mg.] ⟨[the belonging] of man (of my human being [*Sein*]) to the world and to the world as the apperceptive being-sense for the human I (and for the universe of men apperceived in it).⟩

115. [Alt.] ⟨Thus⟩ transcendental experiential life ⟨which gives sense to the world⟩ and the ⟨world itself as transcendental apperceptive being-sense is⟩ laid bare.

Epoche and the action of reduction proper are the two internal *basic moments* of the phenomenological reduction, mutually required and mutually conditioned. If by the epoche we understand *abstention from belief*, then under the concept of "action of reduction proper" we can understand all the *transcendental insights* in which we *blast open captivation-in-an-acceptedness* and first recognize the acceptedness *as* an acceptedness in the first place. Abstention from belief can only be radical and universal when that which falls under disconnection by the epoche comes to be clearly seen precisely *as a belief-construct, as an acceptedness*. Through reductive insight into the transcendental being-sense of the world as "acceptedness"[116] the radicality of the phenomenological epoche first becomes possible. On the other hand, the reduction, consistently performed and maintained, first gives [117]*methodic certainty* to the reductive regress. The special, reciprocal conditioning relationships have a highly differentiated structure. Without going into it in detail, we cannot make any headway in[118] understanding. Only by thematic explication of the two basic moments of the phenomenological reduction can the reduction become completely transparent in its methodological essence, and our work yield understanding of the phenomenologizing I (as performing both the epoche and the action of reduction).—At this point we wish to turn to these two moments by taking a brief look at two typical misunderstandings.

One sense in which the phenomenological epoche can be misunderstood may be expressed perhaps by the following question. If philosophy is seeking a final *clarification of the world* and of the sense of *being*, do we not by a universal epoche precisely *lose* the thematic field of philosophical problems? How then are we to clarify these problems if we make no use of belief in the world? This and similar objections to the phenomenological epoche on the whole rest on the *misinterpretation* that takes the epoche to be a universal abstention of belief within the *straightforward attitude* of our experiential life. Instead of being wholly taken up in the unbroken belief-performance of our customary life in the world, we are now supposed to let go this belief in the world and simply leave it alone. This way, among others, of representing the phenomenological epoche is altogether *ambiguous*. It *can* be *correct* if the *subject* that precisely thus leaves things alone is correctly understood. The possibility of ambiguity has

---

116. [Ins.] ⟨or the concrete life of taking-things-as-holding [*Geltungsleben*] [and thus] as effecting their being-sense⟩

117. [Alt.] *methodic* ⟨unity and inferential coherence, in which alone transcendental phenomenology has its consistency.⟩

118. [Ins.] ⟨concrete⟩

its basis in the still problematic *unity of the three I's* of the phenomenological reduction. The *human I*, with its belief in the world, with its inclusion of itself in
its account of that world, does *not* interrupt its belief in the world.[119] Nor does
the *transcendental-constituting I* concealed in the former let go its constitution
of the world. Who then works the universal epoche? None other than precisely the transcendental I of reflection, the *phenomenologizing onlooker*. This onlooker *does not stop* exercising a belief in the world because he *has never lived in
belief in the world* to begin with. He is after all first formed precisely in the action of not joining in with, of not participating in world-belief. As reflecting
I he does not share in the life of belief on the part of the theme I; in his thematic stance toward this life of belief he works an epoche, but only in the
sense of *not going along with it*, or not joining in.[120] With respect to his *object*,
world-belief *as such*, he is in an unbroken attitude of belief.

[121]The point is that by the epoche we do not *lose* a previous thematic field
at all. Quite *the contrary*. By the production of the phenomenologizing onlooker we *gain* an immense new thematic field, the sphere of *transcendental subjectivity*, which was hidden in the natural attitude. *What we lose is not the world*,
but our *captivation by the world*, the restrictedness of the natural attitude which
looks upon the world as the universe of all that is existent, which is "blind" and
closed off to the true universe of that which is existent (in which the world
lies as only an *abstract stratum*). We recognize that what we think of under the
title world is a relative and[122] abstract universe that is absolutized, the sense
of which can be first understood when the [123]abstractness is brought back to
full *transcendental* concreteness. Instead of being *captivated and caught up* in the ac-
ceptedness-*constructs [Geltungsgebilde]* of transcendental subjectivity in a way
that is blind to them, by performing the reduction we achieve *transcendental un-
captivation* and openness to everything that, in an *ultimate sense*, "is"[124]. (Naturally we must *not* use the concept of being, which first arises in the "abstract"
natural attitude, in an *unreduced way*.)

---

119. [Mg.] ⟨nor can it ever do so. That would be analytically countersensical.⟩
120. [Mg.] ⟨[in the sense] accordingly of a change in the mode of performance.⟩
121. [On this paragraph see below, Appendix I.]
122. [Ins.] ⟨in a certain way⟩
123. [Husserl puts quotations marks around "abstractness," to which he makes a
marginal comment:] ⟨Abstract and concrete are certainly dangerous expressions, as
are all other concepts that originate from naturalness.⟩
124. [Sup.] ⟨and thereby [openness] to the ultimate sense in which all natural being is rooted and to which its worldly being is relative in its sense⟩

The misunderstanding that takes the phenomenological epoche to be a *straightforwardly thematic* abstention from belief (instead of understanding it as transcendentally *reflective!*) not only has the consequence that we believe we have to fear the loss of the thematic field, but is also intimately connected with a misunderstanding of the *reductive* return to constituting consciousness. It can happen in this way, that one indeed takes transcendental consciousness as a thematic field for a possible new science and as a field which in principle does not lie in the world, but at the same time one misinterprets the sense of this *"outside-of-the-world-ness"* of transcendental consciousness, precisely because one explicates the *epoche* in the mistaken sense given above. One remains stuck in setting the world and transcendental subjectivity *in opposition*[125]. When it comes now to a constitutive analytic, to a concrete phenomenological under-standing of the construction of all the acceptednesses in which we stand re-ferred to the world in our acts of meaning, the *separation* of "the world" and transcendental subjectivity, held to from the beginning, easily tempts one to a false *interpretation* of the concrete constitutive analyses. Such as the thesis, for instance: in actuality the world just is not, what alone is is only transcendental subjectivity and its constituting life, its life of performing acts of meaning.

However, if we have *rightly* understood the epoche as an epoche of the tran-scendental *I of reflection*, then we are safe from this temptation. We then have the insight that by the epoche we in no way set the world out of acceptedness, that in no way, after as it were annihilating the world (by inhibiting all posit-ing), do we have left over as *"residuum"*[n] only transcendental subjectivity as that which is truly existent; we see rather that we have kept the world, [126]of course *not with the absolutization* taken in the natural attitude, but as the unity of all *final acceptednesses* in the constitutive construction of acceptedness.[o]

(Note [to *"residuum"*].

In *Ideas,* motivated by the sequence of thought pursued there, transcen-dental subjectivity was designated as the *"field"* and *"region* of pure conscious-ness." Certain as it is that the expressions[127] are *unsuitable* as characterizations of transcendental subjectivity, this must nevertheless be understood *in terms of the way the work proceeds.* After the general presentation of the reduction, the transcendental attitude is once again *suspended* for a while in order first to gain

---

125. [Sup.] ⟨as two spheres of being co-existing [*koexistierender*] in one ensemble, harmonious or struggling against each other.⟩

126. [Alt.] of course *not with the* ⟨thematic⟩ *absolutization* taken in the natural atti-tude, but ⟨in the transcendental correlative attitude,⟩ as the unity of all [etc.]

127. [Mg.] ⟨understood naturally⟩

a few basic intentional concepts[128] and to make essential distinctions. The *sphere of human immanence* is thereupon exhibited in its proper essentiality and *closure* and made to stand out against "transcendence" taken in the most general sense. The closure-into-itself of immanence justified the designation *"field" and "region."* After these elementary distinctions, which really ought to have been already provided by mundane psychology, *the attitude* of the phenomenological reduction is *once more restored,* yet the terminology of "region," among others, is *unfortunately retained.* That "consciousness," however, has now taken on a totally new sense, [129]that thereby "region," field, etc., have simply become *expressions that create awkward problems,* expressions which one must in no way take in their *mundane meaning*—all that remained hidden from the understanding of *most* readers of *Ideas,* so that they made no advance whatever toward genuine *transcendental* sense.[130]

The *grossest* misunderstanding that relates to the use of the expressions "region," etc., is basically to dispute the *transformation* of *human* immanence in and by the *reduction* and to try to establish phenomenology on a *speculative absolutizing of human immanence.)*

We also understand, then, that the theme of phenomenologizing, as disclosed by the reduction, is not a *region* or a new *field of being,* transcendental subjectivity *in antithesis to the world,* but that it is *constitutive process* that must be comprehended as the *object* of phenomenologizing[131]. This process goes *out*

---

128. [Mg.] ⟨which by their nature psychology ought to have developed as basic psychological concepts.⟩

129. [Alt.] that thereby "region," field, ⟨and so all words taken from natural language⟩ have simply become *expressions that create awkward problems,* ⟨expressions however which are totally unavoidable,⟩ which one must in no way [etc.]

130. [Mg.] ⟨Region as higher genus in mundaneness leads therein to the cognizing of the world as total region, as the region of regions. By the phenomenological reduction consciousness gains the totally new sense of transcendental consciousness as a new region, into which, as new total region, transcendental subjectivity enters. That lies in the consistently conveyed sense of the transcendentality laid bare by *Ideas;* and what is lacking in *Ideas* is only an emphasis upon this distinction that explicitly draws it again in broader fashion and gives explicit indication of the alteration of sense in language, which arises from natural mundaneness as the only one at one's disposal. Thus that *all* talk in transcendental phenomenology holds good only in alteration of sense, etc.⟩

131. [Sup.] [*,constitutive process*] ⟨in the being which, as universal performative happening, transcendental subjectivity is what it is ("is" in *its* way).⟩

from constituting transcendental subjectivity and *terminates* in the *end-product, world*.ᴾ Constitutive genesis, however, is not something that *goes on merely* ¹³²*"attributively"* in transcendental subjectivity, as if that subjectivity first already were (as substance, as it were) and then would in addition engage in constitution. ¹³³Rather, subjectivity is nothing other than the *wherefrom of this genesis*, it is not there *before* the process, simply and solely *in the process*. And the world (the natural attitude) is likewise not the "substantival" opposite member of the constitutive correlation, but the *whither of constitutive termination*. Not the *"members"* of the correlation, but the *correlation* is the prior thing. It is not that subjectivity is *here* and the world *there* and *between* both the constitutive relationship is in play, but that the genesis of constitution is the *self-actualization* of constituting subjectivity in *world-actualization*.

The sense of the epoche, on the one hand, and of the action of reduction, on the other, is liable to a misinterpretation which has its basis likewise in the mistaken view that the ¹³⁴epoche has a *"simple straightforward aim,"* namely, that it is nothing but a *method of confirmation*, an "exaggerated methodism." The question will be asked, is not a *decision* already taken on the sense of philosophical knowledge when one wishes to construct it upon some final, ultimately grounded truth? Is not the *ideal of certainty* already primarily normative here? Is not the intent here to take one's beginning in an *altogether secure cognition* and, best, in the *most secure* cognitions? Is not the *telos* of "presuppositionlessness," which is to be realized in the disconnection of all prejudices (epoche), a *primarily "methodological"* point of view? Do we not stand under the spell of certain *traditional* ideas about science if we require philosophy to start off this way with the most certain (*apodictic*) truths? But is it so settled that the *most certain* cognitions are also the *most original?* Or is it not also possible that the truths that are illuminating in original ways regarding human existence [*menschliches Dasein*] precisely *do not have the formal rank* of apodictic certainty, but are given *questionableness and ambiguity*, just as is that which they illuminate? Is it not perhaps just *utterly wrong* to wish to draw one's conception of the originality and

---

132. [Alt.] ⟨on occasion, accidentally⟩

133. [Alt.] Rather, subjectivity is nothing other than ⟨the where and, in conformity with its I-centering (polarization)⟩ the *wherefrom of this genesis*, it is not there *before* the process ⟨but⟩ simply and solely *in the process*. [To which Mg.:] ⟨World and transcendentality—not coexisting or not-coexisting [*nicht koexistierend oder nicht-koexistierend*], not in accord or in strife, not regions that are together or not together in a total region, not correlation in a more comprehensive universe of being—transformation of all natural concepts.⟩

134. [Ins.] ⟨transcendental⟩

depth of a truth from the *degree of its certainty (clara et distincta perceptio!)*? Perhaps it is a fateful prejudice to demand for the beginning of philosophy—since Descartes—a minimum of presuppositions, or even *presuppositionlessness* (by analogy to the mathematical reduction of truths to a few "axioms"). Has not the philosophy that aims primarily for *certainty* already passed over *all fundamental truths*, and opened out into the [135]inconsequentiality of a "wholly secure" knowledge? To put the question still "more radically": is not regress to secure and apodictically certain truths an *avoidance* of the real problems, a *flight* from the *insecurity* and *eeriness* of unsettled human existence? Does the method of the epoche originate in a *tendency to security*?

The seemingly radical "objections" formulated in questions like these lead one, then, to particular misinterpretations of the reduction. One substitutes for phenomenology a *self-reassurance* through the *apodictic* mode of givenness of *inner experience*. However outer experience may deceive, however doubtful and questionable that which is experienced therein is, by contrast we clearly have in what is given in inner experience a field of thematic cognitions that is absolutely *secured* in cognitive rank. One thus *imputes* to phenomenology *human immanence* as its theme. The region of "pure consciousness" is understood as the island of that apodictically given being [*des apodiktisch gegebenen Seienden*] to which one has retreated from the sea of general insecurity and questionableness.

Inasmuch, however, as inner experience (and its thematic area) is only a "*structure*," only a "*stratum*" in *concrete man*, the "formal phenomenology of consciousness" (Heidegger's expression!), which is motivated by the above mentioned *tendency to security* and *exaggerated methodism*, has become an *abstract* explication of "existing" subjectivity [*der "existierenden" Subjektivität*]; and the latter has to be once again brought back to the "concreteness of existential wholeness" [*Existenzganzheit*]!

This is how objections to the epoche might run. The only thing that need be said here is that they do not apply to the [136]*phenomenological* epoche, and so as *objections* are irrelevant. Nothing is as far removed from the phenomenological epoche as is a *method of safeguard*, of *reassurance* in apodictically certain knowledge—in the natural attitude. Instead, the epoche risks *more* than all philosophical beginnings made with the questionableness and insecurity of human existence. It puts into question what all "existential" philosophies of this kind presuppose, that upon which they rest assured: *human being itself [das Menschsein selbst]* (the natural attitude). The phenomenological epoche in no

135. [Husserl puts quotation marks around "inconsequentiality"]
136. [Ins.] ⟨transcendental-⟩

way stops at the cognitive excellence, *mundanely* considered, that inner experience possesses; rather, [137]"immanence" and "transcendence," the whole natural acceptedness of the world with all its distinctions of truths certain and uncertain, original and non-original, are what it puts into question. Not only does it not reassure itself with mundane knowledge, but it precisely makes the world *questionable* in a way in which this is never possible on the basis of the world—despite all existential perturbation and agitation. It is after all in principle false to insinuate human-mundane tendencies (the striving for security) into phenomenologizing as a *transcendental* (non-human) cognitive movement. Hand in hand with this misunderstanding of the epoche goes a falsification of the sense of the *action of reduction* proper (the move back behind the self-objectivation of transcendental subjectivity). The latter is rejected as *speculative construction*, for instance when one says: in actuality the phenomenologist has no other theme than *human* inwardness. Instead of consulting and explicating this inwardness psychologically, one falsifies one's "concrete" detailed analyses ("concrete" taken of course in the *abstract* attitude held toward the "stratum of consciousness" of concretely existing man) by a speculative interpretation, in that one makes an *antecedency in being* out of the *cognitive antecedency* of consciousness before the existent that it experiences.

This misunderstanding also touches upon the action of reduction (in the proper[138] sense). What shows in the action of reduction as immediately *open to the insight* of transcendental cognizing is this: that human immanence is nothing other than transcendental constituting subjectivity enveloped by enworlding self-apperceptions [139]and "stationed" in the world.q But this cannot be demonstrated to natural consciousness, it can never be shown to consciousness as long as it is naturally stationed, i.e., as long as it does not perform the reduction. Still this much can be said in response here: [140]phenomenology in no way "mistakes" (or speculatively reinterprets) the *mundane* cognitive antecedency of consciousness before the objects of experience for a *mundane-ontic antecedency in being* on the part of experiential life before that which is experienced. The phenomenological reduction does not at all overlook and deny the at first simply intentional antecedency of consciousness, just as little

---

137. [Ins.] ⟨human⟩

138. [Ins.] ⟨transcendental⟩

139. [Alt.] and ⟨constantly already included⟩ in the ⟨flowing total apperception,⟩ world.

140. [Alt.] ⟨it is not⟩ phenomenology ⟨but the insinuating interpretation of its critics that⟩ "mistakes" [etc.]

as it denies or speculatively interprets man in the world[141]. [142]Rather, what it does is *interrogate* them and make them the theme of a *transcendental clarification*. It also does not object to giving [143]inner experience the distinction of being apodictic. But it does not make this apodicticity "absolute being"[144]. Rather, in the reduction it *reaches beyond* the natural attitude and the whole horizon of *truths belonging to it* and takes *transcendental* subjectivity as the object for concrete demonstrative investigations, it demonstrates this subjectivity as altogether *taking precedence constitutively* over the being of the world (and that means: also over the being of mundane-apodictic immanence). This "constitutive antecedency," however, [145]cannot be comprehended by taking one's lead from an ontic-mundane dependency relationship.

Our characterization of phenomenologizing as an action of reduction in its two basic internal moments (transcendental epoche and reduction proper) has been only *indirect*. It was done by drawing a contrast to misunderstandings that amounted to apprehending the action of reduction with the means used by understanding in the natural attitude. (E.g., epoche as a tendency in human life to "security"; reduction as "speculation.")

We have still not gained a representation that outlines the task of a phenomenology of the phenomenological reduction. Yet in the end it has become clear that making the action of reduction the object of reflection, taking as one's express theme the transcendental process that is enacted under the problem title "phenomenological reduction," can for the first time produce an adequate understanding that not only has the appropriate answer ready for all objections and misgivings but also first makes possible final transparency and transcendental intelligibility for a *literary presentation* of the reduction.

§6. Phenomenologizing as a process of regressive analysis

We have become acquainted with regressive phenomenology in its first stage. This consisted in explicating transcendental being, given to us in the phenomenological reduction, and in providing us with a first survey of the

---

141. [Ins.] ⟨and the world itself⟩
142. [Alt.] Rather, what it does⟨, and it is the first to do this,⟩ is to *interrogate* [etc.]
143. [Alt.] ⟨pure immanent⟩ experience
144. [Ins.] ⟨for it discovers the horizonal pregivenness of the world as the basis for this apodicticity.⟩
145. [Alt.] cannot ⟨in principle⟩ be comprehended

problematic of regressive constitutive inquiry. Once again, this took place by our first seeking to bring into view the *field of action* for making the first regressive moves. Yet the phenomenological reduction had not in any way opened up the realm of transcendental being [146]in an *articulated* horizonal consciousness; from the very beginning it had in no way presented us with a wealth of transcendental knowledge but rather had left us in an *extreme poverty*.[147] Transcendental subjectivity was first only given to us as the [148]*"living present" flowing in the actual moment* in my own (egological) experience of the world. The horizons of this *narrow point of breakthrough* to transcendental subjectivity lay at first wholly in the dark[149]. The task that first arose was the intentional explication of this flowing life, the analytical study of the interweavings and syntheses, the unitary formations and differentiations [150]in the living flow-time of my transcendental experience of the world.[151]

With a first understanding of intentional examination and disclosure thus readied, we were then quickly able to show by analysis that this flow is not only the coursing of intentional *acts and act-complexes* in the actual moment, but that "in this actual moment" there is also a *sedimented possession* always included in the living present of this flow, even if in a way all its own. In these habitualities, on the one hand, as well as in the presentifying acts [*Vergegenwärtigungsakten*] of *memory*, on the other, a transcendental *past* was indicated. We were therefore faced with the problem of a passage beyond the [152]presentness of transcendental life that was first given by the reduction, the problem of "genetic" phenomenology. In the generality of our further elaboration, however, we did not get closer to the problematic that lay in this broadening of the transcendental field of being. That is, we did not carry out a *transcendental critique of recollection*, of the consciousness of the past that is indicated in the habitualities of this actual moment.

---

146. [Alt.] in a horizontal consciousness articulated ⟨in a generally familiar predelineation.⟩

147. [Mg.] ⟨that of the most extreme "mute concreteness"⟩

148. [Alt.] ⟨primal⟩ *present*

149. [Ins.] ⟨as quite undeveloped, bare of any predelineation⟩

150. [Alt.] in the living ⟨flowing temporality⟩ of my transcendental experience of the world.

151. [In what follows cf. Fink's revision texts for Meditation III in the *Ergänzungsband*, Text No. 5 (pp. 220–224); for Meditation IV, Texts No. 8 (pp. 233–234), No. 9 (pp. 234–236), and No. 12 (pp. 239–242).]

152. [Alt.] ⟨nowness⟩

But is not this kind of critique of recollection, for example, first a task for the transcendental *theory of method?* Is it not the latter that must first give methodological transparency to this methodic procedure in the transcendental theory of elements? Not at all! The opening of the transcendental-egological past by a critique of present memory, for example, is a *reductive step;* it belongs as such in the expanding and unfolding of the reduction, i.e., in the thematic complex of *regressive phenomenology* itself.

It is not the critique of the transcendental experiences and habitualities in which a transcendental past announces itself but the *critique of the action that thus functions in that critique* that, among other things, is the task of the theory of method, [153]inasmuch as the latter, in relation to regressive phenomenology, is the thematization of regressive phenomenologizing.

What are the problems that enter here? Let us indicate them briefly. The *central question* here is: how is the phenomenologizing I in on things [*dabei*] in carrying out the analytical explication and constitutive examination of transcendental subjectivity? The answer, formally correct but trivial, is: it is in on things *as* explicator and *as* constitutive analyzer. But precisely the "how" of being-in-on-things, being-there-on-the-job [*Dabei-Sein*] in doing the explication and constitutive questioning is the real problem. What is the *situation of phenomenological analysis?*

Constitutive analyses result in truths *about* constituting transcendental life. But *for whom* do these "truths" obtain? Obviously for the phenomenologizing onlooker. There are, therefore, no truths "in themselves," but rather *truths for phenomenologizing.* For example, if we go back into the deeper strata of constituting life that are involved in the transcendental experience of the world, if we deconstruct the transcendental subjectivity [154]that is *"finished and ready"* in the flow of the actual moment, such as in regression to "hyletic" fields, we still never reach the inner constitutive structure of transcendental life as it proceeds *in itself.* We gain no understanding of the transcendental inner horizons of subjectivity that are concealed in the natural attitude, as they are there and functioning *before* the reduction, as they are in play *"in themselves."* We only catch sight of them *as given for* the phenomenologizing onlooker.

To what extent, however, should we see difficulty in that? As long as one naively keeps to the *natural attitude concept of experience,* according to which the

---

153. [Alt.] ⟨for the latter in our sense,⟩ in relation to [etc.]

154. [Ins.] that ⟨continuously has the world as phenomenon, that thus in world-constitution is, so to speak, always⟩ *"finished and ready"* [etc.]

existent experienced is there in exactly the same way "in itself" *before experi-ence*[155] as it is given *in experience,* one will certainly not get into trouble. One then takes phenomenologizing itself as an act of experience (with the usual mundane experiential structure), only here it relates to a new region of being, one which hitherto lay hidden but has now come to givenness by the reduc-tion. The constitutive processes that were hidden and covered up in the nat-ural attitude in human experiencing are now only "laid bare," "discovered." [156]But in this "laying bare" of constitution *we annul precisely the "natural" concept of experience* by the constitutive analysis of it. We recognize, for example, that the *independence* of the existent from experience, its being-already-there-beforehand, in other words, its *"being-in-itself,"* [157]is itself a *bestowal of sense by ex-periencing consciousness,* that constitution is not only constitution in the *momen-tary act,* but that in present-moment actual constitution potential and habit-sedimented consciousness is always *co-functioning;* and that in co-functioning consciousness there is and has been *constitutively constructed* precisely the "being-in-itself" of the object, its independence in being with respect to actual-moment perception.

In carrying out the constitutive analytic we thus overcome the "natural con-cept of experience," in that we uncover the *"receptivity* of human experience" as a concealed and unexamined constituting *productivity.*

But have we not unwittingly once more *taken over* this natural concept of ex-perience in precisely this characterization of phenomenologizing? Are we not accepting it [158]as the action of taking theoretical cognizance of something which is *"in itself" independent* of this becoming-known and is also in no way al-tered by this knowing?

If, however, we see through this view as a *worldly prejudice* and suspend it, [159]can we then perhaps construe phenomenologizing cognition as *"constitu-*

---

155. [Mg.] ⟨or—as it may be put—even if it is not experienced, is there in that way⟩

156. [Alt.] But in this "laying bare" of constitution *we annul precisely the "natural" con-cept of experience.* ⟨In its place steps the new, transcendental experience and its explicat-ing forms as⟩ the constitutive analysis of it. [i.e., of that "natural" concept of experience. —Tr.]

157. [Alt.] is itself ⟨[a] sense-formation come from⟩ a *bestowal of sense* [etc.]

158. [Alt.] as the action of taking cognizance ⟨, in a⟩ theoretical ⟨stance,⟩ of some-thing [etc.]

159. [Alt.] ⟨then⟩ can we perhaps [etc.]

tion"? Will the thematic objects of phenomenologizing experience be first *constitutively produced* in this experience?[160]

Neither from the naive—in the natural sense—nor from the transcendental-constitutive concept of experience can that be comprehended which is special to the *phenomenologizing* experience of the transcendental onlooker. The problem of the situation of phenomenological analysis is the transcendental interpretation of the [161]*givenness of all analytical components and complexes of matters [Sachverhalte] for the phenomenologizing onlooker.* In what sense is the "onlooker" the *presupposition* for all phenomenological truth?

This is the altogether general formulation of the problem here of the transcendental theory of method. For we should conceive phenomenologizing cognition neither after the manner of mundane knowing nor even in the light of the constitutive clarification of worldly knowledge and *reflection*. The transcendental *differentness* of the phenomenologizing I—in contrast to the constituting I—is, as we have seen,[r] precisely the *basis of the problem* of the theory of method.

How is the phenomenologizing I *there on the job* anytime the analyses of regressive phenomenology are performed? We shall only use a few indications to give an *explicit trenchancy* to this question. (At present we cannot do more. The theory of method refers to regressive phenomenology, and it could obviously only be sketched out in regard to the matters that it sets as its most general problems if in the theory of elements we had actually gone all the way through regressive phenomenology and not stopped at the first stage.)[s]

I find transcendental life, given immediately to me by the phenomenological reduction, as living and flowing, I find it as a [162]*"living present"* ["lebendige Gegenwart"]. "Present" here in no way has the temporal sense of a present that stands *in* time, but signifies the [163]flowing self-presence [Selbstanwesenheit] of my transcendental life; we designate it as a "present" ["Gegenwart"] only with every reservation. But is my transcendental onlooking I [164]also "present" ["gegenwärtig"] in this sense? Do the theme, transcendentally flowing life, and the thematizing action stand in the *unity of a "now"*? Do both belong to *the same* transcendental stream of experience? We see returning here in more specific contexts

---

160. [Mg.] ⟨Phenomenological experience too presupposes for the one experiencing transcendentally that what is experienced is pregiven to him as there. Only what is pregiven to him can he look at, receiving it. Only by receiving it can he explicate it in whatnesses, in its determinations, relations, etc.⟩

161. [Alt.] ⟨pregivenness and receptivity⟩ *of all analytical components* [etc.]

162. [Alt.] ⟨primally flowing⟩ *present*

163. [Alt.] flowing ⟨nowness,⟩ [the] self-presence [etc.]

164. [Ins.] *also* ⟨now⟩-*"present"* in this sense?

problems that we have already indicated in formal fashion, viz., the problems of the *"identity"* of the phenomenologizing I and the constituting I *in the difference* of their transcendental kind of being.ᵗ Is the transcendental *stream of experience* that together with its thematic reflective acts is getting explicated also the comprehensive life unity *in which* phenomenologizing takes place? Or does the latter have its *own temporality and temporalization?* Does the constitutive temporal analytic of the *temporalization* ¹⁶⁵*of this "stream"* and of the reflective iterations of reflection that might come forward within it already make possible an understanding of *phenomenologizing reflection and of its temporalization?* Is not the stream of experience which figures in the theme merely the *universal time-form* of transcendental *constituting* life? With these questions we get into deep trouble, precisely if we bear in mind that the phenomenological onlooker stands in a *"difference"* with respect to the constituting I. We may not, therefore, give the answer that "suggests" itself, that *transcendental* reflection—as with *any* reflection whatsoever—stands united with the theme of its reflection in the unity of a *single* life-complex, in the unity of *the same "now"*¹⁶⁶. If we reject this answer, however, we have not understood anything more than the *problem.*

How in the end the temporality of the analytical situation has to be conceived, whether we finally have to show an *"overarching"* transcendental stream of life in which phenomenologizing stands in *discordant unity* with its theme, together with it but certainly in a way *"altogether different"* from the way an act of reflection usually stands together with its object—this remains open.

We conceive the regressive explication and constitutive analysis of the transcendental onlooker as a *doing,* and so we use concepts that we have taken from the general understanding of a reflective thematization. In this sense we might say the following: in the theoretical attitude the phenomenologizing onlooker is oriented to the transcendental-constituting life given him by the reduction; he performs *acts of taking cognizance,* forms *polythetic cognitive complexes* in the course of cognitional progress, acquires theoretical convictions, thus sets up a tradition of his own scientific activity¹⁶⁷, etc.

Now, the *clarification* ¹⁶⁸*of* these *theoretical actions* and operations, retentions, habituations, is one of the basic urgent problems of a transcendental theory of method regarding regressive phenomenology, in that—because of the transcendental differentness of the phenomenologizing I—its retaining, its

---

165. [Alt.] *of* ⟨the former, the thematic⟩ *"stream"*

166. [Ins.] ⟨as the same relative to the same temporality⟩

167. [Ins.] ⟨and of his acquisitions⟩

168. [Alt.] of these ⟨experientially explicative and predicative-⟩*theoretical actions* [etc.]

establishing of habitualities, its theoretical acting, etc., are *not* simply a *de facto actualization* of the *"theoretical performance as such"* which in regressive phenomenology is made thematic in essential universality and constitutively clarified.

The theoretical functioning of the onlooker, however, is through and through determined in regressive phenomenology by the *particular* problems in the latter, i.e., it intentionally explicates, it constitutively analyzes, it also reduces (primordial and intersubjective reduction!). That is what makes the questions indicated above *specific.* But we cannot go into that now. We can, however, pose the question whether the sense in which the phenomenologizing I *"is there on the job"* regarding all analytical transcendental *"matter-complexes"* [*"Sachverhalten"*] is *always the same* throughout regressive phenomenology. Even if we still do not yet know how, e.g., in the *primordial analytic* the being-in-on-things of the onlooker has to be determined, we can still remain open to the *possibility* that in the phenomenological explication of *intersubjectivity* this being-in-on-things can take on *another sense of "presupposition."* We certainly bear in mind that it is *I,* as onlooker, who makes *myself* (as constituting ego) the theme, that nevertheless it is also *I* who *reduces* the "Other" first given as "phenomenon" to the transcendental Other. Is the Other, as monad in his own essentiality, also *"like me" insofar as "I" am phenomenologizing?* Is the "phenomenologizing I" *repeatable* in the Other? Can the Other indeed perform the reduction precisely out of himself and establish an "onlooker" in himself? The "onlooker" of the Other is only *given* to me by *empathy* (communication), i.e., he is given me in a kind of experience whose intentional explication and constitutive analytic precisely *belongs to regressive phenomenology as a theme.* He is not at all a "phenomenologizing" Other *on equal standing* with me as phenomenologizing I. I do not share with him the being-in-on-things that is the presupposition of the whole regressive analytic. My phenomenologizing I *even stands over against him* as the I *for which* alone and solely the constitutive components of empathy, along with the *self-reduction of the Other* which it is possible to approach in empathy, are in force.

Naturally the phenomenologizing transcendental Other is not an *irrelevant problem* for the "theory of method," but needs its *own thematic treatment.*

[169]§7. Phenomenologizing in "constructive" phenomenology

The Idea of a transcendental theory of method contains the task of making *phenomenologizing* itself the object of phenomenological investigation and

---

169. [Mg. at top of the page] ⟨[54–88] gone into September 8, 1932, Eugen Fink⟩

cognition, starting with the *particular ways* in which it functions precisely in the transcendental theory of elements (the phenomenological cognition of world-constitution). For merely an *outline* of this idea, it might already be enough to take the most general problems into account. Thus, for example, we were able in a preliminary way to characterize the "phenomenology of the phenomenological reduction"—even if indirectly—by the two lines of inquiry dominant in it.ᵘ Likewise, we are already brought to a preliminary understanding of the problematic of the theory of method in its reference to regressive phenomenology by having established the basic problem, namely, the question of the "situation of phenomenological analysis,"ᵛ or, otherwise put, the question of the transcendental meaning [170]of *being-given [Gegenbensein]* for the phenomenologizing onlooker on the part of all analytical matter-complexes and truths.

These indications were possible because we had already gone through the phenomenological reduction, and therefore had also actually set our hand to regressive phenomenology, although only in its first stage.

But how are we to get a preliminary look at the way the problem of the transcendental theory of method takes shape in regard to another matter special to it, "constructive phenomenology," which we do not even at all know yet? Do we not instead first have to make our own the most general Idea of constructive phenomenology, before we can sketch out the inquiry to make regarding the *phenomenologizing operative in it?*

Even a completely [171]empty and preliminary indication of the material issues that have to be grasped under the title "constructive phenomenology" is bound up with extraordinary difficulties; and the reason for this is above all that it does not designate a *unitary "domain of objects"* within the phenomenological theme, transcendental subjectivity. Constructive phenomenology does not refer to a closed thematic complex analogously to the way "egological" ([172]or better, "primordial") and "intersubjective" phenomenology do; it is not a "content" designation at all, but a *methodological concept* for transcendental cognitions of a peculiar sort. If regressive phenomenology is the whole of the primordial and intersubjective explication of reductively opened up transcendental subjectivity, then there is not alongside it still another new region of *reductively given* transcendental life now to be offered as the theme for a constructive phenomenology. Rather, under the concept of constructive phenomenology we conceive the *methodological unity* of all transcendental

---

170. [Alt.] of *being-*⟨pregiven and ⟩*given for* [etc.]
171. [Alt.] ⟨indeterminately general⟩
172. [Alt.] ⟨here to be understood as⟩ "primordial"

cognitions that are accessible by *"construction"*—in the phenomenological sense!—and which as such can be *heterogeneous in content.*

The concept of "construction" must not, however, be understood here in an ordinary sense (such as hypothesis-making). It has no affinity to any kind of "constructive" procedure as practiced in the worldly sciences, e.g., in mathematics, in paleontology, etc. The *transcendental* title "construction" is only an allusion to the *modes of referral* on the part of phenomenological cognizing with respect to the theme that is here in question, modes of referral which are still completely obscure in their own special character. The "object"—or better, *the objects*—of constructive phenomenology are *not "given."* [173]The theorizing directed to them is not an "intuitive having given" [*"anschauliches Gegebenhaben"*], is not "intuitive" [*"intuitiv"*]; but as referral to something that precisely by its transcendental mode of being is *in principle* deprived of "givenness," is "non-given," this theorizing is *constructive.*

Precisely in these vague indications of the Idea of a constructive phenomenology, the danger that all phenomenological presentations bring with them is especially great. Not only do we not understand the sense of transcendental "non-givenness," but already in our construal of the transcendental concept of "givenness" we are all too easily misled by mundane notions.

"Givenness" does not mean mere[174] presence [*Anwesenheit*], the actual-moment presentness [*aktuelle Gegenwärtigkeit*] of transcendental life to the phenomenological onlooker. In this sense only the actual-moment[175] stream of egological *cogitationes* and the actual-moment having of the I, its present habitual possession, in a word, only the "living[176] present" [*"lebendige Gegenwart"*] of transcendental life, would be "given." Assuredly this living present of flowing egological experience and the egoic having that in a special way flows along with it make up *the core givenness,* the *basic givenness* of transcendental life. In the transcendental breakthrough of the phenomenological reduction we [177]indeed also first run into this primal element of newly discovered "be-

---

173. [Alt.] The theorizing directed to them is ⟨not in any such broad sense something that is itself given in the manner of experience and that has to be brought each time to self-givenness,⟩ is not "intuitive";

174. [Ins.] ⟨perceptual⟩

175. [Ins., afterwards erased] ⟨primal⟩

176. [Ins., afterwards erased] ⟨primal⟩ [to which Mg.] ⟨the primal? Or the present of immanent-egological time-modality? It seems the latter. But this has to be made clearer.⟩

177. ["indeed also" lined through by Husserl]

ing."[178] But we do not stay with it forever. Already in the first stage of regressive phenomenology we necessarily move through the full extent of the transcendental subjectivity given us by the reduction; and we do this by systematically unfolding the implicit content of the reduction, by exhibiting a transcendental egological past beyond the living[179] present of the actual moment, and finally by disclosing the transcendental "others" that announce themselves in egological acts of empathy, disclosing them, that is, as belonging to the full concreteness of the transcendental life that becomes visible as intersubjectively self-communalizing.

"Reductive givenness" is thus the title that takes in the *entire*[180] "being" [*"Sein"*] legitimated by the phenomenological reduction as transcendentally existent [*existent*]: the monad-community centered in the primordial ego. In this context "givenness" thus does not signify being-at-hand and lying before one, for instance, in the way things are given,[181] are there, as objects of natural worldly experience; but it means *possible*[182] *accessibility through the unfolding of the phenomenological reduction.*

Transcendental subjectivity (monadic intersubjectivity), however, is reductively given as *constituting the world*, i.e., as standing *in the process* of the constitution of the world, as actualizing itself in actualizing the world. This is of fundamental significance.[183] Only in consideration of this does the concept of "reductive givenness" gain its *proper precision*. We thereupon realize that by the phenomenological reduction we disclose transcendental subjectivity in a

---

178. [Mg.] ⟨It is a primal element in the movement of transcendental *cognition*, but not the ultimate absolute as is the primal flow.⟩ [To which Mg. at top of the page] ⟨The movement of uncovering: from the time-modality that uncovers itself earlier, the present of the transcendental-egological time-stream, to the primally living "present," which is not a time-modality—the absolute primal element, but not the primal element of transcendental cognition.⟩

179. [Ins.] ⟨egological⟩

180. [Ins.] ⟨temporal⟩

181. [Mg.] ⟨in their spatio-temporal accessibility for me and everyone⟩

182. [Ins.] ⟨transcendental⟩

183. [Mg.] ⟨Reduction to concrete transcendental time—as time in the narrower sense of successive temporality and time in the sense of transcendental spatiality. Intersubjectivity as universal horizon is the "space" for every transcendentally subjective item of any particular present as the Coexistence form for all successive presents—and its concrete transcendental time in the time form, temporo-spatiality. The deeper problem: the transcendental constitution of a higher level, that of transcendental temporality.⟩

particular situation regarding its mode of being, namely, as *engaged*[184] *in* the transcendental activity of world-constitution.[185]

Even if we must not conceive the presentness [*Gegenwärtigkeit*] in which transcendental life at first confronts us [186]by taking our lead from a present [*Gegenwart*] *in* time, even if we first have to set aside all worldly ideas about the present, still the further unfolding of the phenomenological reduction leads us to recognize the actual-moment flowing present as a present *in a transcendental time*.[187] But the essential thing here is not that the actual-moment presence [*aktuelle Präsenz*] of transcendental life stands in a transcendental "history" ["*Geschichte*"], but rather that *the entire being [Sein] that is accessible by the reduction,* thus also the transcendental *past* (the demonstration of which can be given by the constitutive analysis of recollection), already stands in a "history" ["*Historie*"], inasmuch as *world-constitution* is *always already* under way.ʷ

Even where in a "genetic phenomenology" we intentionally and constitutively clarify the actual-moment having (habitualities) on the part of the ego by the analysis of primal institutings, of the processes of formation, out of which the having arose, we also always have within our theme a transcendental life that is already *in the midst of* world-constitution.

However, not only is the being-complex of constituting action, as far as the latter is disclosed and pregiven as theme by the reduction, found to be in a transcendental "situation" (precisely by being-in-the-midst-of-world-constitution), but also the *phenomenological onlooker* is *determined* by this transcendental situation. Although he is not engaged in constituting the world—because of his "differentness"—and thus does not participate in the ongoing process, still he is affected by this situation. He is nothing other than the exponent projected out by the transcendental life that *stands in world-constitution* in order by it to come to itself. However problematic the "simultaneity" of the phenomenologizing I and the constituting I may be, still the "nonparticipation" of the onlooker is only possible in the first place if precisely that *in which it does not participate,* world-constitution, is in progress.

---

184. [Ins.] ⟨from the ego out⟩

185. [Sup.] ⟨or as transcendental intersubjectivity constantly taken up in world-constitution.⟩

186. [Alt.] by taking our lead from a present *in* ⟨world-⟩time, even if we first have to set aside all worldly ⟨and even all transcendental⟩ ideas about ⟨temporality⟩, still the unfolding [etc.]

187. [Mg.] ⟨[in] intersubjective [time]?⟩

This *communality* in the transcendental situation for the life of constituting action and the phenomenologizing onlooker completely determines that which, in reference to regressive phenomenology, we have named the basic problem of the transcendental theory of method.ˣ The "situation of constitutive analyses," that is, the givenness *for* the phenomenologizing onlooker of all analytical components and truths, can receive its final [188]elucidation only after *prior* adequate explication of the special kind of *"simultaneity"* between world-constituting transcendental activity and the action of thematizing that, while not participating in it, makes it its theme. The necessary *presupposedness* of the phenomenologizing I *for* the analytical exhibitings of constitution has its *counterpoint* in the *presupposedness* of world-constituting life for the possibility of establishing a transcendental onlooker.

What this correlativity of mutual self-presupposing means constitutes among other things the special problematic of the transcendental theory of method in reference to regressive phenomenology.

[189]These indications, however, are only supposed to bring out for us the impact of the problems that the transcendental theory of method must pose in relation to *constructive* phenomenology. But we still do not have a concept of constructive phenomenology itself. The indications we have given for determining the concept of *reductive givenness* prove now to be the guide by which we can press on toward getting a rough idea of a constructive phenomenology. The latter is nothing other than the sum total of all the problems that go beyond the reductive givenness of transcendental life. But is a problematic of this kind at all conceivable? Can one attribute any sense to an inquiry that goes beyond the transcendental subjectivity that in the full breadth of world-constitution is "given" to us in the phenomenological reduction? The *basis* for constructive phenomenology is laid down by the development of the motivations that lead us to sketch out problems that are basically *no longer resolvable* in the horizon of regressive phenomenology. These motivations indeed arise still within regressive phenomenology, in quite diverse "places," and each in diverse ways; they are its *"exempla crucis."* Because of their diversity they[190] do not constitute a problematic in terms of theme and content. It is for this reason that at the outset we called constructive phenomenology simply[191] a

---

188. [Alt.] ⟨clarification⟩
189. [Alt.] These indications ⟨now⟩, are supposed to bring out [etc.]
190. [Mg.] ⟨at first?⟩
191. [Mg.] ⟨at first⟩

methodological concept, and rejected as impossible here a characterization
of it that would claim to give its thematic region.

To develop and[192] lay out in detail the motivations in question is once again
not possible before we have gone all the way through regressive phenomenology and seen its limits, the problem elements [in it] that have not yet been
mastered. Only when we have pushed the [193]constitutive analytic right to the
ultimate reach of its ability to understand will we have at our disposal the possibility of posing limit-problems in a suitable form.

Must we not, therefore, give up a preliminary concept of constructive phenomenology? Can we expect more than some empty and general indication
of it, such as that it is the set of transcendental problems that lie beyond reductive givenness? Certainly not before we have brought regressive phenomenology in concrete work to a close. But in our empty and imprecise notices
there is nonetheless already contained a certain *indication* of the problem-
complex of constructive phenomenology.

Reductively given transcendental life, the theme of regressive phenomenology, finds itself, we said, in the transcendental situation in which world-
constitution has already been set going and is in progress. If the first
exhibitable historicity [*Historizität*] of transcendental subjectivity is the historicality [*Geschichtlichkeit*]*y* of the constitution that is *under way in present actuality*,
[194]nevertheless, perhaps misled by worldly prejudices, we can pose the particular question of a *"beginning"* and an *"end"* of this constituting life given as historical. Even if these questions were in the end to be proven transcendentally
inadmissible, still the proof of their eventual inadmissibility must take place
in a problem dimension that in principle lies *"outside"* regressive phenomenology. The thematic treatment of this problem[195] does not have the style of a
constitutive analysis of a *given* transcendental element, it has rather the character of a *"construction."* The phenomenological onlooker, bound up in a personal union*z* with the I that stands in the midst of the constitution of the
world, and "identical" with that I in a special kind of "antithesis," projects the
question of a beginning that is in principle "non-given" to him. Working out
from the given historicity [*Historizität*] of constituting life the onlooker inquires into the temporal wholeness, into the totality of transcendental being,

---

192. [Ins.] ⟨concretely⟩

193. [Alt.] the ⟨problematic of the⟩ constitutive analytic

194. [Alt.] ⟨then, to begin with, the very obvious question is that of⟩ a *"beginning"*
and an *"end"* [etc.]

195. [Ins.] ⟨clearly⟩

which is not given to him in totality. The motivation for a question like this comes from consideration of some particular content of the "phenomenon of the world," for example here, the mundane time-whole [196]of human subjectivity. [197]If by the phenomenological reduction human "immanence" is reduced to the transcendentally existing stream of experience [*den transzendental existenten Erlebnisstrom*], then this reduction includes the explicit disconnecting and bracketing of all worldly representations of the wholeness-structures of this stream, which we constitutively analyze now purely in its transcendental temporality. That is, we inquire back from the temporal unities of flowing life into the performative processes of temporalization [*Zeitigung*], as a constituting action, that are implied in it. We thereby gain the most original and most radical understanding conceivable with respect also to the psychic immanent time that is found in the "phenomenon," inasmuch as it is from the constituting sources of sense-bestowal that we are able to understand psychic immanent time as the *time that is* [198]*constituted in end-constitution.* There results now a special *"coincidence"* between the temporality of bracketed human immanence and that of the transcendental[199] stream of experience inasmuch as both are "the same" flowing temporality, only in the one instance it is enclosed in transcending,[aa] enworlding apperceptions, in the other it is freed from these mundane construals by the reduction.[200] It is a decisive question, now, *how far* this "coincidence" reaches, whether a pure stream of experience transcendentally corresponds *throughout* to the time of human immanence which is found in the "phenomenon," namely, whether it corresponds above all to the *structures of wholeness* in human lived time. The time man in the world has begins at birth and ends in death; does the transcendental *time of world-constitution*[201] likewise have a "beginning" that corresponds to worldly birth and a transcendental "end" that corresponds to worldly death? Or are "birth" and "death" only ele-

---

196. [Alt.] of ⟨any individual-human⟩ subjectivity.

197. [Alt.] If by the phenomenological reduction ⟨my individual-human⟩ "immanence" is reduced to the transcendentally existing stream of experience, then this reduction includes the explicit disconnecting and bracketing of all worldly ⟨apperceptions⟩ of the wholeness-structures ⟨and individual experiences⟩ of this stream [etc.]

198. [Alt.] *constituted* ⟨as world-time⟩.

199. [Ins.] ⟨egological⟩

200. [Mg.] .⟨Cf. above! Acceptedness in being [*Seinsgeltung*] is bracketed and *in that way* "freed" from acceptedness. But world-temporalizing apperceptions are discovered, become thematic, and now yield the concrete correlation.⟩

201. [Ins.] ⟨corresponding to man's time⟩

ments of sense constituted in reductively given transcendental life, does human beginning presuppose a transcendental existence [*Existenz*] *that already is*, that enworlds itself as man and must constitute its own worldly beginning; and perhaps death in the world as well, to-be-no-more as man, presupposes an *existing [existierende]* transcendental subjectivity that constitutes "death" by withdrawing itself from worldly self-objectivation?

This crude alternative is not, of course, a suitable way of formulating the problem. We do not in any sense have at our disposal an "either-or" of real possibilities here. However, this much may become clear to us, that we have to take up the transcendental problems that are *indicated* in the "phenomenon" of birth and death as given in the world, and that we have to do so in a way that is fundamentally different from the procedure followed in regressive phenomenology. Even there, to be sure, we do not have constituting life given in the sense of simple presence at hand [*Vorhandensein*]; for the constitutive processes of sense-bestowal are first laid bare by the method of intentional *regressive inquiry* into constitution. Still these are[202] *implied* in the given transcendental experience and having of the world, and they need only be analytically "extracted." In contrast, here we have neither a givenness of the kind of thing with which regress into deep constituting strata could begin[203], nor an implied givenness of constituting life itself. When we phenomenologize, we *always already*[204] refer to a world-constitution in progress, but we never at any time refer *with intuition* to one just beginning or just ending. Translated back into mundane ideas: [205]we make subjectivity, i.e., ourselves, a theme only insofar as we are already born and have not yet died. However *questionable* it is whether the great [206]realities of human existence [*des menschlichen Daseins*], birth and death, even point to a transcendental actuality, it is nonetheless evident that the constitutive *sense-bestowings* that transcendentally underlie these mundane *sense-elements* cannot be exhibited in an immediate way in the being-context of on-going world-constitution, which of course is given by the reduction and by it is made a possible theme for intuitive analyses. It is evident instead that, in order to gain any understanding at all, we have to "*construct*." Obviously this construction must not be an arbitrary, more or less fanciful invention, but can

---

202. [Ins.] ⟨intentionally⟩

203. [Sup.] ⟨[and] which would have to be transformed in reflective intuition⟩

204. [Ins.] ⟨with intuition⟩

205. [Alt.] ⟨I⟩ make subjectivity, i.e., ⟨myself,⟩ a theme only insofar as ⟨I am born⟩ [etc.]

206. [Alt.] ⟨facts⟩

only draw its *cognitive standing* exclusively from a prior *differentiated* study of given genetic processes, of the demonstrated temporalizations [207]in which a having is built up, etc., in order to be able, then, in an appropriate *motivated* way, to abstract "constructively" from the common presupposition of all given, demonstrable "developments" and genetic procedures, namely, from the transcendental *time* that is found already under way in self-temporalization and which is there as the universal horizon *in* which all process and genesis arise and come to an end. Only fully mastered analytic understanding of the transcendental events of beginning and end *in* time lends methodological security and material insight to the constructive project of inquiry into a beginning and an end *of* transcendental time.

However, it is not only the worldly facts of birth and death through which transcendental questions about a genesis are to be "constructed," but also the world phenomena of *early childhood development*, insofar as precisely this early period lies beyond the reach of our memory; these are all questions that are raised [208]in psychology under the titles "the origin of the idea of space, of the idea of time," etc., and of course at the essentially inadequate level of the natural attitude.[209] The *transcendental* response to [210]all these questions cannot proceed in intuitive fashion, i.e., it cannot bring the archaic building processes actually to a present or recollective self-givenness, it can only "construct" them.

Alongside the question of *egological* wholeness, however, there enter in here also, as tasks for constructive phenomenology, all the problems pertaining to the form of wholeness of the *intersubjective community of monads*, and above all the totality-form of[211] monadic *history [Historie]*.

[212]And again it is not through the problem of totality alone that constructive phenomenology is determined: rather, it begins in quite *different* problem regions in regressive phenomenology, and in every case does so in a style of

---

207. [Alt.] in which a having is built up, etc. ⟨That is clearly the presupposition for being⟩ able then, [etc.] [Obviously what Husserl does here is break up Fink's longer sentence. The English here retains the full awkwardly extended sentence that Fink wrote in order to allow Husserl's alteration to have its effect. —Tr.]

208. [Alt.] ⟨in psychological knowledge-theory⟩

209. [Mg.] ⟨moreover by the lack of a genuine intentional psychology [they] have not even been answerable as mere psychological questions.⟩

210. [Alt.] ⟨all the transcendental⟩ questions ⟨corresponding to those [just mentioned]⟩ cannot proceed [etc.]

211. [Ins.] ⟨intersubjectivity-related⟩

212. [Alt.] ⟨But⟩ it is not [etc.]

"construction" that is in each case *particular*, that is only understandable in view of each problem situation. It thus shows an intrinsic multiplicity of methods, a manifold of heterogeneous problem-complexes, that make it quite impossible to sketch out an adequate preliminary concept of it.bb

(Note.   The characterization of constructive phenomenology as "transcendental dialectic" has, in its echoing of the Kantian concept, and despite the essential difference, the following in common with that concept:

1. that in one as in the other there is an inquiry into structures of wholeness that are in principle non-given: here concerning the totality of transcendental subjectivity, there the totality of "appearances" (the cosmological antinomies);

2. that in the one as in the other what is in question, in a way that overcomes the dogmatism of the metaphysics of faith, is "immortality": here the question is the coincidence in Existence between the transcendental subject and its enworlded self-objectivation (therefore also concerning the problem whether an end to life is at all possible in principle in the sphere of transcendentality), there it is the "paralogisms of pure reason";

3. that in the one as in the other a basic distinction in the principle of understanding lies before us in contrast to the "transcendental analytic": here understanding is no longer "intuitive" but "constructive," there it is no longer of "constitutive" but only of "regulative" employment.

These "common points" are only external analogies, but in one instance there is a material affinity, namely, that in both cases it is a matter of the basic problem of the relation of the "given" to the "non-given.")

If, now, we want to bring into view[213] the most general problematic of the transcendental *theory of method* as far as it relates precisely to constructive phenomenology, if we raise the question of the particular mode of *functioning phenomenologizing* found in it, [214]then because of the relative intangibility of the Idea of a constructive phenomenology this can only be done by way of indication of an all too general sort.

True, from a formal point of view, the basic problem presents itself here as well in a fashion similar to the way it does in the theory of method with respect to regressive phenomenology, namely, as the question of what it

---

213. [Ins.] ⟨at least⟩

214. [Alt.] then ⟨of course⟩ because of the relative ⟨indeterminateness⟩ of the Idea [etc.]

means for the phenomenologizing I *to be in on things there [Dabeisein]* by its thematic object. What does the *givenness*[215] of the transcendental complexes of matters which come to disclosure through "construction" mean, the givenness, that is, *for* the phenomenologizing I? Clearly now the relation here between phenomenologizing and its theme is fundamentally *different* from what it is in regressive phenomenology, where it is a matter of a relationship of *givenness*—which to be sure is very problematic in its intrinsic nature. There we found a theoretical experiencing that cannot be made comprehensible by taking as a clue either a worldly ("receptive") concept of experience or one of "productive" constitution. The problem consisted instead in the transcendental interpretation of the relationship of givenness and, correlatively, of the sense of the presupposedness of the phenomenologizing I for this *givenness*.

If, now, with "constructive" phenomenology too [216]we speak of the problem of the "givenness" of the theme for phenomenologizing, then the concept of givenness is *formalized* to the extreme and [217]designates nothing more than the "thematic" relationship. Formulated as a paradox: the givenness of the theme for phenomenologizing is in constructive phenomenology a *non-givenness;* the being-in-on-things-there *[Dabeisein]* of the theorizing I is really a not-*being-in-on-things-there [Nichtdabeisein].* In other words, the phenomenological onlooker does not stand in a[218] demonstrable and given *"coincidence of identity"* with the transcendental life that is accessible only "constructively," he has his theme here in contrast to the indisputable *privileged status in being* of transcendental existence *[Existenz]* in present actuality.

In contrast, in regressive phenomenology no such distinguishing of the phenomenologizing act over its object occurs. Both "subject" as well as "object" of the theoretical correlation stand in one and the same transcendental rank in being of present moment actuality.cc The basis for that is ultimately that the phenomenologizing I is nothing other than the [219]exponent of transcendental self-reflection which is projected out by world-constituting life itself, and in which the becoming-for-itself of constituting life is to be made possible.

In contrast, the transcendental being *[Sein]* that is *constructively* disclosable does *not in principle* have an "onlooker" established by itself; *non-given* transcen-

---

215. [Mg.] ⟨the exhibitedness, the uncovered goal⟩

216. [Alt.] we ⟨should want to⟩ speak of the problem of the "givenness" of the theme for phenomenologizing, then the concept of givenness ⟨would be⟩ *formalized* to the extreme [etc.]

217. [Alt.] ⟨would⟩ designate

218. [Ins.] ⟨[an] intuitively/*originaliter*⟩

219. ["exponent" lined through by Husserl]

dental life can only "come to itself" in the onlooker of *given* transcendental life. This state of affairs determines the whole sense of the point under discussion, viz., the "presupposition" of the phenomenologizing I for the thematic elements and matter-complexes of constructive phenomenology. Even if the world-constituting life that is given in transcendental present actuality [*Aktualität*] places itself, by the constructive projection of the phenomenologizing I that is originarily established out of it, into transcendental contexts that in principle lie beyond reductive legitimating demonstration, if, for example, world-constituting life thereby relativizes itself as an episode in the open-ended history of transcendental life, nevertheless all genuine transcendental actuality [*Wirklichkeit*] lies in the reductively *given* sphere of transcendental being. And inasmuch as the onlooker that phenomenologizes in constructive phenomenology participates in his own way in actual present-momentness [*an der wirkliche Aktualität*], whereas his thematic object does not, *the being of the phenomenologizing onlooker in a particular respect precedes the being of his "constructed" theme.* Determining the more precise sense of this "precedence" constitutes the *basic problem* of the transcendental theory of method in relation to constructive phenomenology. What difficulties then show up, what apparently altogether paradoxical complications come to light, what *"dialectical"* formulations become necessary here—of all that we cannot even give an inkling. We are simply sticking to the *basic problem*, the question of the *intrinsic sense of the relation* of "constructive" phenomenologizing, which is given the distinction of the *privileged status in being* of actual-moment (given) transcendental existence [*Existenz*], to its object, which does *not* partake in this same privileged status in being. It is only after the phenomenological interpretation of the sense of the relation here in question that the different ways in which constructive phenomenologizing is done, all of which are determined by that relational sense, can be made thematic; it is only then too that the basic tasks of a transcendental theory of method, in the particular problem it has of thematizing the phenomenologizing that functions in "constructive phenomenology," can be taken up successfully.

§8. Phenomenologizing as theoretical experience

The project of the Idea of a transcendental theory of method, as the phenomenology of phenomenology, has received a first, preliminary determination through our having indicated the basic problems that are set as tasks for this theory of method by virtue of its reference respectively to the modes of phenomenologizing that are determined through the articulation of the transcendental theory of elements. What remains now is to sketch the *fundamental questions* of the transcendental theory of method that pertain to phenomenologizing *in general*, i.e., in abstraction from any particular functional mode. We turn first to the most basic question that in a way is the presupposition for all others, namely, the question in what sense phenomenologizing, that which basically goes on in phenomenological cognitive performance, is on the whole to be addressed as *theoretical experiencing*. In our [220]indicative presentation of the reduction[221] we spoke of how the established transcendental I of reflection finds itself in a theoretical attitude, of how in theoretical habituality it keeps itself referred to its cognitive object, etc. We spoke further of how the aim of the cognitive activity of transcendental life is not one that is occasional and more or less accidental, one that results from some kind of personal interest, but rather is thoroughly "scientific," that is, one whose goal is ultimately valid, methodologically secured *systematic* knowledge. The *problem*, now, is in what sense this kind of characterization is at all admissible, how the concept of science, a concept that first arises in the natural attitude, as does likewise the concept of the "theoretical," must be taken *transcendentally*.

Clarifying the possibility and proper sense of the science of phenomenology begins with the question of the "theoretical experience" that constructs this "science." To what extent is there at all a problem here? Is it not obvious that phenomenologizing (the action of philosophizing brought to transcendental radicality) is "theoretical" cognition, is theoretical experience, is the rational systemization of what is gained from this experience? The formal, empty characterization of phenomenologizing activity as a realization of a cognitive process is altogether undisputed. But it is precisely the particular how of this cognitive process, its *specific intrinsic nature*, indeed even its possible start, that is for us a troubling problem.

In the horizon of the natural attitude the concepts of the "theoretical" and of theorizing human activity are familiar and common. We do not need to go into them in detail. We shall only highlight a few of the structures and presuppositions of mundane theoretical cognition in order thereby to be able to explicate the problem of phenomenologizing theoretical activity. For is it not conceivable that in the worldly Idea of knowing and cognizing, and in the

---

220. [Alt.] ⟨general⟩

221. [Cf. Fink's revision texts for Meditation I in *Ergänzungsband*, Text No. 2, d (pp. 119–133), and Text No. 3, f (pp. 158–191), as well as Chapter 2 of his "Entwurf zu einem Anfangsstück einer Einleitung in die Phänomenologie" (*Ergänzungsband*, pp. 63–105).]

conditions that make it possible to begin, particular material elements are contained that only apparently belong to the formal Idea of cognition as such, but which in truth constitute precisely the *worldliness of theorizing?* In other words, must we not in the end before all else formulate the concept of theoretical experience in a radicality such as is not possible on the basis of the natural attitude? But seen more exactly, in this case it is not a matter of "formalization," but of *analogization* of formal Ideas that are worldly and transcendental. (The "logical" problem of the *analogy between mundane and transcendental* involves a major transcendental-logical discipline!)[222]

Already allusion to the *start* of phenomenological theorizing gets us into trouble. How is it at all possible that phenomenological "theoretical experiencing" can *begin?* This question does not pertain to the founding of the possibility of real phenomenological cognition in and by the phenomenological reduction, but rather to the *mode* with which phenomenologizing *starts out* insofar as it proceeds from the reduction as an *ability all ready-to-go*—like fully-armed Pallas Athene sprung from the head of Zeus.

In the natural attitude we as adult humans always have the [223]possibility of taking the step of beginning a theoretical cognitive practice; this is potentially always pregiven to us. We have *reason in trained and developed form* at our disposal, we have the most elementary *categorial insights,* we have *logic, concepts,* and *language.* Every initial move of theorizing activity presupposes the *ability* to theorize as a pregiven and established *habit.* The *forming* and genetic development of this ability [224]does *not first occur in* actualized theory, but in the *daily practice of life* that precedes any theoretical performance. Theoretical practice, i.e., practice exclusively set up for cognition, is in principle a *temporary modality* (even though it may extend over periods of activity) of this life in the world, which is not primarily governed by theoretical aims.

For phenomenologizing theoretical experience to *start,* there is *not* presupposed a *pre-theoretical* transcendental experience in which the habitualities that make possible a transcendental theory could have been formed.[225] Rather, the theoretical experience of the phenomenological onlooker begins with *already*

---

222. [A question mark stands in the margin alongside this whole sentence in parentheses. To which Mg.] ⟨The problem of a logic of the transcendental in "analogy" to mundane, natural logic, the question of a supra-formal logic, that asks about the supra-formal common element of both logics—questions like this.⟩

223. [Alt.] ⟨capability⟩

224. [Alt.] does *not first occur* ⟨within the actualization of⟩ theory, but ⟨within⟩ the *daily practice of life* [etc.]

225. [Mg.] ⟨That should have been said before the theory of the natural attitude.⟩

given habituated theoretical abilities.[226] That is where a central problem lies. If we have actually carried out the phenomenological epoche in utmost radicality, then must not the disposition to theorize which is acquired in mundane processes of development, i.e., *reason, logic, conceptuality, and language, all arisen in worldly fashion*, thereby also *implicitly* fall subject to bracketing? Or is rigor of this kind simply not possible in carrying out the phenomenological reduction? Must we not leave certain items of acceptedness (i.e., the laws of formal logic) in unbroken validity in order to be able to get our enterprise, the theoretical cognition of transcendental subjectivity, meaningfully under way at all? The way out of this dilemma appears to lie in the direction of our saying: It is not at all necessary to carry out the epoche with some kind of diminished rigor in order to be able still to utilize theoretical abilities *after the reduction*. For despite the extreme strictness of the epoche, they do *survive* for us *transcendentally*, just as the whole of human immanence, the actual-moment stream of experience with its habituality-sedimented components—only freed precisely from human apperception—is kept for us and is given as first transcendental being. Has not *transcendental reason*, purified of human apperception, only come from *human* reason? And are we not quite obviously allowed to exercise this transcendental reason in the self-explication of transcendental life? [227]Certain as it is that human theoretical abilities are disclosed by the phenomenological reduction as, at their deepest fundament, *transcendental abilities* and habitualities of the transcendental ego, still they may not without more ado be utilized in the explication of transcendental subjectivity. The reason for this is the *"differentness"* of the phenomenologizing onlooker, which governs the whole problematic of the transcendental theory of method. Transcendental reason and transcendental logic and all the theoretical habitual dispositions of the ego are ultimately nothing other than *reduced* worldly-human reason, worldly logic, etc. By the phenomenological reduction these theoretical abilities indeed have themselves come to be properly demonstrated as transcendentally existent [*existent*], but they belong in the *being-context* of *world-experiencing* and ultimately *world-constituting life*. The world-constituting ego stands as such in the habitualities that make theoretical experience possible. But this is not so of the phenomenologizing I—which is separated from the constituting I by a transcendental *antithesis in being*. Does the phenomenologizing I perhaps first develop a transcendental reason, a theoretical ability, of its own? Clearly not.

---

226. [Mg.] ⟨But abilities for natural theory, of course, [which] nevertheless in some way or other get turned around into abilities for transcendental reason.⟩

227. [Ins.] ⟨Nevertheless⟩

Nonetheless immediately after performing the reduction we begin with the explication of transcendental life. We thereby are faced with a problem of a special sort.

It is a question here of a *particular mode* of the transcendental antithetic "identity" of the phenomenologizing and the constituting I, a mode that is revealed in the way the theoretical dispositions of the constituting I are *taken over* by the established phenomenological onlooker. That this [228]taking over does not represent a simple appropriation of the dispositions but a peculiar and remarkable *transformation* precisely of these dispositions and habitualities—to show that would be a major particular and far-reaching[229] task of the transcendental theory of method. Only then would the ambiguity disappear that lies in the expressions "transcendental reason," "transcendental logic," the ambiguity of designating, first, transcendental reduced human reason and reduced human logic, and, second, the *reason and logic of the phenomenologizing onlooker.*

The possible start of the "theoretical experience" of the phenomenological I of reflection does indeed introduce a series of problems; the set of these problems culminates in the question of the *sense of the relation theorizing bears* to its "object." We have of course already indicated this question[dd] as the particular problem of the relation of phenomenologizing to its theme respectively in regressive and in constructive phenomenology. But now we are framing the problem in a *radical universality.*

The concept of theoretical experience[230] is first given us *in the natural attitude.* We understand by it the whole of coherent perceptions, or originary intuitions, in which the thematic region comes to evident givenness for us, together with the *activities* of categorial determination, predicative explication, etc. After the phenomenological reduction we recognize that theoretical [231]experience is itself a *basic form of world-constitution,* that in the operations of logical performance determinate objective units of sense are constituted. The question now is whether precisely in the natural and then in the transcendentally interpreted concept of theoretical experience *content-laden presuppositions* remain that already completely determine the whole sense of theorizing, and that must first be *eliminated* in order to gain that concept of "theoretical experience" which designates the *cognitive practice of the phenomenologizing I.* All nat-

---

228. [Husserl puts quotation marks around "taking over" —Tr.]
229. [Mg.] ⟨an important⟩
230. [Mg.] ⟨=theoretical evidentness, the giving of something itself⟩
231. [Alt.] ⟨evidentness⟩

ural cognition is cognition of what is *existent*, all experience is experience of what is *existent*. *Being and knowing*, these are the two inseparable components of the cognitive relation. Every cognition only has its truth insofar as it measures up to the existent itself, "accords" with it. There can in principle be no other object of cognition than what is existent. And if cognition refers to itself, it is only possible because cognition itself is "existent." Not only is the object "an existent," not only is cognition "an existent," but the relation [between them] is a relation that is existent, a *"relationship of being between two existents"* [*ein "Seinsver-hältnis zwischen zwei Seienden"*]. Thus in its most intrinsic sense, and not merely extrinsically and accidentally, knowing is always referred to what is existent. This relation lies, as it were, "analytically" in the concepts of knowing and theoretical experience.

The natural concept of cognition, which analytically involves the concept of theme *as existent*, undergoes through the phenomenological reduction precisely its transcendental interpretation as constitution of *being*. All constituting is a constituting of *the existent*, even the constitution that functions in theoretical acts. Already in the transcendental theory of method referring to regressive phenomenology, we were confronted by the special situation that resulted from our not being allowed to take hold of phenomenologizing either by taking our lead from the mundane receptive concept of experience or from the concept of transcendental constitution.ee Ultimately, now, the reason for this is that the theoretical experience of the phenomenologizing onlooker does not represent *an experience* (or constitution) *that relates to what is existent*. Does that not entirely annul the sense of experiencing? Can we form even the slightest idea of a cognitive relation that is *not directed to what is existent?* Does phenomenologizing cognition ultimately refer to "nothingness"? Is world-constitution, the object of phenomenologizing, perhaps nothing?

Progress on the problem of the proper sense of the "theoretical experience" of the phenomenological onlooker can only be made if the *sense of being* [*Seinssinn*] of its theme has reached explicit clarification and the question of the *objectiveness of the transcendental object* is settled. As little as one may designate the theme for the phenomenological onlooker, world-constitution, as something existent (in an uncritical sense), just as little can we characterize it with the naive counterconcept to being, the concept of "nothingness." What is needed, rather, is a *thematic reduction of the Idea of being*.

Here there are enormous problems that we cannot even roughly indicate. By this required reduction of the Idea of being the whole of phenomenology is stamped with its final and fundamental character.

The Idea of being is no longer left in the *indeterminacy and ambiguity* that the first carrying out of the transcendental theory of elements required. No longer can it be used in a, so to speak, "neutral" sense for characterizing the existent in the natural attitude and also for world-constitution itself. We have to make clear to ourselves that "transcendental being," as a counterconcept to "natural" or "worldly being," is *not a kind of being [Sein] at all,* such as the kind that has the highest rank and metaphysical valence, but that fundamentally it cannot be comprehended out of the [232]formalized Idea of being.

What is "existent" in the natural and thus in the *original* sense is the existent [*das Seiende*] [233]which is to be met with in the horizon and circuit of the natural attitude: that which is *existent in the world.* It is in the *captivation in/by the world* in the natural attitude that the *Idea and concept of being* first arises for us. Even if performing the phenomenological reduction then gets us out of the restrictedness of the natural attitude and opens up for us the never suspected dimension of world-constitution, [234]even if we gain the insight that what we commonly understand as the totality of that which is existent represents in truth only a stratum in newly discovered world-constitution, that is, precisely the stratum of constituted end-products,[ff] [235]still we have not for the most part got beyond *captivation in the mundane Idea of being.* Ensnared in it we interpret what comes to givenness for us through the phenomenological reduction in the light of the, of course, formalized concept of being, namely, as a sphere of "transcendental" being. Although necessary, this is a *phenomenological naiveté* insofar as, under the covert guidance of the natural concept of being not yet properly overcome, we at first seek to grasp transcendental being as an autonomous dimension of the existent which as such represents the substrate of our theoretical-phenomenologizing experience. We are caught in the quite obvious belief that transcendental being would be a new mode of being discovered precisely by the reduction, one now to be set *alongside* the mode of being of mundane being.[236]

---

232. [Alt.] ⟨empty-⟩formalized
233. [Alt.] which is to be met with in the horizon ⟨of the world as [the]⟩ circuit of the natural attitude: ⟨something or other exists [*existiert*]—that is, naturally speaking, to be in the world somewhere, sometime or other.⟩
234. [Ins.] ⟨then⟩ we gain the insight [etc.] [Husserl makes this the conclusion of the conditional sentence, rather than a second condition in a longer sentence, as Fink has it. —Tr.]
235. [Alt.] ⟨Nonetheless,⟩ [Husserl makes this begin a new sentence. —Tr.]
236. [Mg.] ⟨One has to distinguish the naiveté of interpretation in reflection that draws a comparison, viz., between something naturally and something transcendentally existent, from the naiveté in which we, in our phenomenological assertion-making, theorizing, make use of natural language and its meanings: being, being such-and-such, logic in general, secretly transformed meanings, without at first noticing

This naiveté is harmless as long as it is only a matter of first getting transcendental subjectivity in sight and explicating it in an initial, preliminary way. But once we have entered into the constitutive analytic and have made the insight our own that all that is mundanely existent is in principle a *constitutive result*, then there results an incompatibility in simply placing side by side the transcendental and mundane concepts of being. The explicit reduction of the Idea of being itself becomes necessary. The difference between transcendental and naive being can now no longer be taken in terms of mere "content," simply as the distinction between the existent which constitutes and the existent which is constituted; rather, at bottom it lies in a *fundamental difference in the ways* in which something transcendentally existent and something mundanely existent respectively "are." That here the universal concept of being, which presents a *unity of analogy* (cf. Aristotle)[237] with regard to the manifold ways in which the existent is *in the world*, does not comprise transcendental and mundane being within itself even as *particular* modes is of quite central significance.

And yet we can press on toward a close determination of the transcendental concept of being only by taking our lead from the *analogy relationship*. In the theorizing experience of phenomenological cognition we indeed relate *not to something existent* (insofar as something existent is originally[238] an existent in the world with the transcendental rank of constitutive result); rather, we relate to transcendental *world-constitution analogously to the way we relate to an existent.* The *"analogia entis"* between mundane and transcendental being is not an *"analogia attributionis"* but an *"analogia propositionalis."*[gg] Just as theoretical experience generally relates to what is existent, so in phenomenologizing we *analogously* relate to world-constitution, which is not "in itself" existent but also not nonexistent. If everything existent—according to the transcendental insight of phenomenology—is nothing other than a constitutive *having-come-to-be* [*Gewordenheit*], then the *coming-to-be* [*Werden*] *of the existent in constitution* is itself not already existent.[239]

---

the transformation. *Here* is where the problem lies. It belongs to the general problem of the pregivenness of the transcendental on the basis of the reduction of the pregivenness (quite another kind) of the mundane. It is the inner change that experience, thinking, and every activity take on "of themselves" through the reduction.⟩

237. [Mg.] ⟨Quotation⟩

238. [Ins.] ⟨understood [as]⟩

239. [Mg.] ⟨Obviously too, however, not a coming-to-be in the sense of a worldly coming-to-be, of a mode of what exists as a [process of] happening—but again an analogue to it.⟩

And yet, we must posit transcendental subjectivity *just as if* it were some-thing existent. [240]We have no other possibility for disclosing and explicating it, if we do not thematize it following the guidance through analogy of the Idea of being.[241] The reason for this ultimately is that we can reach transcen-dental subjectivity only by *starting out from the natural attitude,* and by breaking out of it. The natural attitude is itself a *transcendental situation:* the *situation of ori-gin and home for the Idea of being and the concept of being.* Living in it I am, as "subject," already a unity constituted in *end*-constitution, man in the world; and in prin-ciple I experience only *end*-constituted objectiveness. The genetic processes of constitution that first lead to the apperception of that which is "existent," but do so through various constitutive strata of *"pre-being" ["Vor-Sein"],* are al-ways *already concluded,* if we are "stationed in the natural attitude." We find our-selves "existent" within a world of that which is "existent."

Since it is precisely only by working from this specific transcendental *situ-ation of end-constitutedness* that we can achieve de-restriction out to the full di-mension of constitutive genesis, [i.e.,] the phenomenological reduction, [242]we are also *spellbound by the concept of being* when we explicate newly discov-ered transcendental subjectivity. But we will not get free of bondship to the Idea of being by simply *abandoning* the concept of being. For we would thereby lose the last possibility of making verifiable explications and asser-tions in regard to transcendental subjectivity. We would fall into the danger of an incurable "mysticism." Only be *reducing the Idea of being itself* and forming a

---

240. [Open square bracket before "we have no other." To which Mg.] ⟨dangerous as apparent mode of argument⟩

241. [Mg.] ⟨[Put] thus it is misleading. By the move into the reduction there arises a new kind of "identifying," "experiencing," intuiting, anticipating, ideating, predicat-ing, etc. The whole of language with all linguistic meanings receives new sense—wholly of itself and surely not as if thereby an action of *taking over* the natural meanings of all these words with the old meanings of existent and modes of being, of subjec-tive modes of consciousness, etc., were performed. There is no need first for a "re-duction" of the supposed taking over. But in reflection on the relationship of natural and new meanings and in the coming forward of the mere analogy, what is needed is to establish the merely "formal" parallel (the mere *analogia entis,* etc.), to change over to transcendental logic as absolute, to make explicitly conscious the constitution of a new concept of being, etc. We are not spellbound by the old concept of being, but we are unclear, in danger of paradox, as long as we have not explicitly carried out re-flection. Cf. marginal remark [note 236 above].⟩

242. [Alt.] we are ⟨at first spellbound because of the unnoticeability of the trans-formation of the idea of being⟩ when we explicate [etc.]

new transcendental concept of being will we escape from captivation in the natural Idea of being. "Transcendental being" must thus not simply signify the world-transcendent constituting universe of monads, but has to indicate primarily the special *way* in which this universe of monads in its life of world-constitutive effectuation "is,"[243] namely, that it *is in a way that precisely transcends the*[244] *Idea of being.*

The obscure and abstruse problematic concealed in the concept of transcendental being altogether determines the sense of the relation which theoretical experience has for the phenomenologizing onlooker. How can and must phenomenologizing be determined as the experience[245] of *transcendental* being? The question aims at the puzzling *"productive"* character of the theoretical experiential life of the I of phenomenological reflection.[246] Given how complicated the problem is, we just cannot give more than a vague indication.

By the phenomenological reduction the dimension of depth, the dimension of world-constituting transcendental life, which was covered up in the natural attitude, is dis-covered [*ent-deckt*] and made accessible. Of course we recognize immediately that transcendental subjectivity does not have a being [*Sein*] that is detached and separated off from the being [*Sein*] of the world, but that it stands in necessary constitutive "relation" to it, that further the world forms the[247] *plane of the constitutive terminations* of the life processes of transcendental subjectivity.[248] The natural attitude consists in the *restriction*[249] of being only open to this plane of the worldly existent and[250] closed to the[251] depth-strata that do not exist [*nicht . . . existierenden*] in the worldly sense, and that constitu-

---

243. [Mg.] ⟨Monadic being, however, is not yet ultimate being and it is "constituted"—⟩

244. [Ins.] ⟨natural⟩

245. [Ins.] ⟨and predicative determination⟩

246. [Mg.] ⟨It is a matter of a necessary reflection on a higher level, one coming after something else, after the phenomenological work is already done, or as the case may be, already under way.⟩

247. [Mg.] ⟨ideal! [*ideelle!*]⟩

248. [Mg.] ⟨That is perhaps still dubious in respect to the naiveté in which one presumably always "has" a worldly existent.⟩

249. [Mg.] ⟨[The restriction, that is,] of the active I because of the forming of a universal theme-ensemble, of the outline of a world as universe of the wherewithal for all plans and pursuits, thus [the restriction of being only open, etc.]⟩

250. [Ins.] ⟨thereby⟩

251. [Ins.] ⟨correlative⟩

tively construct the being of the world.²⁵² Inasmuch now as the theme of the
theoretical experience of the phenomenologizing I is world-constitution,
the phenomenologizing onlooker relates cognitively to a constitutive strata-
structure the uppermost stratum of which (world) is borne by all the others
²⁵³and, in a natural sense, is *alone existent.* ²⁵⁴All the rest of the constitutive structure can become thematic in a mode of experience *that only forms an analogy* to
an experience of what is existent. ²⁵⁵Phenomenological experience does not
cognize something which is *already existent,* as what and how it is; it cognizes
the sort of thing which is "in itself" not existent; in cognizing it it objectifies it into something that is (transcendentally) "existent," it lifts the constitutive construction-
processes out of the *condition of "pre-being" ["Vorsein"]* proper to them and for
the very first time in a certain sense *objectivates* them²⁵⁶. In other words, the theoretical experience of the phenomenological onlooker *ontifies the "pre-existent"
life-processes of transcendental subjectivity*ʰʰ and is therefore in a sense—a sense
not comparable to any mode of productivity pregiven in a worldly way—
*"productive."*²⁵⁷

---

252. [Mg. explicitly linked to the end of this sentence] ⟨but that [is so] as long as
they have not become a correlatively infinite thematic in a new constitutive production, have not been constituted in regard to being as a higher universe.⟩
253. [Alt.] and ⟨is the one that in the natural attitude is⟩ *existent* ⟨as end-themati-
cally existent in it.⟩
254. [Alt.] ⟨But subsequently all⟩ the rest of the constitutive structure ⟨together
with the world as such therein constituted can become thematic in a productive
theme-ensemble, and in the end can even become a thematic universe, by the establishment of which the being of transcendental events as such is first completed *in* an
in itself existent "world" of the transcendental (transcendental inexistence [*Inexistenz*]).
Only after that does "transcendental experience" as theoretical experience of something *existent,* of something determined in itself, of something determinable from experience—in this "world"—first have its full sense.⟩
255. [Alt.] Phenomenological experience does not cognize something which is *already existent* ⟨for it ahead of time⟩, as what and how it is, but cognizes *the sort of thing
which is "in itself"* ⟨not yet⟩ *existent;* [etc.]
256. [Ins.] ⟨(productively) constituting a new thematic universe of being⟩
257. [Mg.] ⟨Thus at the start of the reduction. However, it is not that, as soon as
the ontification is under way, immediately the open horizon and universal horizon of
that which is transcendentally existent is coproduced. [The] phenomenon of the
world as clue means at once [the] turn to the universe of world-constituting, constitutive performances in the ego—which is not yet something existent. The production, however, first creates *the existent* in the new transcendental universe, the all of
monads in its monadic community of time, [and] in it everything which is subjectively
and empirically constituted. To describe that universally in its essential structures in

(Note: The productivity of philosophical cognition was already surmised by philosophers who were still caught up in the natural attitude. Thus, for example, already in German idealism there was the recognition that the traditional antithesis between *"intellectus archetypus"* and *"intellectus ectypus,"* which constituted the metaphysical difference between human and divine knowledge, in truth signified the antithesis between human and un-humanized [*entmenscht*] philosophical cognition. The concept of "intellectual intuition" and above all that of (Hegel's) "speculative knowledge" is a genuine presentiment of the productivity of phenomenologizing "theoretical experience.")

§9. Phenomenologizing as an action of ideation

The basic question of the transcendental theory of method, the question of the phenomenologizing onlooker, branches out into a series of particular problems that are conditioned by the multiplicity of ways in which phenomenologizing functions, but which all interconnect most closely. [258]The theoretical experience of the I of phenomenological reflection has an autonomous, if also still thoroughly problematic, basic character that opens up a chasm separating that experience [259]from the natural concept of experience as well as from the worldly concept of theoretical experience. If indeed every theoretical experience has its logic-forming structural elements, all of which are determined by the basic character of the particular theorizing action in question, then one should expect the peculiar productivity of phenomenologizing theoretical [260]experience also to determine the *particular way it is formed as a logic* [*Logifizierung*], what we are accustomed to designate as the *eidetic method* of phenomenology. Does the *ideating action* exercised by the phenomenologizing on-

---

transcendental evidentness, however, is the task. Addendum: In the change of thematic position there arises "of itself" a *thematic horizon* as potentiality *through transformation.* But by [the] *productive* forming of *existents* as always re-experienceable and theoretically determinable for anyone there is constituted the transcendental universe as universe of transcendental existents—the world of the transcendental in which the human world is phenomenon. "An existent" only makes sense as something existent in a world—even that which is transcendentally existent.⟩

258. [Alt]. The theoretical experience ⟨and predicative evidentness, in short the theoretical cognition of⟩ the I [etc.]

259. [Alt.] from the natural concept of experience ⟨and the theoretical⟩ concept ⟨of cognition⟩

260. [Alt.] ⟨cognition⟩

looker have the same methodological sense as the ideating done by the worldly scientist? In introducing the eidetic procedure into transcendental explication, have we not perhaps secretly taken over particular worldly prejudices, because we were not yet capable of explicitly grasping the distinction between the mundane and the phenomenologizing eidetic? Does the transcendental theory of method here too have an overhauling function to perform?[261] In any case, the problem is there, how the transcendental eidetic has to be conceived in contradistinction to the worldly eidetic.

What is first needed is to determine more exactly what is meant by the expression *"transcendental eidetic."* One thing that can be understood by it is the entirety of the transcendental clarifications that pertain to the *worldly* eidos, thus the transcendental theories of the mundane a priori. Not only does that which is individually existent, the totality of real things [*der realen Dinge*], make up the world which is constitutively examined and clarified, but the regions of the ideal essences of formal and material nature also compose the object of the constitutive interpretation of the world. Beginning with the unities of a particular essence or essence-complex, we inquire constitutively back into the transcendental presuppositions and conditions of the existent essence [*des seienden Wesens*]. We thereby open up the possibility of final insights into the range of the eidos in question, insofar as we can follow the latter back to its *constitutive origin* in the invariant structural constitutions of transcendental life. The apodictic evidentness of the eidos which confronts us in the natural attitude undergoes by this constitutive retro-inquiry a clarification that not only legitimizes the unconditional acceptedness of the essence, but also unveils the ultimate grounds[262] for the necessity of this essence, its why. If in exhibiting an a priori someone standing in the natural attitude, man, stops with its acceptedness as a validity not open to further questioning, for someone who has passed through the phenomenological reduction this acceptedness gains a new dimension of possibilities for more radical understanding:[263] he performs

---

261. [See Fink's revision text for the Fourth Meditation in *Ergänzungsband*, Text No. 11, pp. 238–239.]

262. [Ins.] ⟨and background⟩

263. [Mg. to the passage from "but also unveils" to the present point, as indicated by a line drawn down from the edge of this passage] ⟨Here there are still some things to be said: the setting of every a priori into a universal ontology.—But this has never been made possible! Why? One always remains stuck on the part [which is the] ontology of nature. The psychology problem. The problem of the ontology of the world of the spirit.⟩ [This note is numbered 264 in the German text. —Tr.]

a reduction of the thematic ideal unity of sense [264]to the *sense-bestowing performances* of transcendental horizon-constitution. The eidos is set into a larger context of sense-bestowing life. The mundane essence becomes the clue for displaying the transcendental processes of constitution, becomes the point of departure for the transcendental theory of the eidetic.

If this is what we understand by the title "transcendental eidetic," then we have[265] *another meaning* to confront, namely, the *eidetic with respect to transcendental being:* the logic-form given to the phenomenologizing explication of world-constitution[266]. If transcendental subjectivity becomes the object of the theoretical experience of the phenomenological onlooker not just as *factual* but above all in its *essential possibilities*, then the question immediately arises whether the eidos with respect to transcendental being is to be set forth at first in the naiveté of merely referring to the *ideal unity of something accepted as valid [Geltungseinheit]*, without going into the constitutive performances that underlie this kind of unity itself; or whether with the transcendental eidos we simply cannot make this distinction between the *straightforward attitude* turned toward the thematic essence and the *reflective attitude* turned toward the transcendental constitution of this essence. Are we allowed at first to exercise the transcendental eidetic naively (thematically)? Does investigating the acts that bestow sense on the transcendental eidos itself mean only a higher problematic of constitution? This is a problem similar to one already familiar to us, viz., whether the theoretical experience[267] of the phenomenologizing I is to be grasped by following the lead of the natural-naive concept of experience or by its transcendental interpretation as constitution. And the resolution of the problem is similar to what it was there. The phenomenological onlooker's eidetic neither is of the same type as the eidetic in the natural attitude, nor shows an affinity to the transcendental constitutive clarification of that eidetic. The constitutional analytic of the eidetic (of the a priori) is not yet the transcendental clarification of that eidos which the phenomenologizing onlooker "looks at" in the transcendental subjectivity that is his theme. Precisely because constituting (and, among other things, also eidos-constituting) transcendental subjectivity is separated from the phenomenologizing I by a *fundamental antithesis in being*, the *eidetic procedure* the latter puts into operation has a

---

264. [Alt.] to the *performances* of transcendental horizon-constitution ⟨that constitute sense in sense-acceptedness.⟩ [This note is numbered 263 in the German text. —Tr.]

265. [Ins.] ⟨still⟩

266. [Ins.] ⟨by the phenomenologizing I⟩

267. [Ins.] ⟨and cognition⟩

basically different structure from the eidetic exercised in the natural attitude
but transcendentally clarified after the phenomenological reduction. This last
is an eidetic *with respect to that which is existent*[268], the theory of the essentials, of
the *invariant being-possibilities* of any *existent* that comes to factual realization. The
eidetic which the phenomenological onlooker must carry out in his theoretical experiencing is essentially an eidos [269]with respect to "transcendental" being, and that means an eidos of the sort of thing that properly is not, but which
has what can only be paradoxically described as the "being-mode" of *pre-being*
[Vor-Sein].[270] The problem has now been formulated for us. It is the question
of how phenomenologizing as an ideating action participates in the *productiv-*
ity[271] of phenomenological theorizing experience. May we take the worldly
ideas about the eidos and eidetic possibility, about the necessity of essential
laws, and the like, which we bring along from the natural attitude, and in some
way make use of them in regard to the *transcendental* eidos? Or do the transcendental clarifications of the constitutive sense-bestowings that underlie
mundane essentialities perhaps give a certain outlined pre-understanding of
the problem? We cannot yet give an answer to this. We must, however, also
be careful not to *exaggerate* the *differentness* of the transcendental eidos—over
against the mundane essence—into an all too radical difference, and thereby

---

268. [Ins.] ⟨in the natural worldly way⟩

269. [Alt.] with respect to "transcendental" being⟨s⟩, and that means an eidos
of the sort of thing that properly ⟨in the original and linguistically usual sense⟩ is
not [etc.]

270. [Mg.] ⟨1) *Spatiotemporal existent* on different levels, of different horizonality,
lastly, of the natural totality of *idealiter* fully determinate beings, which have inexistence *[Inexistenz]* in the mathematically infinite world. 2) *Transcendental existent*: on different levels—finally the transcendental universe as "world" of monads in monadic
temporality (and quasi "spatiality" as monadic coexistence form *[Koexistenzform]* of the
total allness of monads—of course mutual implication of monads, of all horizons).
Every transcendental existent as existent, in the full transcendentally constituted
world, is "presented" *["vorstellig"]* in the actual-moment field of experience of every
monad, "presented" as itself there or as included in the external horizon. —The transcendental "world" as constituted also has the distinction between world itself and
world-presentation *[Weltvorstellung]*. We always called "pre-existent" what is existent
in the relative universe, from the first open horizon on, which already indeed has the
form of an unknown "allness." Every pre-existent on one level becomes on the higher
[level] that which *exists-in [inexistierenden]* with [an] apperceptive horizon; presentation
[Vorstellung], something subjectively existent.⟩

271. [Mg.] ⟨productivity by constant modes of repetition⟩

relinquish the problem entirely.272 But just as we could still conceive the "productive" experience of the onlooker analogically as *experience,* so we also have
to emphasize the analogical relationships between the eidos with respect to
mundane being and the eidos with respect to transcendental being.273 For this
reason, contrasting the transcendental concept of essence against the worldly
(and its constitutive analytic) gives us insight into the *difference* and at the same
time the *analogical similarity* between the two.274 Naturally we cannot develop
this contrast *in extenso;* we are letting it go with a few indications that are meant
only to give the problem a sharper profile.

However multifarious the natural concept of eidos is as a result of the difference in the existent that is grasped in eidetic universality (the eidetic of nature, of the historical, of the inorganic, of the organic, etc.), we can still draw
certain general features from it.

In the natural attitude we have to distinguish 275*knowing about the essential structures of the existent,* as that occurs before every intellectual operation, and the
mode of givenness of essentialities *in the act of ideation.*276 The first is nothing other
than the completely unthematic *knowing of what is pregiven* that illuminates our
whole life of experience. 277In it there is a pre-understanding of the most general articulations of that which is existent whatever it may be; habitual horizons of acquaintedness are laid out in the apperceptive schemata of which we
apprehend every newly met existent always *as* a thing of nature, *as* a living being, *as* an organism, etc.278 The knowing of what is pregiven already contains

---

272. [Mg.] ⟨yes⟩

273. [Mg.] ⟨Isn't there already exaggeration in this?⟩

274. [Mg.] ⟨What kind of analogy is that? Natural experience is after all a transcendental mode, existent in the transcendental world as self-apperception of the natural attitude monad in the apperceptive universal-horizon, the natural world. The
new, uncovered activity of the transcendentally redirected I, redirected from the
epoche on, is precisely again an activity of the transcendental I of a new mode, and
on altered background.—It [the activity] is always a life of consciousness with all the
modes that belong to it, perception, memory, modalization, etc. But in the new attitude a new constitution of a new world, [and a] new temporalization and time.⟩

275. [Alt.] ⟨preknownness regarding⟩ *the essential structures* [etc.]

276. [On the passage that begins with this sentence, cf. Appendix XII.]

277. [Alt.] In it there is a pre-⟨knowing of⟩ the most general ⟨set of types for⟩ that
which is existent ⟨individually and in its constellations⟩ whatever it may be [etc.]

278. [Mg.] ⟨Every set of types (every pregiven individual has its individual set of
types) stands under the regional universal set of types—in the unity of the ontological totality type of the universe-region as top region.⟩

all knowledge of essence precisely *in the mode of the unthematic*,[279] [280]and we can at any time take possession of that knowledge by the activities of the categorial intuition of ideation. Ideation is only the thematic *appropriation* of a knowing [281]that we already have, is an ἀνάμνησις. It only objectifies the knowing of the pregiven that functions beforehand in nonobjective fashion, and it articulates it in a particular way.[282] Seen thus, there is already a certain productivity that befits the act of ideation in the natural attitude. But this productivity is proper to every intellectual spontaneity, and so has not the

---

279. [Mg.] ⟨This "unthematic," however, is problematic. 1) Thematic in the sense of active directedness. Here the actual background of the field of perception is indeed "unthematic." 2) What is potentially (or actually) thematic in the horizonality of the *spatiotemporal world* as world of spatiotemporal realities: nature in the broadest sense, something individually apperceived or apperceivable—world the universe of objects of "possible experience," the individual as such which possibly becomes known, which is to be brought, and at some given time is brought, to recognition. 3) The associatively constant set of types by virtue of constant analogizing and fusion in coexistence [*Koexistenz*] and succession.—In the individually constituted world complete homogeneity of analogy and a corresponding structure. Every real thing has its horizon of similarities, into which its horizon of actually known matters reaches.—But it has an anticipated horizon of unknown "similar things" as things possibly to-be-made-known. The universe is a universe of the real, which by essence stands in a horizon of analogy and is given in typicality immediately as that. There is a division between the primarily thematic, the individual distinctive trait (internal and external) and the thematic to be made, the type. —Type not a proper attribute that pertains to something's own essence—not arisen from constituting activity as individually constituting something real, but *co*-arisen, something to constitute by analogization in passive process and only subsequently in an active way as regards being, and already constituted in the normal human environing world (language). The ontological form of the total, of the world, is accordingly distinguished as "nature" and as form of the "universe-region" ["*Allregion*"] in particular regional forms. *Human* world already actively constituted in its material set of types over against those of animal environing worlds.⟩.

280. [Alt. to beginning of sentence as required by the previous Mg.] The knowing of what is pregiven already ⟨implicitly⟩ contains all knowledge of essence, [etc.] [To which Mg.] ⟨"Implicitly" means: by essential necessity, with de facto pregivenness is given the possibility of practicing variation and ideation, etc.⟩

281. [Alt.] that we already have ⟨as pre-existent, as a passively constituted a priori⟩, is ⟨as it were⟩ an ἀνάμνησις.

282. [Mg.] ⟨By essential necessity the capability of reason for free variation and essence-constitution belongs to the articulation of the pregiven world in the regional set of types.⟩

least to do with the problem that concerns us here. When we designate ideation as categorial *intuition*, [283]that signifies less that the eidos is *receptively experienced* in the act of seeing the essence [*Wesensschau*] than that thereby the *self-givenness* character of the essence is to be indicated. In actuality one does not first experience the essence by ideation; rather, in a way that is methodologically special, one *"remembers"* a previously unthematic knowing of what is essential in any thing. The variational rethinking done while adhering to an invariant identity as the method of grasping the essence is already *guided by the knowing of the pregiven*, inasmuch as in an intuitive *antecedent look [Vorblick]* upon what is essential we hold on to it *as invariant*. The eidos is always given to us in *"a priori"* fashion in the natural attitude, i.e., given in the unthematic knowing of the pregiven *before* its express thematization and objectification in ideation.[284] If ideation therefore, only has the function of *raising up* something that knowing possesses in a state of submergence in the obvious, then the proper locus of the transcendental constitutive interpretation of the mundane eidos is not the analytic of the ideative act but the *analytic of the pregivenness of the world*.

The eidos referring to transcendental being *differs* in a fundamental way from the worldly essence. To put it in a word: the transcendental eidos is *not an "a priori"*—if what is supposed to be meant by a priori is the *antecedency* of a knowing of the pregiven before the objectification of the pregiven by an act of ideation. In principle, transcendental subjectivity, which is laid bare by the phenomenological reduction, does not stand in a *pregivenness* of its most general, essential articulation.[285] The ideation that refers to it is not a simple re-membering (ἀνάμνησις), not an objectification of a knowing already possessed, not a mere method of accession and appropriation, but has a fundamentally *more eminent* function with respect to the essence. The productivity that befits the theoretical experience of the phenomenological onlooker as the positing as existent (transcendentally existent) of the sort of thing that has the constitutive nature of pre-being [*Vor-Seins*]—this *productivity* is proper also to the *transcendental ideation that gives logical form* to this theoretical experience. It

---

283. [Alt.] that signifies ⟨not so much⟩ that the eidos is *receptively experienced* in the act of seeing the essence ⟨but⟩ that thereby [etc.]

284. [Mg.] ⟨The eidos has the apriority of something produced, but the production presupposes a deeper a priori, the a priori that lies in flowing world-experience itself, the necessarily antecedent regional structure of the world, etc.⟩

285. [Mg.] ⟨Pregivenness as pregivenness of what is existent. But the "reversal," the "turn around," draws a kind of pregivenness out of the transcendental.⟩

ontifies [ontifiziert] the "pure possibilities" of that which is preexistent into validity-constructs in a transcendental eidetic.

§10. Phenomenologizing as predication

With the question of phenomenologizing in its particular functional mode as predication, we come to a complex of problems in which *two directions* of questioning cross. If until now in our inquiry into phenomenologizing our objective has been the modes of phenomenologizing life which have theoretical, i.e., scientific, effect, then what also always stood in the horizon of inquiry was the *internal structure of the scientific action* of the phenomenological onlooker, that is, his transcendental activities first in their specific particularity as reduction, regressive analysis, and phenomenological construction, then in their generality as theoretical experience and ideation. Living in these scientific actions, the transcendental observer builds his science, phenomenology, as a systematic unity of cognitions.

The problem of *transcendental predication* designates the *shift to the outward expressional form* of this science, what we wish to call its *"appearance" ["Erscheinung"]*. The transposition of cognitions *into sentences*, their preservation in predicative linguistic configurations, would continue to be only a problem of the way phenomenology has the transcendental structure of science as an *internal* matter *if* there could be a proper transcendental language. The predicative formulation of transcendental cognitions would then only signify a method of stabilization.[286] The problem of the "outward expressional form" of transcendental science is based on the *necessity* that phenomenologizing *in some way exit from* the transcendental attitude.[287] What this means we are not yet able to see.

---

286. [Mg.] ⟨Science is a product arising in acquired subjective activities, which from now on is there for "everyone" by virtue of the linguistic outward expression of constructs that from the beginning are produced as meaningful words. In speech the discourse which at first is a subjective product externalizes itself; thus too scientific discourse and science with its expressional truth-products. What is the situation with regard to the "externalization" and "outwardness" of transcendental discourse and science? To what extent does transcendental predication offer a particular problem for the transcendental theory of method? Is it a matter of merely suitable (equivocation-free) expression?⟩

287. [Mg.] ⟨but on the dubiousness of the use of customary language, or language come into its natural meaningfulness in the natural attitude. What is problematic here is, on the one hand, the predication of someone thinking and discoursing in the egological sphere, on the other hand the possibility of intersubjective predication and of

We shall approach this obscure area of inquiry preliminarily by way of specific issues.

All predication, as the articulative interpretation of cognitions by the "Logos," is accomplished *in the medium of a language*. Language arises in the *natural attitude;* and, depending on the empirical concreteness of the speaker via his participation in a particular linguistic community, a language is primitive or evolved, predominantly rational or affective, and so forth. That language has its home in the natural attitude is given expression in this common basic trait of all languages, namely, that all *concepts* are *concepts of being*. The natural human I, the bearer of language, in principle only speaks in regard to *what is existent*, interpreting his experience of the existent and his bearing toward the existent as questioning it, [288]appealing to it, desiring it, commanding it. [289]Furthermore, he speaks in regard to the existent's being-at-hand or not-being-at-hand (actuality and non-actuality). Now, through the phenomenological reduction, the I indeed loses its natural-attitude restrictedness; but it in no way loses the habitualities and dispositions acquired in the natural attitude, it [290]*does not lose its* "*language*." The *constituting* I, as the proper I that is concealed by human being, is [291]also the *proper speaker;* [292]predication is a form of its life activity, is a mode proper to *constituting action*. Elucidating the constitutively implicated bestowal of the sense which underlies the action of speaking is a special and in no way easy problem of constitution taken from the phenomenological theory of elements. (For example, we find in this instance that the constitution which is primarily

---

the intersubjective being of scientific truths (as constructs) for everyone, whereby getting beyond the transcendental attitude seems to become necessary.⟩

288. [Ins.] ⟨determining [it,]⟩

289. [Alt.] Furthermore, he speaks in regard to the existent's ⟨occurring or not occurring in all spatiotemporal modalities: to be in the world, in existence [*Existenz*], as actually to exist [*existieren*] in a spatiotemporal place.⟩

290. [Ins.] ⟨thus also⟩

291. [Alt.] ⟨in a certain way⟩ [To which Mg.] ⟨1) Human language-ability as developed capability for human language. It is something existent belonging to man, something existent in the world, just as is the existent spoken of in it. 2) This human feature is reduced to its transcendental, to its transcendental truth as its transcendental being: the transcendental correlate of worldly language. Here language is 3) language as expression of the transcendental I, existent in transcendental intersubjectivity and first of all in its egological immanence.⟩

292. [Alt.] ⟨mundane⟩ predication is a form of its life activity, is a ⟨function⟩ proper to *constituting action*. [To which Mg.] ⟨Here, then, it is a matter of worldly predication, of the transcendental corresponding to it in the transcendental ego, or, as the case may be, in intersubjectivity. Over against this: the *linguistic expression of this transcendental* by the theorizing-phenomenologizing ego.⟩

intersubjective has a definite antecedency to egological constitution, which, following after it, appropriates a language handed down in a tradition.)

Language is indeed retained as habituality right through the epoche, but it does not lose the *expressional character of referring solely to what is existent.* True, it is a transcendental capability, just as is every disposition and ability of the ego ultimately; but it is *not a transcendental language,* that is, one that can with genuine suitability *explicate and give predicative safekeeping to* transcendental being.[293]

Nonetheless, the phenomenological onlooker must make use of it, if he at all wants to give predicative expression to his cognitions. He must *take over from the constituting I* the habituality of language and *participate in* the latter's constitutive life, against his own wish to be non-participant. But this participation is merely *apparent [scheinbare],* inasmuch as in taking over[294] language the phenomenologizing onlooker *transforms* its natural sense as referring to what is existent. If this kind of *transformation* did not occur, then the phenomenologist would *slip out of the transcendental attitude* with every word he spoke. Since phenomenologizing assertions on the one hand transform the natural sense of words, and on the other can nevertheless only express new transcendental sense with mundane concepts and terms (which are one and all concepts of being and not concepts of pre-being),[295] phenomenologizing moves in a certain way[296] out of the transcendental attitude; but it does this in such a fashion that in[297] *exit-making words its being in and remaining in that attitude are indicated and "outwardly expressed,"* and it speaks of what properly is not existent (what is pre-existent) in ontic concepts and words.[298] In this only apparent [schein-

---

293. [Mg.] ⟨In thematic ascertainment: the human habituality (that which is existent in the world) changes its sense-of-being to an habituality of the transcendental ego—this is something I, the onlooker, *state,* and at the very same moment I become thematic as this onlooker; again I state this, and I always speak natural language, but in transcendentally altered sense. I have the same transcendental habituality as the transcendental ego has, with whom I am at one: my onlooking is a reflecting by that onlooking itself upon its naturalness.⟩

294. [Mg.] ⟨Already the expression "taking over" misleading.⟩

295. [Mg.] ⟨The miracle of the transformation of the mundane into what is preexistent [*Vorseiendes*]—that is precisely the problem and one actually solvable. A phenomenological language in principle only has sense, only has possibility, as transformed natural language, just as the transcendental phenomenon, world, only has sense as the transformed sense-of-being, world.⟩

296. [Mg.] ⟨seemingly [*scheinbar*]!!⟩

297. [Ins.] ⟨—naturally understood—⟩

298. [Alt. to this sentence but written in the margin] phenomenologizing ⟨proceeds in an essence-imposed doubleness of meaning in its discourse, one that ac-

baren]²⁹⁹ abandoning of the transcendental attitude phenomenology goes over into its *"appearance"* [*Erscheinung*].³⁰⁰ Preliminarily we understand then by "appearance"³⁰¹ the outward expressional form³⁰² in which the inner transcendental form of phenomenologizing finds its predicative safekeeping and *objectivation.* For the time being we shall put off formulating the concept of "appearance" in a more fundamental way.

It is not in its external *vocabulary* form³⁰³ that natural language suffers a "transformation" in being claimed by the transcendental onlooker for the expression of his transcendental cognitions, but in the *way it signifies.* When enlisted in the language function of the phenomenologizing I, not a single word can retain its natural sense. Instead, the natural meaning that is indicated by the particular verbal unit now serves *only as an* ³⁰⁴*indicator* for a transcendental linguistic sense.³⁰⁵ Again, it is not as if there were an *indicative*

---

cordingly is completely unavoidable and that is the greatest constant hindrance to the understanding of phenomenological presentations, in that it perpetually tempts one to lapse back into the natural attitude and into psychological or mundane misinterpretations.⟩

299. [Mg.] ⟨yes⟩

300. [Mg.] ⟨at the same time?⟩

301. [Mg.] ⟨*Appearance* [*Erscheinung*] is an unsuitable expression.⟩

302. [Mg.] ⟨Until now the discussion was not about "outward expression." That has two senses, first, the transcendental intersubjectivity of transcendental language and theory—their coexistence [*Koexistenz*] in the transcendental world-totality [*Weltall*] (in monadic temporality (spatiotemporality)), second, the secondary existence-in [*Inexistenz*] of phenomenology in the natural-human world and its natural world-space, as cultural constructs related to humans, as are the positive sciences.⟩

303. [Mg.] ⟨not to mention that verbal units are human bodily products and as words are idealizations.⟩

304. [Husserl lines through "indicator" and then makes this Mg.] ⟨as indicator? Then I would still stand in the world. Instances of discourse that enter the scene in the phenomenon of the world, that arise from natural instances of talk as [their] clues. But not those of the onlooker.⟩

305. [Mg.] ⟨for whom? For the listener, the reader? But he too must already be in the phenomenological attitude, and if he is already himself a phenomenologist, then he already has his reversed natural-phenomenological language. But how is it at the beginning, with first entry into the phenomenological reduction, where I nonetheless speak in it without more ado and quite naively? Does not the proto-instituting of phenomenology require, besides the reduction of the world to phenomenon, still another special reduction of my phenomenologizing action of speaking (as phenomenologizing I)? Or is this not the place for the proto-instituting of the transformation of language—of the language that is *functioning,* not the language in the world

system[306] settled and agreed upon ahead of time; but in a *living, analogizing affinity* a transcendental meaning (a meaning referring to that which is pre-existent [*Vorseiendes*]) is expressed through a meaning that refers to the existent [*Seiendes*]. The special *mode of apophansis* at hand here shows a strange internal tension and dynamic structure.[307] [308]It is not a quiescent, as it were *static* relationship that obtains between the expressional body (the public voicing [*Verlautbarung*]) and the meaning adjoined to it, but a relationship of *opposing movements* that are difficult to characterize. [309]On the one hand, the natural

---

that is thematic in humans who are speaking—; must it then first be practiced further? All the same, only in the way the reduction has to be practiced. The transformation as that of natural language, as the ability to speak German, etc., is a continual accompaniment.⟩

306. [Mg.] ⟨The problem of indication: by phenomenological activity itself from the reduction on, every natural existent becomes the index for its constitutive system. —There is necessarily and intelligibly accomplished the formation of a "relationship"-property on the part of the ontic with respect to the manifold that has been brought, or is to be horizonally brought, to thematic experience (apperceptive transference). At the same time also the natural linguistic expression becomes the index for the transcendental description. Subsequently, the clarification of the doubleness of meaning, which at first is unnoticeable.⟩

307. [Mg. at the top of the MSS page] ⟨October 5, 1932⟩

308. [Mg.] ⟨The phenomenology of phenomenological language is a problem in phenomenology itself (which naturally includes its iteration). It requires a specific reflection on phenomenological language and its intentional implication *as* language. Implied in it is [its character of] being transformed from natural language, it is an intentional modification of natural language; it is part of its being-sense that as a product in the reduction it "refers" to life as set in the natural attitude, as does also the reduction as such. In the change of attitude (by the founding of the transcendental attitude through the natural) lies a "coinciding" (analogy), first between world purely and simply and world-phenomenon subjectively taken. But for language here there is a still more particular phenomenon, as is also the case for that which comes to utterance. We have the analogy between transcendental world-perception, transcendental memory, transcendental life, and psychic life, [we have] in the phenomenon of world, or in the world of the natural attitude, transcendentally functioning subjectivity as constituting and holding the worldly sense of being, predicatively expressed in functioning transcendental language, which is not as that lodged in the phenomenon of the world, accordingly is not that intentional modification of natural language which the phenomenological reduction brings about. And yet as intentional modification it points to human language.⟩

309. [Alt.] On the one hand, ⟨a parallel⟩ natural meaning of the word and sentence ⟨lies in every transcendental word and sentence; we can "understand" every word "in

meaning of the word and sentence points analogously to a corresponding transcendental sense, while, on the other hand, the intended transcendental meaning *protests*, as it were, against its expressional formulation; the sense to be expressed does not rest quietly in the expressional form, it is in constant rebellion[310] against the constraint imposed upon it by the formulation in natural words and sentences. Thus all transcendental explications have a special *inadequacy*,[311] all concepts and sentences in one way or another fall short and in a particular sense fail before the demand that is, it seems, to be placed upon every predication (but especially the scientific).

[312]This inadequacy on the part of the transcendental assertion—and so generally of transcendental apophansis as a whole—must not in any way be measured by the inadequacy relationships that are possible even *within* natural speech. It is instead an independent problem that can only be clarified transcendentally. If we have spoken till now of an "analogical meaning-function," in a strict sense this is false. The inadequacy of natural speech, which we designate as a symbolic mode of speech, as an analogical mode of speech, among other things, is for the most part transparent in its inadequacy, always allows

---

a natural way" without more ado.〉 On the other hand, the intended transcendental meaning *protests*, as it were, against 〈the parallel natural sense of the word, although the latter is always there in a certain way〉; the sense to be expressed [etc.]

310. [Mg.] 〈In what does the rebellion consist? The unity and consistency of natural life is a unity of a constantly instituted habituality that continues to be instituted, activating itself in the primal mode of custom, in a primally modal form of tendential movement onward. The epoche inhibits this universal tendency and transforms world-life as intentional modification—itself a tendency, except deliberate, which, opposed to the natural tendency, constantly refers to it intentionally, institutes a new life from the I of willing, but as a constant countering against naturalness, in order to phenomenologize it transcendentally. Natural custom is in constant "rebellion" against phenomenologizing, however much the latter also institutes custom and then proceeds on its course following custom; the custom of the phenomenologist too, his general mode of life, is in constant tension against natural custom. Finally, this is also decisive for transcendental language.〉

311. [Mg.] 〈only for the one who does not explicate and describe in actual phenomenologizing—and for every presentation of phenomenology that addresses itself to not-yet-phenomenologists.〉

312. [Alt.] This 〈internal divisiveness and tension〉 on the part of the transcendental assertion—and so generally of transcendental apophansis as a whole—must not in any way be measured by 〈occurrences of divisiveness (e.g., a poor sense of logic, symbolic mode of speech),〉 that are possible even *within* natural speech.

translation into exact, [313]adequate expressivity, and in the final analysis rests
upon *metaphors*, which represent primitive rudiments in speech. (Archaic
speech, as the expressional form of thought that proceeds more in "images"
than in abstract concepts, is altogether *metaphorical*. On this, cf. the occasional
emergence of archaic language in folk and poetic speech.) It is nevertheless
quite evident that analogical and symbolic speech (the two main forms of inadequate natural predication) can be understood in their "metaphors" only because in the end a *comparison* of that which is compared in the "metaphor" is
after all possible. Beyond all particular common traits that make individual
metaphors possible, what in natural inadequate speech can always be brought
into the relationship, in the bond of common affinity, is: there "is" [*es "ist"*].
Natural analogy and symbolism compare *existent with existent*, precisely with
respect to specific elements of their general or individual being-such-and-
such [*Sosein*].

If, now, natural language, which is exhibited by the phenomenological epoche as a dispositional habituality of the *constituting* I, is claimed by
the *phenomenologizing onlooker* [314]for the explication of his "theoretical experience"—which does not deal with what is "existent" (with that which is end-
constituted), but with that constituting life which actualizes itself and the
world in stages of *"pre-being"*—then the natural meanings of words and sentences cannot stand in a relationship of analogical predication to the intended transcendental sense-elements. This is because *ontic* meanings just
cannot form an analogy to *"non-ontic"* transcendental meanings, for the two
cannot be at all compared with one another. Instead we have to admit that
talk about an "analogical function" possessed by natural meanings for the
predicative explication of transcendental complexes of matters has simply
become an *expression that causes a predicament*. And yet this predicament-causing
expression has a certain material justification. Just as in an analogy (*analogia
propositionalis*) we understand certain meanings first in their own normal apo-
phantic sense, but then always *along with that* the "analogous" sense indicated
in it, so analogously when we use natural language to explicate phenomenologizing experience we understand the proper thematic transcendental sense
through the mundane sense of words and the usual meaning of sentences.
The *"transcendental* analogy of signifying" which governs the whole of phe-

---

313. [Alt.] ⟨so to speak, smooth, tension-free, etc.⟩

314. [Alt.] for the explication of ⟨the data of his theoretical experience and his
theoretical thinking (given thinking),⟩ then the natural meanings of words and sentences [etc.]

nomenological predicative explication is thus *not* an analogy possible *within* natural speech, but an *analogy to the analogy* that is found within natural speech; and it is the phenomenological reduction that makes that possible. We cannot now in our vague preliminary sketch of the most general problematic of all indicate the great methodological problem that thereby results. Let us only allude to the fact that the source of this special structure of transcendental apophansis lies ultimately in the *substratum* for all transcendental predication: in the "mode of being" peculiar to transcendental subjectivity. Just as we first gained[315] the transcendental concept of being through a *thematic reduction of the Idea of being*, and accordingly in it took up precisely the concept of that which is *"not-existent [nichtseiend]* in the sense of worldly Existence,"[316] and just as we had to determine the *"analogia entis"* between mundane and transcendental being as an analogy between what is existent (the constituted) and that which is pre-existent [*Vorseiendem*], so now too the analogical function of meaning in the transcendental assertion is *not an ontic* but precisely a *transcendental* analogization.

[317]The phenomenologizing I has to take over language as the sedimented disposition of the constituting I in order to conceptualize its theoretical experiences. This necessity, now, is the basis for the inadequacy of phenomenological predication, but at the same time is also the basis for the possibility of numerous *misunderstandings* to which not only the reader but also the phenomenological researcher remains exposed. The living actual-moment theoretical experience of the one phenomenologizing, which proceeds in an evidentness of immediate insight, now transposes itself into predicative formulation, and is preserved in concepts and sentences in the medium of a language[318] that provides no expressions that are genuinely suitable, but only

315. [Mg.] ⟨made sure of it fully⟩

316. [Mg.] ⟨Here's where the main issue is, but it doesn't quite come out.⟩

317. [Alt.] The phenomenologizing I has to ⟨use⟩ language as the sedimented disposition of the constituting I ⟨in transformed sense and can have no other language but this intentionally transformed language,⟩ in order to conceptualize its theoretical experiences. This necessity, now, is the basis for the ⟨doubleness of meaning⟩ of phenomenological predication, but at the same time is also the basis for the ⟨continually threatening⟩ possibility [etc.]

318. [Mg.] ⟨that indeed can achieve expression unambiguously and in full adequacy and yet even where it does so implies a doubleness of meaning in that its sense is a transformation of a natural sense, which shares in the immense power of the customariness of natural life in the world and its ways of taking things as holding in being [*Seinsgeltungen*].⟩

ones that work by analogy [*analogisierende*]. Because of this, the danger arises that the natural, original sense of the words will lord it over the "transcendental" sense analogically indicated by that natural sense and overrun and conceal it, so that an attempt to understand that reverts back to taking words only as they literally sound [*auf den Wortlaut*]ii must necessarily fall into error. 319Phenomenological sentences can therefore only be understood if the *situation of the giving of sense* to the transcendental sentence is always *repeated*, that is, if the predicatively explicating terms are always verified again by *phenomenologizing intuition*. There is thus no phenomenological understanding that comes simply by reading reports of phenomenological research; these can only be "read" at all 320by re-performing the investigations themselves. Whoever fails to do that just does not read *phenomenological* sentences; he reads queer sentences in natural language, 321taking a mere appearance for the thing itself [*die Sache selbst*] to his own self-deception. But even someone *doing the investigation* is himself subject to self-deceit, if he does not continually test his predicative gains 322by living intuitional illustration in the "thing itself," if he does not continually and explicitly disconnect323 the mundane ideas inaugurated by the sense of words in their natural meaning. It is therefore quite impossible to want to give phenomenological "definitions," to establish basic predicative concepts and meanings that are supposed to stand fast once and for all. Rather, precisely this inadequacy specific to all phenomenological predica-

---

319. [Alt.] Phenomenological sentences can therefore only ⟨actually⟩ be understood if the *situation of the giving of sense* to the transcendental sentence is always *repeated*, that is, if ⟨the epoche as the withholding of the usual worldliness is actively sustained and⟩ if the predicative explicating terms are always confirmed again by ⟨actually transcendental⟩ *phenomenologizing intuition*

320. [Alt.] by ⟨actually⟩ re-performing ⟨the reduction and⟩ the investigations themselves ⟨in it⟩.

321. [Alt.] ⟨taking the mere reflection [*Reflex*] of transcendental theory in the natural world for the thing itself⟩ [etc.] [To which Mg.] ⟨One could state at any point whatever that every transcendental sentence, that transcendental science by essential necessity has a "reflection" as a manifold of words and sentences [composed] by man [in] the world—but therefore in no way in [the] form of a system of sentences with unitary sense. This is significant for the secondary enworlding of phenomenology itself.⟩

322. [Alt.] by ⟨actualizing the reduction and in it⟩ living intuitional illustration in the "thing itself," [etc.]

323. [Ins.] ⟨as slipping out of the reduction⟩

tion entails that all conceptuality is in a strange way *fluid* and open.[324] This, however, in no way precludes that transcendental matter-complexes, which represent the theme of the particular explicative predication concerned, be quite *unambiguously determined and determinable.* It is precisely the *rigor* of transcendental concept formation that requires the fluid transcendental apophansis that, rather than being frozen in "natural" meanings, analogizes right through them. The transformation that natural language, as expressive of that which is existent, undergoes in being claimed by the phenomenologizing I must always be kept in mind *as a transformation* of ontic-naive meanings into "analogically" indicated, transcendental-ontic meanings. It signifies a lapse into "dogmatism" (that of the natural attitude) if explicit knowledge of this necessary transformation dies away, and the phenomenologist thereby in his explications falsifies the object of his theoretical experiences. The reduction has overcome dogmatism, but along the path of the detour that phenomenologizing takes [325]through appearance [*Erscheinung*] the intrusion of dogmatic prejudice is still possible. As a result the phenomenological reduction gets extended further in that it not only makes possible [326]and ensures the theoretical experience of phenomenologizing by disconnecting all dogmatic prejudices, but also inasmuch as it has a particular function to fulfill in the predicative *explication* of that experience: precisely to expel all naively ontic representations regarding transcendental subjectivity to the extent that such representations may seem motivated by the way the transcendental assertion, in its analogizing utilization of ontic concepts, literally *sounds [durch den Wortlaut].* The *reduction of the Idea of being* which is implied in the phenomenological reduction thus, as we see, brings with it a *reduction of language.*[327] By that, how-

---

324. [Mg.] ⟨That belongs in a quite different chapter. What belongs here is only the wrongheadedness of the readers who, still phenomenologizing in naiveté, miss having definitions, which they naively presuppose as natural definitions composed of ultimately self-understandable elementary concepts.⟩

325. [Alt.] through ⟨the natural language mode of⟩ appearance [etc.]

326. [Alt.] and ensures the theoretical ⟨evidentness of⟩ phenomenologizing by disconnecting all dogmatic prejudices ⟨and the basis of worldly preacceptedness⟩, but also [etc.]

327. [Mg.] ⟨It is not really a broadening, but an ensuring of the sense of phenomenological ascertainment against misunderstandings. It is also not permissible to speak of a reduction of language. The natural sense of language is not to be brought into the transcendental by a reduction to be therein exercised.⟩

ever, is not meant the simple insight that language is ultimately a capability
of the transcendental constituting I; the "reduction of language" is rather the
transformation of it as a transcendental capability of the I of world-final constitution, a transformation *done in the taking over*328 *by the phenomenologizing onlooker*.
This onlooker "reduces" language by demoting the natural-meaning sense of
language in the explication of transcendental constitution to a mere *"analogization,"* he makes language into a *mere means* for the explications for which he
himself has at his disposal no suitable language of his own.

   That he relies, however, on this "means," that he can have no language of
his own, no concepts of his own, has its basis in the phenomenological reduction. In a way, the reduction places the just-established "onlooker" before
329*nothingness*: the world is bracketed and thereby as well 330the whole *pregivenness* of the world, all world-possibilities; there remains as the single first theme
for the onlooker nought but actual-moment flowing transcendental life with
its undisclosed horizons. But it is permitted neither to apprehend the "flow"
by way of clues from mundanely pregiven time-structures, nor to apperceive
the undisclosed horizons as implications of being. Strictly speaking, it cannot
designate the flow at all *as* a flow.331 All concepts such as the actual-moment
life of the I, and so on, are from the bottom up worldly concepts, already wed-
ded to quite determinate representations which it is important to keep expressly out of the sphere of transcendental subjectivity.332 All apperceptions

---

   328. [Mg. partly erased] naturally no [such taking over]
   329. [Husserl puts quotation marks around "nothingness"]
   330. [Alt.] the whole *pregivenness* of the world ⟨in universal temporality⟩, all world-
possibilities. ⟨The world, however, is for the natural human I the "universe of the existent."⟩ There remains as the single first theme for the onlooker nought but ⟨the
phenomenon of world in⟩ actual-moment flowing transcendental life with its ⟨correl-
ative⟩ undisclosed horizons.
   331. [Mg.] ⟨Would it not have been a great help to the problematic of transcendental language to put all that at the head of things and start with it?⟩
   332. [Mg. to the whole passage beginning with this sentence: "All concepts" etc.]
⟨Here [is] an important point, which requires more careful consideration. As phenomenologist I am in transformation at one with the phenomenological givenness
[*Gegebensein*] of experience, etc., in my speaking and expressing; to look for expressions
is only to look for "more exact" explicative expressions which I can scientifically use.
The first discussion [I give] is not yet a speaking in phenomeno*logical*, scientific language, which I must first fashion out of originally adequate description on the basis
of pure intuitive-phenomenological explication. Already in inner psychology [it is]
thus for a systematic intentional explication, which had never as systematic been car-

are lacking, the phenomenologizing onlooker has no sedimented acquaint-edness regarding his theme, no tradition of knowledge and thereby no con-cepts. He must instead consistently hold fast the "phenomenological attitude" and first acquire for himself and lay down as sedimentation these traditions of knowledge and habitualities of acquaintedness, in order to reach unambigu-ous transcendental meanings, in order to be able to form unambiguous, cir-cumscribed concepts. The process of forming transcendental apperceptions does *not*, however, lead to the construction of an autonomous transcendental language, nor can it ever do so. [333]Rather, to have at one's disposal a system of transcendental apperceptions that emerges in the cognitive life of the phe-nomenologizing I is simply the *indispensable presupposition* for the transcendental-analogical *assertability* of transcendental matter-complexes in the alien medium of natural language. When phenomenologizing begins its action immediately after the reduction, at this stage of inception it is not only without concepts but also in principle [334]*lacks language.* ("Lack of language" means too the in-ability to assert transcendental cognitions by means of natural language as a

---

ried through in adequate description. Prescientific language in "everydayness" also, when the meaning of *words* is refuted, yields something valid for the experiential ob-ject as apperceived. In adequate phenomenological description I am not allowed to make use of any anticipations belonging to words, I have to form a new language on the basis of a speaking that is first naive and [then] as phenomenologically trans-formed. The natural worldly meaning of words has the tendency to be claimed totally as transformed. But it is supposed to describe *adequately*—thus the problem of ade-quation!⟩

333. [Alt.] ⟨Rather, just as the being of the world precedes the being of the tran-scendental phenomenon of the world and thematically, as it were, repeats itself in it—so natural language precedes language in parentheses, and gets reversed to become a new actual language (actual language—one that talks about what is existent). Along with that the natural language of psychic intentionality (intentional psychological discourse) gets reversed to become transcendental-noetic discourse (transcendental-psychic discourse) and so the language of the worldly correlation of the ontic and the subjective (world and world-presentation) is reversed as such to become the language of the universal transcendental correlation.⟩

334. [Alt.] ⟨lacks scientific language.⟩ [To which Mg.] ⟨not entirely lacking lan-guage. Right away I say: that there, what shall I call it? or right away I say: percep-tion, then memory, in memory "lies" transformation, etc., I distinguish things and have to create a terminology, to name and contrast different "modifications," etc. Thus there is the problem: what does the *first* language after the instituting move that starts the reduction look like as transformed language, and what is the situation with respect to the intention directed to science, which itself [is] a transformed natural in-

simple medium of presentation.) The onlooker has not the slightest possibility of predicatively expressing his theoretical insights. This means: the phenomenological onlooker's action of taking over natural language for the purpose of explicating his theoretical experiences *presupposes* that he has already gained possession of certain *universals* in transcendental knowledge, before he can judge the *suitability* of mundane concepts and representations for analogously indicating transcendental concepts. For by no means are all mundane meanings *en bloc* false when it is a matter of expressing transcendental matter-complexes. Otherwise, a transcendental explication would indeed be absolutely impossible. There are instead quite definite *relations of affinity*[335] obtaining between matter-complexes that are transcendental and those that are designated in each instance with the naive verbal sense of natural expressions (naive, i.e., acquired without consideration of the analogy function). These affinities are what first make it possible for the phenomenologizing I—in apparently speaking the language of the natural attitude—to be able to explicate predicatively precisely in natural concepts and modes of representation its theoretical experiences referring to the transcendental constitution of the world. It is in them [i.e., these affinities] that the *problematic* of transcendental explication is concentrated. Even just to sketch out the first move of the methodological clarification of these special correspondences between *concepts of what is existent [Seiendem]* and *concepts of what is "pre-existent" ["Vorseiendem"]*, clarification which in the end is the "logical" obverse of the ontological *analogia entis* between the mundane and the transcendental ("*transcendentalis analogia entis*"), demands such an extensive preparation that we are not able here to carry it out.

Phenomenologizing predicative explication is done in *levels of methodological naiveté.* Understandably, first explications, those in which the phenomenologizing onlooker is first able to have at his disposal a *restricted store* of transcendental apperceptions, are naive and permeated with dogmatic beliefs;[336] but

---

tention, in that it is the motivation for fashioning a language, with its terminologically stabilizing effect, on the basis of adequation and identification of what is adequately grasped. Prescriptive identification then: this shall be the set name for this item itself, etc.⟩

335. [Mg.] ⟨for higher level reflection! Naive direct phenomenology expresses what is actually seen phenomenologically and does not first need to take note of and present the fact of having double meaning!⟩

336. [Mg.] ⟨The natural custom of verbally expressing natural experience in such a way that the explicational units of linguistic meaning are claimed as valid for experience beyond the explication done during actual experiencing gets accepted in phe-

these will be of no harm just as long as one remains aware of the preliminary character of this first-effort explication. As the processes of transcendental cognition advance, there is an ever-increasing broadening of insight into the "nature of the being" ["*Seinsnatur*"] that is peculiar to constitutive subjectivity; and a critical *overhaul* of the first explication takes place, in that on the basis of the cognitive dispositions that have been acquired certain beliefs can now be separated out as prejudices that were dragged in by way of the natural verbal sense found in that preliminary transcendental explication.

The danger of seduction by mundane meanings with their merely analogizing function is smaller in concrete constitutive analyses of details than it is in the case precisely of *fundamental* characterizations of the transcendental, those which endeavor to synthesize these detail-analyzing studies in general cognitive realizations. For example, talk of "constituting subjectivity" is misleading as long as one is guided by mundane representations of substantial and accidental being and construes the adjective "constituting" as an *accident* in a transcendental subjectivity understood as substance. Only later insight shows that this *substantialism* in regard to transcendental subjectivity is a prejudice, that subjectivity is not something that first is and then constitutes, but that it is in the constitutive process in which the world comes about [*Weltwerdungsprozess*] that it constitutes *itself* for the first time. Indeed even this conception is encumbered with possible misunderstandings and is in a certain sense *false*. The refusal of a substantialist conception of the transcendental must not shift into the contrary belief that transcendental subjectivity is nothing else but an

nomenology to its detriment in this way, that after adequate description by return to what was just said or said earlier on, linguistic connotations, although in transformation, are taken as also holding good, as if they had previously been adequately established. That is just what concerns the experience of apperceptions. One has first got to learn not to let the natural co-holding-good [or: co-acceptedness] of what is adperceived [*Ad-perzipierten*] get mixed in with transcendentally transformed holding-good [or: acceptedness]. Difficulties in holding transcendental life actually in pure transcendentality, in the unity of a new custom and custom-forming process that is always an *overcoming* of natural customary life. Natural custom—a totality that has to be overcome as such but at the same time as one that works its holding-good in every particular. Whoever has a universal will for the normative, even in constancy, is still not protected against the intrusion, in individual instances, of customary life unconcerned about norms. The universality of the reduction is a total act, one that however must be constantly exercised as here and now [*aktuell*] participating and *actual [wirklich]* in every particular act. That belongs therefore to the phenomenology of the reduction itself.)

existent process [seiender Prozess]. (A dynamic conception, therefore, instead of a static one!) The transcendental constitution of the world is not conceptualizable by taking one's lead from either a static-substance or a dynamic-process relationship in being. It is just that the "process" conception is more appropriate for an *analogical* presentation; it has a certain *affinity* to the special transcendental "mode of existence" [*Existenzweise*] proper to world-constitution, which of course cannot be comprehended by means of the ontically mundane categories of existent genesis (process)ʲⁱ, although it can indeed be thereby *explicated*—precisely in analogizing fashion. [337]

Even if with ever greater advances in phenomenological knowledge the naiveté of predicative explication is overcome and mundane concepts are freed more and more from the natural associations that adhere to them, still one can *never* succeed in *abolishing* the *divergence of* [338] *signifying* that is present in every transcendental sentence between the natural sense of words and the transcendental sense that is indicated in them. Rather, there always remains an immanent conflict and contradiction in every transcendental predication. Indeed it is not even a *desiratum* that this divergence ever altogether disappear. The Idea of a transcendental language that would not need the mediation of natural language at all is in itself countersensical. [339] Full insight into this state of affairs is, to be sure, not easy to gain.

Immediately after performing the phenomenological reduction we as phenomenologizing onlooker begin with our theoretical experiences. However, as we have seen, these experiences necessarily "lack language" in the first stage of our new experiental life. But could not this experiental life remain then *forever* without language? Is there any necessity that knowledge gained be expressed? And does phenomenologizing stand subject to some such necessity, must it necessarily "explicate" itself predicatively? Is a consistent life of knowledge conceivable that, while constant in holding to the transcendental attitude, would never pass into linguistic [340]self-explication? Certainly—there is

---

337. [Mg.] ⟨The necessary inner transformation of all modes of being and correlative subjective modes also includes all levels of temporalization, and so also all concepts of becoming, of happening—even the happening of constituting genesis is temporal happening and in a different way egological and intermonadic.⟩

338. [Ins.] ⟨equivocal⟩

339. [Mg.] ⟨Even if the phenomenologist should want to invent a new language, he would need for that purpose natural equivocal language as first expression of his phenomenological ascertainments, as the most direct expression of them. And this indirect new language would be precisely thereby itself defined again equivocally.⟩

340. [Alt.] ⟨expressivity⟩

no reason and *no compulsion* for predicative outward expression lying in phenomenologically theorizing experience as such. And yet predicative outward expression is in a definite sense *transcendentally necessary*. The transcendental motive for it arises in a *tendency to the universal* on the part of constituting life, which *co-affects* the *phenomenologizing* I, although in a way of its own—despite its *differentness* and its *antithesis in being [Seinsgegensatz]* with respect to the constituting I. All constituting, as we already know, is a constituting of the existent in the universal complex of the world. The constitutive process terminates in the world as the sum of all constituted end-products. We name this *proper* or *primary enworlding*. We must strictly distinguish from it a *non-proper* or *secondary enworlding*. What might be meant by this will at first appear obscure and puzzling. And yet only from it will we be able to reach an understanding of the transcendental impulses that push and lead to the outward expression of transcendental cognitions[341]. Preliminarily, let it be put this way: non-proper enworlding is the summation of the constitutive process which places *phenomenologizing* itself *into the world*, that is, *into the natural attitude*, it "localizes" and "temporalizes" it there; in other words, it makes it *"appear" ["erscheinen"]* in the world.

Phenomenologizing first becomes predicatively explicable, becomes [342]explicating action *[Explizieren]*, when through secondary enworlding it is transferred—seemingly *[scheinbar]*—into a *worldly situation for the sake* of which it has to express itself. The path of phenomenological cognition thus not only moves out from the natural attitude into its reductive overcoming, but leads back into the natural attitude because of the *enworlding of phenomenologizing*, which rests upon transcendental acts of sense-bestowal. The natural attitude is not only the *wherefrom [Wo-von-aus]* but also the *whither [Wo-für]* of philosophizing. In it the individual who philosophizes takes charge of the task of following the path of pure knowledge to the end for himself and for the others with whom he stands in the natural community of life. If he thus from the outset *performs an official service* [lit.: is a *functionary*], then enacting the phenomenological reduction takes him, as it may seem at first, *out of* all humanly mundane communities and the purposes that are rooted in them, and places him in the *monstrous solitude* of transcendental existence *[Existenz]* as

---

341. [Ins.] ⟨and therefore to the divestiture outwardly *[Entäusserung]* of its transcendentality⟩

342. [Alt.] ⟨the action of predicating transcendental occurrences, becomes communicative utterance⟩, when through [etc.] [To which Mg.] ⟨I use "Explizieren" for explicating while experiencing *[erfahrend auslegen]*⟩

ego. However, in consequence of the transcendental cognitions made possible by the reduction he gains the insight not only that *others* as *transcendentally coexistent [mitexistierende]* others remain in an unbroken *community of life* with him, but that also the natural attitude itself has a *transcendental existence [Existenz]*, precisely as a specific *restricted life-situation* on the part of the transcendental subjectivity [343]not aware of itself. The natural attitude is "in itself" transcendental, but not "for itself"; it is in a way transcendental subjectivity's *situation of "being-outside-itself" ["Aussersichsein"]*. The process of "becoming-for-itself" on the part of transcendental life must not only necessarily move out of the natural attitude, but also *return*[344] into it, *if* precisely the one philosophizing *co-philosophizes for the others* with whom he stands in an ultimate transcendental community of life but who are still caught in the restricted situation of the natural attitude. The necessity that phenomenologizing be expressed outwardly, the necessity of phenomenological explication, is thus first grounded in the *communicative tendency* of all philosophizing, the deepest source of which arises in the *"metaphysical" unity* of all transcendental life. We are not, however, in a position here to show that[345]. But we can see that the *"enworlding"* of phenomenologizing, which begins with its predicative presentation, is a tendency that seems to grow out of *transcendental pedagogical impulses*: a tendency to a universal becoming-for-itself on the part of an all-inclusively communal transcendental life.

§11. Phenomenologizing as "making into a science"

The predelineation of the Idea of a transcendental theory of method reaches a *preliminary end* in the characterization of the general problems that are presented by the fact that phenomenologizing is made into a science. The term "make into a science" [*Verwissenschaftlichung*] does not at all mean raising the *cognitive rank* of transcendental experiences and acts of taking cognizance to that of a knowledge that has some kind of *final validity*; for that is an operation that belongs thematically in the transcendental *theory of elements*. We are now, however, in the transcendental theory of method, and so the question

---

343. [Ins.] not aware ⟨of its very transcendentality⟩.

344. [Mg.] ⟨Is that actually "to return"? Even this return has undergone its modification of sense.⟩

345. [Ins.] ⟨involving as it does the clarification of the phenomenologically genuine sense of the metaphysical⟩

we pose is that of the transcendental being[346] peculiar to the *phenomenologizing onlooker.* We have broken this topic down into a series of particular questions concerning specific functions and theoretical operations of the "onlooker." There yet remains for us only the question how the phenomenologizing I "is" in the remarkable happening that we can characterize as the passing of phenomenologizing into its mundane appearance [*Erscheinung*], into the "piece of philosophy"[kk] that enters the world and addresses itself to co-worldly others. The problem of transcendental science is not principally the question of the *system and inner architectonic* of the transcendental knowing that accrues to the phenomenologizing agent in his cognitive life; rather, it presents itself first of all as the *problem of publicly voicing* transcendental acquisitions, thus as the *problem of communicating and announcing* transcendental knowledge *in the world*, in the natural attitude[347]. This cannot be emphasized enough. It is of all the greater importance because all questions about the transcendental concept of science can only be satisfactorily and methodically posed when one has learned to distinguish strictly the scientific nature that phenomenologizing adopts precisely by its enworlding into "philosophy" appearing in the world, and the scientific nature that befits transcendental knowing purely as such, independently of all "localization" within the world. Secure mastery of this distinction first affords insight into the variously *reciprocal double-sidedness* of the transcendental theory of science, in which the theory of method reaches completion. With it we have at the same time a *transcendental "canon"* of phenomenological reason in judgment on its own self-organization and self-unfolding into the system of the science of phenomenology. We are capable of distinguishing between *seeming*[348] [*scheinbaren*] truths regarding phenomenologizing, which concern only its *mundane appearance* [*Erscheinung*], and *proper* transcendental truths.

In what follows, however, we shall make do with a few basic, general indications; for any attempt to give more specific contours to the problematic would inevitably have to take us into wide-ranging investigations.

A) The *problem* of the scientificity of phenomenologizing

We are inquiring into phenomenologizing from the point of view of "scientificity." As was already said, by this is not meant a certain cognitive rank,

---

346. [Ins.] ⟨or the doing⟩
347. [Sup.] ⟨—with the further purpose of producing a mankind that forms itself into a community in transcendental research.⟩
348. [Mg.] ⟨enworlded⟩

but the *presuppositions* that in a specific sense *ground* this "rank." To be sure, the expression "presupposition" is easily misunderstood. Still we use it for the most part to indicate certain relationships of foundation on the part of cognitions and, correlatively, truths. But in our posing of the question of the "scientificity" of phenomenologizing, it is now not a matter of ways in which *truths* are presupposed, but of the way in which *subjective life-structures* are presupposed for it to be possible that transcendental phenomenologizing be objectivated [349]into "science" in the first place. It is the basic question whether and how the *objectivation* of phenomenological cognition into a science that makes its entrance *in the world* participates in the subjective conditions that hold for every mundane science, whether and how it takes part in the *dependence* which the *institutional organization* of worldly science has upon certain basic phenomena of *human existence [Existenz]*.

Let us first of all attempt some indication of the corresponding state of affairs as found in the worldly naive sciences. Does "scientificity" here consist only in a particular ultimately valid rank held by knowledge? Or is that wherein[350] "scientificity" consists perhaps first a form of the intersubjective objectivation of this "ultimately valid knowledge" which is tailored to the *aims* of human cognitive effort? What we shall do here in the question of scientificity—and let this be the way it is termed—is draw attention to the *institutional organization* of knowing. In this sense a "science" is for us not primarily a unified complex of finally proven and systematically grounded *truths*, which is conditioned by the unity of the thematic field, [351]but a theoretical *practice of human being [des menschlichen Daseins]*, which terminates in truths as the results of this practice. Science is thus a *free possibility in man*, which he can decide for or which he can refuse. That in human being a universal posture of will arises that we call the "theoretical attitude" is a "presupposition" which, rather than being a "premise" for the truths known in science, has the character of an *ontic condition*. Prior to all thematic truths of a science there is the actuality of a *life* that pursues science. The "subject" of science is "man," not man the indi-

---

349. [Alt.] into ⟨"objective science" among other objective sciences⟩ in the first place.

350. [Ins.] ⟨Objective⟩

351. [Alt.] but a theoretical *practice of human* ⟨social⟩ *being*, which terminates in truths as the results of this practice ⟨—as the practice of men of science formed into a community.⟩ Science is thus a *free possibility in man* ⟨as member of an open scientific community⟩, which he can decide for or which he can refuse. That in human being a universal posture of will ⟨that reaches into the practical life of an open fellowship and counts on its joint willing⟩ arises that we call the "theoretical attitude" [etc.]

vidual, but the historico-generative complex of life standing in the unity of a cultural tradition[352]. "Science" thus is an *intersubjective,* [353]historically transmitted habituality of will on the part of the human race, into which the single individual fits as functionary, as link in the chain.[354] But man's "subject-being" ["*Subjektsein*"] in the doing of science is not only a *life of cognition* continuing through history and reaching a term in truths known, is not, as it were, only the subjective-noetic side as against the construct "science," which presents the objective-noematic side. Subject-being also means [355]that it is man *for whom* there is "scientific" knowledge in the first place. That is, it is not enough for scientific truths simply *to be known;* they must be *objectivated* [356]in sentences, in research reports, in textbooks. [357]This *objectivation for man,* however, is altogether determined by definite structures of finite human life; "subject-being" prescribes forms of objectivation to the *construct* "science." "Making knowledge (or a unitary cognitive complex) into science" is not least of all the *preserving* of it in the medium of intersubjective language (and intersubjective writing) and thereby the *raising* of it out of the *transitory subjective time* of [358]the cognitive process into the Objectivity of a duration superior to that of all human duration. Only through the "outward expression" of the individual cognitive process in the sentences that make assertions about it does something like the intersubjective Objectivity of science become possible, together with the continuity of the tradition of scientific knowing. In a word, only through the organization of thought performances into *institutional expressional constructs*

---

352. [Sup.] ⟨and in which there is the closer complex of the open scientific community.⟩

353. [Alt.] historically transmitted ⟨and community-forming⟩ habituality of will on the part of ⟨a community of researchers stretching down through the ages within its humanity,⟩ into which [etc.]

354. [Mg.] ⟨In serving an official function for [literally: being a functionary for] the community of men of science, he at the same time does so also in a certain way for unitary mankind, which profits and wants to profit from science, and furthers it by supporting researchers and their organizations.⟩

355. [Alt.] that ⟨the man of research has an audience,⟩ for ⟨which⟩ there is [etc.]

356. [Alt.] in sentences ⟨that abide, that are at all times accessible for everyone, for every man who is in the research community or who enters it in the future (and then for everyone interested in science),⟩ in research reports, [etc.]

357. [Alt.] This *objectivation* as ⟨abiding existence [*Dasein*], being accessible, being at the disposal of every⟩ *man,* however, [etc.]

358. [Alt.] the cognitive process⟨es of individual knowers in living discussion with one another⟩ into the Objectivity [etc.]

for intersubjectively accessible ³⁵⁹(learnable) truths is science even created as a *supra-individual and collective habituality*, and then the *possibility* also founded of entering any time into this habituality. Objectivation (outward expressional form) is not an element that is extra-essential to the scientificity of a science, but rather precisely that which makes *subjective*³⁶⁰ knowledge into an *Objectivity for everyone*.³⁶¹ To what extent, now, is this objectivation related to basic structures of human existence? As certain as it is that in all worldly sciences the "subject" who does science is *man*, just as certain also is it that the *temporality* of the development of a science is nothing other than ³⁶²the *historical temporality of human life*. But then is not the horizon of the future for any science precisely "infinite"? It is just because ³⁶³human being [*das menschliche Dasein*] in its doing of science is *"finite"* (limited by birth and death) that the Objectivation of scientific truths in a *relatively non-transitory medium* is at all necessary.³⁶⁴ Science can only be infinite (i.e., extend right through all the finite spans of future generations of researchers) precisely because the *Objectivation* of knowledge makes possible *transmission (handing down)* from generation to generation.³⁶⁵

To summarize the point of what has just been indicated (all too briefly, of course), what results is:

1. It is a fundamental characteristic of every *worldly* science that the "subject" of the action of doing science, from whom it nevertheless springs, is *man*; and thus that every science is *human* science. The doing of science and the result of this action are together in the unity of the world.³⁶⁶

------

359. [Alt.] ⟨(which can at any time be followed and understood, grasped again insightfully)⟩

360. [Ins.] ⟨and already here and now communalized⟩

361. [Mg.] ⟨for everyone understood as of all places and all times, as far as possibilities of connection are conceivable.⟩

362. [Alt.] the *historical temporality of human life* ⟨formed generatively into a community, or, as may be, [the historical temporality] of that part of history which is ordered toward its universality.⟩

363. [Alt.] ⟨individual⟩ human being

364. [Mg.] ⟨One has to distinguish here: [1] the actual present communal doing of science in the unitary fellowship of men of science and the tradition that is actual and present in this finitude and the corresponding everyone—[2] on the other hand the open environing world as a whole, with its humans (non-scientists too), but in the unity of a mediated connection, unity of a concretely complete history.⟩

365. [Sup.] ⟨Likewise in the open infinite coexistence [*Koexistenz*]—but as far as the possibility of connection reaches. That too is history—historical present.⟩

366. [Mg.] ⟨This world, however, is first the surrounding life-world and not the infinite world of the exact idea. Every man has his universe of humanity as belonging to

2. Every science, whether in fact actualized or not, lies basically within the *horizon of human possibilities*. (That these possibilities are as such revealed is not yet thereby said.) No project of any science whatever *transcends* the range of human possibilities; in the case of no science does man go beyond himself.

3. All sciences, both those that men have developed and any that are yet to be developed, are *communicative*. And are so in several respects:

    a) All sciences refer cognitively to *that which is existent* in the world. That which is existent, however, is always existent for everyone; the Objectivity of things of the world signifies accessibility in principle for everyone. Every science is communicative because its *object* is basically an intersubjective Objectivity (which in addition is made thematic not in some particular empirical individuality but in the moment of universality.)

    b) To the intersubjectivity of the *object* and correlatively of the *truth* referring to it there corresponds an intersubjectivity of the *"objectivation"* of this truth in the collectively understandable sentence, etc.

    c) The "infinity horizon" of mundane science relates to the *historico-generative communication* of individual finite life, which is only capable of handing down its scientific acquisitions thanks to the "objectivation" of those acquisitions.

We have thus given a basic characterization of worldly science with regard to its "who," its potentiality, and its communication. If we take this as a *clue* for a corresponding inquiry into the "scientificity" of *transcendental phenomenologizing*, we then find sketched out for us the *problem* of the special kind of relationship, extremely difficult to grasp, that *phenomenologizing* has [367]to its "appearance" [*Erscheinung*].

1. Who phenomenologizes? Is *man* the subject of the science of phenomenology? Does phenomenologizing permit of being at all within reach of some kind of *"existential"* treatment and perhaps critique?

2. Is phenomenology a possibility that is pregiven within the horizon of *human possibilities* and, as it were, lies ready and waiting? Is it a possibility left up to man's freedom, to take or to leave?

3. Are the thematic *objects* of phenomenological knowledge *"intersubjectively"* given? Does the one phenomenologizing find himself from the very first in a

---

this environing world, he and they all live out in it, not men on the moon. Thus the first "empirical" science. Then, however, exact science—but can every man idealize?]

367. [Alt.] to ⟨its construal, possible at any time, as human action in the world and [so] to phenomenology itself as a fact of human cultural development.⟩

potential knowledge community with "others"? [368]Are the truths known by him truths for "everyone"? Is there an intersubjective objectivation of these truths? Is, furthermore, the historicity [*Historizität*] off phenomenological science related to the historicality [*Geschichtlichkeit*] of generatively connected human life, thus to a historicity *in the world*?

In all these questions what is being asked about in a pointed way is the being of the phenomenological onlooker. The transcendental theory of method is able to answer them only in a specific *divisiveness*. However, this is not through lack of capability on the part of its knowing, but is based upon a divisiveness in the "matter at hand itself," a divisiveness ultimately comprehensible only in a *dialectical-paradoxical* fashion.

B) The enworlding of phenomenologizing

If the basic central problem of the transcendental theory of method—sketched, to be sure, only in its *most general Idea*—consists in the transcendental *antithesis in being* between the phenomenologizing onlooker and the transcendental constituting I, then it seems that by taking up the problem of the "scientificity" (objectivation) of phenomenologizing we have in a way annulled that antithesis in being. How? The universal theme for the onlooker as nonparticipant in world-constitution is constituting life in the multiplicity of its strata, constituted stages, and intermediate levels. While the phenomenologizing I refrains from all participation in constitution and only performs a transcendental, theoretical experience (one which cannot be apprehended by taking one's lead either from the naive conception of experience or from the constitutive interpretation of that conception), in the life that is thus thematic to the onlooker the constitution of the world is accomplished [369]in a direction articulated in *basically two ways*: in one way as the constitution of "objects" (identical unities in the multiplicity of subjective adumbrations, perspectives, presentations, modes of givenness, etc.), in another as the constitution of the *world-character* of subjectivity, as the constitution of "*humanity*" as the mundane self-apperception of the constituting subject.[370] Otherwise put: *in one* with

---

368. [Alt.] Are the truths known by him ⟨from the beginning⟩ truths for "everyone" ⟨—and if to be so taken, does "everyone" signify originally every man?⟩

369. [Alt.] in ⟨two directions that are always interwoven with each other and that move through all levels⟩: [etc.]

370. [Mg.] ⟨as man having himself a body and soul, among fellow men having bodies and souls, who for their part are, likewise as enworlding themselves, transcendental subjects for themselves, humans among humans.⟩

"objective" constitution (environing world, outer world) there also occurs, always in an essential correspondence, the "self-constitution" of the transcendental subject into man[371] in the world. The constituting subject enworlds itself as man existing in the world, in that it[372] settles down and, as it were, takes up a place *in the midst* of the complex of being it[373] itself has constituted. The world-aiming tendency of transcendental constitutive process terminates not only in mundane *"Objects,"* as the end-products of constituting performances, but just as much in the mundane *subject*: in man, who likewise represents a *result* of a constitutive sense-bestowal.[374]

---

371. [Ins.] ⟨among fellow men⟩
372. [Mg.] ⟨and they⟩
373. [Mg.] ⟨or they themselves⟩
374. [Mg.] ⟨World constitution goes on constantly as a constitution that produces the being-sense "world" in such fashion that in it constituting subjectivity is at the same time constantly enworlded and constituted as humanity, as a totality of humans living with one another in open, finite mediation, existing [*daseiender*] for one another, having experiences, thinking, acting with one another. As living in the world that is existent for them, they are aware of the existent world and also of themselves as living in it and as existent in the world with a body and a soul, as functioning subjects of acts and at the same time as Objects, [which] just as with other Objects [are] possible thematic objects, especially every human subject for itself in possible self-reflection. Constituting subjectivity always constitutes itself and has all along constituted itself as humanity. —The concrete ego is not constituted simply as individual man, as I-man, without more ado; instead, enworlding, which lies within world-constitution, consists in this, that in the ego, the I-center of all constitution, the I of the acts functioning in it, a primordial universal sphere is concentrated as a performance-unity specifically belonging to it, but that also in the ego, on the basis of this primordiality and by virtue of the "empathetic movements" belonging to it, a horizon of presentified primordialities and I-centers which comes to acquire acceptedness in being [*Seinsgeltung*] in the mode of other subjects, co-subjects, comes to constitution and in this way then becomes on its part a founding agent always capable of constituting the objective world. The ego can only have being [*Dasein*] in the world as something in human form that has the world, as I-man, I-person with psychic being, in such a way that in the ego the division of constituting being and living as primordial in primal modality and as alien, as other, has been accomplished and is always being accomplished, that in the ego a transcendental intersubjectivity, a universe of monads is constituted, which for its part is constituting in relation to the world. The universe of monads is objectivated in the world as the universe of mankind, while in the constituted community of monads nature is constituted as core of the world, to which the bodily organisms belong upon which worldly souls must be founded. By virtue of the

The phenomenological reduction signifies now the awakening of a transcendental tendency which in a certain way goes counter to the pull of life in the constituting I that, directed out to the world as its end, is *dazed by that world*. It is a tendency precisely of self-clarification, of theoretical inquiry moving back from the end-products of constitution into the constituting sources of sense-bestowal. This tendency is nothing other than the cognitive habituality of the phenomenologizing I which is established in the phenomenological epoche. Only because the "onlooker" does *not* take part in the action of constitution that aims teleologically at worldly being[375] can there be accomplished in and through his experiental life a *"coming-back-to-itself"* on the part of the cosmogonic constitution process that otherwise lives in unconcern about itself in its orientation to the world, only thus can there occur a transcendental *"becoming-for-itself."* Beyond all "antithesis in being," nevertheless, the phenomenologizing I stands in a *transcendental unity of life* with the constituting I; in the final analysis the "onlooker" is for all that only an I of reflection that is projected out from the life of constitution[376] (not of course in a [377]constitutive way). And now this I becomes, as it were, *passively* participant in world-constitution insofar as, in a way that is very difficult to analyze, it is encompassed by the self-enworlding of the constituting I, carried off by it and made mundane. [378]The enworlding of the constituting I into man in the world, the constitution of its "self-apperception," we already termed proper or primary enworlding.[379] It is a transcendental constitutive *activity;* the constituting I

---

constitution of the transcendental universe of monads as necessary "means" for world-constitution, there then of course takes place, thus mediately, the remarkable fact that my *soul* has not only enworlded my I of acts, but my whole ego. It is the objectivated ego-monad in and in unity with the universe of monads, and in that measure this universe is a first objectivation of the ego. But my monadic ego already encompasses all others as implied in it, and, objectivated in the *world* as soul, [as] my concrete psychic being, my whole ego finds itself enworlded in it.⟩

375. [Mg.] ⟨namely, in acts of living in the world which, on the basis of the world that is already horizonally pregiven, that is thus already constituted, continue world-constitution, temporalizing the results as events in the world.⟩

376. [Mg.] ⟨as center of the new activity that is, so to speak, turned away from the world.⟩ [This note is numbered 377 in the German text. —Tr.]

377. [Alt.] ⟨constituted⟩ [This note is numbered 376 in the German text.]

378. [Alt.] The ⟨self-⟩enworlding of the constituting I into man in the world, ⟨[which self-enworlding is] inseparable from world-constitution,⟩ the constitution of its "self-apperception," we already termed proper or primary ⟨self-⟩enworlding.

379. [See §10, p. 99.]

makes itself mundane through its own active constitution performances.[380] These sweep the "nonparticipant" phenomenologically theorizing I along into the mundanization that, for it, becomes only a *non-proper and seeming [scheinbar]* enworlding, for it does not rest *upon its own activity*. Phenomenologizing becomes *"appearance" [Erscheinung]*. As a transcending of the world, it now falls back again into the world—seemingly [*scheinbar*], i.e., if one judges by appearances [*nach der Erscheinung*]—it now becomes a transcending attempted in the world.[381] As an "un-humanizing" on the part of the reduction it is now made human.[382] [383]Phenomenologizing becomes a science *in the world*. That the transcendental cognizing of the phenomenological onlooker is enworlded and passes into mundane appearance as the result of a self-concealment, a self-apperceptive *constitution lying back over* constituting life, this is a necessity that affects phenomenologizing whether it *objectivates* itself as "science" *or not*. But *in the objectivation* of phenomenological cognitions into intersubjectively accessible knowledge, this becomes clear to a particular degree.[384] By mundanization phenomenologizing is returned precisely into the *situation of the natural*

---

380. [Mg.] ⟨That is a dubious way of expressing things. As against what other constitution? *Everything* real is constituted intersubjectively, all mundane constitution rests upon the activity that produces primordial nature and as empathizing actively constitutes alien subjectivity and thus the togetherness of I and Other and identical nature, identical world, etc. Where are the acts of self-mundanization that are "its own"? It is from the first the intentional web of the activity in which an existent world is [there] for me. How is it now with the enworlding of the transcendental phenomenologizing I and the world of monads that constitutes itself in the ego, as possible phenomenologizing monads? On this see the supplementary page.⟩ [See Appendix II.]

381. [See Appendix III.]

382. [See Appendix IV.]

383. [Alt.] Phenomenologizing becomes ⟨a scientific doing and its acquisitions become⟩ a science *in the world*.

384. [Mg.] ⟨Surely what is meant here is not the route taken through language? It is simply a return to the natural attitude. That can of course mean two things: 1) restoration of the world as final thematic ensemble in abandonment of the epoche and 2) remaining in the epoche so that the world now is the phenomenon of world, but consistently remaining in the relative theme-domain of the world continually taken as phenomenon. E.g., developing a mundane ontology and positive sciences of facts—only precisely not in naiveté, but as transcendental theme, as component region of constitutive phenomenology. That is the way in which all positive sciences find their place once more in phenomenology, only divested of naive absolutization. If I go "back" into the natural attitude in the second sense, then I have enworlded the

attitude, for which it expresses itself. That, however, does not mean *renouncing the epoche* and the whole reductive cognitive stance. The one phenomenologizing does not actually revert to the natural attitude and fall into naive dogmatism regarding the world, but the "transcendental attitude," which he consistently holds fast is the very thing that, consequent upon an "enworlding" that rests upon transcendental acts of sense-bestowal, *appears in the world, in the horizon of the natural attitude.* The task, now, would be to display in concrete analyses this non-proper ("secondary") enworlding of phenomenologizing (the falling back of transcending action into the world, the humanization of reductive unhumanization, etc.), so that our presentation might get beyond these very general indications. But the immensely involved problematic compels us to forgo that. We wish to suggest only a few essential clarifications in order to show the *style of answer* that the transcendental theory of method as the *canon of phenomenological reason* has to offer in distinguishing *"appearance-truths"* ["Erscheinungswahrheiten"] from *transcendental truths* with respect to phenomenologizing.

With our first attempt to give an answer to the question proposed above regarding the *"who"* of phenomenologizing, we immediately get into a certain difficulty. In the transcendental attitude, which we gained by performing the phenomenological reduction and which we consistently held to, there is no answer but the compulsory one prescribed for us by the understanding of what takes place in the reduction: the subject of phenomenologizing, i.e., the one phenomenologizing, is the *transcendental ego*, or, more exactly put, the *I of reflection* which forms itself in the living complex of transcendental subjectivity by a special immanent self-division [*Selbstentzweiung*].[385]

On the other hand, it is quite undeniable that phenomenologizing is a theoretical cognitive practice on the part of a *man* "philosophizing" there. Is not the phenomenologist a man like any other, with particular habits of interest and intention that govern his waking, active existence in the world? He certainly does not live in his specific cognitive attitude in unbroken permanence, but in a periodic actualization, broken by recreation or sleep, or everyday actions, etc. Is not "phenomenologizing" as mental labor a *human activity* like any

---

world-constituting agent as something psychic and, for positive scientific research, as something psychological. Phenomenologizing then also presents itself as psychological. But I know that a universal worldly psychology is in truth impossible and its universality is annulled in phenomenology. In the descriptive psychology of finitude I find enworlded nothing but the constitutively subjective, but not the action of phenomenologizing, etc.⟩

385. [Mg.] ⟨of the life of *acts*⟩

other? We cannot simply reply to this question with a "No." But one could at first think the difficulty here is not at all a serious one. After all, precisely by performing the phenomenological reduction we gain the fundamental insight that *all* human actions are basically *transcendental* actions and activities. *Before* reductive disclosure their "transcendentality" lies in an unrecognizable hiddenness, just as does the whole life of constitutive performance. "In themselves" all human activities are indeed transcendental. Phenomenologizing therefore is only *one among the other* transcendental activities that are constituted and apperceived *as human* by the self-constitution of the transcendental subject into man in the world.

The "difficulty" is not, however, eliminated in this way. Phenomenologizing is not an activity that can or does lie on one and the same level, so to speak, with other human activities. It is not first there in the natural attitude and then revealed in its transcendental properness by the reduction; it is never at all purely transcendentally existent [*existent*] "in itself." Rather, in order to set phenomenologizing in motion at all we have to get precisely beyond the natural attitude and achieve insight into the transcendentality of all human actions. In other words, the construal of phenomenologizing as a human action (cognitive practice) does not arise from a *naive captivation* in the natural attitude that would be got rid of and could be annulled by performing the phenomenological reduction. It is not a *dogmatism before the reduction*, but a *dogmatism after the reduction*. [386]What is meant by that is nothing less than this: the so-called *transcendental* cognition according to which all human actions are properly transcendental and can be ultimately understood only through a transcendental interpretation is itself a *human* cognitive stance. Or, put another way: the interpretation of man as a constituted objectivation-construct of transcendental subjectivity [387]is a *human interpretation*, a human theory. Or even a human "speculation"? Is it in the last analysis *man and man alone* who "phenomenologizes"? How might this phenomenologizing done by man stand up to a serious and relentless self-criticism? If the phenomenologist asserts as content for his more or less questionable "insights" that by the fundamental reflection of the "phenomenological reduction" he has in a quite definite sense gone beyond a restrictedness and captivation which is otherwise common to all men, that in some ultimate depth within his "self" he has discovered "world-constituting" (world-creative) subjectivity, and is capable of making it the

---

386. [Alt.] What is meant ⟨by the construal [of phenomenologizing] as human activity⟩ is nothing less than this: [etc.]
387. [Alt.] ⟨would be⟩

theme of strictly scientific knowledge, this seems still to be outright *arrogance,* an extravagant presumption, an unparalleled hubris, or, to speak in religious terms, the usurping of creation by putting oneself in the place of God. And an "existential criticism" would perhaps dig even deeper: Is this bold "titanism," documented in the construction of the transcendental subject, ultimately but mental sloth, a frivolous intellectual contrivance by a life that is alienated from the truly menacing and terrifying realities of human existence (death, fate, guilt, and other "Last Things")? Or is what lies behind this indeed the eeriness of human existence, which one tries to hide from oneself; is not phenomenologizing, as pretending to overcome the natural attitude, a *"flight from finitude"?*

If we had to grant this, then phenomenologizing as a mode of human philosophizing would be an *evasion* of the actuality of human being, a self-deceit lacking any ultimate truth. [388]But the criticism conducted from an "existential" consideration of things *goes wrong from the start.* To a certain extent it presupposes as proven that phenomenologizing is nothing other than a human action. Its counterargumentation is simply an *"argumentatio ad hominem."* Nonetheless, it clearly has *appearances [Augenschein]* in its favor. Who would want to deny that the phenomenologist is a man in the world, a fellow human, with strange views that one can nevertheless come to know. The question is only whether *all* truth regarding phenomenologizing (or the subject functioning within it) lies in the obvious look of things [*im Augenschein*], whether the look of things is a *final authority* or whether it is not precisely an extremely *questionable matter* that stills needs to be *elucidated.* Is phenomenologizing then actually on hand in the world "in the obvious look of things" [*augenscheinlich*]? As long as one believes that phenomenology, or phenomenologizing, can be at all *criticized existentially,* one just cannot have understood it. One remains stuck in mundane and naive meanings, which function in proper phenomenological sentences with only "analogizing" significance, and insinuates an abstruse sense into them. Thus, for example, sentences in which the one phenomenologizing makes statements about the phenomenological reduction are not understandable at all if one does not *oneself* perform the phenomenological reduction. Such statements are not reports about something which would be pregiven and known in its possibility, but are *imperative pointers* to a cognitive action of a hitherto unknown radicality *which can be compre-*

---

388. [Alt.] But ⟨this kind of⟩ criticism conducted from ⟨the⟩ "existential" consideration of things *goes wrong from the start.* To a certain extent it presupposes ⟨as obvious or⟩ as proven [etc.]

hended only in being itself performed. If the "existential critic" really takes the discussion seriously, and has his understanding follow the phenomenological reduction as he performs it, he *eo ipso* gives up the basis for his "critical stand-point." He can no longer carry out his proposal, because he has overcome captivation in the natural attitude, i.e., (among other things) *captivation in be-ing a human [im Mensch-Sein];* and he has recognized himself as transcendental subject. Cognition has thereby broken its way through to the realization that—[389]*despite* the perfectly obvious way it all looks—phenomenological knowing and its *habitus* do *not* represent a *human attitude,* that an *argumentatio ad hominem* is in principle meaningless. Performing the reduction produces the un-ambiguous, secure, and unforgettable certainty that the proper (ultimately actual) subject of phenomenologizing is the *transcendental* onlooker. Phenom-enologizing proves itself to be something that takes place *transcendentally,* namely, the transcendental *self-movement of constituting life.* How is the expression "self-movement" to be understood? The reductive disclosure of transcenden-tal life yields the recognition that this life, even *including* precisely this disclo-sure, has proceeded "anonymously," that the whole of transcendental life has habitually held to an invariable orientation of constitutive processes to the telos of all constitution, the being of the world. Only with the reduction does a *disturbance* enter into this, as it were, "statically" steadfast process of world-constitution: within transcendental life there springs up a *countermovement,* the constitutive "retro-inquiry" [*"Rückfrage"*] of the phenomenologizing onlooker. This signifies a *primal event* in the life of transcendental subjectivity, *it comes to itself,* it "awakens"—to speak in a metaphor—out of the age-old "sleep" of *be-ing-outside-itself;* it passes from the stage of sheer *"being-in-itself"* into the stage of *"being-for-itself."* The phenomenological reduction (when it is first performed) is the *peritrope*[ll] in the drama of world-constitution, and phenomenologizing is a transcendental procedure [390]which introduces a decisive caesura into the "history" of world-constituting life. However, the self-movement of transcen-dental life is not only a *counterplay* of world-oriented constitution [on the one hand] and phenomenologically theoretical cognition countering it ("retro-in-quiring") [on the other]; it is a *circular turn into itself* inasmuch as phenomenol-ogizing is itself *taken along* once more by the world-aiming tendency of the life of[391] constitutive process. The transcendental operation "phenomenologiz-

389. [Ins.] *despite* the perfectly obvious way ⟨the man who proclaims phenome-nology⟩ looks [etc.]

390. [Alt.] which ⟨makes⟩ a decisive ⟨cut in⟩ the "history" of world-constituting life.

391. [Ins.] ⟨now of course disclosed⟩

ing" is thereby *made mundane*, is carried back into the natural attitude of which it had rid itself.[392] It enters into the midst of a life-situation in the horizon of the natural attitude as a cognitive action on the part of a man, in the manifest look of things it becomes human philosophizing sustained by a particular attitude, and thus[393] it presents an *area of vulnerability* for the naively dogmatic "discussion" which common sense (that of "natural-attitude" man) holds with it.[394] In other words, phenomenologizing as a mundane event becomes [395]interpretable in mundane terms. But the principle holds: *every mundane interpretation falls short*, it touches only the outer form, "appearance" ["*Erscheinung*"]; the inner (transcendental) essence remains necessarily closed and inaccessible to it. And it remains *forever* alien, if the interpreter or critic does not himself perform the reduction *from out of himself*, and thereby abandon the basis of all attempts at mundane and naive interpretation.

After this *defense*, however, one has got to determine somewhat more closely the positive sense of the enworlding of the subject of phenomenologizing action. "Man" is the *subject of the appearance [Erscheinung]* of phenomenologizing, that is, man is the subject that appears in the natural attitude, the *seeming [scheinbar] subject*. This "seeming" on the part of the being of the subject [*Subjektsein*] altogether determines the problem of the relationships between certain basic (existential) attitudes in human being ("authenticity," etc.) and the awakening of the disposition to make the breakthrough in those flashes of transcendental preknowledge that first motivate the performance of the phenomenological reduction. Here is a whole realm of obscure and puzzling problems. To tackle them would presuppose having *already carried out* a constitutive interpretation of human being [*Menschsein*].

However that may be, however a particular ethical self-activation by man might be presupposed for successfully carrying out the phenomenological reduction as disclosure of the constituting "ground of the world," an "anthropologistic" interpretation of subjectivity (i.e., one that is caught up in man as constituted construct) can never reach and get a grip on the "actual" subject of phenomenologizing. On the contrary, the phenomenological transcendental philosopher does not mistakenly think it is obvious from the look of

---

392. [Mg.] ⟨but in such a way, of course, that this is now recognized *as* transcendental process and thereby also the world [is recognized] as transcendental correlate.

393. [Mg.] ⟨in the human connection with other men on the part of the one philosophizing⟩

394. [Regarding pp. 112–114, see Appendix V.]

395. [Alt.] ⟨subject to predication⟩ in mundane terms.

things [augenscheinlich] that it is a "man" who philosophizes. For him this "obvious look of things" ["Augenschein"] is always transparent with respect to the transcendental truth that lies behind it.[396] He sees through the "appearance," whereas
the dogmatist takes the appearance for an ultimate reality, behind which we
simply cannot inquire further. To the "child of the world" [Weltkind] appearance is not transparent, is just not given him as appearance; and so he falls into
a deception which he is quite unable to detect.

If, now, the enworlding of phenomenologizing is itself a constitutive necessity
that rests upon transcendental sense-bestowals and tendencies, then the ques-

---

396. [Mg.] ⟨Not entirely free of misunderstanding. The phenomenologist has
acted out and theoretically cognized all possible attitudes. He now masters the possibilities of running through them one after the other in their coherence in a unity;
and he can now see how, in the return to the natural attitude, which now has its transcendental horizon, the transcendental ego has performed in itself a psychic and human self-objectivation as I-man, and [how therein], as with everything egological,
phenomenologizing activity and habituality lie co-objectivated. Likewise with respect to the constitution of the whole universe of monads, the "coinciding" of it with
its objectivation as mankind. It lies in the constitution of monads that the phenomenologizing of the absolute ego figures into the I-monad. Every other monad also
has all my possibilities, it can phenomenologize; just as I have my temporospatial location for the other monads, so, as it turns out, do they and in them their phenomenologizing, and that enters into souls in natural mundane objectivation. Transcendental science quite rightly has its ideal being in the world of monads, but also
in the mundane world, and the phenomenologizing activity that works this science
in an actual present moment has spatiotemporal locations here and there in the corresponding sense. On both sides this performative action of phenomenology is addressed to eventual cophenomenologists and has a horizon of monads and human
subjects that are dogmatically naive. They can, however, be taken as subjects that
could phenomenologize and remove their dogmatic blinders, and science can be done
from the beginning with the intention of gradually opening mankind's eyes, etc. In
this sense accordingly phenomenology is itself and in a good sense in the world and
analogous to a positive science in its intentions of addressing [someone], etc.

That is all truth for me, the phenomenologist. Systematically explicating myself as
ego, I find each and every existent intentionally included in myself, and existent in
every sense as constituted, therein too each and every possibility, also all the follies
of dogmatism that arise from philosophizing that still knows nothing about [its]
blinders. The naive man hears and reads "phenomenology," but cannot understand it
and only has natural language words without their sense.

A problem proper here is how far it is possible to follow and understand [phe-
nomenology] without actually concomitantly performing the reduction.⟩

tion about the "who" of phenomenologizing must not be answered by simply
pointing to the transcendental onlooker, recognized in performing the reduction as the proper "subject." The *full-sided subject* of phenomenologizing[397]
is neither the transcendental I (sticking to its transcendentality), nor "man"
closed off against the transcendental, this closure being what constitutes the
naiveté of the natural attitude; the full-sided subject is rather *transcendental subjectivity "appearing" ["erscheinende"] in the world*—by non-proper enworlding. I.e.,
the "who" under inquiry is a theorizing subject that must be characterized *both
as transcendental and as mundane.* What is involved here is a "dialectical unity" between the spheres of the transcendental and the mundane, and that is what
comprises the "concrete" concept of the "phenomenologizing subject." This
unity is the result of non-proper enworlding, which is not a process whereby
phenomenologizing transcendentally objectivates *itself,* but one in which phenomenologizing as a transcendental occurrence is *passively taken along* by the
general self-objectivation of transcendental subjectivity into man within-the-
world and naively caught up in it. This "being taken along" that phenomenologizing undergoes is, however, radically *distinguished* from the enworlding
of constituting life[398]. For not only does this latter enworlding consist in the
work of transcendental subjectivity turning its constitution action back upon
itself so as to come forth in an objectivation form ([399]man) in the midst of the
complex of being it has itself constituted, but above all it is characterized by
the fact [400]that the life that constitutes itself as "worldly," in having its term in
constitutive end-products, *forgets its transcendental origin, knows itself only as man,*
and does not reach behind its own humanness in its return to itself in self-
consciousness. [401]Secondary (or non-proper) enworlding of phenomenologizing, now, is not the kind that leads to a *forgetting* of its transcendental origins, but is precisely the worldly objectivation of *knowing about transcendental
origin.* Accordingly the transcendental process of the self-cognition of consti-

---

397. [Mg.] ⟨if by that is understood the activity in which phenomenological science is worked as addressing itself to a circle of researchers??⟩

398. [Ins.] ⟨in the natural attitude⟩

399. [Alt.] ⟨⟨I-man⟩⟩

400. [Alt.] ⟨that the transcendental I-substrate of the activity *is all taken up* in bringing things to their term, etc., and thereby is, as it were, blind to the transcendental-
constituting processes and intermediate formations, etc. So it happens that the I in
the natural attitude knows itself only as man⟩ and does not reach [etc.]

401. [Alt.] Secondary (or non-proper) enworlding of phenomenologizing ⟨on the
contrary⟩ is not the kind that leads to ⟨being blind to⟩ its transcendental origin [etc.]

tuting subjectivity is not *properly* enworlded, it is not objectivated into a merely human cognitive operation by constitutional processes *that remain "anonymous."* Instead, not only the transcendental process as such which is masked in "appearance," but even this *mundanization* becomes *transparent* in its transcendental constitutive essence.

There is a *twofold transparency* in the mundane [402]appearance of phenomenologizing: 1) transparency with respect to the transcendental process of *phenomenologizing*, and 2) transparency in the "appearance" with respect to the *constitutional processes* that fashion that "appearance." This twofold transparency provides the phenomenological cognizer with the possibility of forming at any time an insight-based judgment regarding that which is only a truth [403]with respect to worldly appearance, and that which is a truth that forms the proper transcendental essence of phenomenologizing. He certainly concedes that "phenomenologizing" is a cognitive action of *finite man;* but just as much he stands by the discerned truth that it is *no merely human* cognition that is being presented. Both the thesis, "the subject of phenomenologizing is the transcendental ego," and the "counterthesis," "the subject of phenomenologizing is man," are *"true."* Yet this is *not a contradiction in truths.* Between appearance-truths and properly transcendental truths no conflict is at all possible, since they just do not lie on the same truth-level. They are simply not in competition with each other. They are neither compatible nor incompatible, in the manner of two opposite truth-claims regarding the same thing. Just as the transcendental clarification of the world does not in any way deny and disparage truths known in the natural attitude, but *"completes"* them through their *transcendental interpretation*—for they are the kind of truths that arise in a transcendental situation of confinement—and finally makes them radically, i.e., *constitutively*, understandable, in the same way there is also no conflict between transcendental cognitions referring to *phenomenologizing* and truths that are naively caught up in the world, that are only concerned with appearance and do not push on to the transcendental essence concealed therein. Instead, the transcendental self-interpretation of phenomenologizing leaves naive truths standing, but interprets them by pointing out the *restriction* (*"abstractness"*) they have in referring to a *constituted situation of acceptedness* [*Geltungssituation*], and by working them in now as "captivated," *one-sided* truth into the "concrete" constitutive *truth* that comes to light with phenomenological analysis. The *superiority of transcendental truth* is thus not a matter of being more true comparatively (not a

---

402. [Alt.] ⟨localization⟩
403. [Alt.] with respect to ⟨subsequent enworlding⟩,

greater degree of truth), but consists in this, that mundane truth is itself *en-compassed* by transcendental truth and in it gains its own final lucid intelligibility. Otherwise expressed, in the transcendental self-explication of the one phenomenologizing, the appearance-truths that refer to him and his theoretical activity are *"sublated"*; i.e., they are *negated*, insofar as they become evident in the restriction and the "dogmatic" situation of acceptedness that are theirs; and they are *preserved*, insofar as they are not themselves "crossed out" but illuminated in their transcendental constitution. This *"sublation" as negating and preserving* is what is characteristic in the style of answer given by the transcendental theory of method in its capacity as the *canon of phenomenological reason* when it divides appearance-truths from transcendental truths in regard to phenomenologizing, which is its continual theme.

Fundamental insight into the subject of phenomenologizing also determines the answer now to the broader question posed earlier about the way in which phenomenologizing subsists *as a possibility*, and how the *potentiality* for it must be characterized. Whereas the question of the potentiality for any worldly science presents no particular problem, insofar as every one of them already lies *from the very first in the horizon* of man's possible ways of behaving in relation to the existent, *phenomenologizing is not a possibility given beforehand to man.* In this, however, do we not contradict the preceding clarification we gave regarding the subject of phenomenologizing, inasmuch as that subject as proper subject is indeed transcendental, but in appearance is *human?* Must not the potentiality for this cognitive action, at least in appearance, be open to being addressed as a *human potentiality?* Must not the ability to phenomenologize *appear* [*erscheinen*] as a possibility for utmost, radical self-reflection on man's part that is always ready and can always be freely seized by him?

The first thing we must do is determine more closely the concept of the potentiality of a science.[404] A basic distinction to make here is one between the way a science is potential *before any actualization* and the way it is potential *after it has been actualized.* For example, mathematically exact science, which reached its decisive breakthrough in the Renaissance with Galileo, was always given to man prior to that in its possibility. (This, of course, does not mean [405]that this possibility was in any way *"on hand,"* that it could have been as available to prehistoric man as to Renaissance man, that disclosure and opening up

---

404. [On this paragraph, see Appendix X.]

405. [Alt.] that this possibility was "on hand" ⟨as an actual ability or one actually needing to be developed empirically;⟩ that ⟨this science⟩ could have been [etc.]

of this possibility would be a matter of accident. 406Rather the revealing of human possibilities is dependent upon quite determined existential presuppositions.) What is essential here, however, is that in opening up a new science *man* recognizes it as one *that was ideally possible for him* 407*at any time*, that he has thereby *not transgressed the horizon of his possibilities* but only fulfilled them.408 At the same time he is aware of the fact that the disclosure of this particular possibility of theorizing had been possible409 from the outset to *each and everyone*. The genius who founds a science opens up *not a mere private potentiality*, but one that is *intersubjective*.410 Even though a particular new science has been actual-

---

406. [Alt.] Rather the ⟨developing⟩ of human possibilities ⟨into actual abilities⟩ is dependent [etc.]

407. [Alt.] ⟨in his time, in his cultural world⟩

408. [Mg.] [This sentence marked with a question mark, and then Mg.] ⟨That is not as simple as it seems. A primitive child brought into our European surroundings, into our school. Any child from a [variety of] humanity, from any era, can be thought of as transplanted into our European world and era and would take on European traditions here and so acquire scientific potentialities. Likewise the reverse. We, thought of as transplanted into some other and possibly primitive [variety of] mankind of any era, and our doctors, would have become more or less "medicine men" in it, etc., "The same man" conceivable in all eras and surroundings, as able to be transplanted into all of them—thus I put myself in the place of anyone else next to me, no matter who— others modification-possibilities of myself; with the totality of phantasy modifications of my I there coincides the totality [of] the others one might conceive of. But every self-modification changes the whole world, and in putting myself in the place of the other I am an I transformed in phantasy, transformed in thought into the other, into the other of his surroundings, of his generative origin, of his experiences, feelings, etc. *But thus one can say:* By virtue of constitution, as man in the natural attitude I have my horizon in possibilities of variation of myself as man as such, that is, as man in a possible world and therefore as man in a possible world-past and world-future, in a possible world-historicality. In what does the possibility reside of putting myself in the place of all men in all eras and all conceivable world-historicalities? This horizon is the same for any man. To it belongs every de facto science, every unknown science conceived of as variation (such as in the indeterminate variation "possible"). In my variation I have included all actual and possible cultures.—That is the furthermost horizon of human possibilities, of what can be conceived of for human being [*menschlichen Daseins*], for structures produced in human performance, etc. Right there no phenomenology can take place.⟩

409. [Mg.] ⟨precisely by "transplanting," upbringing, etc.⟩

410. [Mg.] ⟨in his era, in his stratum of educational formation, his stratum of normally educable people, etc.⟩

ized, nevertheless the actualization is not one of uninterrupted continuity on the part of scientists pursuing it. The *periods of non-actuality* of this science are here a *new mode of potentiality*. The pregivenness of a potentiality now means a *consciously known* habitual disposition for freely bringing the scientific attitude on stage [411]at any time.

The distinction between, on the one hand, an unconscious, undisclosed human possibility and, on the other, one that is conscious and actualizable is important now in order to characterize the *potentiality of phenomenologizing*. First of all we unconditionally hold that phenomenologizing is *not a human possibility at all*, but signifies precisely the *un-humanizing of man*, the passing of human existence [*Existenz*] (as a world-captivated naive self-apperception) into the transcendental subject. [412]Yet we leave undisputed the *appearance-truth* that the subject of phenomenologizing is man. How is the potentiality for phenomenological cognition codetermined now by this appearance-truth? *Before* phenomenologizing is actually realized in carrying out the reduction there is *no human possibility* of cognizing phenomenologically, no human possibility that is [413]*simply undisclosed* and *unconscious*. Just as man is the transcendental subject *closed off* to its own living depths, so too *all* human possibilities are *closed off* to the inner transcendentality of the subject. Man cannot *as man* phenomenologize, that is, his human mode of being [*Menschsein*] cannot perdure through the actualization of phenomenological cognition. Performing the reduction means for man *to rise beyond* (to transcend) *himself*,[414] it means[415] to *rise beyond himself in all his human possibilities*. To express it paradoxically, when man performs the phenomenological reduction ([416]un-humanizes himself), he carries out an action that *"he"*[417] just cannot carry out, that just does not lie in the range of his possibilities.[418] This paradox is made clear if we keep in view that

411. [Alt.] ⟨in the future, from now on⟩

412. [Alt.] Yet we leave undisputed the ⟨secondary mundanization of phenomenology, according to which⟩ the subject of phenomenologizing is man.

413. [Alt.] ⟨real but⟩ *simply* ⟨unforeseen, or a constructed possibility in the total horizon of phantasy, but conceivable.⟩

414. [Mg.] ⟨to put his simple, straightforward being (being that is oriented to end-themes) out of play by the epoche⟩

415. [Mg.] ⟨to put [all his human possibilities] out of accepted validity.⟩

416. [Alt.] (⟨releases⟩ himself ⟨from his humanity⟩)

417. [Ins.] ⟨as man⟩

418. [Mg.] ⟨To man it belongs to see exclusively the world and in it his worldly existence [*Dasein*] and correlatively to be blind to the transcendental. To see and to

it is not properly man who performs the reduction, [419]but the transcendental subject that, awakening within him, presses toward self-consciousness. If then, *before* phenomenologizing *becomes actual*, its appearance as a human potentiality is not given in the natural attitude, if the self-satisfied naiveté of that attitude consists precisely in *blindness* to the transcendental interiority of life and thus in a restricted and biased openness for *possibilities that are only human*, then there occurs with the fact of the (non-proper) *enworlding* of phenomenologizing an[420] *apparent enlargement* of the realm of man's possibilities. It is not *before* but *after* the reduction that the ability to cognize phenomenologically *appears* [*erscheint*] as a theoretical attitude that is attainable by man out of himself at any time and that is given to him beforehand potentially. But this [421]appearance-truth is also *"transparent"* as to its inner transcendental essence, is *"sublated"* in proper transcendental constitutive truth, so that the potentiality for phenomenologizing is a *transcendental* potentiality.[422] The distinction between appearance-truth and properly transcendental truth,[423] which forms the special problematic of the *canon* of phenomenological reason as a part of the transcendental theory of method, must now still be applied above all in the inquiry into the *"intersubjective"* character of phenomenologizing, which in a certain sense is synonymous with the question of its scientific character. After all, the scientificity of a science—seen from one particular viewpoint—consists precisely in the *intersubjective Objectivity* of its knowledge and the *objectivation* (predicative outward expression) of that knowledge in[424] *expressional constructs* which make possible an institutional habituality in knowledge ("science") that persists throughout all the change intrinsic to human transitoriness. The decisive question now is whether phenomenologizing is or can at all be an *"intersubjective science" in this sense.* To begin with we certainly cannot deny that—seen from a wordly viewpoint—it seems to have the same structure that every [425]worldly science has. Phenomenological cognition does

---

be able to see in this exclusive way is to be in an exclusive and consistently onward developed theme-domain that has ended up as a fixed, closed habituality, that is directed to a predelineated polar system of end-themes.⟩

419. [Alt.] but the transcendental ⟨life⟩ that, awakening ⟨"⟩within him⟨"⟩ ⟨thematically,⟩ presses toward self-consciousness. [Quotation marks put in by Husserl.]

420. [Ins.] ⟨only⟩

421. ["appearance-truth" lined through by Husserl]

422. [On this see Appendix VI.]

423. [Mg.] ⟨truths before and after the reduction⟩

424. [Ins.] ⟨predicative⟩

425. [Alt.] ⟨positive⟩

make an entrance into the world in the horizon of the natural attitude as the common concern of philosophizing individuals who refer to the *same* theme and attain the *same* cognitions and truths, does it not? Obviously! And is not this community of knowledge, then, a community that is in principle open and available to everyone who puts the requisite attitude into effect? This too must be conceded—in a certain sense. Despite this, however, the scientificity of phenomenological knowledge, organized as it is into the unity of a science, is *toto caelo different* from that of [426]mundane sciences as a whole. Here also a canon of phenomenological reason is to be set up with the distinction between the *pseudo-mundane*[427] "intersubjectivity" that proceeds from the constitutive process of the ([428]non-proper) enworlding of phenomenologizing, and the intersubjectivity that belongs to phenomenologizing as a *transcendental cognitive process*. In other words, phenomenological knowing and the intersubjectivity proper to it, which is documented by the community of those philosophizing, simply does not allow being conceived according to the clue provided by the intersubjectivity structure that belongs to every world-referred naive science. The positive grounds for this way of discriminating the "intersubjective" character of phenomenologizing we shall indicate only briefly. In radically bracketing belief in the world, the phenomenological reduction takes the one phenomenologizing out of the situation of intersubjective-communal reference to that which is existent in the world and accessible to everyone, and places him in the *solitude* of his transcendental egological existence [*Existenz*]. As phenomenologizing onlooker he consistently thematizes his [429]own constituting life to gain a wealth of cohesive cognitions that in their systematic linkage comprise something in the manner of a *solitary, solipsistic* science. [430]The *objects* of his cognitive life are at first not (*in any sense*) "intersub-

---

426. [Alt.] ⟨positive⟩

427. [Mg.] ⟨but secondary enworlding is a necessary "localization" of the transcendental in the world and to that extent precisely not seemingly [*scheinbar*] existent in the world and yet, on the other hand, not in the world in the natural sense, thus nonetheless pseudo-mundane⟩ [This note is numbered 428 in the German edition. —Tr.]

428. [Alt.] (⟨secondary subsequent⟩) [This note is numbered 427 in the German edition.]

429. [Alt.] ⟨primordial⟩

430. [Alt.] The *objects* of his cognitive life are at first *not* (*in any* ⟨intelligible⟩ *sense*) *"intersubjective"*; even the essential laws he sets forth are only pure possibility modifications of ⟨this absolute, plural-excluding⟩ egological de facto existence. The object of egologically phenomenologizing cognition now ⟨has⟩ as little intersubjective ⟨sense⟩ as the resulting truths.

jective", even the essential laws he sets forth are only pure possibility modifications of his *own* egological de facto existence, and do not in the least supply a validity that goes beyond the transcendental ego. The object of egologically phenomenologizing cognition now is as little intersubjective as the resulting truths are truths for everyone. The one phenomenologizing finds himself in neither an actual nor a potential cognitive community with others.[431] In unfolding the phenomenological reduction from its egological to its intersubjective character, now, in the concrete constitutive explication of the intentionality of empathy he arrives at the *transcendental acknowledgment* of others as co-subjects *that constitute*. But the reduction of others, first given in the phenomenon of the world, to their transcendental existence [*Existenz*] is nonetheless carried out by the ego in its action of constitutive explication[432]; it does not go beyond the solipsistic character of its cognition. "Others" are transcendentally existent as constituting monads with whom the ego stands in a community of constitution, but *not* in a community of transcendental self-knowledge. When phenomenological knowing is enworlded, i.e., becomes[433]

---

431. [On this see Appendix VII.]

432. [Ins.] ⟨of itself⟩

433. [Mg.] ⟨The "becomes" ["*-werden*"] is dangerous. The world *is* constituted, for the ego is ego in possession of a world. And therefore this becoming-placed-in [*Eingestelltwerden*] is always already an is-in-place-in [*Eingestelltsein*]. The ego is a phenomenologizing ego, but it needs (within the epoche) a change of thematic stance in order to find itself and what is its own in its psychologization in man. It is perhaps *important* to *distinguish* from the start, with respect to the phenomenologizing ego, the different thematic attitudes: 1) the first fundamental attitude that occurs at the start of the reduction, 2) [the] transcendental-ontological attitude as "return" to the mundane attitude, particularly that of positive science, although the latter is, of course, no longer naively blind to constitution. Therein the attitude taken toward the psyche, toward intentional psychology. 3) Or, as 2) will sometimes be, the monadological attitude. 4) The attitude of reflection upon the phenomenologizing absolute ego and its "transformed" language. 5) The attitude toward the monadic ego as phenomenologizing and its language.—Phenomenologizing in my I-monad and as possibility in other monads. Intersubjectivity is constituted beforehand at different points, it becomes thematic at 5), likewise at 2). It should not bother anyone that the ego was presupposed as possessing a world, that its world-constitution, however, takes on a new form by phenomenologizing, that the mode of being of the ego itself makes a turn, namely, in such a way that it is no longer the natural-naive ego but the ego become thematic and patent to itself that has to make itself mundane as man. Man is also thereby transformed, the whole occurrence of transcendental-phenomenologizing *eo ipso* enters his psyche. [Husserl's point at the beginning of this remark depends upon

placed in the natural attitude,[434] and the possibility is thereby given of addressing oneself to fellow humans living in their world-captivation and even of conveying phenomenological knowledge to them, in order thereby to set phenomenologizing in motion within them—all by means of the objectivation of transcendental knowledge in the medium of natural language—then for the first time something like a *transcendental intersubjectivity* is formed. Transcendental intersubjectivity, then, is the community relationship, played out purely in the transcendental theater, on the part of the *many who perform the reduction* and achieve phenomenological knowing and which now "appears" in the world as the intersubjectivity of those philosophizing.[435] One must, however, be altogether clear about this, that in the end the intersubjectivity that forms itself in the transcendental sphere through the empathy-mediated community of phenomenologizing is never comprehensible under the guidance of the way [436]*mundane* structures of intersubjectivity are understood. First, the thematic object of phenomenological knowing is not *intersubjectively* accessible in the same sense [437]as that which is existent in the world. The reason for this is that what is existent precisely in a worldly way as the stratum of "end-constitutedness" [*End-Konstituiertheit*][438] is determined by an accessibility that is intersubjective in principle, and that the "Objectivity" of that stratum has precisely the constitutive sense [439]of being for everyone [*Sein für Jedermann*]. The constitutively antecedent strata that in the entirety of their layered structure (to be disclosed by regressive inquiry) form the theme of phenomeno-

---

the distinction made in German between the use of *werden* with a past participle, forming the grammatical passive voice, and *sein* with a past participle. The first indicates an *action* or *process*, the second a *state* or *condition*. This distinction is usually blurred in the normal English use of "is/are" with a past participle. Thus Husserl's emphasis on the "is" in the first line calls attention precisely to the abiding condition character of the world: "Die Welt *ist* konstituiert."—Tr.]

434. [Mg.] ⟨not in the natural attitude simply—it is transcendentally transformed⟩

435. [Mg.] ⟨which for them actually *is* in the world—in the world that, however, for them is now understood transcendentally.⟩

436. [Alt.] ⟨naive-⟩*mundane* [To which Mg.] ⟨in the sense of positive science, in the world⟩

437. [Alt.] as ⟨the totality of that which is existent ultimately, absolutely is [accessible] for the naive person in the naive⟩ world.

438. [See Appendix VIII.]

439. [Alt.] of ⟨true⟩ being for everyone. [To which Mg.] ⟨for everyone as man who in naiveté or positivity takes the worldly existent as that which is ultimately, *absolutely* existent.⟩

logical theory cannot in principle be taken [440]in the way that items constituted in end-constitution are. In other words, phenomenological experience does not refer at all, as we know, to something existent[441], but to the *constitutive becoming of what is existent* (to the stages of "pre-being" ["*Vorsein*"], in which that which exists (the world) is constitutively built up). Just as phenomenological experience makes its object thematic in a way that we have to determine by *analogy* to the experience of something existent,[442] so also the intersubjective Objectivity of the phenomenological "object" and correlatively the intersubjectivity of cognition and truths referring to it are only determinable by *analogy* to the mundane Objectivity of objects and the intersubjective cognition and truth that correspond to it. We cannot, however, present here this "analogical" determination itself. We shall have to be content with the mere indication of the problem. Secondly, however, the multiplicity of those phenomenologizing is also not understandable on the model of a mundane community of cognitive subjects. While every worldly "we" is rightly understood as a collectivity of really separate and individualized subjects that stand in a common effort, with respect now to the *transcendental community of monads* it is an open problem whether they are actually built up out of "individuals"[443]. The question thus is whether a common phenomenologizing action [444]is a *plural* cognitive process, or must ultimately be determined as *one* transcendental tendency that only articulates itself in monadic plurality, therefore, whether the process by which transcendental subjectivity "becomes for itself" is not played out at a depth that lies *prior to all monadic "individuation."* This problem of the mutual *implication of monads* is a major one, and it brings with it "metaphysical" consequences of a wholly new style; but unless we enter into this matter we cannot bring the question at issue to resolution. However, this much has become clear to us, that the "intersubjectivity" that befits phenomenologizing in a pure and transcendental way ([445]before any enworlding) is not of such a kind that *from the first* it determines the object and correlatively the cognition and truth of phenomenologizing, but that it must first of all be

---

440. [Alt.] in the way that ⟨absolutely existent things⟩ are.

441. [Ins.] ⟨in the natural-naive sense⟩

442. [Mg.] ⟨It is a re-formation of the concept of being, of the apperception of being, etc., a re-formation of logic into transcendental logic.⟩

443. [Ins.] ⟨in the sense derived from the world⟩

444. [Alt.] is a ⟨plural of separate absolute⟩ cognitive process⟨es⟩, or must ultimately be determined as *one* transcendental ⟨intentionality⟩ that only [etc.]

445. [Quotation marks put around "before"]

built up in the action of the constitutive explication of empathy as demonstrating not only a co-constituting but also a *co-phenomenologizing* Other. It is a special, far-reaching problem to follow this intersubjective construction of the intersubjectivity of transcendental knowledge. Once this is done, then also the properly *transcendental intersubjectivity* of phenomenologizing can be distinguished with "canonic" evidentness from its [446]*mundane appearance*.

A further question, intimately connected with this distinction, is that concerning the sense of the *communicative* [447]*givenness of the objectivation* of phenomenologizing. Here inquiry is made not into the transcendental intersubjectivity structures of phenomenological cognition, nor simply its mundane appearance—as it might well at first seem. Transcendental outward expression is a *bridge* transcendental cognition itself throws over to the natural attitude,[448] *for* which it wants to express itself. Indeed, the possibility of this mediation of phenomenological cognition itself is grounded in the event that we have called the [449](non-proper) enworlding of phenomenologizing. Only because phenomenologizing is localized and temporalized in the world can it objectivate itself in the language of the natural attitude. The natural sentence that is as such enlisted in the transcendental meaning function [450]shows first of all the *mundane* "Objectivity" (intersubjective accessibility) of its natural meanings. The sense-bestowal that follows now in the situation of the explication of transcendental cognition fulfills these mundanely intersubjective meanings with an *analogized* sense that no longer has or can have this "intersubjective Objectivity." Rather, it is now only understandable at all if the one apprehending it altogether *transcends* the sphere of pregiven intersubjective Objectivity, the sphere of what is existent in a[451] worldly way, by himself performing the phenomenological reduction. Thus the objectivation of phenomenologizing that occurs in the natural attitude (by which transcen-

---

446. [Alt.] ⟨transcendental mundanization⟩

447. [Alt.] ⟨outward expression and transmission⟩ of phenomenologizing.

448. [Mg.] ⟨to the [natural attitude] transcendentally understood, at least from the side of the one outwardly expressing himself⟩

449. [Alt.] ⟨(secondary)⟩

450. [Alt.] ⟨on the one hand indicates in its essence-required doubleness of sense⟩ the *mundane* "Objectivity" (intersubjective accessibility) of its natural meanings. ⟨On the other hand,⟩ the sense-bestowal that follows now in the situation of the explication of transcendental cognition ⟨imparts to⟩ these mundanely intersubjective meanings, ⟨as stripped of their acceptedness function by the epoche,⟩ an *analogized* sense [etc.]

451. [Ins.] ⟨naive⟩

dental communication is first possible[452]) becomes the *place where the shift-over occurs* for forming the purely transcendental community of those collectively phenomenologizing.[453] It is only [454]through the *mediation of the objectivation* of phenomenological cognitions that every monad that "becomes-for-itself" can enter into community with another monad that realizes transcendental "self-consciousness." Indeed, the possibility of phenomenological objectivating is grounded in the base-level occurrence of enworlding, inasmuch as it is precisely through it that the relation of the transcendental attitude to the natural attitude becomes possible. This objectivation, however, *is not what does the enworlding*, but rather[455] is what enters the scene in the situation of mundanization as the *expression of the transcendental*. As the bridge from transcendental cognition to the natural attitude, objectivation is itself subject in turn to an *enworlding*, it passes over into appearance [*Erscheinung*]. In other words, the documentation of phenomenologizing in the natural attitude, in which it appears as a human cognitive process, also *appears* itself in the natural attitude as a process of objectivation in play merely between a *human knowing* and *its expressivity*. That is, the appearance-truth that pertains to the[456] objectivation[457] of phenomenologizing does not at all reach to the transcendentally analogizing meaning function as the proper and intrinsic essence of phenomenological objectivation, but stops short in the[458] appearance of that essence, in *mundane* meanings (which as such contain no further "phenomenological" sense at all). Here too we shall refrain from going into the problem in a more specific and differentiated way.

As clue for our inquiry into the communicative structure of phenomenologizing, what we did above was to characterize the corresponding structure of a wordly science in respect to three things: 1) the intersubjective accessibility of the object of a science (or of the cognition and truth that refer to it);

---

452. [Ins.] ⟨as something further⟩

453. [Angle brackets around this sentence, to which Mg.] ⟨Communication functions differently for the naive reader than for the one already reading as a phenomenologist.⟩

454. [Alt.] through ⟨the mediation of the common environing world as common transcendental correlate and in unity with it through⟩ the *mediation of the objectivation* of phenomenological cognitions ⟨(they appear localized in man)⟩ that every monad [etc.]

455. [Ins.] ⟨that?⟩

456. [Ins.] ⟨linguistic⟩

457. [Mg.] ⟨the natural meaning⟩

458. [Ins.] ⟨outward⟩

2) the intersubjective accessibility of the[459] objectivation of scientific cognitions; 3) the relationship of any worldly science to the existential phenomena
of *finitude and transitoriness*, which are documented in the historical handing
down of traditions (every science related in its development to the intersubjective generative historicality of human life!). We have outlined how to pose
the question concerning phenomenologizing in regard to the first two of
these points and indicated the most general problems—even if quite vaguely.
There still remains for us now the question of whether and how *phenomenologizing* relates to *historicality*. Is a "canonic" distinction between appearance-
truths and transcendental truths necessary here too? As indisputably true as
we must allow it that man is the subject of phenomenologizing, if we also take
this as a mere "appearance-truth," just as indisputable is the recognition that
phenomenologizing enters the scene *in world-time*, that it has ahead of itself
world-time yet to come as the future horizon of its further scientific development; and, in addition, that not only does it proceed in world-time and, perhaps, will continue in time to come, but above all it has arisen in a particular
historical situation and therefore is conditioned in the context of cultural history
[*Geistesgeschichte*]. This truth, however, does not pertain to phenomenologizing in its proper transcendental content, but only the *mundane appearance* of that
content. The non-proper enworlding of phenomenologizing as the process of
its being placed in the natural attitude is also what *places it in the order of the historicity of human spirit* [*in die Historizität des menschlichen Geistes*]: it appears in cultural
history [*Geistesgeschichte*]. The phenomenological reduction, however, when it
is actually performed, gives us insight into the principle that *mundane history* is
constituted in a transcendental, intermonadic sense-bestowal, just as is the world
as a whole; that mundane history is nothing other than the universal *constituted
time-form* for constituted beings; that it is fundamentally *something constituted in
end-constitution*, just as they are. Still, the naiveté of the natural attitude consists
precisely in this: unconsciously to consider as absolutized the "stratum" of *those
things which are constituted in end-constitution*, the transcendental *surface*, and to be
"blind" to the *dimension of the constitutive performances* from which the "world" proceeds. By the phenomenological reduction mundane temporality becomes evident as a time constituted in transcendental processes of temporalization, and
mundane historicity as a *constitutive result*. Just as in general the existent, by its
constitutive interpretation as the "abstract" stratum of that which is end-
constituted, comes to be "filled out" in full transcendental "concreteness" by
the exhibiting of the performances and performance products that constitu-

---

459. [Ins.] ⟨linguistic⟩

tively construct it, so also *mundane time-events*, which in their totality make up worldly history, get *transcendentally interpreted* and thereby finally clarified. In worldly cultural history we, under the spell of the prejudices of the natural attitude, become familiar with motivation contexts in human cognition which satisfy the demands of the intelligibility expected of worldly science, but which in no way are "philosophically" adequate. It is through the *transcendental interpretation of history*, in regress back to the constitutive processes that construct it, that the *destinies of spirit* in this world first gain a *transcendental-rational* "sense" which can be demonstrated. The phenomenological reduction thus [460]comes to *lay the foundation for the* "philosophy of history." In it is achieved the *immense breakthrough from* constituted "history" (as an [461]abstract moment) *into* the *transcendental-concrete history of world constitution*[462]. It means therefore the *end* of captivation in world history, it means bringing world history into constituting *intermonadic historicity [Historizität]*.[463]

[464]But just as the action of reductively transcending the world *falls back into the world* [465]as "appearance"—precisely by non-proper enworlding—so also the *breakout from captivation* in "abstract" world-history falls back *again into world history*:[466] phenomenologizing "appears"[467] in a particular historical situation within western cultural history. The transcendental thematizing of the constitution of world history is itself[468] *enclosed and swept along* by constituting life, it is enworlded within the constituted context of time. But just as the phenomenological reduction is *not within reach of* an "anthropological-existential" characterization (and critique), phenomenologizing in itself is as little able to be explicated by "historicizing" interpretations.[469] It is not a "piece of philos-

---

460. [Alt.] comes to ⟨inaugurate for the first time a proper⟩ *"philosophy of history."*
461. [Quotation marks around "abstract"]
462. [Sup.] ⟨and of absolute concrete subjectivity.⟩
463. [Sup.] ⟨as transcendental, absolute history [*Historie*].⟩
464. [On the next two paragraphs, see Appendix IX.]
465. [Alt.] as ⟨transcendental phenomenon⟩—precisely by ⟨transcendentally secondary⟩ enworlding [etc.] [To which Mg.] ⟨in a secondary mundanization necessitated by essence lies back into the already previously constituted world⟩
466. [Mg.] ⟨but transcendentally understood⟩ [world history]
467. [Ins.] ⟨in worldly fashion⟩
468. [Ins.] ⟨in a secondary concomitant constitution⟩
469. [Mg.] ⟨The subsequent existential function of phenomenology—the transcendental problem of existence [*Existenz*]—enters the scene in phenomenology as a higher-level problem. What must be avoided in the whole presentation is for things to look as if the mundanization of phenomenology, as well as the continual psychol-

ogization of transcendental performances that phenomenologize and get phenomenologically displayed, were an evil thing that only occasioned errors and misunderstandings. [But] man, breaking through his humanity in transcendental cognition, achieves thereby the possibility of a new, higher humanity. In it he shows
himself as transcendental ego, which has objectivated itself as man and has moved
out of the particular attitude of transcendental blindness into transcendental self-
cognition; further, that, necessarily moving at the same time in this higher station, he
must find every acquisition made into something human [vermenschlicht], historically
objectivated. Now he gains the possibility of a new mundane being [Dasein] in transcendental self-cognition, everything transcendental projected back into mundaneness and determining worldly life in this new mundaneness. But this moving
mundaneness that again and again takes up into itself whatever is newly cognized
transcendentally is always understood as continually arising out of secondary constitution. The life of man in transcendentally clarified humanity is basically different
from naive natural life, which for the serious phenomenologist just ought not really
to be put forth any more. His life is a new life, and to this newness belongs the change
in transcendental attitudes, namely, in the sense of thematic directions within transcendentality. His "return into the natural attitude" is a thematizing of the world,
which for him is a correlate. He holds himself to this correlate, which has the cognitive sense "correlate" only for him in his transcendental self-consciousness. And for
him the world itself now receives a new dimension in the transcendental which flows
into it. But he also has transcendental knowledge of fundamental happening, of the
event of his absolute transcendental historicity, of the intrusion of the phenomenological reduction and the collapse of the world in its originally naive sense, the world
into which the disclosed transcendental has flowed and flows on further.

Precisely thereby the world for him is not merely world in the ordinary sense (and
even that of positive science) plus a transcendental explanation; rather, it is for him a
world of new worldly sense, and his life in the world and in community with other men
has a new worldly style, it gives him as man in the world new tasks.

(Accordingly, the problem of transcendental misunderstandings stands in another order,
misunderstandings, e.g., on the part of readers of transcendental writings who just do
not stand in the transcendental attitude, but also those who already "have understood
something" but do not know how to "hold on to it" (here the real questions).)

In the new world of the phenomenologist there are his fellow men, that is, in part
phenomenologically naive men with their transcendentally concealed natural world,
in part phenomenologists. Here we have the problems: 1) Phenomenologists in intercourse with one another, as phenomenologizing with others, practicing criticism of one
another, etc. Intersubjective phenomenology as science for all who might possibly
phenomenologize. What is their attitudinal stance? They speak to one another, they
live in the new world as a common "new" world (now only as theoretically new men), and
phenomenology is the ideal structure in their new world. 2) Phenomenologists in intercourse with non-phenomenologists, guiding them to the phenomenological reduction and

ophy" [*"Philosophem"*] within the world historically, having arisen in human cultural history. It is only this kind of thing [470]*in its appearance*. All previous philosophies stand basically in the horizon of the [471]natural attitude, i.e., they conceive their own historicality [*Geschichtlichkeit*] only as *worldly historicity [Historizität]*; the transcendental dimension of history is closed to them and unknown. If, now, phenomenologizing, become worldly appearance, enters the scene of mundane cultural history, [472]it obviously also continues in world time, not, however, in that time as a time *still closed off* to transcendental horizons of constitution, but as "appearance" it proceeds in *already transcendentally interpreted* world time. The "transparency" of its appearance in world time not only gives the one understanding it an unhindered view into the *transcendental procedural temporality* of phenomenologizing and into the constitutive processes of temporalization that underlie mundane appearance itself, but it also allows one to recognize that with the *phenomenological opening up* of the[473] history of constitution (in which world history lies only as a "stratum" constituted in end-constitution) *this history* [i.e., of constitution] has *itself entered a new stage*. The "Eon" in which transcendental subjectivity is outside itself [*Aussersichsein*] is at an end. The *history of its "anonymity"* closes and terminates with the phenomenological reduction, and enters the "age" of the *transcendental process* of coming-to-oneself [*Zusichselbstkommen*]. If one has grasped the proper transcendental truth concerning phenomenologizing—which is only thus indicated—(i.e., has performed the reduction), then once and for all it is seen that a comparison of phenomenologizing with any form of philosophizing that has arisen *in* the natural attitude is in principle false. Only its [474]appearance can be placed

---

into following and understanding phenomenology. From the side of the phenomenologist: the understanding of the natural attitude, of the natural naive world, the naiveté of which he nevertheless can only have by abstraction (one quite other than the blindness of the naive man), in like manner the understanding of his fellow men who do not understand, and that they take him and his claim of a wisdom superior to the world to be folly. 2a) Phenomenologists in intercourse with non-phenomenologists in daily life—similar to scientists with non-scientists, etc.⟩

470. [Alt.] in its ⟨secondary enworlding⟩

471. [Alt.] ⟨naive-⟩natural

472. [Alt.] it obviously also continues ⟨natural history [*Historie*];⟩ however, ⟨it does not continue it⟩ as a ⟨history⟩ *still closed off* to transcendental horizons of constitution⟨.⟩ ⟨Rather⟩ as "appearance" it proceeds [etc.]

473. [Ins.] ⟨transcendental⟩

474. [Alt.] ⟨worldly outward expression⟩

in this comparison, and then only so long as one is incapable of looking through it as appearance.[475]

But it is still an open question how phenomenologizing as appearance in the world, and that means as appearance *in worldly history*, is related to the transitoriness of the appearing "phenomenologizing" subject, and thereby to the forms of historical tradition. This question first of all has nothing to do with how phenomenologizing, which represents an egological cognitive habituality, may continue[476] in a transcendental historical monadic tradition; but it is a problem that relates to the *objectivation of phenomenologizing*. Objectivation is the *outward expression* of phenomenological cognitions [477]*into and for* the natural attitude. It participates, in a way difficult to describe, in [both] the transcendental and the natural attitudes: in the transcendental attitude insofar as it objectivates *transcendental* cognitions, i.e., with respect to their "what"; in the natural attitude by the "how" of its objectivating: natural concepts, language, etc., and then, above all, by its relationship to the existential structures of the appearing phenomenological subject. For the sake of the objectivation of phenomenologizing[478] for the natural attitude[479]—even though the one doing the objectivation is coming from the transcendental attitude—the mundane structures of finitude and transitoriness in the appearing subject are taken seriously, altogether despite their transcendental interpretation, in a way that has a certain *similarity* to *pre-phenomenological naiveté*. *Phenomenologizing objectivates* itself *into* a "*phenomenology*" that expresses itself in its worldly situation of appearance. This "phenomenology" is wholly determined by *worldly* motivations (which to be sure undergo in this phenomenology their transcendental clarification[480]); the phenomenological cognizer philosophizes as a functionary of the human community, he fits himself into the human generative habituality of philosophizing, he transmits, lectures, publishes, etc.[481]

---

475. [Mg.] ⟨[as] secondary transcendental enworlding? But even that is dubious.⟩

476. [Here Husserl inserts a reflexive pronoun needed grammatically in the German but not in the English.—Tr.]

477. [Alt.] ⟨in⟩ [Husserl's alteration makes the preposition one indicating place within rather than movement into.—Tr.]

478. [Ins.] ⟨in the human world⟩

479. [Mg.] ⟨of others?⟩

480. [Mg.] ⟨yes, precisely⟩

481. [Mg.] ⟨The world and mankind and we in it—all that is still actuality in the transcendental universe of being in its transcendentally true sense of being.⟩

C) The concept of "science"

The general question that guides our inquiry into phenomenologizing as an action of *"making into a science"* can receive its final precision only in the determination of the concept of "science." By that, however, is in no way meant a phenomenological clarification of what we generally understand by "science," namely, the mundane idea of science; rather, what is in question is the concept of science that is actualized *in phenomenologizing* itself. That can *never* be grasped by taking one's lead from the[482] worldly concept of science. The Idea of phenomenological science altogether *transcends* all known notions of science or any that are ever possible in the natural attitude. [483]Mundane sciences are one and all *sciences of that which is existent;* phenomenological science refers to the constitutive *becoming of the existent.*

The general characterization that we have outlined for worldly science[484] with regard to its "who," its potentiality, and its communication had only "negative" value for first indicating the phenomenological concept of science, the negative value, namely, of being the background against which something else could stand out. It yielded nothing more than the point that the corresponding structures in phenomenologizing are from beginning to end *entirely* "*different.*" And yet setting things into this relationship was not in vain. We came to see that a kinship in structure holds between the *mundane appearance* of phenomenologizing and [485]*mundane science.* [486]Now because appearance is itself necessarily constituted in transcendental sense-bestowal and first creates the possibility that phenomenologizing be able to express itself for the natural attitude, appearance forms precisely a *moment* in the phenomenological concept

---

482. [Ins.] ⟨natural⟩

483. [Alt.] Mundane sciences are one and all *sciences of* ⟨"⟩ *that which is existent,*⟨"⟩ ⟨of which the concept of totality, of all-inclusive unity, is the world⟩; phenomenological science refers to the constitutive ⟨"⟩*becoming*⟨"⟩ *of the existent* ⟨and thereby of its being in the absolute concreteness of this becoming, of which the all-inclusively unitary concept of being is transcendental all-inclusive unity.⟩ [Quotation marks by Husserl in both instances here.]

484. [Ins.] ⟨in naive positivity⟩

485. [Alt.] ⟨naive-⟩*mundane*

486. [Alt.] Now because ⟨self-presentation-as-worldly⟩ is itself necessarily constituted in transcendental sense-bestowal and first creates the possibility that phenomenologizing be able to express itself for the natural attitude, ⟨self-presentation-as-worldly⟩ forms [etc.]

of science. In no way is it *alone* transcendental truths regarding phenomenologizing that contain the integral elements of the phenomenological concept
of truth. Rather, this concept is determined [487]precisely by way of the *mundane
appearance* of phenomenologizing. In the opposition and "canonic" distinction
between proper transcendental truths and mere appearance-truths, in this antithetic delimitation, we are working *within* the phenomenological concept of
truth, which is nothing other than the *"synthetic" unity of antithetic determinations.*[488] But the "synthesis" lying before us here is not a "sublation" of one-sided
truths in a higher truth that includes them as moments. Appearance-truth does
not stand, so to speak, with equal rights alongside transcendental truth, but in
the final analysis is a *seeming truth [Scheinwahrheit]*[489] which is always "transparent" for him who philosophizes—a seeming truth which of course itself rests
upon a transcendental sense-bestowal. And inasmuch as a seeming truth is
transparent not only as to the *transcendental nature of phenomenologizing*, hidden by
the appearance, but also as to the *"constitution"* (enworlding) that underlies it,
seeming truth is itself "sublated" in transcendental truth—for the one philosophizing.

In what sense, now, is the phenomenological concept of science the "synthetic uniting" of the mutually opposed appearance-truths and transcendental truths, with respect to phenomenologizing? The answer is that in the
strictest sense the synthesis here is not between *truths that are distinct from one another*, but rather between the *transcendental characterization* of phenomenologizing *and the reference to a transcendental condition* for phenomenologizing that
documents itself in "appearance-truths." Or, otherwise formulated: the *mundane situation* in which phenomenologizing enters the scene as "phenomenological philosophy" (and which is expressed in appearance-truths) is *in no way
irrelevant* for framing the phenomenological concept of science, but represents

---

487. [Alt.] ⟨only aporetically⟩

488. [Mg.] ⟨This is surely correct: In the world, which [is] perpetually a stratum
of "things existent," which in its being originally relates to a natural naiveté—even after this naiveté has become transcendentally intelligible—, constitutive cognition,
the world too as clarified phenomenon, have no business. The enworlding of all transcendental cognition and of things transcendentally existent, e.g., even monads (not
souls), is in this sense non-proper enworlding, namely, it yields nothing that is a
worldly existent.⟩

489. [Mg.] ⟨That rubs me the wrong way! Spatiotemporal localization that is no
seeming, but has a sense that transcends all worldly localization, [which is] that of the
worldly existent.⟩

a moment integral to it. Of course, we know that as a constitutive result it it-self rests upon transcendental performances (which we named secondary[490] enworlding); but it looked as if the enworlding of phenomenologizing were only a matter of its getting into a sympathetic involvement which was, so to speak, external to itself, which did not give it in itself any further determina-tion, an involvement, that is, with the constitutive world-aiming life-tendency of transcendental subjectivity. Even if this *enworlding* and *"masking"*[491] of the transcendental occurrence in which constituting subjectivity *"comes-to-itself"* is unavoidable in the cognitive performance of the phenomenologizing on-looker, since it arises itself from *constitutive sources*, nonetheless it may clearly be harmless and safe for the one philosophizing, that is, for one who sees through the "appearance."[492] And precisely because by his superior transcen-dental insight he remains protected from the temptation to take the appear-ance as the thing itself, can he not grasp the proper transcendental concept of science in diligently *turning away from* all appearance-truths?

The question now has to be raised whether, then, the enworlding is actu-ally an external and outward occurrence that is extrinsic to the essence of phe-nomenologizing itself, or whether it [i.e., the occurrence of enworlding] is itself determined *essentially* by that [i.e., by what phenomenologizing essen-tially is].mm We find the answer to this question in the discussion of the pe-culiar relationships between the natural and the transcendental attitudes, or, more exactly put, between the two *transcendental modes of existence [Existenzweisen]* of world-constituting subjectivity: mere "being-in-itself" ["*Ansichsein*"] (self-forgetfulness, [493]sleep) and "being-for-itself" ["*Fürsichsein*"] (self-awareness, [494]wakefulness) on the part of transcendental life. In the first place, the nat-ural attitude is the *presupposition of all phenomenological knowing*, inasmuch as phe-nomenological cognition is only possible if world-constitution has already happened, precisely in the "condition of self-forgetfullness." In other words, the *coming-to-itself* of transcendental subjectivity *presupposes its antecedent "being-outside-itself."* What is designated here is not a "logical" necessity derived ana-lytically from the concept of coming-to-itself, but a *transcendental necessity* that is prior to any logical conception. The conditioning of the "transcendental at-

490. [Mg.] ⟨good⟩

491. [Mg.] ⟨Localization, seeming realization—if one is not being careful⟩

492. [Mg.] ⟨Nothing can be dangerous for someone who actually lives and theo-rizes in reduction—he only has to be consistent.⟩

493. [Ins.] ⟨quasi-⟩sleep

494. [Ins.] ⟨quasi-⟩wakefulness

titude" by the transcendental mode of existence [*Existenzmodus*], "natural attitude," consists not only in the fact that constituting life, as the theme and substratum of philosophical cognition, must have proceeded in naiveté before it
could have been "illuminated for itself" precisely by the phenomenological reduction and the regressive inquiry into constitution that was therein made
possible; but beyond this it lies in the way *phenomenological cognition has to rely
upon the mundane situation of outward manifestation*. This means that all transcendental self-cognition, which is realized in regressive inquiry into constitution,
does not merely move out from the natural attitude[495] but *remains also referred
back to it.*

But the sense of this return-referral must be rightly understood and formulated. Since phenomenological cognition represents precisely the *annulment
[Aufhebung]* of the captivation and naiveté that comprise the *closure of the natural
attitude* against the transcendental dimension of origin, it cannot be referred
back to the natural attitude that still rests in its specific "naiveté," but only to
the natural attitude that is *transcendentally interpreted*, i.e, to [496]the transcendental situation of *end-constitutedness*. All regressive inquiry into constitution starts
off necessarily in the sphere of constitutive "end-products." But the phenom-
enological-theoretical identifying of deeper-lying, constitutively founding
strata, of the manifold constituting [497]processes and the formations that always appear in them (that are "pre-existent" ["*vor-seienden*"]), etc., is—despite
their evident givenness—*not an actual move back* by the one phenomenologizing into these earlier strata of constitution and a *move out of* the constituted
"end-stratum." Rather, phenomenologizing analyzes these deeper strata of
transcendental constitution always in the *end-stratum as horizon for regressive inquiry*: by starting out from the transcendentally explicated situation of the natural attitude. Thus all thematic cognitions in the end refer back to that as the
continual situation of the one phenomenologizing. What this means now is
that the knowing in which becoming-for-itself is fashioned for transcendental subjectivity necessarily refers in itself to a transcendental situation that is
exhibited and illuminated by this very knowing as the *situation of "being outside
itself"* on the part of constituting subjectivity.

If we get completely clear about the state of affairs thus indicated, then we
at once reach the insight that *in appearance-truths* concerning phenomenologizing, and thus in its characterizations in the natural attitude, there are quite

---

495. [Ins.] ⟨(as historical situation)⟩
496. [Alt.] the transcendental⟨ly disclosed⟩
497. [Quotation marks around "processes"]

definite *transcendental truths* implied [498]that come to light precisely by the transcendental interpretation of "appearance." [499]In other words, the determination of phenomenologizing that would be *only* transcendental in completely *turning away* from all appearance-truths or their transcendental interpretation does not suffice for exposition of the phenomenological concept of science. For the *appearance* of phenomenologizing is not a covering up[500] and concealing of it in a way extrinsic to its essence, a concealment which the specific nature of the knowing that is realized in phenomenologizing would not later touch upon; [501]but rather this appearance is the result of the transcendental *constitution of the situation of knowing* [Wissen], *of the situation of science* [Wissenschaft], in which situation phenomenologizing *starts off, proceeds, and remains.* The "self-consciousness" of transcendental subjectivity is in principle not possible as an action in which constitution-performing life stays with itself [Bei-sich-sein] at the deepest layers of constitution, but takes place *in the transcendental stratum of end-constitutedness.* In other words, transcendental subjectivity *becomes for-itself* in the constitutive dimension of *"being-outside-itself"*—to be sure, transcendentally elucidated.[502] Once we have gained full insight into these linkages, we shall also understand the character of the above mentioned *"synthesis"* between proper transcendental truths and appearance-truths, which is supposed to comprise precisely the phenomenological concept of science. We will then see that this synthesis presents the *unification* of the *transcendental* truths about

---

498. [Ins.] that ⟨only⟩ come to light ⟨explicitly⟩ precisely by [etc.]

499. [Alt.] In other words, the determination of phenomenologizing that would be *only* transcendental in completely *turning away* from all appearance-truths or their transcendental interpretation ⟨is a sheer abstraction and⟩ does not suffice [etc.] [To which Mg.] ⟨It is a sheer abstraction. The continual secondary self-enworlding of the transcendental belongs to the new constitution that is put into action by the transcendental reduction under the presupposition of and with the reversing of the earlier naive constitution. Whether we look at it or not, the higher constitution of transcendentality in being is at the same time referred back to itself in the form of a transcendental localization in the world. That already concerns the lower stratum of transcendental experience and in addition of course the upper stratum of transcendental theoretical assertion and again its communicative transmission from the transcendental ego to others, etc., and so the transcendental intersubjectivity of science.⟩

500. [Mg.] ⟨really no covering up at all⟩

501. [Alt.] but rather this appearance is the result of the transcendental *constitution of the situation of knowing, of the situation of* ⟨natural-worldly experience and theoretical⟩ *science* [etc.]

502. [Mg.] ⟨good⟩

phenomenologizing, as those truths stand out in relief against appearance-truths, with the *transcendental interpretation of appearance-truths*, as truths about the *constitutedness of the transcendental situation of self-elucidation.*

[503]Now, how can the phenomenological concept of science be set off against the mundane? [504]Do we not find also in worldly science relatedness to the transcendental[505] situation in which constituting[506] subjectivity "is outside itself," and to the stratum of end-constitutedness? Of course—but here the relation to the natural attitude is in principle different from that proper to phenomenologizing.[507] Whereas phenomenologizing recognizes the natural attitude precisely *as* a transcendental situation and in constitutive analysis gives the world its proper identity *as the dimension of "end-constitutedness,"* and whereas it thus knows about the "being-outside-itself" of transcendental subjectivity as the *habituality of self-objectivation* (in the world) formed in its constitutive move of going-outside-itself,[nn] in natural mundane science all this is out of the question. Only *as phenomenologist*—in the phenomenological explication of worldly knowing and of the science that arises out of it—do I recognize its captivation in the natural attitude, do I recognize its necessary relatedness to "the existent" as "that which is constituted in end-constitution." As worldly scientist, however, *I know nothing* of my naiveté and dogmatic restriction[508], which consists not only in the fact that what I do, and the only thing I can do, is to relate thematically to an "abstract" stratum, the world (the totality of constituted end-products), but also and above all in the *manner of this knowing.* Caught in the natural attitude, I have good reason, by formalizing the mundane sciences given me, to construct [509]the formal Idea of "science as such." Without now going into this universal Idea of science and displaying the mundane "prejudices" implied in it, we can still bring out *two main characteristics* of the mundane Idea of science. First: theoretical cognition is cognition of [510]something existent; all science [*Wissenschaft*] is a systematically unified

---

503. [Alt.] ⟨Accordingly⟩

504. [Alt.] ⟨If we already *know* of the transcendental, then we can *also* say: A)lso in worldly science ⟨there is⟩ relatedness to [etc.]

505. [Question mark over "transcendental." to which Mg.] ⟨I do not understand.⟩

506. [Question mark over "constituting." To which, lightly erased, Mg.] ⟨thinking while experiencing⟩

507. [Mg.] ⟨precisely⟩

508. [Sup.] ⟨(both accordingly transcendental concepts to be first understood by phenomenology)⟩

509. [Alt.] the ⟨logical⟩ formal Idea of "science as such"⟨, and thus logic.⟩

510. [Quotation marks around "something existent"]

knowing [*Wissen*] of that which is existent or of the universal structural styles of that which is existent.[511] Not only is the object of science "existent," but the subject also is always "existent" (whether it is a matter of a single or a collective subject). To cognize and ultimately to do science is a particular *existent behavior on the part of the existent subject toward the existent object.* Second: *cognition and object* are *separated* by the cognitive relation. All cognition is *cognition about* ____. If the one cognizing becomes object to himself (reflection), then we divide the cognized, objectified "self" from the cognitively functioning "self."[512] In other words, the *opposition of cognition and object,* of *science and region,* belongs essentially to the natural Idea of knowing [*Wissen*] and science [*Wissenschaft*]. Not least of all, the *finiteness of cognition* belonging to the natural attitude consists in an intrinsic opposition and dissociation in the mundane cognitive relationship (cognizing and its theme) which represents a *mutual delimitation* of the relata themselves. The *phenomenological* concept of science, and thus the characterization of what is properly specific to the knowing that results from the phenomenological reduction cannot be subsumed under the *general concept of science* that arises from the formalization of mundane science. By performing the reduction we altogether *transcend* the universal situation in which all worldly knowing as a whole has its *home and origin, captivation* in the natural attitude; we realize a comprehending grasp, a cognizing, a knowing, [513]and a science of a quite new kind, of a new, hitherto unimaginable radicality. We must never hope, by however extreme a formalization of the worldly concept of science, to gain the *higher order concept* which comprehends within itself mundane as well as transcendental science. It is not through a *formalization* but only by a *thematic reduction of the mundane Idea of knowing and science* that we can push on to an understanding of the phenomenological concept of science. (Thus in the phenomenological reduction is included not only the many individual reductions of the factual world to its transcendental constitution (egological-primordial and intersubjective reductions), not only the reduction of world-possibilities to the constitution of world-style, not only the reduction of the Idea of being and of ontic language, but also the reduction of the worldly Idea of knowing and science!) The phenomenological reduction

---

511. [Mg.] ⟨Something existent in the historically universal sense has its concept of the all-inclusive, its totality concept, under the title, world.⟩

512. [Sup.] ⟨for which at the same time anyone else can step in.⟩ [To which Mg.] ⟨My self as existent is an identical in-itself for all cognizers—humans.⟩

513. [Alt.] and a science of a ⟨quite⟩ new, hitherto unimaginable ⟨kind and⟩ radicality.

opens up not only a *new dimension of "being"* but also a *new dimension of knowing and science.* And just as mundane being does not lie "outside" transcendental being, but only represents a hitherto absolutized "stratum" of the latter, so also the mundane concept of science is contained in the *transcendental* concept of science: *"finite" knowing* is an *abstract moment in "infinite,"* i.e., transcendental, knowing. This is shown, for example, in the fact that the transcendental clarification of the world in no way cancels and discredits mundane cognitions and sciences, but rather comprehends them as "abstract" knowledge-moments in transcendental knowing, moments which can first come to be fully understood and to have their genuine sense worked out through the "all-sided" (concrete) exhibiting of the constitutive truths that precede and found all worldly cognitions. In other words, mundane cognition, mundane science, the mundane Idea of science as such, is a counterconcept to transcendental science only in the *absolutized* form in which mundane science enters the scene in the natural attitude. Rightly understood, that is, *referred to the acceptedness situation constituted in end-constitution,* mundane cognition itself forms but *one* structural moment in the whole of the *system of transcendental truth.*

The reduction of the worldly Idea of knowing and science (with its home in the captivation of the natural attitude) represents a large and comprehensive *theme for the transcendental theory of method.* In the pursuit of our intention to outline only the most general Idea of a transcendental theory of method, we cannot carry out the requisite reflections, we cannot actually present the concept of phenomenological science in its internal structure. Only by way of anticipatory *preliminary indication* do we wish to get in sight that to which a transcendental reduction of the Idea of science may lead. What finally happens then in this "reduction" is nothing other than *laying the foundation for the phenomenological concept of science* in its determination as *"absolute science."*

In what sense is phenomenological science characterized in a *decisive sense* by the attribute, absolute? It is not by a return to any of the usual meanings of this term,[514] nor to the historical echoes given with it, that we can understand the sense of this characterization, but only in the express adoption of the *phenomenological* concept of "absolute." For that some preparation is needed. We first disconnect the undeterminate, fluctuating, and obscure concepts of "absolute" that are supposed to indicate in some way a special rank, a certain degree of knowing. We also repudiate the popular conception of "absolute," expressed in the phrases "absolute art," "absolute religion," etc., and properly

---

514. [Mg.] ⟨But it is! By the analogy drawn from what natural science should do. See below.⟩

meaning only a mode of exclusivity for existence [*Dasein*] lived within those activities; and we do the same with all *"metaphysical" concepts of "absolute"* that suggest themselves from the history of philosophy. (We leave open, however, the *problem* of the extent to which such traditional ways of framing the concept in question stand in immediate proximity to the phenomenological sense of this term.)

The phenomenological clarification of the attribute "absolute" applied to phenomenological science with the intention of centrally characterizing it must begin with the determination of the nominal concept, therefore with an explication of the *concept of the "Absolute."* We must from the first be explicit and firm about intending thereby a *transcendental* concept, which we can only designate by a specific "analogization" that *makes use of a mundane concept.* To be able to be enlisted in the analogy-function at all, the mundane concept must stand in a definite affinity to the *transcendental* meaning indicated by it. To begin with, the mundane concept of "absolute" is a *counterconcept to "relative"* and means a *mode of being,* namely, being as non-relative, self-sufficient substance (οὐσία). Against the non-self-sufficient, relational being of accidents, which are relative precisely to the being of substance, this latter is itself the non-relative, the self-supported, the bearer of all relativities. Strictly taken, however, a single substance may well be non-relative as against its accidental determinations, but is not unqualifiedly non-relative. Every substance as an individual existent is *in the universal being-complex of the world,* every substance is linked with every substance in the correlativity of the *"commercium."* It is with a certain right, now, that, against the relative being of individual substances, we can designate the *being of the world* itself as *"absolute,"* and the world as the "Absolute" (the absolutely existent). Against this *mundane-ontological* concept of the Absolute, now, we pose the transcendental concept, and in such a way that what we do is precisely to designate and *analogically* indicate the latter with the mundane expression. In this indication by analogy, however, there is included precisely a *reductive transformation* of the mundane sense of absolute and of the Absolute. As long as we stand in the natural attitude, the world rightly holds for us as the all-inclusive unity of that which is existent, as the absolutely existent in which every individual existent is contained and outside of which there is and can be nothing. In performing the phenomenological reduction, however, we recognize that what we have taken to be the non-relational and ultimately self-sufficient totality of that which is existent represents in truth *only an abstract stratum* in constitutive becoming, that the universe of the existent, the world, is only a *relative "universe"* which in itself refers back to transcendental constituting subjectivity. At the same time we understand that this "relativity" must not be construed as a relationship between two "substances" (as if here

stood the world as formed something, there subjectivity as constituting, forming agent), but as a relation in play *within* transcendental life itself. The world
becomes understandable as the *sum total of ends* in the constitutive life-processes
of transcendental subjectivity; it therefore does not lie *outside* this life itself.
Furthermore, we recognize that the Idea of an "outside" that would lie beyond
constitutive becoming is in principle altogether meaningless; that world-
constitution, in which transcendental subjectivity *and* the world lie as the
poles of the "whence" and of the "whither," is the universe that is fundamentally ultimate and no longer cognizable as "relative."

Is now this *"universe of constitution"* the *Absolute* in the phenomenological
sense? That cannot simply be answered in the affirmative. We must rather
make an essential distinction. *Before* the phenomenological reduction transcendental world-constitution (transcendental subjectivity "unconscious" of
itself and at one with the world that is formed in its anonymous performance)
is the "Absolute" in phenomenological understanding. *After* the reduction,
however, constitutive "cosmogony" (world-constitution) can no longer *alone*
be designated as the Absolute. Rather, the Absolute is precisely the *unity* of
transcendental *constitution* and the transcendental process of *phenomenologizing.*
That is, the Absolute is the overarching total unity of transcendental life as a
whole, which in itself is articulated into opposites. This division between constituting and phenomenologizing life determines now the concept of the Absolute: the Absolute is the synthetic unity of antithetic moments.

However, not only is the Absolute, when it has reached "self-consciousness," determined by a certain internal oppositeness, but so also is the
Absolute when—before the reduction—it is *"existent in itself."* Whereas the
mundane concept of "Absolute" is an *ontological* concept, i.e., means a totality
of that which is *existent*[515], the phenomenological concept of the Absolute can
be characterized as *non-ontological,* i.e., it does *not* mean a *totality of that which is
existent*[516]. The reduction is not simply the unlocking of a hitherto concealed
larger complex of being, in which the previously meant totality, world, is set
as bounded and relative; it is not that "transcendental being" is only more comprehensive, but otherwise is "existent" in the same sense. The natural attitude
is "relativized" by the phenomenological reduction not by way of a de-
restricting of the region of being, but by way of a *constitutive de-restricting:*[oo]
Through the recognition that something "existent" has the constitutive rank
of end-product, of result, the universal horizon of *all being* (the world) is set

---

    515. [Ins.] ⟨in itself⟩
    516. [Ins.] ⟨in itself⟩

into the *universal context of world-constitution*. In other words, the Absolute is not, so to say, a *homogeneous* universal unity of that which is existent (analogous to the world), but precisely the comprehensive unity of *the existent as such and the pre-existent [Vor-seiendem]* (of *mundane and "transcendental"* being), of *world and world-origin*. It thus embraces within itself "opposites" that are *not opposites of being*, and is in a non-ontic sense the *"coincidentia oppositorum."* (This is, of course, not meant in some "mystical" sense, but aims at the unity in opposites that cannot be grasped with the categories of formal logic—which ultimately is a *logic of being*.)

The concept of the Absolute thus indicated seems to be *identical* with the concept of the "transcendental" so far used. This is also in a certain sense correct. Nevertheless it is with the concept of the Absolute that central structures of the constitutive becoming of the world first came into view. First of all the expression "transcendental" designates the constituting subjectivity that is *disclosed in transcending the world* (by the phenomenological reduction)—*in antithesis to the world*, or, respectively, to the natural attitude. It is indeed from the beginning a thematic designation, yet one that has arisen by transference of a *direction-giving concept* to that which is accessible in the direction thus indicated. When, then, *after* the constitutive interpretation of the world we also designate the world itself as transcendental, the *original directional sense* still resonates in this expression; and therein is to be seen a source of misleading interpretation. If, therefore, the term "transcendental" is primarily an *oppositional concept [Gegenbegriff]*, which, used thematically, means precisely the transcendental-constituting life that is, in a certain sense, *removed* from the world (of the natural attitude) and *set up* [517]*over against* it *[entgegengesetzt]*, then in contrast the *concept of the Absolute* is an all-embracing *inclusional concept [ein universaler In-Begriff]*. An essential problematic of the transcendental theory of method is redrawn by the task of *methodically unfolding the concept of the Absolute* and bringing the wealth of its inner moments to presentation. A few indications will have to suffice as a *preliminary notice*.

The determination of the Absolute given above as the synthetic unity of the world and the transcendental subjectivity that constitutes it is indeed not incorrect in this formal generality, but it needs to be put still more exactly; at the least the *problems* given with it must become clear in their most general outlines. The *world* as the total unity of the really existent, boundlessly open in space and time, with the whole immensity of nature filling it, with all the plan-

---

517. [Mg. at top of the MSS page, which corresponds to this point] ⟨[142–159] October 21, 1932⟩

ets, Milky Ways, and solar systems; with the multiplicity of existents such as
stones, plants, animals, and humans; as soil and living space for human cultures, for their rise and fall in the turn of history; as locale for final ethical and
religious decisions; the world in this manifoldness of its existence [*Dasein*]—
in a word, *being [das Sein]—is only a moment of the Absolute*. The awful tremor
everyone experiences who actually passes through the phenomenological reduction has its basis in the dismaying recognition that the inconceivably
great, boundless, vast world has the *sense of a constitutive result*, that therefore in
the *universe of constitution* it represents only a *relative "totality."* (One can characterize the phenomenological reduction directly under a *central aspect*, if one
keeps in view the "revolution in the way of thinking" that occurs with respect
to the *concept of totality*. The *de-absolutizing of the world* (which in the natural attitude is *absolutized*) signifies a more radical "Copernican revolution" than the
conversion from a geocentric to a heliocentric system—one more radical than
all philosophical revolutions in world outlook which take place on the basis
of the natural attitude.) But how is the *other moment of the Absolute*, constitution
as terminating in the world as its result, to be determined? We have in fact
already recognized in the first stage of the transcendental interpretation of
the world that what lies at hand under the title "world" is *not, so to say, a private*
(primordial) constitutive construct of the individual transcendental ego, but
the correlate of a transcendental *communalization* of the living constitutive
processes which are realized by the *transcendental community of monads*. Must we
now take *monadic intersubjectivity* as the "other moment" of the Absolute, and
conceive the latter itself as the unity of the transcendental community of monads and the world actualized in its constitutive life? Right here lies a *fundamental
problem*. Inasmuch as the phenomenological concept of the "existent-in-itself"
Absolute aims for the inclusional unity of constituting *life* and of the result proceeding from it (world), the question first has to be raised whether with the
analytical demonstration of transcendental *monadic intersubjectivity* transcendental life as a whole is already *ultimately* determined, whether in the regressive movement of "constitutive retro-inquiry," which goes from the world as
the end-stratum of constitutive becoming on through the founding stages and
strata of the constitution process, we have already reached its ultimate *depths*
when we make thematic precisely the *transcendental plurality* of constitutive-
communicating *monads*. Questions arise here concerning the *universal living
complex* of the monad community at first given as "open," concerning the transcendental meaning of the mutual intentional *implication* of monads, etc.—all
questions and problems that can only find their solution in the context of the
methodic development of the concept of the Absolute. More precisely put,
their solution is precisely this *development and presentation of the concept of the Ab-*

solute. What perhaps is shown, then, is that the *community of monads* itself represents one more *constituted stratum* in the constitutive becoming of the world. The question is therefore posed whether the *transcendental individuation of plural monads* is a final and reductively irremovable determination of constituting life. What may then be proven is whether the *Absolute* itself is *articulated in the plural* and subjected to an *individuation*—or whether all articulations are only *self-articulations within it*, and it itself can only be thought definitively under the *Idea of the "One."* As long as all these problems are still not overcome, an indicational notice about the phenomenological concept of the Absolute as the inclusional unity [*Inbegriffseinheit*] of world and world constitution must of necessity remain formal and empty.

However, even with the determination of the concept of the Absolute by way of formal indication we have to struggle with basic difficulties for the *possibility of presentation.* If in one's own performance of the phenomenological reduction one has actually lived through *the shift in the representation of totality* and made it one's own in theoretical cognition, nevertheless *apperception* is for the most part under the spell of mundane prejudices. One well understands the enormous *de-restriction* that is achieved in recognizing the "relativity" of the worldly universe, but one all too easily succumbs to the temptation to apperceive this de-restriction (annulling of the restriction of the natural attitude) *after the manner of a relationship of being* (for example, by representing the phenomenological Absolute under the Idea of the "Greater," "the More-Encompassing,"[518] etc.). In all this *ontic apperception* there lies a *dogmatism* which fundamentally prevents grasping the concept of the Absolute with phenomenological *suitability.* And yet these ontic-mundane concepts are not dispensable. We must not, of course, *think philosophically* in them, but rather *by means of them predicatively assert* philosophical cognitions. The explication of the concept of the Absolute cannot do without them, since they are needed in that explication as the *medium for transcendental analogizing.* The inadequacy of every ontic characterization of the Absolute has its basis in the fact that "being as such" makes up but one moment of the Absolute. But just such talk of a *"moment"* must only be understood as "phenomenological *analogy.*" Taken crudely and directly, the representation of an Absolute as articulated in moments is false. "Being a moment" is a *mode of being* (e.g., of accidental being). The Absolute is not a being-unity, not a totality of existent moments, but the inclusion together of the *"pre-existent"* becoming of being (constitution) *and being* (world).ᴾᴾ A dogmatic mistaking of the nature of the Absolute is the idea, im-

---

518. [Sup.] ⟨the infinite Whole⟩

plied in the representation of things as "moments," that "constitution" and "world"—precisely as two moments in something *existent*—stood in some way *beside each other*. The truth is that the Absolute is not the unity of two non-self-sufficient moments that, while indeed mutually complementary, also delimit and *finitize* one another, but is the *infinite unity of the constant passage of one "moment"* (*constitution*) *into the other* (*world*). All expressions such as opposition, otherness, delimitation, and finitization have basically no ontic sense, i.e., sense that is comprehensible with ontological categories, *when* they are used in the explication of the concept of the Absolute but intend *transcendental* concepts—in analogical rejection of ontic meanings. In what sense, now, the Absolute itself is to be addressed as the *"infinite"* we cannot even suggest, although a *central characteristic* is contained in that very designation. For this would presuppose a preliminary look at least into the most general problematic of the *Idea of a "transcendental logic."* (This title does not designate here the phenomenological problems that, by reason of the task of transcendentally interpreting "formal logic," arise in demonstrating the *constitutive sense-bestowals* that underlie it, but rather the *transcendental theory* [519]*of the "phenomenological proposition."*) But this much we can see by way of anticipation, that the ontic Idea of infinity can only serve as an *analogue* for the *predicative outward expression* of the theoretical cognition of the transcendental infinity of the Absolute.

(Note: True, the ontic Idea of infinity is itself twofold: 1) infinity as "continuum" on the one hand, and as iterative infinity on the other (e.g., number series and other iterative processes); 2) infinity as world form, as totality. Whether both ontic representations of infinity can and must be maintained together for the analogical presentation of the infinity of the Absolute is an open question.)

Methodologically, all this implies the following: the Absolute becomes *explicable* at all only by virtue of the fact that ontic categories and concepts function meaningfully in "transcendental [520]analogy"; however, insofar as "being" (the world) is itself a moment of the Absolute, the problem of explicating the Absolute presents itself as the question of the sense of the application of the conceptuality that has its home *in one* moment to the whole of the Absolute itself. Only if the desideratum of an adequate framing of the concept of the Absolute, methodologically constructed and thoroughly clarified, is fulfilled can one handle the special problems in the transcendental theory of method,

---

519. [Alt.] of ⟨phenomenological theory⟩
520. [Alt.] ⟨transformation⟩

already indicated earlier (see §10), which refer to phenomenologizing as an explicating action; and only then too can one develop the full Idea of a transcendental logic (as the phenomenological theory of the *self-explication* of the Absolute).qq

If through such indications—indeed quite "unsystematic" as they are—we have brought the concept of the Absolute into initial view, then we have only fulfilled the *precondition* for the task set for us, namely, to take the phenomenological *concept of science,* in accord with which phenomenologizing (the constant "object" of the transcendental theory of method) as knowing is organized in the form of science, and to set it forth and explain it as *"absolute science."*

We must now go on to redraw this *concept of science* in consideration of the preliminary insights we have gained into the nature of the Absolute. The decisive point, now, is to bring to light in the determination of *absolute science* as well the [521]*inclusional synthesis* that lies in the essence of the Absolute. This may be done in a threefold respect, by characterizing absolute science 1) with regard to the *object,* 2) with regard to its *"subject,"* 3) in the *mode* of its knowing.

1) The object of absolute science is the Absolute (in phenomenological understanding). Should we now simply insert into the point put thus the characterization of the Absolute as the synthetic unity of *constitution and world* given above? And is the object of absolute science thereby adequately determined? Not at all! Rather, when absolute science becomes actual there takes place a *transformation in the Absolute itself,* i.e., it moves out of the "condition" of being-in-itself into that of being-for-itself. With that an immanent *new antithetic element* is articulated in its synthetic inclusionality [*Inbegrifflichkeit*]: specifically the *dualism of two absolute tendencies.* Before the phenomenological reduction there "is given" [*es "gibt"*], so to say, in the unity of Absolute only *one* continuous[522] tendency: *world-constitution* with the antithetical distinction pertaining to it between constituting *pre-existent* [*vorseiendem*] performance and constituted *existent* [*seiendem*] "result." In performing the reduction a new tendency breaks out in the unity of the Absolute: *the tendency of self-elucidation,*[523] of coming-to-oneself, which now by the phenomenological epoche (by the nonparticipation of the phenomenologizing onlooker in constitution) *sets itself antithetically against* the[524] world-constitutive tendency. Both [525]the constitutive and the counter-moving "transcendental" tendencies (we use the word "transcendental" now in

---

521. [Alt.] ⟨totalizing⟩
522. [Ins.] ⟨intentional⟩
523. ["-elucidation" lined through by Husserl]
524. [Ins.] ⟨naive⟩
525. [Alt.] the ⟨naive-⟩constitutive

its original directional sense) compose in their *play "together" against each other* precisely the *synthetic unity*[526] of the Absolute. It is not therefore only the *being-in-itself* of the Absolute but together with that its *becoming-for-itself* in the transcendental occurrence of phenomenologizing that makes up the thematic *"object"* of absolute science. This means, after all, that phenomenologizing as absolute science, referring as it does to the Absolute, also *refers to itself,* inasmuch as it is itself an occurrence that goes on *in* the inclusional unity of the Absolute. It is as the transcendental *theory of elements* that absolute science is thematically directed to the mere *being-in-itself* of the Absolute, i.e., to the synthetic unity of world-constitution and world; it is transcendental world-interpretation in regression to constituting subjectivity. But as transcendental *theory of method* it refers to itself, it is the *thematization of the absolute tendency of becoming-for itself.* The problem now is whether the cognition of phenomenologizing that has hitherto been possible could apprehend phenomenologizing itself in *final self-elucidatedness* as a *tendency of the Absolute,* or whether here too we are faced with a preliminary, more or less *naive stage* of the transcendental self-understanding of the phenomenologizing I. Parallel, so to say, to the question whether the *individuation* of the transcendental ego (as an individual monad in monadic intersubjectivity) is not a *level of the self-objectivation* of a transcendental life which is *"one"* and lies *before all individuation,* we can now ask whether the phenomenologizing I, as the I of reflection, is in the last analysis projected out from the ego as standing *in* transcendental individuation, or whether the dimension of the *ultimate* determination of phenomenologizing (and therefore of the transcendental theory of method) must not be sought by a regressive move to a *more original depth* of absolute life. However, we shall have to let this stand simply as a *problem.*

If we characterize the phenomenological concept of science first from the determination of the "object" of absolute science, which is to say by designating the Absolute as this object, namely in the stage of being-for-itself, then there is need for explicit indication of the *synthetic structure of this theme.* Every mundane science refers to something existent. From its object it is characterized as *ontic* science. The thema of absolute science is the Absolute and, to be sure, the Absolute as the *synthema of the constitutive and "transcendental" tendencies.* The internal opposition of these two tendencies is the *first synthesis-encompassed antithetic articulation* in the unity of absolute life. And once again the constitutive tendency itself is the *synthetic encompassing* of the antithetic opposition of

---

526. [Mg.] ⟨That, however, is a dubious mode of expression. What kind of "synthesis"?⟩

"pre-existent" constitution and its result: being. While mundane science thus *alone* stands in theoretical relationship to the existent, in the Idea of absolute science the relationship to the existent is only *one* structural moment of the thematic relationship; put more exactly, it is a component directedness in a component directedness [*ein Teilrichtung in einer Teilrichtung*]. Of course the *sense of the theme of the existent*, as this enters into absolute science, is altogether different than in mundane science. Worldly science, originating in the natural attitude, refers to the existent as if beyond it *no thematic inquiry* were possible, that is, in the stance of *closure* against the transcendental subjectivity that constitutes the existent. Absolute science, on the contrary, when it refers to the existent, is from the outset *open* to the constitutive horizon of the existent, it takes the existent *as a result* of constitution. That means: mundane sciences and the cognitions attainable within them do not stand *outside* absolute science; rather, they are *legitimate branches* of it, without of course knowing it. Only through the *phenomenological reduction* and the transcendental insight into the constitutive sense of being (as end-product) made possible by the reduction does the restrictedness of the sciences that make the existent their theme become evident, and only then do these sciences themselves become understandable in the *ultimate sense* of their relation to the existent. We do not thus set absolute science at all *against* mundane science, since worldly science precisely lies *in absolute science*. The closure first becomes manifest by the reduction. (The closer characterization of the relationship of mundane and absolute science is the task of an *"absolute theory of science"* made possible by exhibiting the phenomenological concept of science.)

2) the *"subject"* of absolute science is the *Absolute itself*. In the transcendental tendency of phenomenologizing it achieves its own *becoming-for-itself*, in that, starting out from the world, in which it always has already reached a certain illumination in the form of *human* self-consciousness, by the phenomenological reduction it *discloses* its depths, constitutive *"pre-being"* [*Vor-Sein*], and realizes transcendental self-consciousness. We have, however, already characterized phenomenologizing as to the subject functioning in it by distinguishing the *proper* subject, the transcendental onlooker, and the *"appearance"*-subject, man. We have, to be sure, not stopped at mere antithetic separation, but have recognized appearance-truth itself as the result of a transcendental constitution (specifically, "non-proper enworlding"). At the same time, however, in a specific sense not enough was done for appearance-truth as such; for it was constantly referred back to its *constitution*, it was discussed primarily in its *transcendental transparency*. That is, it was explicated according to what it signifies *transcendentally*, the explication went in the *direction of regressive inquiry* into constitution. If we now designate the Absolute itself as the subject of ab-

solute science, this is, materially considered, not an explanation that goes beyond the earlier one, but to some extent has the *methodological superiority* of being a *synthetic* determination. The earlier characterization was predominantly the resolution of an apparent antithesis by way of the constitutive interpretation of appearance-truths, a sublation of them in transcendental truths. Now, however, we are first able to do justice to the *mundane* truth of phenomenologizing, in that we no longer at all *set aside* the *opposition* of man and transcendental onlooker, but comprehend it as a necessary antithesis *in* the synthetic unity of the Absolute. That is, the thesis: man phenomenologizes, as well as the counterthesis: the transcendental ego phenomenologizes, are both *sublated in the absolute truth* that phenomenologizing is in itself a cognitive movement of the Absolute. Just as the Absolute when "in-itself" ["*ansichseiende*"] is the unity of "being" ["*Sein*"] and (constituting) "pre-being" ["*Vor-sein*"], so also the *becoming-for-itself* of the Absolute is just as much something *mundanely existent [mundan seiend]*, i.e., human philosophizing, as it is something "*transcendentally existent*" ["*transzendental-seiend*"], i.e., the cognitive action of the phenomenological onlooker.[527]

3) The *mode of cognition* of absolute science, i.e., of the self-cognition of the Absolute, is *itself* [528]*absolute*. What might that mean? We are incapable of performing in its basic traits the exhibiting that is in question here. Whereas more or less all the structures of the Absolute and absolute science that have been indicated are to be developed out of the understanding of the phenomenological *reduction*, that is not the case here, unless we once again repeat the reduction in a new and more *radicalized* form. But that cannot be done within the limits of a general sketch of the Idea of a transcendental theory of method. A brief indication and we shall let the matter rest.

One way the *mode of a cognition* can be examined is with respect to the *degree of certainty possible for it*. We distinguish, after all, between assertoric and apodictic evidentness in mundane scientific cognition. (Thus, for example, the cognitive mode of a priori science is apodictic, and that of inductive factual science is assertoric.) The question now is whether "*absolute*" as a mode of a cognition means a particular *degree of certainty* for it. The reply is that the modality of a cognition designated by the term "absolute" does not directly aim for a degree of certainty, but rather is connected with the evidentness and rank,

---

527. [Mg.] ⟨In addition the concepts "mundane" and "transcendental" equivocal! Naively mundane—transcendentally mundane. Transcendental as any particular [action of] transcendental constituting. Transcendental as the total Absolute.⟩

528. [Quotation marks around "absolute"]

superior to all worldly "apodicticity," which are distinctive of *transcendental* cognitions. In the phenomenological reduction there is also implicit a *reduction of the Idea of evidentness*, which may lead to a transcendental *new framing of the concept of apodicticity*, as the mode of transcendental insights.—If not directly a degree of certainty, therefore, what else may it be that is to be designated as the *"absolute" mode of cognition* of absolute science?

What is involved is nothing less than a *reduction* of the *Idea of the "thematic domain,"* an Idea which belongs to every worldly science. Mundane science is science by man about that which is existent. Man is himself an existent among existents. The totality of the existents which man is not is the *external world* for him. Originating in the natural attitude, science is first of all a particular theoretical behavior on the part of man *toward his external world.*[529] That means: *the original sense of theme for theory is outer-worldly.* Cognizing is "relative" (i.e., 1. is *relational* as a relationship between man and that which stands counterposed to him *in the external world,* the object;[rr] 2. [530]is *finite* as referring to something existent that *delimits* the cognizer and also finds its *limit* in him: *finite object and finite subject!*). Even in *psychological-reflective* cognition the thematic domain is still determined as *outer-worldly* (I cognize myself 1. in my *referral* to the external world, and 2. as demarcated off (as "immanence") *from* the external world).

These primitive suggestions do not bring us to recognize the greater problem which is posed by the fact that the thematic relation in all mundane sciences is determined by the *subject-object correlation* (the immanence-transcendence relationship), and which becomes comprehensible in elaborating the *finitude of all worldly cognition.* As suggestions, however, they are to serve to bring into relief the impact of a formal *indication of the absoluteness character* of the cognitive mode of absolute science. If the "object" of absolute science was determined as the Absolute, then it may in no way be comprehended by taking one's lead from a *mundane* concept of *object-being.* The object for cognizing here is given neither as something *outer-worldly* nor in the manner of an experience of self that demarcates itself *off from the "external world."* The *self-cognition of the Absolute is not "relative";* there is no external world for the Absolute, and therefore also no *self separated off* from some such world. That is, the mode of cognition of absolute science cannot be comprehended with the apperceptive schema of a *transcendent* or *immanent* experience and cognition, it cannot be at all comprehended with the *schema of a finite cognition.* Talk about the "self-cognition" of the absolute is thus a *transcendental analogy.* The affinity that makes the anal-

---

529. [Mg.] ⟨"external world"? Ambiguous⟩
530. [Ins.] ⟨cognizing⟩

ogy possible, the affinity, namely, between *finite reflective* cognizing (psychic or perhaps psychological self-experience) and *infinite, absolute self-cognition*, is something we cannot now show. (At the same time this would also give the phenomenological justification and clarification of the "infinite knowledge" of the one philosophizing that is always asserted by philosophy caught up in the natural attitude: the transcendental interpretation therefore of "intellectual intuition," of "speculative thought," etc.) The guiding question for the whole transcendental theory of method, viz., the question of phenomenologizing, reaches its final answer in the determination of absolute science. All particular issues (regarding phenomenologizing 1. as reduction, 2. as regressive analysis, 3. as "construction," 4. as theoretical experience, 5. as ideation, 6. as explication,[531] 7. as the action of making into a science) *coincide* in the Idea of absolute science as the synthetic unity of all the various aspects. In distinguishing it with this honor, if in a wholly preliminary way, one also completes the *project-outline of the Idea* of a transcendental theory of method, which in a way now *sublates itself* in the concept of absolute science, insofar as the *antithetic distinction* of the transcendental theory of elements and the transcendental theory of method disappears in the final synthesis of absolute knowing.

  Absolute science, toward which phenomenologizing is organized, is, as the *actuality of the being-for-itself of the Absolute, the system of living truth* in which *it knows itself absolutely.*

§12. "Phenomenology" as transcendental idealism

  In setting the theme of this section, we clearly move out of the problematic of the transcendental theory of method. And in fact the predelineation of the Idea of a theory of this kind has found its *end* in the endeavor to indicate the concept of absolute science. Considered *in itself,* phenomenologizing is neither an "idealism" nor a "realism," nor any other kind of doctrinal point of view, but the *self-comprehension of the Absolute* sublime above all human doctrinal opinion. But why should we conclude the outline of the Idea of a transcendental theory of method with the characterization of "phenomenology" as a transcendental idealism? Is something thereby said about *phenomenologizing* after all? We have to admit, of course, that we thereupon no longer have phenomenologizing as our object—*in contrast* to the world-constitution that is thematized in the transcendental theory of elements; but we still thereby ex-

---

531. [Mg.] ⟨predicative determination surely meant⟩

press something about phenomenologizing in an *indirect way*. That phenomenology is transcendental idealism can be shown only in a return back to the *cognitive gains of the theory of elements* which ground this idealism. Ought not, then, the characterization of phenomenology as "idealism" have its place there, too? No, for to characterize phenomenology in this way is nothing other than a *self-characterization of phenomenologizing* with reference to its thematic cognitive performance; it is a self-explication of its self-understanding—namely, in and *for the mundane situation of its "appearance"* as phenomenology. In its *outward objectivation* as a piece of philosophy [*Philosophem*] in the world, phenomenologizing, in announcing itself as transcendental idealism, speaks out, not only about the sense and range of its cognitive performance, but also about its *conviction*, its world-outlook: the one phenomenologizing as "phenomenologist" characterizes himself as "idealist." Although he always sees through his mundane situation as being the result of a constitutive bestowal of sense, still he develops a "self-awareness" deliberately for this mundane situation of "appearing" phenomenologizing. This self-awareness is summarized in its *self-conception as "transcendental idealism."* Inasmuch, now, as the phenomenologist as a philosophizing human stands in natural living community with his fellow humans, he must, in order to be able to talk with others about his theoretical activity, *explicate this self-conception,* he must formulate his "standpoint" in *discussion.* "Phenomenology as transcendental idealism" is nothing other than the *thesis that presents phenomenology for discussion.*

Every discussion presupposes some common ground; a *philosophical* discussion presupposes the communality of the *problems and problematic.* Does the phenomenologist now actually have a *common problem-space* with the man who philosophizes in the[532] natural attitude, to whom he constantly turns, with whom he shares his philosophy, and for whom he brings it under the generic aspect of transcendental idealism? Or has he not precisely through the phenomenological reduction *lost* the communality of ground, the natural attitude, and therefore the communality of philosophical problematic possible within its horizon? Has he not *"transcended"* captivation in the world altogether and so likewise the whole *style* of world-captivated, dogmatic philosophical inquiry? Certainly! [533]Does not "idealism" mean in the first place a doctrinal opinion that arises from a philosophizing that is *bound to the world?* That too we must admit. What, therefore, is transcendental idealism in the self-explication of

---

532. [Ins.] ⟨naively⟩

533. [Alt.] "Idealism" ⟨after all⟩ mean⟨s⟩ in the first place a doctrinal opinion that arises from a philosophizing that is *bound to the world.*

phenomenology for the mundane situation supposed to mean now? In characterizing itself by a title (idealist) whose home ground is first of all the natural attitude, phenomenologizing throws a *bridge* over to men in the natural attitude, thus awakening the *semblance [Anschein] of a like problem situation* and thereby creating the disposition for a possible discussion with the proponents of other philosophies [*Philosopheme*]. But once the discussion is under way, then phenomenological self-explication (as transcendental idealism) immediately *transcends all forms of mundane idealistic philosophy;* it revokes the deceit that was necessary in order for the discussion to take place.

It would be a *major task,* now, to carry out this discussion between a doctrinal opinion that presented itself as transcendental idealism and other philosophical views—at least in their main features—beginning with the seeming appearance of a like problem situation and going on to the dissolving of that semblance. But in the general character of our considerations we cannot take up this task. We are condensing the declaration of transcendental idealism as the self-conception of phenomenologizing in the mundane discussion situation into a few essential *basic thoughts.* We shall proceed first in a negative way by *destroying* the presuppositions of and bases for mundane idealism (and for its counterconcept: mundane realism), thus preparing understanding for what is distinctive of phenomenological idealism. Then, secondly, a few essential indications will lay out the positive sense of the doctrinal view adopted by the phenomenologist in the mundane situation.

As premise to the discussion, let us recall briefly the sources of the *equivocation* in transcendental concepts. Even if the concept of transcendental idealism is given out as one that is intelligible in the horizon of the natural attitude, still in itself it is a *transcendental* concept and as such is equivocal in a special way. There always exists the danger of confusing it with the mundane concept which only stands in analogy to it. (This of course does not concern so much the concept of idealism itself as precisely the terms with which it must be formulated for the natural attitude.) Apart from the possibility of equivocation lying in the structure of phenomenological *statements,* the representation of transcendental idealism (in the phenomenological sense) is all too easily liable to misunderstanding by construal of it in the "light" of historical knowledge. And since it is an appearance-truth about phenomenology that it must enter the scene in the midst of the continuum of the history of philosophy as one philosophy [*Philosophem*] among others, having a place with them in the *common* culture-historical tradition, etc., for all the more reason, then, "phenomenological idealism," i.e., the self-characterization of phenomenologizing *in and for the situation of "appearing" [Erscheinung],* cannot first start out by rejecting *a limine* every historical aspect. Rather, the phenomenologist classifies himself in the *history of the problem of idealism.* If he thus immediately agrees with the man of the natural attitude when the latter wishes to use *traditional problem motifs* to comprehend phenomenology in the context of the historical tradition, nevertheless he (the phenomenologist) leads the other *out of this naiveté* with the *explication* of the idealism. The connection with the problematic found in past philosophy is therefore in no way denied but only *interpreted more deeply* than is ever possible *within* the natural attitude, namely, inasmuch as now mundane (idealistic) philosophizing *becomes transparent as a transcendental tendency that had remained concealed,* that had not yet reached the breakthrough to proper self-understanding. In this kind of *transcendental interpretation of the history* of philosophy, what may show is that fundamentally *"idealism"* in all its various forms is *superior to the position of realism,* that in it the *first tremors of the unsettling of* the natural attitude are already heralded, which in the phenomenological reduction then lead to its collapse. The phenomenologist, standing in the mundane situation of his "appearing philosophy," characterizes that philosophy as transcendental idealism in order thereby to express his acknowledgment that he is the *legitimate heir of the great idealistic tradition,* and to lay claim to the role of bringing to final settlement *all the genuine motifs of thought* in this tradition by laying the foundation for a *new Idea of philosophy.*

Insight into these equivocations that threaten the concept of transcendental idealism is what motivates setting it in express *contrast* to *mundane idealism.* One cannot subsume under the common genus of "idealism" mundane as well as transcendental idealism as merely different types respectively of one common basic idea. But before we can even begin this job of making the contrast, a preliminary clarification is still necessary regarding that *against which* the contrast is to be made. What, then, is "mundane" idealism? This expression does not designate a *self-characterization* of any idealism, but is the general formula which transcendental phenomenological idealism has available for all "idealisms" distinct from itself, those which arose precisely in the horizon of the natural attitude and are held captivated in it. If we look more closely, the concept of idealism as it enters the scene in human intellectual history displays an ambiguous profusion of meanings, and this makes it impossible to fix it in any way in a definition. We can, however, distinguish in the totality of the idealistic systems that have developed historically *four basic forms of idealism,* which of course represent crude generalizations: 1) ontological idealism, 2) epistemological idealism, 3) activistic idealism, and 4) "absolute" idealism. Ontological idealism is in a certain sense also the first historically. It breaks through in the Platonic interpretation of the world when that which is properly existent is determed as *eidos,* as Idea. Transcendental idealism is to be set in relief, however, not against *ontological idealism,* but only against *epistemological* idealism—even if quite *decisive* insights into transcendental idealism are to be gained precisely in the development of the problematic of ontological ideal-ism. It is epistemological idealism above all that dominates most of modern philosophy and therefore also is the prevailing determinant for the mundane situation in which phenomenology enters intellectual history. The two other basic forms of idealism (such as represented by Fichte and Hegel) have a *more intimate affinity* with the transcendental idealism of phenomenology than any form of epistemological idealism ever has. Precisely because of this, however, they are harder to interpret; the explanation has to be more intensively drawn and simply does not allow being done in a few brief remarks. We shall there-fore restrict ourselves to bringing out a *distinction of principle* between transcen-dental and mundane idealism by marking *epistemological* idealism off from the "idealistic position" adopted by phenomenology. (In order to prevent a fatal misunderstanding, let it be said that the Kantian expression "transcendental idealism" is in no way identical with the phenomenological sense of this term—and this for as little reason as we have for seeing in Kantian idealism a particular form of mundane idealism. Of course, we have to forego explaining that here.)

We have distinguished epistemological from ontological idealism, and that is in a certain sense correct; but it does not preclude the fact that idealism it-self has to be expressed primarily *ontologically*. Every philosophy in the hori-zon of the natural attitude is a particular *interpretation of the being of the world*, and is formulated in a *basic ontological thesis*. Epistemological idealism, now, gets its ontological thesis in a *theory of knowledge*. And insofar as knowledge precisely is primarily a way man relates to his *external*[534] *world*, the problematic of epis-temological idealism is condensed into the question of determining the rela-tions of *immanence and transcendence*. At the same time it always keeps "realism" in sight as counterposition to itself; it is to realism that for the most part it makes explicit reference and against which it sets itself off. But the two, ide-alism and realism, come together in this: they both start out from the *pretheo-retical attitude of man* toward the things he has to deal with, that he experiences, becomes acquainted with, determines more closely, about which he can be mistaken, which hold good in harmonious experiences, etc. This pretheoreti-cal life-attitude that a man bears toward things in *immediate confidence* is neither "idealistic" nor "realistic," neither entertains doubt about the being of the ex-ternal world nor expects proof of it. We call this attitude the immediate liv-ing attitude of human subjectivity leading its life in the world and engaging in practical activity in it. This attitude, however, has already become as a

---

534. ["external" lined through by Husserl]

whole *questionable* if the problem surfaces to which both mundane idealism as well as mundane realism mean to be an answer. The "idealist" and the "realist"—although they no longer themselves stand in this living immediacy of original familiarity—both make that attitude thematic in regard to particular elements [*Momenten*] that have to be assessed *by argument,* in order in that way to gain *testimony* for their theories by returning to the pretheoretical attitude.

Idealism reduced to its most general form argues in the style of a *universal reflection* on the *givenness of the existent* in our (or, respectively, in my) experience. Do we have another world besides the one experienced, meant, and judged by us? Is it not an absurd doubling of that which is existent to posit hypothetically still another *"world in itself"* behind the world that is given to us and demonstrated in our experience in lived processes of verification? Must not rather the sense of being for the world be precisely derived from the fact that it is what it is only as the *universal unity of acceptedness* for our life of believing, experiencing, and meaning things? Are we not compelled to refuse it any *being* which would be *free* in principle of subjective givenness? The continuation of this course of thought, which in no way need be empty speculation but can be motivated by concrete, systematic investigations into the universal reference of all beings to subjective modes of givenness, etc., leads at once to the formation of the idealistic thesis: the *being of the "external world"* has in principle only the sense of a *correlate* to lived subjective processes that mean being and confirm being.

Realism, likewise understood quite generally,—and when it does not have the antiquated form of realism oriented to the "the theory of images"—does not in any way dispute the exhibitings that play the role of testimony in idealistic argumentation. Only it does *not go along* with their assessment, with the way they are used in argumentation. In returning to the immediate attitude of pretheoretical life in the world, realism recognizes that everything of which we can say: "it exists" ["*Es ist*"], is only *accessible* to us in *lived processes that demonstrate being.* It concedes further that the *Idea of being* is *inseparable from the Idea of accessibility* and therefore that the existent is *inseparable* from givenness for humans. But the realist will always then be able to say: Even if the existent is not just contingently but necessarily the correlate of our actual and possible experience, and thus only makes sense *in* our experiential life, still it does not have its sense *from* our experiential life, it is not *ontically dependent* on our (or my) existence [*Existenz*]. The experiential relationship of the existent to the knowing subject does not exclude but—rightly understood—precisely *includes* the ontic *independence of the existent* from the life that experiences it.

However realism and idealism may vary in particular systems, there always remains, as the common foundation that makes their conflict possible, the *basis for their problem,* viz., the *relation of experience between man and external world,* or, expressed formally, the *intramundane* subject-object correlation. The unfruit-fulness of the dispute between idealism and realism ultimately consists in this, that both are held fast in a common *naiveté* that neither one has ever itself made thematic, namely, they remain held fast in the *horizon of the world*. The idealist may in principle look on the being of transcendent objects as the result of sub-jective constructions of unity, as in some sense a *subjective product*, and so may formulate his ontological thesis thus: what is *properly existent* is the *subject*, whereas the "object" participates in being only *by the grace of the subject*—still he thereby *remains in the horizon of the world*. The world is not only the *external world*, but the inclusional unity of immanence *and* transcendence. He has not re-duced the world to the subject, he has reduced *transcendence within the world to the subject within the world* (whether this subject be taken as man in a global sense or more constructively as consciousness, as the "epistemological I" (Rickert), among other possibilities).

Considered *doxographically*, now, transcendental idealism appears to have the *same thought-content* as the idealism indicated above. And yet it is separated from it by a *chasm*. In what does the distinction *most essentially* consist? a) Tran-scendental idealism, established by the phenomenological reduction (by tran-scending the world), is *not captivated in the horizon of the world*. b) It does not share with mundane idealism and realism the common problem-basis, man's prethe-oretical experiential attitude toward that which is existent. It does not seek re-course in the finding that this immediacy is the *forum of ultimate demonstration*. c) Transcendental idealism does not consist in an interpretation of the *intra-mundane subject-object relationship*, the thesis of the *ontological primacy of the mundane subject*. d) Thus it is *not an absolutizing of "consciousness"* (taken as an abstract stra-tum of concrete man), not a *philosophy of immanence*. e) Furthermore, it does not skip over the givenness character of the existent in human experience—which is emphasized by realism especially—the *independence*, the *self-sufficiency*, etc.; it does not make the external world into *man's construct*.

But what positive sense does transcendental idealism have? Does it not also mean an ontological thesis? Certainly—but in a *quite new sense*, such as is not pos-sible with any philosophical interpretation of the world that originates in the horizon of the natural attitude. Only by the phenomenological reduction is the *dimension* at all opened up from which *being [das Sein], that which is existent as a whole [das Seiende im Ganzen]*, becomes determinable. It is not a matter here of an antecedency of one mundane existent (the subject) over another (the object), but of an *interpretation of being* which also fundamentally affects each and every existent. The basic central thought of transcendental idealism is: *the existent is in principle constituted*—in the life processes of transcendental subjectivity. Not only the existent in the kind of givenness termed *"transcendence,"* but likewise that which is existent as *"immanence"*; the whole world as the *ensemble* of the immanent interiority of experiencing life and of the transcendent external world is a *unitary constitutive product*. Transcendental idealism is best characterized by the designation *"constitutive idealism."* Whereas mundane idealism seeks to explain what is existent *by* an existent, the ontological world-thesis of *transcendental* idealism represents the *interpretation of being out of "pre-existent" constitution [aus der "vor-seienden" Konstitution]*. This means above all that transcendental idealism is not a hypothesis resting on arguments but is the summation of the *concrete demonstrations* of the phenomenological analytic. Because with the phenomenological reduction the existent acquires a horizon of final examinability and intelligibility in the regression to its transcendental constitution, namely, in a scientific method that as absolute science is *superior* in cognitive rigor and rank to all de facto or imaginable mundane sciences, transcendental idealism is the philosophical world-interpretation which can have *no counterconcept*. (So, for example, the idea of a transcendental realism is absurd!) The fundamental *superiority* of transcendental idealism over mundane realism is manifest in the fact that the whole *dimension of dispute* between idealism and realism: the mundane experience-relationship, is, as *constituted situation* in the transcendental idealistic clarification of the world, referred back to the *constitution that fashions it*. Realism persists in the dogmatic belief in being, and thus has a mundane kind of truth; but it never reaches the *problem-sphere of philosophy* at all. Mundane idealism, however, comes *close* to transcendental truth, except that it refers the *external world* to a subject that itself *belongs to the world*; it *"subjectivizes"* the world in an inadmissible sense. Thus it seeks to apprehend the *transcendental* dependence of *the existent* as such upon *pre-existent* subjectivity as the *dependence of transcendence* upon *existent immanence*. Insight into these connections allows clear recognition of how transcendental idealism is *beyond idealism and realism*.

Appendices

A. APPENDED PAGES AND INSERTIONS

(From Summer 1933 to January 1934)

Appendix I [to p. 42][a]

The point is that by the epoche I do not at all lose the world, the universe of all thematic activities in the naturalness of ongoing human life, hence the basis of acceptedness, continually pregiven to it, for all theoretical, axiological, and practical questions and endeavors. As phenomenologizing I, in practicing the epoche I only deny myself the use of this basis for thematic activities, I deny myself the actions of inquiry, of thematic experience, of judgment, of axiological and practical projection, of deliberation, of decision, that insert into the horizon that pregives the world. The acceptedness of natural pregivenness always means the thematic habituality of having it beforehand as thematic field, of directing effort into it beforehand in actualizations that set the doxic, axiological, and practical predelineations which course through it in structured preknownness. But with the inhibiting of this universal thematic domain, the possibility is opened of turning it around into a new kind of thematic arena. In unity with the epoche and as the one practicing it, I become precisely the "nonparticipant" onlooker of transcendental life, in which the acceptedness of the horizon, as giving the basis for all natural themes, and these themes themselves course on.

Appendix II [to pp. 108–109][b]

How does the activity of the transcendental onlooker, now, make itself mundane? All its doing rests upon the epoche and reduction. The latter, however, consists in this, that life in the world is "inhibited" in its whole being-constituting activity as well as in all-inclusiveness (in the all-inclusive anticipation of the acceptedness of the horizon as the acceptedness of totality) and at the same time in every individual act that goes on one after another to form actual-moment life in the world, that what is thematic in it is put outside thematic focus, is made end-thematic, is posited with the altered sense: something that holds good *as* something taken in ways of holding good [*Geltendes* als *das der Geltungen*], and world *as* constituted in the all-inclusiveness of constituting actions that take things as holding good [*der konstituierenden Geltungen*]. Thus the constituting ego and that which is inseparable from it, that which is its very own, become the all-inclusive theme in which the whole thematic complex of the natural I is taken up, annulled, and raised to a higher level. To this theme, ego, also belongs phenomenologizing action, and, as the occasion demands, its iteration in the reflectivity proper to the ego. The underlying world-constitution revealed by phenomenologizing action is by essential necessity of such a kind that my ego, in a move of return into the natural attitude is enworlded as I-man and each of its own correlates is enworlded as psychosubjective. All possible acts and products of acts of the natural attitude belong in the framework of human possibility, and hence every reflection upon them and theoretical thematization of them no less so—they belong in the framework of an intentional psychology. If in the phenomenological epoche, as in historical fact happened, there took place for the very first time a systematic investigation of psychic life, namely, in the reversal of the natural attitude into the attitude attentive to the constitutive correlation, that changes nothing, as obvious, of what was gained in the transcendental attitude, of what could have been gained by transcendental reversal if an intentional psychology had already been under way there and systematically developed. Indeed what would have been needed in regard to psychology is the decisive will to set as research task the totality of psychic being in its full concreteness, including the infinity of reflections found there and in the method of psychological-phenomenological reduction.

If we consider, now, that what was ascertained in the first step as the thematic, explicated ego is inseparable from the functions which we apprehended under the title phenomenologizing I, which as anonymous are nonetheless accessible to reflection, then it is clear that, just as the "phenomenologizing I," and hence these anonymous strata of the ego, are also taken into account, they are also immediately included in the thematic transposition into worldliness. That which at first became thematic as transcendental ego changes into the human soul^c with all that belongs to it of world-constituting functions; and since the phenomenologizing functions are inseparably one with this ego, they thus *eo ipso* also receive their place in the soul, hence in the world of the natural attitude. Here, however, the situation is such that they do not from the outset and in a proper way belong to the soul in the form of psychic possibilities, for they are not the functions in which the soul has already been constituted as correlate of experience. I cannot as man (or as psychologist) come upon functions in which the psychic annuls itself as natural-worldly and stops being able to be in the universal end-theme world. That, however, does not prevent me, in passing over into the natural attitude, from finding enworlded my phenomenological all-inclusive theme, ego, together wtih phenomenologizing action.

Likewise, naturally, in regard to the separation of the transcendental I and transcendental others, included in the concrete ego as a functional distinction for world-constitution. Every Other "is" himself man, when I pass over into the natural attitude;

as transcendental I within thus constituted transcendental intersubjectivity, I am a monadologized ego and every Other is another ego. My transcendental-phenomenologizing being belongs to "myself," every Other, as like me, could also phenomenologize, and so phenomenologizing at once belongs as a subsequent over-lay to every human soul as a possibility.

Appendix III [to p. 109]ᵈ

If I "turn back" into the natural attitude, while remaining in the reduction, if I on-tically explicate "the life-world of the natural attitude" and in it men and that of them which is psychic, then the natural attitude is a transcendental attitude and as tran-scendental a conscious stance of the ego, which has become thematic for itself.

Now, in the "world" I have human subjects who have consciousness of the world in any given moment respective to each [in Jeweiligkeit], who have a world holding good in common among them, but who have it as "the" world in their subjective—in-dividual subjective and common subjective—modes of belief, modes of appearance. The way one presents the world to oneself [Weltvorstellung] and the world itself are dif-ferent things, because the world is presupposed as the world of this natural attitude (as its correlate of acceptedness)—it lies antecedently there as the acceptedness of a basis for me as ego standing constantly in the natural attitude. If I make the natural attitude of the ego and its correlate world thematic, then I have thematic in the ego a special attitude in which it is not the full ego that becomes thematic. As phenome-nologist I say "natural attitude of the ego"—but I have the full ego in view and as theme and already disclosed, if I have gone far enough. In what is disclosed, now, there enters the scene that which gives understanding for man, for human presenta-tion to oneself [menschliche Vorstellung], for consciousness of the world, etc., and I now understand that monadic structure lies in the concrete ego, that monad has become soul in the natural attitude, that the relationship of monad to nature constituted jointly in the connection of monads with monads, and to the respective bodies [Leibern] there, has become a soul-body relationship in the world, and the soul now has its place in the world, and in the world of naturalized realities is united with the body as a single psycho-physical thing.

Appendix IV [to p. 109]ᵉ

The (phenomenologizing) methodological demonstration of primordiality in my ego, as that in which an alien ego constitutes itself and thus an open totality of alien egos is temporalized, shows that every alien Other has his primordial environing world, and that right through all these givens of presentification [Vergegenwärtigungs-gegebenheiten] there necessarily runs an identity of acceptedness, the same nature for all, for my proto-modal primordial environing world and for everything empathetically presentified. Therein for any ego its organic body—"monads," subjects have their bodies, their localization in the one all-inclusive nature for every one of these subjects.

What, therefore, are the monads other than human subjects, and what is the methodological exhibiting of the way monadic subjects come to constitution in the ego, together with the constitution of an identical nature therein made possible and occurring in unity with it, other than the exhibiting of the way human subjects are only in the world by the fact that, as bearers of world-consciousness, they produce the sense, world, for themselves at every moment respective to each. Nevertheless, in the natural attitude, in which for ourselves and for others we are called and are humans, to everything worldly there belongs the being-acceptedness: existent in the world [*in der Welt seiend*], in the world that is always existent beforehand [*im voraus seienden*] as constant acceptedness of a basis. So also man's being is being in the world that is existent beforehand. In phenomenology this being-beforehand [*Im-voraus-Sein*] is itself a problem, and the monads are not in the world that is existent beforehand, but are the subjects that constitute it and [its] always antecedent being [*Voraus-Sein*]. Thus they are themselves antecedent—with respect to the world, while in naive naturalness the world is antecedent.

Appendix V [to pp. 112–114][f]

Within phenomenology, within the different attitudes systematically brought into action, the different "regions": the attitude toward the world as phenomenon of the universe of spatiotemporal being, explication in ontology and in positive science, the description of the form of a life-world, of a native human group, etc. That is the operation, "natural attitude," within the phenomenological reduction.

1) Attitude to the world in the relativity of its naive holding good for "us" as existent. Relativity of existents in the revaluation of what is precisely still "existent" in mere appearance. Existents are subjectivized, into "merely subjective" modes of appearance. Subjects, cognizing persons, each in his respective orientation; space, perceptual field, etc. Always in the attitude toward the relativity of "the existent," of *onta*.

2) Attitude to new modes of the subjective, of that in which first subjective things (the relative *onta*) are "constituted" (their perspectivation—in regard to nature): system of the "constitution" of *onta* in accord with their own systematic foundational structure, nature, etc. The attitude toward I-subjects, toward their bodies, etc. New dimension and new sense of constitution.

If all that is brought to development and we place ourselves again purely and systematically in the "region," phenomenon of world (ontic, standing in the reduction), then in it we have all that is existent in a worldly way and all mundane truths with respect thereto. But that which is existent in a worldly way now has, beyond its mundane truth, beyond mundane determinations, "phenomenological" determinations, is known in its respective constitution.

Still, that is a misleading expression: as if every real thing were constituted for itself, although in interinvolvement, like to the way real things in the world are constructed in their properties each for itself and form a universe in the universal form of
spatiotemporality by the dependency regulation of causality that links all real things
and the determinations that are proper to their essence.

The constitution of the world is a performance of the absolute ego which is thoroughly unitary within all variation in single performances, and in which the acceptedness of the world is always already acceptedness of the word, and not first the
acceptedness of individual real things, out of whose particular constitution that of the
world is in some way assembled.

But the world has its ontological foundational structure, every real thing is *res extensa*, the world has an all-inclusive core stratum, nature, and in it are localized psychic subjects and the meaning relating back to psychic subjects—intellectuality
[*Geistigkeit*].

Psychic subjects are localized in nature and have natural spatiotemporal position
and expanse (form, duration). On the other hand, as subjects living the world, living
in the world, they are bearers of every sense-of-being, [of what is meant by] world.
The world only makes sense, only has content and acceptedness as to being, in human I-subjects as experiencing, knowing the world, as continually fashioning the
world in activity, as fashioning and possessing in their consciousness of the world the
being-sense of the world, as the world existent for them. The world has the ontological structure that it is only thinkable as world with the sense of being which can be
recognized by the human subjects existent in it—experienceable by everyone, acquiring its experiential sense, etc., hence perspectivated, building itself up in each in
childlike innocence[g] [of the fact that all this is going on].

In that, now, reduction is performed and the constitution of the world explored,
or, respectively, the ego is made concretely thematic as world-constituting and in its
absolute being, the world as naively and straightforwardly existent acquires the sense:
transcendentally constituted world, hence a cognitive construct of the transcendental ego; and this new determination of sense is also shared in a certain way with every
mundane real thing and all mundane truths. The clarification of constitution, however, leads now, as functioning for constitution, to various concepts of subject, it leads
respectively, besides the absolutely constituting ego, to the ego that embraces all being in every sense, to the monadic ego, as relatively concrete monad (with its monadic
I as pole of I-acts and habitualities) in the universe of monads, whereby other monads are intentional modifications of the monadic ego with the being-sense: other transcendentally monadic I's, their primordial life, and their primordial habitualities.

Appendix VI [to p. 121][h]

In naiveté, in the attitude of being engrossed in worldly interests, there world-
constituting performance, that which produces monadization and mundanization,

cannot be seen. For the phenomenologist who "returns to the natural attitude," and thereby abstractly screens off that which makes up constituting life, the task ensues of carrying out a fundamental separation: 1) Nature and world in the naiveté of the natural attitude have their prescientific and exact-scientific essential structure—task of a mundane ontology. What is of special importance in this connection is to bring out the ontological essence of the soul as framework for a possible mundane psychology of de facto man. 2) Nature and world after the ego's transcendental change of stance. Consideration of monadizing and mundanizing performances and of the realization that monadizing and enworlding action is itself again monadized and enworlded, and that accordingly the phenomenologist has to find in the phenomenon of world, that is, within the human soul, everything in him which is exhibited of transcendental constitutive action, as something made natural and mundanely temporal in the form of the psychic. Thus phenomenologizing means an intentional process, or a capability, of psychologizing everything transcendental in infinitum. That, however, is itself nothing other than a special attitude and mode of constituting performance, while the absolute ego is the absolute totality of all attitudes and all performances, actual and possible.

I am the transcendental "onlooker"—that is not an adequate expression—; I am the one phenomenologizing, who discloses all that I myself am and thereby make it into that which is existent in the true sense, existent cognitionally.

Over against the enrichment of the content of the soul by virtue of phenomenologizing scientific performance there stands the original worldly content of the soul, precisely that content which is the theme of psychology as mundane science in the natural sense. What can a mundane ontology in the natural attitude, without any idea of the phenomenological reduction, achieve, particularly in view of the divorce of nature and soul? What rightful scientific task is to be defined for a psychology? Disclosure of the basic error of modern psychology, or of universal ontology, as if the soul were an in itself something finished and ready.

Appendix VII [to p. 123][i]

Reduction to myself as ego in the full concreteness of the life of taking things as holding good [*Geltungsleben*] which belongs to me (and the concreteness of things that therein hold good as existent, among them everything that gets verified as "existent":) that which holds good, however, purely as correlate in constituting life. This life itself, however, is contained in the universe of that which holds for me. What I am lies in it, is explicated in my phenomenologizing action, an action which belongs again to myself.

In this self-explication I come upon various presentifications [*Vergegenwärtigungen*] and in them presentified things as such, among them instances of empathy. More precisely: there is a distinction between memories as presentifications "purely and simply," and, relating to them, empathetic presentifications. By memories my successive-temporal life is constituted in modes of past, present, future. I find in myself as ego my I (the pole to which all egological life and being and everything constituted therein is related) temporalized as past, present, future I, and as the same something in temporal continuity that was constantly present, in unity therewith was continu-ously earlier, and will be in continuously different modes. To each modality of time there belongs the life that corresponds to its time-modal I—so taken all together, the life that is mine, of the same I, and which in the same course of time was my own, is now my own, and is future. In empathy there is constituted, and always constituted, a co-present belonging to an alien something which has its being-sense only as pre-senting itself empathetically (similar to the way something does in memory). The alien something is an alien I with an alien I-life, I-acts, with unities of being holding for the I, etc.

Accordingly, the I in its transcendental all-inclusive field is constantly existent for itself in this way, that in standing-flowing transcendental life it is the one, the single I-pole, which has its unities of acceptedness in this life and in addition also has itself as this I. Its life is a life that continually constitutes unities of acceptedness in such a way that in the flow it has memories and empathizings, both in a certain way as self-temporalizing presentifications. In them the ego finds itself temporalized (as accept-edness-unity), as I that has its past and future and at the same time "a space," a realm of coexistence [Koexistenz] of alien I's (so to say, making themselves alien in em-pathizings) of such a kind that to any given actual present, but also to every earlier and future present, there necessarily belongs the co-accepted horizon of alien I's, hence as I's that are co-past, co-future, in each particular mode. By this self-temporalizing, that is, by this monadizing as self-explication of the ego into a monadic multiplicity, that is, into an endlessly open totality in a monadic tem-porospatiality, the ego constitutes first before anything the world of naturalness, in such a way that in it a new temporospatiality is constituted, one in which the mo-nads are made mundane as psychic subjects psychically related to nature, nature communal to them all, nature cognitionally identical for them, and each of them is related in firm fashion to its own body and is thereby inseparably one with it. Some-what later the "humanization" [of] nature and of man himself as significance, imbue-ment with spirit [Vergeistigung], and thereby constitution of the historical world.

Absolute ego and my life, as that wherein I have the universe of that which for me is existent; therein I and this life constituted for itself as existent, namely, constituted as that which is existent immanently for itself, constituted as in immanent being an alien's universe, that is, as a coexistent something with the sense, alter ego, and as monadically existent in the time-structured [gezeitigten] being-form of ego and alter ego, and in connection with co-monads as others.

The constituted connection is itself again functional for the constitution of the world, in which subjects are constituted unities come from this constitution. In the phenomenologizing explication of my being as the ego that I am, in the life that makes up, effects, constitutes my concrete being, is contained as constituted all that is existent, in it all levels of the existent on the part of self-constitution, of self-constitution as time-structured ego [*als gezeitigtes Ego*], that is, as immanently time-structured, and as time-structured in a coexistence [*Koexistenz*] (monadic space), as that in which I am a monad in the universe of monads, wherein each monad intentionally implies each and the whole universe, one and the same monad-universe for all, in which all are as members. And yet what is not to be forgotten is that everything, my very own temporality and my monadic coexistence [*Koexistenz*] at any point in time, that monadic spatiotemporality and "world" itself, which presents itself in orientation to me and to every monad, is implied in me, in the concrete ego of the reduction, as the primal ego. This ego is the only one in an absolute sense which does not allow meaningful duplication, even more sharply put, excludes it as meaningless. Implication means: the "higher being" ["*Übersein*"] of the ego is itself nothing other than a constant primally streaming constituting action, an action of constituting various levels of universes of existents ("worlds"), belonging to each [level or world are] actual-moment and habitual acceptedness of being in modes of horizonality belonging to each, which modes of horizonality, in the present-moment actuality of performances of fulfillment, harmoniously bring individualized, i.e., "spatiotemporal," universes to acceptedness, namely, by corrections in modes of modalization.

Appendix VIII [to p. 124][1]

What does *end-constituted being* mean? Transcendental subjectivity lives in a constant, original having of tendencies in such a way that in a progressing, synthetically linked activity it has ever new themes as relative ends (as aims to be actualized), that these ends become passages, become means to new activities, and that all these activities predelineate an infinite horizon of possible further activities and aims, in which there becomes manifest a harmonious universe-system of aims which seem to point to an ultimate ideal pole that lies at infinity,[2] as that to which all striving ultimately is to relate. The world is constituted in the relativity of environing worlds as arisen from interests and as infinite field of interests or field of aims for the I.

However, the fact that in its exclusiveness world-constitution is tendential—we perpetually having the world and living on in the world—also means: the I is engrossed in attaining and appropriating the world (practically and then also theoretically, and that again then put to practical use), in constituting the world—it is at first incapable

---

1. ⟨Cf. [pp. 129-132] and [Appendix IX, 171–173] thus unusable.⟩ [While Husserl's note here to his own manuscript makes reference to both a further passage of Fink's and further remarks of his own, the present Appendix VIII is explicitly referred by Husserl to p. 124 in Fink's text, where the point under discussion is indicated by note 438.—Tr.]

2. ⟨That, however, would already be naturalization. That is why I say "seem."⟩

of seeing its all-inclusive life of final constituting action, the life that afterwards, however, can also be discovered as this life. Also it is "something conscious," although not in the mode of actual or potential world-thematic material. By essence, however, directedness to the constitutive presupposes transcendental reflection in a move from that which is constituted to the performance which does the constituting. Along with that, however, the problem of all-inclusiveness—the all-inclusive tendency perpetually to move to mundanization and not stay put and in all subjective reflections to make the subjective mundane. Then only, after world-life constantly promises in its progress the unity of a satisfaction of interests and appears at times to fulfill it, the growing feeling of the inadequacy of a satisfaction that is thus never actually to be gained and the motivation for the breakthrough of a new tendency, a turn away from worldliness, finally a resolute epoche and now in relation to that: science and its function—all-inclusive science of the world, all-inclusive science in the epoche.

Appendix IX [to pp. 129–132]ʲ

The phenomenologist living in the world, the "new" world for him, finds his phenomenologizing and that of his associates as a new something psychic in the intersubjective whole of worldly humanity.

In naturalness he finds his personal being and that of every other dominated by the unity of a tendency that moves through all individual activities in aim after a universal accord through correction. In return to the transcendental ego I find my transcendental activity in itself in its central unity directed to "self-maintenance," to accord with itself. The in itself first form of this endeavor and life of tending is the constitution of the natural environing world, and in it [are] human persons struggling for their "Existence" in life in the world. The "Existence" that they reach as men in belonging to this open-ended environing worldliness—the kind of self-maintenance, of normal satisfaction of their endeavors, of their "needs," in the personal horizon of their whole life—is one that is eudaemonistic, relative, temporary, with a finitude that never stands firm. Abstractions: egoistic satisfaction, family egoism, "national" egoism, internationality in the stance of egoism. Man in historical time, in unsettled, legendary historical tradition, in the normal environing world of the nation in normal hopeful existence. The individual and his fate in this normal existence of the political whole. Belonging to normalcy, the ruling power that makes the political whole, the government. The rulers as functionaries of unitary political mankind—every people has its ruling leader. Accord and discord among peoples in egoistic togetherness—one's own people in conflict with other peoples, its interests—alien interests. That is the continual concern of statesmen, of leaders, they have the horizon of internationality, their eyes are on the dangers of loss of national Existence, the possibility of the breakup of the environing world of the nation in its normal form, in which is included the possibility of individually personal Existence as of one citizen, who has as his purpose the familiar historical environing world of this national form and historicality, who affirms it as the sort of thing in which he can fulfill his needs or which lets him hope for a unity for his life in satisfactory form. Of course, not in individual isolation. All needs [are] already historically formed and the individual in the national, generative context is immediately and mediately interwoven with his countrymen in his personal existence: however egoistic he is, regard for others also living is not to be wholly written out of his endeavors and life.

The life of reason in the normalcy of the countryman, in the horizon of ethnic groups (national unity), hence in the normal growth of the "people." Life purely in customary tradition (tradition within the period of normalcy), successful, unsuccessful life. In practical life in individuals rational reflection and decision. Motives for a universal rational reflection, various kinds of universality. Individual life constituted in its all-inclusiveness as universal horizon and endeavor to be able by reflection to give the whole of life the style of something striving upwards, continuously and harmoniously affirmable—as a whole. Government—solicitude for the whole people, for the best form of its life, in which every "citizen" could have the best life-possibilities, first in familiar style, then eventually in change of style. Government—care for the outer, care for the inner.

Egoistic motives and the individual's passions against reason—likewise for the politician conflict of political reason with individual-egoistic passions. Traditional motivation and rational motivation—rational motivations on the basis of tradition, bound by it and not yet conscious of the bond (as bond of rational freedom).

Man, the people in abnormality. The rupture in normal existence by "destiny," fate—individual and of a people. The rupture in individual Existence within a national Existing in good fortune—further still, life under the threat of a disastrous fate, the rupture in existence as possibility constantly belonging to normal life. For the nation as nation among alien, *eo ipso* "enemy" nations (as egoistically interested) life in constant danger of loss of Existence. Various possibilities. The people remains a national unity, but enters into service, becomes a servant people, a people enslaved. Or the people loses its national unity as unity of a nationality; the nation is shattered, the individuals become individual slaves or are transplanted into strange surroundings, denationalized. Possibility of forming a quasi-national unity out of historicality, a people in the diaspora.

New formation of peoples out of peoples. Among them, therefore, the formation of stateless "peoples" as generative-historical communities of life on the part of foreigners and associations of foreigners within the peoples of a nation, among which they themselves have no part as citizens. Further transformation: naturalization of these foreigners while their national bonds beyond the state cannot yet be dissolved. The community, that which institutes personal bonds, lies as historical tradition further in persons.

The intrusion of scientific reason into mankind, which lives prescientifically in finitude and knows the world only as open horizon of life. Disclosure of the open endlessness of the world by the rational form of infinity. Supposed "discovery" of the infinite world, in which all relativity in one's belonging to an environing worldliness and everything that exists within an environing world is annulled by this, that in a universal attitude encompassing all possibilities precisely the totality of relativities is taken in and considered, that in an action of idealization it carries out the anticipation of an infinite ontological structure of identically worldly being as Idea, which as invariant rational form has to guide all empirico-factual determinations in the pregiven world in the sense of approximations of "true being," which lies at infinity. The infinite world presumably apprehensible in the form of infinite nature—physical—psychophysical. Breakdown of this conception. Breakdown of ontology and of the hope of world domination as domination of nature.

The error of ontology: all ontology takes the world as universal nature, the intellectuality of the soul, all personality natural. The critique of ontology and of universal philosophy in its ontological way of proceeding—of the *universitas scientiarum* as positive sciences by phenomenology. Or the discovery of universal phenomenological psychology and therefore of transcendental philosophy first made the critique possible and showed the essential unintelligibility of the world as nature. Radical alteration of the concept, a being ([*to*] *on*). Phenomenology discovers the universe of intelligible being and makes possible on the ground of self-understanding and phenomenological understanding of the world the possibility of autonomy.

The powerful instinct for self-preservation, for an existence that one can universally affirm. Living in finitude man stands before the riddle of the world—the world is senseless, all human endeavor is ultimately senseless, a chase after unreachable goals, "life-goals," ultimately a will to life under the practical ideal of "happiness." This is senseless, even if individual life looks upon itself as a function of national life. For the latter can only temporarily (in the contingent absence of ill-fated occurrences) remain propitious. As soon as man leaves restricted finitude and enters into a knowledge of the world that reaches further, particularly a wide-ranging historical knowledge, something which belongs to every higher culture, he will not be successful in coming to terms with the sense of the world. Man rescues himself by absolutizing religious powers.

Science—infinity—but in science there is above all alteration of the natural stance in traditionalness—attitude of autonomy.

In naive worldliness man suffers under restraints, accidents, fates, which break into the normalcy of his traditional existence and do not make possible a ruling of his life by reason, by reflection and foresight. Man, projected beyond familiar finitude and knowing himself in the infinite (endlessly open) world and in the infinity of incalculable possible contingencies, sees in the world and his existence in it an incomprehensible riddle. Positive science with its naturalistic objectivation of the infinite gives him new hope of grounding Existence through reason. But there he founders. Now the world of scientific reason becomes incomprehensible—new absolute reflection, epoche, highest level of rationality.

B. COMMENTS AND RESEARCH NOTES

Appendix X [to p. 118]ᵏ

Idea of universal human capability—particularly
truth for "everyone" (First days of July, 1933)

[Contents:] Essence of man (in unrestricted essential universality—not merely earthly)—personal, the ideal whole of his abilities and the order of their levels—the highest ability, reason. Correlatively: truth for everyone and every era—Science, science ability, scientific reason. To what extent does every man have the ability to acquire science as theory?

The essence of man—not merely of earthly man—the ideal whole of his abilities, the order of their levels (old talk about lower and higher abilities), usually named as highest ability "reason." Correlatively: truth for everyone and every era. Theoretical truth—science as theory and science ability (scientific reason). To what extent is there actually for everyone, let us say also on earth, this potentiality for being able to acquire science in one's investigation and study? That belongs to a phenomenology of universal teleology.

Human potentialities, abilities—the universe of the capabilities that belong to man by essence. The ability of cognition—scientific truth as truth for everyone and in every era. But the ability for science nonetheless was not a developed power in all historical periods of our culture and not at all for lower cultures. To what extent is it still a potentiality belonging to everyone? Something existent for everyone as possibility for his development?

The natural science of Galileo: Galileo himself in his Renaissance world, in his stratum of the "new man," man of a new educational direction and formative upbringing [*Bildung*], belonging to it, in the tradition of revivified and transformed ancient phi-

174

losophy and science. Everyone from this stratum—everyone who grew up into it as mature man, and into its coexistential tradition, would have the developed abilities from which by active tradition, by association with others, by understanding Galileo's writings, Galileo's ability (natural science) could have become an actual ability in everyone as fellow scientist: if he listened patiently and experienced anew the original motivation in its origin character. Prior to that he would have the pre-abilities, conditioning abilities, for entering this circle in which Galileo's motivation was taken over and, in a way, his actual abilities. So for all of Europe—in the stratum of the humanists, or the personalities of the Renaissance. And the other Europeans? Some would have mediate access in that they fulfilled in their capabilities the preconditions for being able to be receptive to the new formative upbringing and from there to come also under Galileo's "influence." The large remaining sector, farmers, the bourgeois common man—if, that is, as children they were raised accordingly, presupposing their normalcy—and then of people who were already precisely "new men."

If we ask about the relationship to Galileo of the old people and of their human abilities, they of course would have had access to Galileo's motivation either not at all or only in times of sufficiently developed ancient science, and that only if the writings of Galileo or those who came later had come to their notice, hence if Galileo had lived then—or we new men of science as teachers of the old. And likewise with regard to the "uneducated" and the possibility of their training—by "us."

Does that lead to an empiricist historicism, scepticism, relativism? Is our science thus merely ours, as the science of every era is its science, for the one chemistry, for the other alchemy, etc.? Does the science of one era have a prerogative, may it appoint itself as norm for criticism of other eras? Does every era have its logic as its formal system of norms for its scientificity, etc.?

By the study of history [*Historie*]¹ we disclose the historicality of our human world, of our humanized environing world: we "reconstruct" past mankind, a past environing world, past objectivated intellectuality [*Geistigkeit*]. We acquire modes of the presentification men as such had in ancient times, we co-construct their accomplishments, which have come down to us in Objective documentation (or by mediate reports about it). Or rather, from their accomplishments we construct the persons and from the persons, the more completely they are put in evidence, the accomplishments whose actual motivation becomes intelligible, and by way of that, their concretely complete sense, and thereby in turn the persons, and so on. That, however, in the whole cultural and ethnic life—hence correspondingly also for ethnic individuals in their subjectivity and their objectivation in their environing world. Of course the "actual past" is an Idea which we only endlessly approach. But is it otherwise in regard to our "present," the spatiotemporal environing world in its human form and its humanity? We live in this now world, but what it is in truth, beyond our subjective, flowing understanding of it, taking it as reality (in meager one-sided ways of being given), it is that as infinite Idea. In it the open horizon of men, the few that we actually have in view, the few that we have become directly acquainted with, an open "infinity" of unknown people—yet remaining in part, by way of their Objective accomplishments, not wholly unknown to us. Every worked piece, even if manufactured, tells of man as worker, as inventing, as executing, etc., however ambiguously, however indeterminately, still worker as working subject for this work, etc. As long as man makes himself known Objectively, so long do we in a certain way stand in intercourse with him, although not immediately and in mutual exchange. In a certain way even in mutual exchange, in mutual connection, inasmuch as, e.g., the manufactured item has in every part the sense that it is intended for users and buyers, and this consignment to others for whom the produced goods are goods is, if I experience the thing concerned, consignment to me, and so I am with others, whom I have never seen, in mediate connection, and perfectly so when I not only understand the thing as to what it is, but put it to use. I do something and fulfill what those others had in mind, their intention. So I am with others partly in direct, partly in indirect empathy. Even the direct is construction, inasmuch as I become acquainted with the Other only by what he does, by his deeds, by his working and by his works, thus by way of a constructing. I have direct intercourse with another, direct community with him, communal action, etc., and here individually. The indeterminateness in which the Other remains pertains here only to his being-such-and-such [*Sosein*], not his being-individual [*Einzigsein*] as this alter ego (just as my being-such-and-such too is for the most part closed off and indeterminate for myself). I can be in connection with specific individuals in mediateness, I have my, and everyone else has his, circle of definite persons which he indirectly knows insofar as he knows of them by their "outward expressings," by their actions, works, etc., and with whom he is in association in I-you acts. And added to that the circle of unknown individuals one knows of, but not as specific individuals whom one can give a place in the environing world, who as individuals make a specific association possible. Although, as shown above, there is still something remaining of a connection, in a certain way, in ambiguous indeterminateness.

I am motivated by my fellow humans inasmuch as in some way they are connected with me; if I am motivated by the intellectual environment, then they share in this motivation themselves. To live in the world and first of all in the present environing world is constantly to live involved in motivation from one's fellow man. To live is to live in living motivation from and living construction of the environing world, of things themselves in becoming acquainted with them, of others and their objectivated intellectual products; through these products [one becomes acquainted with] the others themselves. That is *history of the present*. Likewise we live in ordinary history and particularly by means of historical science [*Historie*], which itself is the path toward constructing "eras," the men, peoples, cultures, environing worlds in those eras in their truth—in relative truths—and this historical past is the past of our present and the continuity of past presents of the same mankind that stretches generatively into pasts. We are motivated, now, by all that is thus disclosed by historical presentification: we are in intercourse, in levels of mediacy, with the people disclosed out of ourselves. We fulfill the testament of a deceased father, his past will reaches into our will and comes to realization in it. However, we also honor the family traditions of earlier ages, the unity of a way of thinking that was meant by our forebears as not only their own, but as one to be adopted and carried on by their children's children. We become acquainted also, however, e.g., with a geometrical or other task set by the ancient Greeks, we take it up and read it—it was directed to one's fellow men in its time, but as having an open life that continues, and not only in the present but in the future.

But however much the unity of tradition, and in historical reconstruction the unity of tradition that with a motivation that always transcends eras continues to have a living effect, moves through history and the historically disclosed world and constitutes unity for a mankind that lives in historical connection and in the historical unity of this mankind's world—however much this takes place, the concrete world is still always a different world. Historical mankind is the mankind of whatever given present in the present of the respective environing world—this present is not a point in time, it is something existent [Seiendes] in relative normalcy in the movement of life and in the mobile change of men and humanity, in a persistent type, in that it makes possible a typicality of motivations, a typicality of transient humanity, of its interests, its actions, its plans in life, its political projects, etc., without which human being would just not be possible. This normalcy, however, is fluid and has its revolutionary breaks too, which lead to a new normalcy, which is one that is new and yet bound to the old by tradition that is retained. All that is to be thought over for our inquiry.

And now in addition: how man as man, through all historicity and all modes of modified humanity which he historically reconstructs, understands, experiences as reality, is still in essential coincidence with himself as man: in every mode of empathy self-modification lies in a condition of coinciding, and with this coinciding an essential composition is given. To it belongs, as something ontologically formal, the environing world structure with its typicality, to which the typicality of man living in this world belongs: de facto typicality, the de facto typicality of men, of their apperception of the world, of their humanly spirit-imbued nature; that is for every "era," every relative present is a different one. But the form is the same. With that also counts the play of being and seeming [Sein und Schein], of aiming and missing, of abiding interests and fleeting ones, of false purposes, false values and true, the play of modalization, of correction, the building up of a life grasped by a universal vision, conceived in a universal project according to an Idea of a right life, one that is satisfying, one never to be regretted, one never to be given up as worthless, etc. To life belongs normalcy not only as type of the pregiven environing world, into whose typical structure one grows up, whose types one takes up, but also active norm-setting and, out of oneself and in union with those who are like-minded, fashioning of the environing world into one in accord with norms. The distinction is made between the normal in accord with a kathekon[m] and the normal in accord with that which is willed or is to be willed unconditionally, the absolute Ought [das absolute Gesollte]. So to human beings belongs absolute critique, but also critique of the Absolute in regard to its absoluteness and the possible relativity that may still cling to it.

What sense and what right, now, does a critique have that reaches beyond the historical present into the past?[1]

Appendix XI [to §3 and §4]ⁿ

Two levels of phenomenology. Straightforward phenomenology and phenomenology of phenomenologizing.
(End of 1933)

[Contents:] The transcendental ego—thematic by reduction—has two strata and a double theme: 1) the straightforward theme of world-constitution, and 2) founded therein the theme of the phenomenologizing life of reason of the transcendental ego. Iterability. The transcendental ego as infinite theme in twofold respect. Infinity in the straightforward direction and in the founded reflective thematic direction.

The reduction in the epoche in regard to every worldly cognitive theme is reduction to subjectivity purely as that subjectivity in which the world has constant acceptedness for it as existent and acquires acceptedness in flowing modes of consciousness in change of content (of presentational sense [*des Vorstellungssinnes*]), wherein the world in each case has acceptedness.

This ego is a concrete ego, one at first "mute"; its explication is phenomenology. In practicing the reduction, I am the reducing I which is thematically directed to itself as that which presents the world [*als Welt vorstellendes*], has the world in acceptedness, and is directed to the world itself as the world therein "conscious," and as constituting phenomenology practices an activity—phenomenologizes. Herewith I can distinguish: 1) I as I of acts and what makes up acts themselves as such, their varying modes, their aims as guiding the act-I, their aims as aimed for in the mode of fulfillment, etc., 2) that which the acts of the I continually presuppose, what for the active I is presupposition for all its doing, is foundation, ground.

Just as for the natural I living in the world the world is constantly pregiven in horizonal consciousness as the continuous all-inclusive horizon of the existent, so in the reduction the pregivenness of the world is "pregiven" as horizonal consciousness (in its flowing modes) in unity with the acts of the I referring to it, in its living change it is the ground of reflective and reductive activity.

Along with that, however, another distinction has to be made: As ego I am, in the reduction, the one phenomenologizing, as was said, I am the subject of theoretical

---

1. ⟨Unfortunately broken off. The whole thing must, of course, be carried on in connection with the total problem of universal teleology, the totality of teleologically attuned abilities, of the universal drive moving through them all toward the completeness, or the "completion," of transcendental interpersonality.⟩

acts, of a theoretical I-life; by my direction of interest I am thematically directed to the "phenomenon of the world" and its subjective (egological) constitution, to that which is precisely thus given, precisely world-constitution, to the whole accepted-ness life in which the world is for me as existent and becomes present [to me] [*vorstel-lig*] with such and such contents.

This is accordingly the theme of thematizing action—this latter as the function-ing action of phenomenologizing is not thematic. In the reflection which we called reductive, however, it does get included, not pregiven in the simple sense of some-thing pregiven in the environing world, something in preknownness, although pre-given in another way than the phenomenon of the world. In the theme, therefore, is the ego in all the active and habitual life of world-constitution with all its substrata. This first theme, now, can be distinguished from that of further reflection upon my-self as the act-I of phenomenologizing action, which clearly is an abstract stratum of the full concrete ego, which stratum it, which stratum I as ego make thematic in re-flection upon my phenomenologizing action and the thematic-theoretical constructs that arise from it.

How can the ego in concreteness be for itself, come to thematic acceptedness for itself? Only with a special infinite horizon of iterative anonymity. But nonetheless the "concreteness of the ego"—accordingly an infinite Idea—makes good sense, one that can be grasped thematically. What stands out from the very first is that in thematiz-ing the concrete ego (as all-inclusiveness of the subjective something which consti-tutes the world, and with all that makes this subjective something into a totality) I have a structure of thematic breadth and anonymous (and in this sense latent) depth. In this thematic breadth, as the sphere that at times is to be investigated without phe-nomenologizing reflection, I acquire an infinity which, as the constitutive infinity of the correlation of world as acceptedness phenomenon and subjective modes of ac-ceptedness-crediting [*Gelten*], of world-presenting [*Weltvorstellen*], world-having, of placing worldly being-sense in acceptedness, is only (and in principle) knowable as a drawing into cognitional focus of essential phenomena that, beyond what is de facto lived and beyond living process, bring the infinite range of possibilities to predelin-eation and at the same time bring my transcendental abilities in this stratum to out-line form. On the other hand, in regard to the depth of the anonymity of phenomenologizing performances in all their habitualization.

But while I perform these reflections, this reflective, previously anonymous some-thing is grasped as such and now further still is comprehended theoretically, and for its part further my anonymous functioning is comprehended as phenomenologizing I of a higher level, whose theme is the first phenomenologizing I, and more concretely the latter together with its substratum in world-constituting life and world itself as unity of subjectively constituting modes. Reflection has its noteworthiness. It is already a prob-lem how it is motivated, and how, when it is entered into, without more ado the con-sciousness of "I can reflect again" occurs and then the "I can always do it again"—as consciousness of an open-ended infinite iteration. But disregarding that and presup-posing the ability of iteration, I stand before the astonishing fact that I as my own theme (that is, in the epoche) imply the iterative distinction between the phenomenologizing ego and the ego become thematic; or, that my concrete ego can only be the theme with a phenomenologizing act-I that in principle functions anonymously.

We have as egologically recognizable the ability to iterate reflection. With the first reflection and by carrying out thematizing activity directed to first thematizing reflection, we immediately have the possibility, on the one hand, of thinking this thematizing activity carried out in its own infinity as first phenomenology, and then of reflectively tracking down its structures in their essential forms. This very system of forms is constituted in the anonymity which to make thematic in its correlative forms is the task of proper transcendental logic as the logic of transcendental phenomenologizing (as transcendental theory of method). And in iteration the same thing necessarily repeats itself, the constitution of nomological descriptions and theorizings is the same over and over again.

Must we not say: Even for intentional psychology, undertaken in the natural attitude, we have this double thematic direction and double infinity: 1) the theme of consciousness of the world, 2) the theme of psychologizing life? But the latter itself, and likewise the ability to iterate, belong in the psychological theme as something existent psychically.

[Probably to §3, p. 15ff.] Transcendental disclosure as performance of the phenomenologizing ego.

By this means the world and positive science are comprehended as constituted, and with that brought into transcendental intersubjectivity as the intersubjectivity of constituting agents.

But this ascertainment is the product of reason, of the method of the transcendental-phenomenologizing ego of reason.

In saying that, I perform a new reduction and reflection. Thereby the life of phenomenologizing performance becomes thematic, the life in which the monadic world is constituted for me and by me, with all that is therein constituted: thus in the monadic world is implied the natural world and in it all that my human I and my fellow men perform in presenting the world to themselves [*Welt vorstellend*] and cognizing it.

If I hold fast the ground of the transcendental monad world, then reflection upon my monadic action would itself be given a place in my monad and monadic world, analogously to the way it is with the natural world. By a reflection at a second level I absolutely and concretely obtain the phenomenologizing I and life, both "worlds" become phenomena at a second level. Each straightforwardly existent in correspondingly different anonymity.

At the hitherto highest level I have therefore the third I, the third I-life, perceiving, etc., eidetically—the eidetics of the I that phenomenologizes, that constitutes the universe of monads, and that thereby constitutes the world.

The life disclosed by phenomenologizing is richer than natural human life, richer in the disclosed performances by which world-life is constituted in the world. The phenomenologizing I recognizes that. In further reflection I recognize my naively

functioning phenomenologizing cognition and function now as higher phenomenologizing I. My eidetic action in phenomenologizing activity, my predicating—that
now does not lie in the monads, not in my monad, it lies in me—a new ego. But is
that not the same as the one that by constitution of the monad world becomes a
monad in it?

Appendix XII (to p. 81)°

Consciousness of the horizon of the world and its struc-
tures. Attempt at a full systematic treatment.
(End of 1933)[1]

World-horizon, particular horizon—type of the total, and type of the individual
real thing. The preknownness of essential structures implied in the pregivenness of
the world, and in contrast to that the giving of essences themselves in ideation.

The first is nothing other than the constantly horizonal consciousness in which
with all its change, by virtue of a continual passive synthesis, "the" world, the one
same universe of continually coexistent realities [*koexistierender Realitäten*], is given. Seen
more closely, this change is one of ever new particular apperceptions in which various individual real things come consciously into the foreground, together and one after the other, but in such a way that any one real thing and all real things apperceived
at some same given time are necessarily conscious as real Objects (or properties, relations, etc.) *from* the world, as existing in the one spatiotemporal horizon of being.
Coexistence [*Koexistenz*] for a real thing never ever has a sense other than inexistence
[*Inexistenz*], than being in the universe, in the open horizon of spatiotemporality, in
the horizon of real things that are already known and not simply conscious in a present actual moment, but also those unknown, those possibly coming to experience
and future knownness. Individual apperceptions make the individual real thing conscious, but unfailingly with a stock of sense, even if not thematic, which reaches out
beyond that apperception, beyond the whole set of individual apperceptions.

In progression from some one set of posited individual perceptions to a new set
(and especially from those that are thematically apperceiving in one case to others
with new thematizations) synthetic unity prevails: The new apperceived item occu-
pies, as it were, the previously still empty, still content-undetermined horizon in pre-
acceptedness, fulfilling a sense that is already predelineated but not yet particularized

---

1. ⟨(Pertaining to this: that everything which explicates horizon implications, that
everything real that comes to be known has its individual type (its distinctive traits in
turn have trait-typicality), world-totality has its universal ontological type. Analysis
of typical apperceptions—indeterminateness as determinability, range, etc.)

Written down on the occasion of checking over the "Sixth Meditation" as given in
Dr. Fink's draft.⟩

and determined. So there is always a horizon of acceptedness, a world in accepted-ness as to being, there is always, beyond that which at a given moment is taken hold of in individuality and relative determinateness and brought to acceptedness, a con-tinually moving anticipation of particularizing and determining fulfillment. Of course, something that would still have to be properly treated, [in] an inner move-ment of the modalization of certainty, of the change of what is modalized by way of correction in producing a new harmonious certainty of the whole.

This transcendence of sense adheres to every individual apperception, to every re-spective total set of individual perceptions not only in regard to the continually an-ticipated potentiality of possible new individual real things and entire real groups as what is yet to come in the course of actualizations in consciousness, in the course of movement from the world into consciousness, but it also adheres as the "internal hori-zon" to every real thing already coming onto the scene with regard to a stock of not yet actually apperceived distinctive traits. Everything individually apperceived in its thisness bears within itself, although unthematically, the distinction (one that has al-ways to be explicitly, thematically produced) between what of the real thing prop-erly enters consciousness and what is merely anticipated, which for its part is sometimes already known from earlier on, sometimes still unknown, and yet with all its "empty" indeterminacy and openness is necessarily co-accepted (such as the re-verse side, still unseen, but a potentiality of able-to-become-visible and then, more specifically, of becoming known). Belonging here too "internal" modalizations and corrections, as possibilities already determining beforehand the horizonal sense.

To passive synthesis in flowing life, as the having of constant horizonal conscious-ness of the world in change, there corresponds the fact that the world, the world al-ways in consciousness as the one spatiotemporal universe, is not conscious, and the identity of the world is not thematically constituted, by an active identification. Just as is so for every thematic consciousness of an individual mundane thing, so too the-matic consciousness of the world presupposes horizonal consciousness with its continual onward course of passive synthesis. The being-sense, world, becoming the-matic, gains elucidated determinateness in its continually anticipated acceptedness as the manifold of real things that in the course of life in the world is harmoniously de-termined, and may remain yet to be determined, in individual apperceptions, and as finally in the totality of real things as existent actualities which is to be brought to givenness in its very self in the infinity of [both merely] possible harmonious experi-ence of the world and that which is [actually] within one's capability. Added to this belongs the great problem of the structure of a possible intuition of the world.

As is shown by the above, the horizonal consciousness [of] the world has a con-stant, essence-determined form: the form of a flowing change and, more closely con-sidered, the structural form of a core set of actual-moment perceptions of individual real things into which new individual apperceptions enter and then new ones again. Individual apperception here means, very broadly conceived, something individually brought to the foreground in a particular acceptedness with its particular sense (with "presentational" content ["*Vorstellungs*"-*Gehalt*]). In this core set there lies in essential, constant fashion a narrower set of intuitive (giving something itself) apperceptions, and in this a still narrower set of perceptual apperceptions, which make up the perceptual field in any one given instance. Cutting across all that is the distinction between thematic and unthematic particular apperceptions, namely, that in essential constancy at any given moment a thematic core of real things in particularized awareness (or in their real attributes, properties, relations, combinations, etc.) is given within an unthematic background which, however, is articulated in particular apperceptions.

Accordingly one distinguishes between [on the one hand] the always full consciousness of the world as horizonal consciousness in a core of totality for any given moment, which consists of particular apperceptions, and [on the other] an all-inclusive horizon of implications, a horizon of that which holds in acceptedness beyond the, so to say, expressly given. That, however, is not to be understood as a mere indication out beyond something which for its own sake is brought in particular apperceptions to acceptedness and to an exclusively accepted being-sense. Therefore the talk of implication. Exterior acceptedness reaches everywhere into particular apperception, into all particular apperceptions, and already co-implies their being-sense. All particular apperceptions are already fulfillments of something meant beforehand, and only as such do they have being-sense (similarly to the way particular apperceptions can only have the being-sense proper to them by their constant anticipation in regard to that which becomes "properly" conscious in them). Along with that one has to consider that, just as world-sense has its unity of identity in passive synthesis and is actively identifiable and explicable over and over again as the same world in the same form of spatiotemporality, so every individual reality that is in it as that which for its own sake can come to acceptedness is and remains an identical item in the horizon of the world, is in it with the sense of identifiability over and over again as the same thing in *its* spatiotemporality, which is given a position as identical in universal spatiotemporality and world.

A fundamental structure pertaining to consciousness of the world, or, in terms of the correlate, to the world as horizon, is the structure of *knownness* and *unknownness*, with the relativity that continually belongs to it and the likewise continual relative distinction of indeterminate generality and determinate particularity.

The world horizonally in consciousness has in its constant acceptedness in being the subjective character of familiarity in general as the horizon of existents that is known in general but therefore not yet in individual particularities. This indeterminately general familiarity is distributed to everything that comes to particular acceptedness as something existent, everything therefore has its form as a known form, within which all further distinctions between knownness and unknownness proceed.

Everything real that enters experience as new stands, we said, in the horizon of world, and as that has its internal horizon. In thematic perception it becomes known, because during the course of experiencing (however far it may reach) [it] is presented as itself continuously identical there, but is displayed in its individual distinctive traits, its what-moments, as for their part self-presenting but precisely with the sense of the sort of thing in which the real shows itself as what it is. Still everything that thus shows itself and already is implicitly there before explication in some act of grasping the perceived, holds essentially in acceptedness as that of the real which genuinely comes to perception in this perception. It itself is more than that which at a particular moment comes, and has already come, to actual cognizance: it comes with the sense that its "internal horizon" always bestows on it, the seen side is only a side in that it has unseen sides that are anticipated as such in a way that determines sense. We can direct ourselves to them at any time, we can ask about them, we can pre-envision them. Perhaps after perception is broken off and from the acquaintance [therein gained] continued acceptedness has come about as an acquired and "still living" cognizance (knownness of the real in regard to that of it which has become genuinely known), we can make present to ourselves in advance what further perception would have been able and would have had to bring forth as belonging to this real thing itself. Every such pre-envisioning of that which "a priori" is to be accounted to this real thing has, however, the essential property of indeterminate generality. That means: If we take the example of visual pre-envisioning, in respect to the visually hidden side of a thing, we get indeed a presentifying intuition (similar to a recollection), but not a fixed determinateness that binds us in individual ways, as is the case with a recollection—in both matters fully elaborated clarity being presupposed. As soon as we actually progress to clear determinateness, we become conscious of the arbitrariness of the determinate color that emerges and that is to hold hereafter as the color of the thing. Every pre-envisioning comes about in a conscious fluid variability, in order to be able to fix conscious variants as a particular color, but as a free variant, for which we could just as well work out another. [It is] otherwise in recollection, in which clarity leads to a limit that binds freedom, to the determinate it-itself as it was. On the other hand, however, the arbitrariness is not one without any restrictions. In the fluctuation of pre-envisioning, in the passage from one variant or directedness toward something temporarily holding steady over to another, we remain in a unity of anticipation, anticipation namely of the color of the hidden side, which, however, is indeterminately general as anticipation, is determined in the manner of a type as an anticipation of something typically familiar. In the explication of this typical generality in the form of determinate "possibilities" which are open for the actual being of this color, there emerges the range of possibilities as explicit "scope" of the indeterminate generality of the anticipation. Because the thing entering experience only has being-sense as a thing with an internal horizon, whereas of it only a core of whatnesses enters into de facto, genuine cognizance, the thing has, absolutely everything real has, as experienceable, its "general a priori," a preknownness, as indeterminate generality that however is always identifiable as itself, an a priori type pertaining to a range of a priori possibilities. Obviously the type encompasses also the properties that enter actual cognizance, if we take the type as a totality. In the change in which whatnesses enter and leave, the real thing is continuously in consciousness as one thing, as something identifiable, and to this unity belongs the total type as total horizon of the typical generality in which everything actually becoming known arranges itself as a particularizing determination that provides more or less complete fulfillment.

As for the external horizon, which in determining sense belongs to this real thing, to some respectively individual thing, it resides in the consciousness of a potentiality of possible experiences of individual real things: of things such as in each instance have their own a priori as their typicality, in which they are necessarily anticipated, and which through every fulfillment in the form of this or that possibility of invariant range remains invariant. Every particular typicality, that of real particulars (and of constellations of real things), however, is encompassed by the typicality of totality, the typicality belonging to the whole world-horizon in its infinity. In the flow of world-experience, of concretely full consciousness of the world in its respectiveness to any given moment [*in seiner Jeweiligkeit*], the being-sense, world, remains invariant and therefore invariant [also] is the structural building up of this being-sense out of invariant types of individual realities. Correlatively, horizonal consciousness, which we have already seen above in rough form in a chain of exhibitings, has its essential structure of noetic forms and syntheses, taken as a whole and in respect to its construction out of individual apperceptions that, for themselves, are altogether dependent in their bestowal of their sense and in their immanent being.

Different "horizons." What is this: the bringing about of horizons?

Natural attitude in the performance of my acts—and of their act-horizons. What is it to perform, to bring about the horizons of an act? What is actual-moment doxa? In all my doing I have a horizon of possibilities, a "living" horizon, in which I "move mentally." This act-horizon can itself have a still further horizon that is now not in question, but which nevertheless is one that determines sense.

I plan a trip, and I am busy with travel preparations—packing the trunk in my room—, then I have to send the trunk by an express company. Now the further horizon comes into consideration, the room is a room in the city with its places of business, possibilities for me to shop there, to take care of the trunk, etc. In my practical possibilities I have levels, what is an active practical possibility, and what is a secondary possibility, one already secondary from the start as an active possibility. In contrast, empty practical possibilities that have another "if–then." The one "if" is "if I did this"—that which lies beforehand in volition and has its time. The other "if" is an imaginary thinking of oneself in a volition (where the volition is a volition as-if) and this modified volition has its practical horizon in different levels that likewise have their primary and secondary activeness. This having, or this activeness, thus requires its explication.

Natural attitude in the performance of acts with their active horizons, the total activity in the flow with its total (as always in different levels) active horizon—positional horizon, acceptedness horizon. Epoche of naive performance. I do not really inhibit that performance. The world continues to hold for me, it is. The universal acceptedness of the world—in the flow of individual acceptednesses and acceptedness horizons. The one world that is constituted therein and always holds good.

Double sense of acceptedness [*Geltung*]. The accepting process as experiential, that which is accepted as holding in that performance.ᴾ The accepted real thing as the perceived in perception, etc., in the how of its content, unity of the accepted in the flow—precisely in a different how. The universal life of acceptedness, the I in performance as "identifying" a continuous unity in harmonious manners of givenness, and explicating this identical something in identical determinations, explicating what is existent in its being-such-and-such, and consequently performing further acts on the basis of that which is existent.

Living in naiveté—world as "basis," as that which the I is occupied with, as the field of being which it has in acceptedness of being, as manifold of existents, those identified and those to be identified prospectively; the existent at a particular actual moment, in actual-moment performance of basis-acts—performance as identifying acts, directed to the identical, to the unity of actual and possible manners of appearance of the same thing.

Inhibiting—not living in this acceptedness of identity, not living in this identifying action and in this already having of something as identical, not living in this act of active reshaping [directed] upon something existent, dedicating [oneself] to the production of a new existent out of what already exists. Rather, beginning a new life of acts, a new identifying and having as identical, a new life in which I have nothing of the universe of the existent that is already given.

Doxic acts and acquisitions from acts—that which is accepted and continues to be accepted as identifiable. The act-horizon, the horizon of that which is already accepted as existent—the horizon of being. That, however, is a ticklish matter. Different concepts of "horizon." 1) Potentiality, capability of repeated identification—recollection of the retentional, repeated recollection, re-cognizing, identifying—recollection here repeating what is "still" in retention, still in living grasp. 2) Further: horizon of submerged memories and the capability of awakening and identifying in recollection. 3) Further: horizon of the unknown, not to be identified by recollection, but "inductive" horizon, projection of a disjunctive sphere of possibilities with the potentiality of the activity of continued experience that decides, and already that of verifying the actual "induction" of some given moment by new inductions. That means, to every perception there belongs the distinction between that which is actually inductively inferred (adperceived) and which has a relative determinateness (indeterminateness is already a first horizon of possibility) and something else not "actually" inductively inferred which has an indeterminateness. What makes the "actually"? It is anticipatory act-rays, while the background-horizon is of course also a potential acceptedness, but in a different potentiality. The potentiality of that which is actually inductively inferred lies in the fact that it is an act-ray but not perception, yet a potentiality of perception. So in the next [horizon], in the horizonality of perception. 4) In addition another horizon. An "obscure" memory, an empty consciousness, which has a role to play in experience as potentiality for fulfillment.

But we have here in experience of the world all the mediacies, the horizonal mediacies, that include the different modes of induction as actual. And different modes of non-actuality; and yet the whole horizon is an acceptedness totality, always "actual" in its own way, determining worldly being-sense, individual being-sense and an individual in the total being-sense. Here research must not fail.

And now we have waking life as a life of acts, where "act" is behavior of the I toward the constantly pregiven world, pregiven as universe of being, the world constantly certain as to its being. Certainty of being in a universal doxa. That as "field," as basis of being for practice, for "acts" in the sense of "acting." Willing as willing something in the world, weighing in the world worldly possibilities—as personal capabilities—, assessing them, making up one's mind, actualizing them in action.

The "general thesis," the universal doxa, is the flowing having of the world, acceptedness of the world, flowing identification, acquiring an identical something and already having acquisitions. To talk of acquisition is dangerous here.

A special treatment of directedness and horizon in the area of perception.

An experience of perception. The clock on the table, during perceptual seeing the change of the manners of the givenness of the clock and the change of my explicating directedness: constantly directed to the clock, which is itself given there identical in mode, I am directed in particularity to now this, now that such-and-such, to that in which the clock is this and that in particularity. In this change identity of the pole of direction, identity first of the substrate pole, and then of the respective attribute-pole, to which corresponds a specific change of manners of givenness referred to it.

The distinction between "experiences" and the manners of appearance of the identical as the identical in the how.

In directedness to, an aiming after, striving toward—with the limit case of attainment, of fulfilled striving in being right there [*Dabeisein*]. Relativity: a manner of givenness itself as relative pole of relative manners of givenness, for example, an appearance in the distance, the thing at a distance—optimally given as against imperfect manners of givenness in kinesthetic change.

On the other hand, "experience" as a problem: here left open. The issuing of directedness toward the pole and its such-and-suchness pole from the I-pole, the I-center, multiplicity of rays of directedness toward the pole, in the continuity of unbroken steady perception, in that from the I-center new rays of such-and-suchness keep issuing. This directedness is the act of perceiving, of doxa as attainment, as a course of continual aiming for more and more perfect attainment, an act that moves in unimpeded course. That which is attained, the existent, toward which I direct my volition at this actual moment, while I am by it but not yet perfectly, not in all that it is. In mere explication I lay out what I already, but not explicitly, have. In the continuation of perceiving one side and then another I actualize that of the object which in a new sense is not yet given.

I already have here too a double horizon: the horizon of the unexplicated side or object in this side, relevant to the explicata of the side; and the horizon of the sides, implicitly their horizons of explicata.

C. UNASSIGNED PAGES

Appendix XIII

The psychological enworlding of the transcendental which is disclosed from the viewpoint of the phenomenologizing ego. *Ad* psychologization of phenomenology.
(December 1993, or January 1934)

Within the absolute universal thematic domain of transcendental attitudes phenomenology calls for particular attitudes with correspondingly subordinate universal themes. Thus the attitude toward the phenomenon of the world, to the naively pregiven world as such, naively pregiven as environing world, in order then to interpret transcendentally the empirical science relating to it. While I, the one phenomenologizing, explore the constitution of the world (as sense of being of the transcendental ego), I perform thereby a continuing constitution of the world itself, namely, by psychologizing the transcendental lived processes which function as constituting the world. So for every transcendental Other and monadic communalization. Everything is psychologized, is thereby put into the world, to be ascribed to human souls. Again and again I, the one phenomenologizing, (and we) can place ourselves "back" in the stance toward the world and humanity and then must find in the world everything transcendental enworlded in souls. Naturally too the action of changing one's stance, of passing again into the natural attitude.

The life of phenomenologizing acts and its performances continually belong themselves to the theme. Transcendental subjectivity is in an infinite reflectivity, in an iterative infinity of actual and possible reflection, and in addition is always constituting the world in such a way that it projects all its transcendental [constitutions], displayed by pure and absolute self-reflection, into the world, into the always already constituted world, into the world that continues to be constituted. That, however, in correspondingly incremental sense: for every such action of projecting is itself a sense-bestowing performance. But what is meant by that is that the sense of the world, issuing from here, from the action of phenomenologizing, is in constant change.

Otherwise expressed: the phenomenologist discovers the true sense of the world. While he, nevertheless, has the already pregiven, preknown world as the presumably concrete world. Doing the discovering in the transcendental present of some given moment, the phenomenologist carries forward the action of transcendentally constituting himself, and in himself gives new sense to the world by inserting that which is disclosed into the psychic, new sense in egological self-temporalization, in the temporality of the world with the temporalized ego.

The always pregiven, preknown world, with which one is to become acquainted in progressive world-experience and science, does not have, in "natural" life in the world, in "natural" life in science, a full and final truth-sense, [i.e.,] the sense of being. It is brought to its full being-sense only when understood as transcendentally constituted. But phenomenology also enters the world as science, it is enworlded as a historical cultural construct. The naturally pregiven world in its psychic side continually receives an increase of being-sense from phenomenology once it is brought into action, being-sense that undergoes worldly objectivation. Man, become phenomenologist, has overcome his naive humanity; but even in the phenomenological change of stance he finds himself "as man in the world," now, however, as "new" man. His transcendentally phenomenologizing action is anonymous and is itself constituted; the subsequent activity of reflection, iterative repetition, makes ever-new enworlding in one's own psychic sphere.

However far I have come as phenomenologist, I can direct myself to the world as correlate. And after I have recognized the necessity of the enworlding of the transcendental in iterability, the world will in advance take on a new being-sense for me, namely, as infinite horizon of transcendentality inserting itself into it and having to insert itself into it. Let us think about what that involves.

The world as nature remains what it was, a construct of sense, a synthetic unity in the infinity of environing natural cores. Prescientifically and then scientifically. Within the natural full world it is a mere stratum; subjectivity in its grip upon it of course changes nature, but alters nothing of the unity of nature as core in its own ontological form.

What comes more essentially into question for us is personal subjectivity (psychic subjectivity) in the world. Souls^q in naive naturalness have, so to say, remained stuck in an unfinished state. By phenomenological activity, which transcends the natural world, they come into movement, their being-sense receives new accrual in the form of new enworldings of the transcendental. This, however, in a double fashion. For one has to distinguish phenomenologizing souls from non-phenomenologizing souls. In our phenomenologizing we understand the latter as naive persons, naive souls, for whom there is only the naive (prephenomenological) world; and if they are psychologists, then they have a "naive" psychology, which they never get beyond. A soul such as this can never get to the truly concrete being of souls.

Appendix XIV

[Absolute transcendental constitution. The self-disclosure
of the phenomenologizing subject] (January 21, 1934)

In the transcendental totality field of the existent in the absolute sense there enters as correlate the natural naive world, the world of men not yet aware of transcendentality; with this accrued being-sense it is itself a moment in the Absolute. That
holds, then, also for historical mankind, to which I, the one phenomenologizing, am
accounted as man and historian (or as knowing something about historical study [*Historie*]), and for the historically engendered and continually developing positive sciences; they are constructs in the complex of the one absolute transcendental
constitution. Along with that the absolute total, in all that it is, is at the same time
constituting and constituted, but of course in such a way that we have to distinguish
[1)] that which is patently constituted cognitionally, that which stands in cognitional
constitution and therefore is existent in a patent sense (explicitly), that which is existent for the ego—I as awake and phenomenologizing—that which holds good for
the ego, verifies itself for it; and [2)] that which is latently existent, the implicit, the
anonymous for the wakeful I.

Final problems tie in here. In wakefulness I am the subject of phenomenologizing;
as such I recognize that in naive-human wakefulness I had a sphere of anonymity in
accord with which I was not phenomenologizing, or I recognize that other men are
transcendental co-subjects with just these anonymities, in which they are not phenomenologizing. As phenomenologizing I constantly have my spheres of anonymity
correlates, that which is patent to me and that which is coming to be patent to me in
the continually relative. But I know [that] the transcendental I [is] not [disclosed] at the
beginning, when the reduction starts, although just as the epoche starts in its motivation and thus is already meant for reduction, a horizon is there as that into which I strive,
as that which is to become known to me. Hence the new transcendental "pregivenness"
without an anticipatable essential style. Afterwards, however, I am ready to carry out
iterated reflections (thus in the "again and again") that are also conceptualized as iteration, and I now have the horizon of constituted constitution which discloses itself
over and over again. In that the phenomenologizing ego is transcendental-
scientific, it is not only one that gets to know something experientially, but continuously patent constitution yields transcendental science, as construct of transcendental
theory about the transcendental Absolute and its components. The phenomenologizing subject, in the wakefulness that produces theoretical cognition, is an ego conscious
of itself; its self-consciousness means here: to be constantly conscious of its I-being as
center of its acts and its act-results and as possessor of its act-basis. The transcendental
I (naturally not as transcendentally phenomenologizing) enters into naive humanity
likewise as conscious of itself, but in "self-concealment" as wakeful human I.

Now, however, arises the problem of sleep. Conceived as transcendental ego in concrete self-constitution and world-constitution, I find myself, the Absolute, in all-inclusive self-temporalization, and therein I find myself in my human spatiotemporality and my psychic immanence as something which has behind it and ahead of it periods of sleep. To that, however, there also corresponds the transcendental mode, "period of sleep," and in monadization I as monad in a period of sleep and others as awake or asleep.

Appendix XV

[The genesis of phenomenological science and the development of the phenomenological community] (January 24, 1934)

Transcendental concrete subjectivity (the absolute universe of being) contains its own science within itself and by it its self-objectification as in truth existent for me as monadic ego and for the co-phenomenologizing others who make themselves known in me. But this too is to be noticed: the transcendentally explicated "I and we phenomenologists" is necessarily enworlded, namely, objectivated into the previously naively constituted world as "we phenomenologizing humans," standing in the historical course of mankind and using phenomenological science to search into the world and its mankind, its human-historical world, and the positive sciences there. Now, however, they will be able as phenomenologizing humans to have an effect upon their fellow men, training ever new fellow men into phenomenology, and then out of phenomenology laying down norms for human being as a whole (keeping constantly in mind the distant horizon of non-phenomenologists) and in accord with those norms endeavoring to train them in a new humanity.

In regard to the genesis of phenomenological science as explicit cognition of truth by the Absolute about itself, this distinction is to be made: 1) I at the start of the phenomenological reduction and then solitarily phenomenologizing, in "solipsistic" solitude, i.e., in which I still have no fellow phenomenologizer. To which the question: How far can this solipsistic phenomenology reach? 2) The progressive development of a phenomenological community by awakening non-phenomenologists into phenomonologists and putting into operation a successful activity in the Absolute, that is, constituted as successful. The activity of the respective already constituted "we phenomenologists," of a "conversion" of ever new co-subjects to performance of the phenomenological reduction and to transcendentally wakeful communalization as co-searching and living life as a whole accordingly. Thus the path to development of a living community of transcendentally awakened subjects widening out to infinity, or a research community as subjective source for an existing transcendental science that widens out *in infinitum* and is transcendentally constituted in infinitum. ʳ(With the question, how long can I phenomenologize as *solus ipse*, as the "only man," how long can I remain at it, I get to the question of the motivation for my passage into the phenomenological reduction and the whole of my phenomenologizing. How long can I *want* to remain at it? Motivating me further is that which motivated the breakthrough of science. Hence in the first place: *I wanted science, serious science, radically self-responsible science. But for what purpose did I want science? I was motivated to self-reflection by the course of my human life, our human life in which the one that is mine is interwoven, as a life on the whole unsatisfying or one that, from its normal, relative satisfaction, which is nonetheless uplifting to me and to us, falls into dissatisfaction, into hopelessness. I become reflectively aware of the fact that through all human existence [*Dasein*] there moves a striving for happiness, life is striving and all striving stands in the unity of a striving for satisfaction, human life however is we-life, and is a striving after self-satisfaction that, in a way which each has to understand in a sense appropriate to himself, is a striving of the we toward unity in a we-satisfaction, the correlate of which is a cultural world constantly in motion, in motion as to the way it already is and in motion with the horizon of future forms of continual self-satisfaction or correlatively of the creation of a new environing human world.

To the Main Text:

TRANSLATOR'S NOTES

and Supplementary Text-Critical Notes

a. Fink's use of the term "addenda" (*Zusätze*) here is indication that this Foreword was indeed written at the period of the entire revision work on the *Cartesian Meditations*. The carbon copy of Fink's revision texts carries the handwritten description "Addenda to Edmund Husserl's 'Méditations Cartésiennes'. Assistant Drafts from 1932" (*Ergänzungsband*, p. 305). This description reflects one of the ideas Husserl had for bringing out the whole work, namely, as a joint publication but with Fink's revisions given as supplements rather than as integrated into a single whole. See the entry in Cairns, *Conversations*, for November 9, 1931, pp. 37f.

b. This is the first of innumerable instances in the Sixth Meditation of a term relating to *gelten* used in its special Husserlian sense. See Translator's Introduction, pp. lxv–lxvi.

c. In Texts No. 5 and No. 8, referred to in note 4, in addition to an explanation of the steps of progression to be gone through in regressive phenomenology one finds a clear statement of the meaning of "*Habitualitäten*," (such as the all-important and foundational one mentioned here, that of "having the world") and their involvement in the "*aktuell strömendes Leben*" (*Ergänzungsband*, p. 222); see also Text No. 9, pp. 234–236.

d. " . . . in der vollen Konkretion seiner lebendigen Gegenwart." On the sense of "*lebendige Gegenwart*," see below, p. 56.

e. " . . . das aktuell stromende Erfahrungsleben." On the translation of *aktuell*, see Translator's Introduction, p. lxvi.

f. As indicated in note c above, Fink provides an explanation of this term in his revisions for the third of Husserl's Meditations. Husserl also, of course, explains the term in his own text, specifically in §32: " . . . with every *act* that emanates from [the centering I] and that has a new sense as an object, [this I] acquires a *new abiding property* . . . an abiding *habitus* . . . an habitual determination." (*Cartesian Meditations*, trans. Dorion Cairns, The Hague: Martinus Nijhoff, 1960, pp. 66–67.)

g. The procedure urged in this paragraph, i.e., that the initial stage of regressive phenomenology must be widened beyond the egological restriction, is precisely what

Fink works out in his revision texts for treating the topic of Meditation 5: Texts Nos. 13–17 in *Ergänzungsband*, pp. 242–275.

h. The sense of the term used here, *Personalunion,* is clearly seen in the explanation as given in *Brockhaus Wahrig Deutsches Wörterbuch,* ed. Gerhard Wahrig, Hildegard Krämer, Harald Zimmermann (Wiesbaden: Brockhaus, 1983), V. 5, under the entry *"Personalunion":* "Unification of two independent states under a monarchy with the preservation of the constitutional independence of both states." Fink quite plainly, then, means the term as a metaphor for the difference in unity of the radically distinct I's he discusses here and elsewhere in the text. See below, p. 60. In Fink's revision texts for the Second Cartesian Meditation Husserl indicates (without explanation) that he accepts the *"union"* part of this term, but not the *"Personal"* part (presumably in the sense given in *Brockhaus-Wahrig*) (*Ergänzungsband,* p. 219, note 368). For another discussion see also *Ergänzungsband,* pp. 83ff., a passage in chap. 2 of Fink's draft for the elaboration of the 1930 *Disposition.*

i. The word used here, *Geschichte,* means the current of historical happening itself and the phenomena that take place in it. *Historik* (theory of historical science) is the study or analytic of the conditions and character of the knowledge of *Geschichte,* i.e., the epistemology of the sciences that study *Geschichte*—at least this is what it means if Fink is discussing the term in the sense given it by Johann Gustav Droysen, as indeed he seems to be. (For a brief explanation of the meaning of *Historik* for Droysen, see Herbert Schnadelbach, *Philosophy in Germany, 1831–1933,* Cambridge University Press, 1984, pp. 52–53.) Fink uses the term *Historie* to indicate the actual account done of a particular *Geschichte.* Husserl seems to use *Historie* in much the same sense as Fink does. See below, Appendix X.

j. Husserl inserts a mark here to indicate the beginning of a new paragraph.

k. Husserl inserts a mark here to indicate the beginning of a new paragraph.

l. " . . . sich als Mensch . . . zu Grunde richtet." Normally *zu Grunde richten* means "to wreck or destroy"; but, as the very next phrase plainly shows, there is a play on words that depends upon taking it in a more literal fashion. Moreover, that this is a move to a fundamental *un-humanizing* of reflection is repeatedly underscored in Fink's personal notes, where the idea of radical phenomenological/philosophical reflection is "die Katastrophe der menschlichen Existenz" (Eugen-Fink-Archiv Z-XII 20c). Elsewhere Fink explicitly identifies the Hegelian derivation of this kind of usage (Eugen-Fink-Archiv Z-XVI III/2a-b).

m. The sense of "freeing" or "laying bare" in the term Fink uses here, *"freilegen,"* has to be interpreted within the special perspective of the treatment of the way the transcendental activity of constitution comes to thematic appearance in phenomenologizing reflection. See below, pp. 64–68.

n. Husserl inserts an asterisk here to specify the exact point of reference of the "Note" of Fink's that follows.

o. Or in paraphrase: "the unity of all final ways things are taken as holding for us in the constitutive construction of those ways": "die Einheit aller *Endgeltungen* im konstitutiven Geltungsaufbau."

p. " . . . und *terminiert im Endprodukt Welt."* This passage gives the explanation for the sense of a term used frequently in the Sixth Meditation: *Endkonstitution.* An earlier discussion also gives relevant explications, pp. 22–24. See also Appendix VIII below.

q. In the phrase here, "in die Welt 'eingestellte,' " "eingestellte" is to be taken as connoting the *consequences* of this enworlding action, in the sense that a station of *unquestioning acceptance of the world*—i.e., the *natural attitude*—is also generated. The expression, in other words, pairs with a similar one a few lines later (in fact it is in the same single lengthy German sentence, here made into two for the sake of more tolerable English), "natürlich-eingestellt," which in turn is directly related to the standard Husserlian expression "die Natürliche Einstellung"—the natural attitude. (Husserl in his alteration, however, changes the wording and thus removes the linguistic linkages.) Similar expressions occur earlier: "der natürlich-eingestellte Mensch"—"natural attitude man" (p. 32), and "natürlich eingestelltes Menschenich"—"the human I standing in the natural attitude" (p. 39). In fact, the expression "natürlich eingestellt" is Husserl's own, from *Ideas I:* Edmund Husserl, *Ideen zu einer reinen Phänomenologie und phänomenologischen Philosophie,* ed. Karl Schuhmann, Husserliana III/1 (Den Haag: Martinus Nijhoff, 1976), p. 59 (§28).

r. See above, §4 and §5

s. Presumably Fink means here the first stage within regressive phenomenology itself, i.e., the first stage of *egology.* The prominence of egology in the Cartesian Meditations is for Fink a sign of their preliminariness and incompleteness. A full development of regressive phenomenology would lead to an adequate treatment of transcendental intersubjectivity. See above, pp. 5–6 and the references there to texts in the *Ergänzungsband.*

t. Again, see above, §4.

u. See §5, pp. 39–41 and 48.

v. See §6, pp. 50–54.

w. Once again, two words for "history" are in use, with a distinction in the meaning presumably much like the one noted earlier (see above, note i). If this is so, then what Fink seems to be pointing out here is this. Whatever the case may be regarding the proper identification of a current of happening (*Geschichte*) on the transcendental level (thus *transzendentale "Geschichte"*), still the transcendental life that one is attempting to reach, and reach in its completeness (hence as including whatever measure of a transcendental "past" there might be for it), would always be reached as already engaged in constituting the world, and as having already constituted the world. But since accession to the transcendental would thus always take place from within some point in the course of the already constituted world's history (e.g., at the time when Husserl or Fink do their phenomenology), the transcendental that would thereby be reached would be reached as "situated" at that point in the narratable *account* of world history, i.e., as standing at that point in *Historie.*

x. See §6, p. 52.

y. The distinction between *Geschichte* and *Historie* proffered above (note i) is not clearly transferable to the two words used here, *Geschichtlichkeit* and *Historizität.* But given some measure of parallel, then the point seems clearly enough to be this: that any coherent identification or account of the historical character (*Historizität*) (both as a structure and as concrete content) of *transcendental* subjectivity will have to be in terms of the concrete historicality (*Geschichtlichkeit*) built up in and forming the life of some particular actual time and place, e.g., in the life of these two men, Edmund Husserl and Eugen Fink, within the intellectual, cultural, and social setting of Freiburg, Germany, in the fourth decade of the twentieth century. See the passage above on p. 58. Perhaps in the end the two terms are verbal variants of the same general concept more than anything else, as one sees for example in Husserl's own usage elsewhere (*Die Krisis der Europäischen Wissenschaften und die transzendentale Phänomenologie*, hrsg. Walter Biemel, Husserliana, Vol. VI, 2 Aufl., Den Haag: Martinus Nijhoff, 1962, pp. 320–323, 378; in English translation by David Carr, *The Crisis of European Sciences and Transcendental Phenomenology*, Evanston: Northwestern University Press, 1970, pp. 274–277, 369). On the occurrence of these terms in the latter of these passages (and presumably in the Crisis texts in general), Ludwig Landgrebe has remarked: "Husserl employs the expression 'Historizität' synonymously with 'Geschichtlichkeit' " ("Lebenswelt und Geschichtlichkeit des menschlichen Daseins," in *Phänomenologie und Marxismus*, Bd. 2: *Praktische Philosophie*, hrsg. Bernard Waldenfels, J. M. Broekman, und Ante Pazanin, Frankfurt: Suhrkamp, 1977, p. 17).

z. On the meaning of this term, see note h above.

aa. The apperceptions spoken of here as "transcending"—*transzendierenden*—are those that invest the apperceived (or perceived) X with the value of in-itself being, that is, with unqualifiedly transcendent being.

bb. Husserl inserts an asterisk here to specify the exact point of reference of Fink's following note.

cc. "In einer und derselben transzendentalen Seinsdignität der aktuellen Wirklichkeit." Here and in the following paragraph, we find in Fink's use of terms the clearest illustration of the need to take *aktuell* as something other than simply "actual." The condition of *Aktualität*, unlike *Wirklichkeit*, specifies (in Husserlian parlance) an actuality with the temporal character of the "now"—actuality in the *now*. (Another example is in Husserl's note 336.) See Translator's Introduction, p. lxvi.

dd. See above, pp. 52, 55, and 66.

ee. See above, §6, p. 52.

ff. "Endprodukte." Here as in many other places the *End-* must be taken in a sense that connotes *goal* as much as (if not more than) "*lastness.*" See above, note p.

gg. One would normally expect to find the term "*analogia proportionalis*" or "*proportionalitatis*," but Fink consistently uses the one given here. It is a unique usage that has nothing corresponding to it in the literature on the doctrine of analogy, nor does there seem to have been any such idiosyncratic usage in Freiburg Scholasticism in the early decades of this century. The only other place it occurs is in Fink's notes for a tutorial on Aristotle given in Freiburg in 1936 (Eugen-Fink-Archiv Z-XXI Ib and 18). It could, therefore, be simply a mistake on Fink's part, and the way it is handled in Z-XXI 18 suggests just that. But it is quite possible also that this is a deliberate modification. The basis for the point of the thus presumed modification is given on pp. 90ff. below, in the context of the whole problem of the possibility of a genuine *transcendental* articulation of meaning. For Fink any proposed analogy between the mundane and the transcendental meanings has to be expressed and stated exclusively in mundane language. A proportionality may hold between mundane situations spoken of effectively in mundane (i.e., natural) speech, but no such proportionality can hold at all between a mundane situation, as expressed in mundane language, and a transmundane (transcendental) condition. When, therefore, one attempts—again, of necessity in mundane language—to express and state any such supposed proportionality, the statement one ends up with is entirely within mundane language, although it *proposes* somehow to project a sense that is properly transcendental. This "proposal" character is presumably what Fink would be suggesting by the choice of the term *"propositionalis"*—i.e., in the manner of a *propositio*, something merely proposed rather than actually carried out. Here, of course, what is proposed is not *able* really to be carried out.

hh. " . . . ontifiziert die 'vor-seienden' Lebensvorgänge der transzendentalen Subjektivität."

ii. The meaning of *Wortlaut* depends upon Fink's earlier explanation of how, in being taken over by the action of the phenomenologizing onlooker, natural language words do not cease to *sound like* natural language words (see above, p. 87). If one takes them, then, to be no more than what they *sound like* (or, if one is reading, *look like*), one is utterly unable to understand their *transcendental* sense.

jj. " . . . mittels der ontisch-mundanen Kategorie des seienden Werdens (Prozess) . . ."

kk. Fink's term rendered here by "piece of philosophy" is not *Philosophie* but *Philosophem*, meaning *a* particular instance of or element in philosophy as such. In the present case, the *Philosophem* is that piece of philosophizing which is "phenomenologizing," i.e., the task of a phenomenology of phenomenology, but as concretely embodied in the normal form of human discourse. The same German term is also used in later passages (pp. 129–131, 153, 154). For a more explicit indication of the contrast between *Philosophie* and *Philosophem*, see Fink's "Entwurf zu einem Anfangsstück einer Einleitung in die Phänomenologie, in *Ergänzungsband*, p. 11–12. The expression is found several times in Hegel's *Einleitung in die Geschichte der Philosophie*, ed. Johannes Hofmeister (Hamburg: Felix Meiner, 1940), while an earlier use can be seen in Schelling's youthful essay "Über Mythen, historische Sagen und Philosopheme der ältesten Welt (1793)" (*Werke*, ed. Manfred Schröter, München: E. H. Beck & R. Oldenbourg, 1927, Bd. 1).

ll. The Greek word Fink adopts here, *peritrope*, simply means "reversal" or "turn about"; thus it is quite similar to some other words frequently used, *Umkehr*, *Umwendung*, and *Umschlag*, translated "reversal," "turning around," or "turning over" (or "shift"). However, in Fink's explication of transcendental phenomenology the word conveys more than a mere change of direction. Within the reduction, reversal of cognitive regard back upon transcendental cognitive processes does not simply disclose them in

some pregiven, preexistent nature, but rather casts them precisely into the kind of fea-
turing that allows cognitive scrutiny, viz., mundane-like objectness; they are, in other
words, constituted according to the same conditions of object-determinacy within
temporality that govern all reflection. An early mention of *peritrope* in Fink's notes occurs in his account (for himself) of a discussion with Husserl on July 10, 1929, on *time*.
The issue is how to understand critically the fact that any talk about time must itself
be *subject to* time. Thus "the fundamental phenomenon of *peritrope*: the retro-
application of the move of origination upon the origin" (Eugen-Fink-Archiv Z-I
150a), or "retro-referentiality" (Z-IV 61a). This, of course, is the key problem of the
"transcendental theory of method."

mm. The bracketed insertions here, by the translator, are an attempt to make the
reference of the indefinite pronouns clear. There is some grammatical ambiguity in
the German phrasing here.

nn. This rendering takes Fink's actual wording, "wahrend sie . . . ," as having to be
corrected to "wahrend es . . . " in order to be grammatically correct.

oo. An unfortunate error in the typesetting of the German text has put *Ein-
schränkung* instead of *Entschränkung*, the actual term in the original manuscript.

pp. "Nicht ist das Absolute eine Seinseinheit und Totalität seiender Momente,
sondern der Inbegriff von 'vor-seiendem' Werden des Seins (Konstitution) *und dem Sein*
(Welt)." On the meaning of *Inbegriff*, keep in mind Fink's explanatory use of the term
on p. 143, ending with the statement: "the *concept [Begriff] of the Absolute* is an all-embracing *inclusional concept [ein universaler In-Begriff]*." The sense of *Inbegriff* here should be
correlated with Fink's parallel phrasing on p. 145: "the phenomenological concept of
the Absolute as the inclusional unity [*Inbegriffseinheit*] of world and world-constitution."
Inbegriff usually means simply "sum" or "sum total" or "quintessence."

qq. Fink's original title for §10 was "Phänomenologisieren als Explizieren," but he
changed *Explizieren* to *Prädikation*. That change, however, was apparently not always carried out in the rest of the text, as, for example, here, where instead of "as an explicating
action" it should read "as predication," and instead of "self-explication," "self-predication."

rr. " . . . als Bezug zwischen dem Menschen und seinem *aussenweltlichen* Gegen-Stand;"

To the Appendices:

TRANSLATOR'S NOTES

and Supplementary Text-Critical Notes

a. In his manuscript Husserl makes explicit reference to a specific page in Fink's text, indicated above in note 121.

b. In his manuscript Husserl makes explicit reference to a specific page in Fink's text, indicated above in note 380.

c. The German term "die menschliche Seele" could equally well be rendered "the human psyche," just as *seelisch* can be rendered "psychic," even if *psychisch* is used just as frequently (and interchangeably) by Husserl.

d. In his manuscript Husserl makes explicit reference to a specific page in Fink's text, indicated above in note 381.

e. The passage to which this appendix probably pertains is indicated above in note 382.

f. In his manuscript Husserl makes explicit reference to specific pages in Fink's text, indicated above in note 394.

g. The reading of this word here is uncertain; it appears to be *kindlich,* which, if correct, suggests a meaning such as that given in the phrase added to the end of this sentence. In fact, on page 115, in the passage following the point to which this manuscript text is referred (see note f immediately above), Fink uses the expression "Weltkind," "child of the world," connoting a natural obliviousness to the transcendental status of appearances as appearances.

h. In his manuscript Husserl makes explicit reference to a specific page in Fink's text, indicated above in note 422.

i. In his manuscript Husserl makes explicit reference to the pages in Fink's text beginning at the point indicated in note 431 above.

j. In his manuscript Husserl makes explicit reference to specific pages in Fink's text, indicated above in note 464.

k. See note 404. Husserl explicitly refers this manuscript to the 6th Meditation, though without tying it to a specific passage.

l. See above, note i to p. 16.

m. *Kathekon* is the Stoic technical term for "duty"—*officium* in Latin, as in Cicero's *De officiis*.

n. See note 17 to p. 13. Husserl explicitly links this manuscript to Fink's 6th Meditation, though without referring it to a specific passage.

o. Reference to this appendix is made in note 276.

p. "Das Gelten als Erlebnis, das Geltende im Vollzug."

q. The term used here and elsewhere in these appended MSS of Husserl's—*die Seele*—must of course be taken not in any religious sense, but as "psyche," as that which is the psychic in man. Accordingly one can just as well translate it "psyche," as is done in other passages in Husserl's notes, for example, in note 31. See also the translator's comment above in note c. to p. 164.

r. The passage beginning here opens as a parenthesis, which Husserl does not bring to a close. In the German edition the text has been placed in the *Textkritische Anmerkungen zu den Beilagen*, p. 241. For all the aptness, poignancy, and irony we may see in it, given the personal and political situation of that darkening period, Husserl himself evidently found it unsatisfactory: from the point indicated by the asterisk on he lined it through. There is, however, something fitting about ending the book with a passage that is open-ended like this one.

INDEX

abnormality, political: 172

Absolute, the: becoming-for-itself, self-elucidation, 148–50; critique of, 177; the infinite, 146; mundane concept of, 141;
non-ontological concept of, 142; not a
being, liii; object of absolute science,
147–49; subject of absolute science,
149–150; phenomenological concept of,
lvi, 140–46; sleep and the A., 191; unity
of being and pre-being, 150; unity of constitution and world, 143–47

absolute science: 140–152; defined, 152

absolute spirit: lvii, 1

absolute subjectivity, ontologically
opaque: xci

acceptedness [*Geltung*]: lxv–lxvi; double
sense of, 185–86

aesthetic, transcendental: 11, 13, 26

affinity: 88, 90, 98, 141, 151–52;
affinity-relations, 96

Albrecht, Gustav: xvi, xix, lxxiii, lxxv, lxxvii,
lxxviii, lxxix, lxxxi, lxxxviii

analogia attributionis: 73

analogia entis: 73, 91, 96

analogia propositionalis: 73, 90

analogization: 68, 91, 93, 141; transcendental, 91, 127

analogy: lv, 73, 76, 81, 88–90, 125; between
transcendental and mundane self-cognition, 151; transcendental, 90–91, 145, 151

analytic, transcendental: 8, 11, 13, 26

anamnesis: 82–83

anonymity: 13, 14, 17, 24, 113, 117, 131,
190–91; of phenomenologizing action,
189

antecedency, constitutive: 48

antecedency, of being and of knowing: 47

antecedency to being: liv

anthropologism: 114

antinomies, cosmological: 64

antithesis in being: 69, 99, 106

apodicticity, transcendental: 151

apophansis, transcendental: 88–89, 93

appearance [*Erscheinung*] (of
phenomenologizing): 84, 87, 93, 99, 101,
105, 114–16, 127, 137, 154

appearance-subject: 149

appearance-truth(s): 110, 117–18, 120–21,
127, 134, 137–38, 149–50, 154

apperceptions, transcendental: 94–95;
thematic and unthematic, 183

beginning and end, transcendental: 11,
60, 63

being: absolute universe of, 191; as end-
constituted, 170; as end-product, 22, 72,
149; idea of, li, 72; and knowing, 71; moment of the Absolute, 144–46 *passim;* and
natural attitude, 107; question of, l; reduction of the idea of, liv–lv, lvii, 71, 73,
74–75, 91, 93; transcended, 75; transcendental b., two realms of, 21; true b. an infinite idea, 173; as world-inherent, xxxix

being-in-on-things, on-the-job [*Dabei-Sein*]:
50–54, 65

being-sense, world: 182, 185

Berger, Gaston: vii, xxi, xxxv, lxviii, lxxvii,
lxxxiii, lxxxiv

Bernau manuscripts on time: xiv, lviii, lxxxi

birth and death: xlii, 61–62

bracketing: 12

Bruno, Giordano: xci

caesura: 113

Cairns, Dorion: xliv, lxx, lxxii, lxxiii, lxxvi,
  lxxix, lxxx, lxxxiii, lxxxix, xcii
canon of phenomenological reason: 101,
  110, 118, 121
captivation by the world: lii, lxxxix, 42, 72
captivation in the natural attitude: 139
Cartesian Meditations: de-Cartesianized, 36–37;
  different versions, lxix–lxx; French translation, x, xii, xlvii–xlviii; Husserl's 1929 revision, x; as prolegomena, 4; second
  revision, xi–xiii, xxxvi
certainty in cognition: apodictic, 45–46,
  150; ideal of, 45–46
certainty of being, universal doxa: 187
Chiavari: xiv
childhood: 63
circularity: 39
cognition, a relationship of existents and
  interpreted as constitution of being: 71
coincidentia oppositorum: 143
commercium: 141
communication, transcendental: 100
community, transcendental: 100, 127
community of monads, a constituted stratum: 145
concreteness, transcendental: 42
construction: 7, 56, 63; non-givenness, 56;
  and the onlooker, 65; speculative, 47
constructive phenomenology: xlvii, 7, 11,
  13, 27, 54–66; as transcendental dialectic,
  11, 13, 64
co-philosophizing for others: 100
Copernican revolution: 4, 144
cosmogony: 10, 14, 142

death. *See* birth and death
de-restriction: 74, 142, 145
Descartes: 46
dialectic, transcendental: 11, 13, 26;
  in phenomenology and for Kant: 64
dialectical unity, of phenomenologizing subject: 116
Dilthey, Wilhelm: xii
divisiveness: 106
dogmatism: 93, 110, 111, 145
doxa, actual-moment: 184; universal, 187
doxic acts: 186
dualism in transcendental life: 20, 22

ego: concreteness of, an infinite Idea, 179; at
  first mute, 178; in first stage, 6; monadic,

167; reduction to concrete e., 168; as
  time-structured, 169; transcendental e.
  and human soul, 164–65
ego-centrality, Husserl's: xliii
egoism: 171
eidetic, transcendental: 78–84
eidetic method: 77
eidos: constitution of the transcendental e.,
  79–81
empathy: xliii, xlviii, 5, 54, 57, 123, 126,
  168, 177
end-constitutedness: 74, 124, 136
end-constitution: 128, 140
end-products, stratum of: 24
end-stratum: 136
enworlding: li, 21, 106–33 *passim*, 164; as a
  masking, 135; of monadic intersubjectivity, 107–08; non-proper, 99, 109, 116,
  126, 128, 129, 149; non-proper/sec-
  ondary, 99, 110; of phenomenologizing,
  99, 109; proper/primary, 99
Eon: 131
epipsychology: 18
epoche: 10, 20, 24, 36, 39–47 *passim*, 69,
  110, 163, 173, 178
epoche and reduction: 41, 48
equivocation in transcendental concepts,
  source of: 154–55
essence, seeing the: 83
essential structures, preknownness of: 181
Eugen-Fink-Archiv: lxvii, lxxxii
existence, two transcendental modes of: 135
existent: a constitutive result, 21–22;
  different levels, 80
existential criticism: 112–13
existential philosophies: 46
experience, natural attitude concept of:
  50–51; natural e. a transcendental
  mode, 81
exponent (explicator): 50, 58, 65

Feuling, Daniel: lxxx
Fichte: lviii, 156
finality: 22
finitude: 112
Fink: arrest in Louvain, return to Germany,
  xxxiii; assistantship with Husserl,
  xxiv–xxv; Cartesian Meditations revisions,
  xv–xvii, xxxvi–xlv, xlvi; collaboration with
  Husserl, viii, xxiii–xxviii; continuing
  Husserlian tradition, xxxiv; differences

with Husserl, xxxi–xxxii; dissertation, xxiv, lxxix; "Draft" for opening section of Husserl's "System," xiv, xxxvi, lxxxiv, 10n, 67n; fidelity to Husserl, xxiv–xxv, xxxix–xxxx; "Foreword" to Sixth Meditation, xviii; German military service, xxxiii–xxxiv; Habilitation, xx, xxxiv, lx, lxxv, lxxvi, lxxxiv; on his years with Husserl, xxvii; independence of mind, xxviii; *Kantstudien* article, xx, xxiii, lx, lxviii, lxxvi, lxxvii, lxxxiii, lxxxix; "Layout" for Husserl's "System," xiii, xxxi, xxxvi, xliv; in Louvain, viii, xxxiii; manuscript notes, xliv–xlv, lxxxii; "non-orthodoxy," xxiii; studies in Freiburg, xxiv; time-book, xxii

foreigners: 172

Formal and Transcendental Logic: xvii, xli, lxxi, lxxiii

Formale und Transzendentale Logik, x

functionary: 99, 103, 132

Galileo: 118, 174–75

Gary, M.: lii

genesis, constitutive: 74

givenness: 56; in construction, 65; reductive, 57, 59

government: 172

Greeks: 177

Grimme, Adolphe: xxiv

habituality, -ies: 6, 49, 54, 58, 68–69, 70, 85, 86, 104, 108, 121

habitus: 113

happiness: ideal of, as will to life, 173; striving for, 192

Hegel: lviii, lxxxvii, 77, 156

Heidegger: x–xiii, xix, xxiv, xxv, xxx–xxi, l, lxxv, lxxix, lxxxii, lxxxiv, lxxxvii, lxxxviii, lxxxix, xci, 46; *Rektoratsrede,* xix

historian: 190

historical knowledge: 173

historical science, theory of [*Historik*]: 15–16, 194

historicality: 60, 106, 131, 175

historicism: 16

historicity [*Historizität*]: 16, 60, 106, 129, 131, 177; intermonadic, 129

historiography: 16

history [*Geschichte*]: li, 16; of constitution, 131; of philosophy, transcendental interpretation of 155; philosophy of, 129; tran-

scendental, 54; transcendental-concrete, 129

history (historical study [*Historie*]): 175, 176, 190, 194; monadic, 63

Hitler: xviii

horizon: different concepts of, 186; external, 184; internal, 182, 184; of possibilities, 185; of real things, 181

horizonal consciousness: 182–83

humanity, constitution of: 106–07

humanization of nature and man: 169

Husserl; 70th birthday, x; 1928 publication of MSS on time, xxx; Cartesian Meditations, *see* Cartesian Meditations; in Chiavari, xiii–xiv; concern for Nachlass, xvii, xxii; Crisis texts, xxxiii, xl, xlii, li; depression, xviii; *Encyclopaedia Britannica* article, xxxi; Fink's *Kantstudien* article, xx, xxiii; *Ideas,* xli; illness, xiv, xv; Jewish origin, xix, lxxv; Paris lectures, x; "System" of 1930, xiii, xiv, xvi, xxi, xxxvi, 8; testimony on Fink, xiv, xxxv, lxxvi, lxxxi

Husserl, Gerhart: xxxiv, lxxv, lxxxiv

Husserl, Malvine: xv, lxxx

Husserl Archives at Freiburg: xxxv

Husserl Archives at Louvain: vii–viii, lxvii, lxviii, lxix, lxx

hyletic fields: 50

I: three I's, 42; reflecting and reflected upon, 178–81; wakeful, 190–91

I, phenomenologizing: anonymous strata of, 164; being-for-itself, 13; difference from constituting I, 52, 79–80, 116; as third I, 180; unity with constituting I, 80

I-pole: 169, 187

idealism: basic forms of, 155; constitutive, 159; German, 77; mundane, 154, 155; not philosophy of immanence, 158; transcendental, 152–59

Ideas, Husserl's: lii, liv, 43, 44

ideation: 77–84 *passim*

identity/difference between transcendental and human subjectivity: xlii–xliii, xlix, l

identity in difference: 23–24, 53

identity of phenomenologizing and constituting I's: 70

immanence: lliv, 43–44, 151; absolutizing of, 44; freed from human apperceptions, 69; and transcendence together, xli, 47; human, 21, 40, 43–44, 46, 47, 61

immanent being, thematized: 22–23
immortality: 64
individuals: 125
individuation: lviii, 1, 125, 148; and the Absolute, 145
infinity, kinds of: 146
Ingarden, Roman: xi, xv, lxxi, lxxiii, lxxiv,
lxxviii, lxxx, lxxxvi
intellectus archetypus: 77
intellectus ectypus: 77
internationality: 171
intersubjectivity: xiv, xliii, xlv; xlviii, liv,
lviii, 5, 6, 10; monadic, lxxxvii–lxxxviii,
57, 144, 148; pseudo-mundane, 122; transcendental, 124–25, 165
intuition: lviii, 26; intellectual, 77, 152
iterability of reflection: 17–18

Jahrbuch, Husserl's, x, xv

Kant: xlvi, liii, lviii, lxxxvii, lxxxix, xc, 64
kathekon: 177
Kaufmann, Felix: xxi, xli, lxxvii, lxxxi, lxxxvi

Landgrebe, Ludwig: xxii, xxiv, lxxix
language: lvii, 69, 84–100 *passim*, 132; and
the epoche, 86; habituality of, 86; home
in the natural attitude, 85; inadequacy of
transcendental l., 89; medium of objectivity for knowledge, 103–04; natural l. and
the transcendental, 94–96, 98; outward
expressional form, 84, 86–87; protest, rebellion in, 89; transcendental indicator,
305–06; transcendental necessity of, 99;
transformation of, 86, 88, 93
life, transcendental. *See* transcendental life
life-goals: 173
life-philosophy: xii
life-world: xl, 104, 166; of the natural attitude, 165
living present: 6, 49, 52, 57; flowing live
present, xiv
localization: 99, 101, 117, 122, 126, 127,
134, 135, 137, 166, 167
logic: 16, 69, 77; transcendental, 70, 146, 180

Mahnke, Dietrich: xlvii–xlviii, l, lxxv, lxxvi,
lxxx, lxxxvii
man: essence of, 174; objectivation of the
transcendental, 116; ontic condition for
science, 102–03; a result of constitution,
107; subject of phenomenologizing, 105,

114–16; transcendentally constituted,
xlii–xliii
mankind, historical: 177
mathematics: 31
memories: 168–69
memory: 49
meontic: xlix, l, lv–lvii, lviii, xci, 2
Merleau-Ponty, Maurice: vii, xxi, lxxviii,
lxxxiii, lxxxix–xc
metaphors: 90
metaphysics: xvi, l, lviii, lxxxviii
method, ambiguity of the concept of: 25–26
Misch, Georg: x, xii, lxxi, lxxii
monad(s): xlviii, 7, 10, 11; become psycho-
physical, 165; enworlding of, 107–08,
109; localization of m. in the world, 166;
phenomenologizing m., 168; transcendental community of, 57, 125, 145
motivation: historical, 176; for the reduction, 30–39
mundane, equivocal concept of: 150

naiveté: 2, 5, 72, 132; methodological, 96;
phenomenological, 72
natural attitude: xli, lii, lxxxix, 4, 166; annulment of, 32, 136; as human being, lii; a
transcendental attitude, 165; a transcendental mode, 14; a transcendental situation, 74, 138; as transcendentally
interpreted, 136
natural stationing, being-placed-in: 47, 123
Nietzsche: lxxxvii
non-givenness: 38, 56, 64, 65
normalcy: 177; political, 171–72
nothingness: 30, 71, 94
now, "nowness": 49, 52, 196

object-being: 151
objectivation into science: 102–05
objectiveness of the transcendental
object: 71
objectivity, intersubjective: 105, 121, 124,
125, 126
onlooker: xxxviii, xlvii, 5, 10, 12, 13,
20, 21, 23, 26, 39, 42, 50, 52, 54, 58, 60,
65, 68, 71, 79, 84, 90, 94, 95–96, 98, 106,
108, 113, 149, 168; differentness of, 58,
69; exponent, 40; and language, 86; mundanization of, 163; non-participant, 14,
20, 163; non-participation, 58; phenomenologizing I, 11; as projected out, 80; reason and logic of, 70

onta, constitution of: 166
ontification: lv, 76, 84
ontology: error of, 173; mundane, 109, 168; of nature, 78
origin, dimension of: 4
Other, the: 176; phenomenologizing, 54, 125–26
other I's in co-existence: 169
others, transcendental: 164–65
ousia: 141
outside-of-the-world-ness: 43

paralogisms: 64
pedagogy: 100
peritrope: 113
personal union: 11, 60, 194
phenomenologizing: appearance of, 109; different from constituting, 22–23; as intersubjective, 105–06; intersubjective science, 121; made mundane, 113–14; movement of the Absolute, 150; mundane appearance of, 133–34; not a human possibility, 120; not human, 113; not idealism, not realism, 152; potentiality for, 118; subject of, lvi, 110, 116–17
phenomenology: beginning of, 30, 68; existential function of, 129–30; genetic, 49, 58; regressive, 5, 6, 11, 28, 59, 62, 65; self-conditionality of, 36; solipsistic, 191; static and genetic, 6; theme of, 60; ways into, *see* ways into phenomenology
phenomenology of phenomenology: xlvi, li, 1, 2, 8, 28, 66, 197
Philosophem: 129–31, 153, 154, 197
pre-being: liv, lviii, 74, 76, 80, 83, 86, 90, 125, 149, 150
predication: 1, 84; conflict in transcendental p., 98
pre-existent, the: liv–lviii *passim*, xci, 80, 86, 91, 96, 136, 143, 145, 147, 159
pregiven(ness): 13, 179; horizonal consciousness, 178; for knowing, 37–38, 52, 81–82, 120, 181; of a possibility, 68, 105; transcendental, 38, 55, 58, 73, 94, 190; of the world, xxxvii, xl, liii–lv, 14, 38, 39–40, 48, 83, 94, 108, 163, 177, 178, 181, 187
presence: lviii, 56
present: 52, 58
presentification [*Vergegenwärtigung*]: 18, 49
presentness: 5, 49, 56, 58
presuppositionlessness: 46

productivity: 51; eidetic, 82–83; transcendental, 75–77, 80, 83
proposition, phenomenological: 146
protest: lvii, lviii, xci; in language, 89
psychologization: 188–89
psychology: 17, 34, 63; basic error of, 168; intentional, double thematic of, 180; and transcendental reversal, 164
pure consciousness: 46

race, Nuremberg Laws on: xix
radicality: of phenomenological epoche, 41; in questioning, 37; of reflection, 32
reason: mundane and reduced, 69; scientific r., intrusion into mankind, 172; transcendental, 69, 70
rebellion, in language: 89
receptivity: 51
recollection, critique of: 49–50
reduction: xlvii, l, 10; double action of, xxxix; egological, 5, 139; of the idea of being, liv–lv, lvii, 71, 73, 74–75; of the idea of evidentness, 151; of the Idea of science, 139–40; intersubjective, 5, 9, 28, 139; phenomenological, 4, 10, 12, 27, 29–48, 74, 93, 114; split caused by, 12
reflection and iteration: 18, 179–80
regress, infinite: 17, 26
regression: 7
regressive analysis: 27
regressive inquiry, retro-inquiry [*Rückfrage*]: 4, 6, 78, 113, 124, 136, 144
regressive move: 21, 148
res extensa: 167
residuum: 43–44
Rickert, Heinrich: 158

Schutz, Alfred: xxi; Fink's explanation of world, xli, lxxiv, lxxxv
science: absolute, 140–41, 147–51, 152; in Europe, 175; as human possibility, 102–05; idea of, as initiating reflection, 31; intersubjective habituality, 102; an institutional habituality, 121; modern s. and infinity horizon, 105; motivation for, 192; mundane, 133; positive, 173; potentiality for, 118–20; reduction of, 139, 140; scientific critique of experience, 30
science, concept of phenomenological: 147–52; absolute science, 140–52; defined, 152; as self-knowledge of the Absolute, 191

self-apperceptions: xlii, lv, 5, 31, 33, 47
self-preservation, instinct for: 173
self-reference in phenomenology: 13–19
    passim
self-reflection: 12, 31; human self-reflection,
    13; in the reduction, 32
self-temporalization: 63, 189
Seventh Cartesian Meditation: xvi
Should, the absolute: 177
situation: 99, 109–10; of end-constituted-
    ness, 74, 136, 140; mundane s. of outward
    manifestation, 136; of phenomenological
    analysis, 50, 55; transcendental, 58, 59,
    60, 74, 117, 136, 138
Sixth Meditation: and Fink's revisions of
    Cartesian Meditations, viii–ix; as Fink's
    work, xxxiii; Habilitation 1945, xxxiv; as
    1933 Habilitationsschrift, xx, lxxv;
    Husserl's readings of, xviii; at Louvain,
    vii–viii
sleep: 110, 135, 191
sociality: li
Société Française de Philosophie: x
solipsism: 122, 191
solitude: xx, 99, 122, 191
soul(s): as unfinished, 189; worldly content
    of, 168
speaker, proper: 85
stateless peoples: 172
Strasbourg: x
Strasser, Stephan: vii, xxxv, lxix
subject, full-sided: lvi; localization of psy-
    chic s., 167. *See also* phenomenologizing,
    subject of
subject-object correlation: 151, 158
sublation: 118, 134, 150
synthetic unity of antitheses: 134
system, Husserl's: as architectonic, 8; open-
    ness of, 7

teleology: lxxxviii, 174; being-tendency, l,
    21, 108; of science, 31
temporality: xviii, 52–53; analysis of, xlii; for
    science, 104; coincidence of human and
    transcendental t., 61
temporalization: 61, 131; being of, xlix, 2
texts and philosophy: xxix–xxx
thematic and unthematic: 82
theorizing, problem of beginning: 68
theory of elements: lxxxix, 11, 12, 14, 20,
    22, 25, 26, 148, 152; outlined, 13, 27

time, modalities of: 169
to on, radical alteration of: 173
tradition: 104, 172; unity of, 177
Tran-Duc-Thao: xxi
transcendental, the: non-givenness of, 38;
    not-existent, 76; psychologized, 168;
    self-objectification of, 32; substantial-
    izing of, 97
transcendental: t. attitude, appearance in
    the world, 110; t. being, 71–75; t. being,
    two realms of, 21; t. communication,
    100; t. community, 100, 127; concept
    equivocal, 150; t. concreteness, 42; t.
    concrete subjectivity, 191; t. definitions,
    92–93; t. dialectic, 11, 13, 26, 64; t. his-
    tory, 58 (*see* history); t. I as wakeful,
    190–91; t. idealism, 152–59 (*see* idealism);
    t. interpretation, 117; t. intersubjectivity,
    124–25, 165; t. knowing, 140; lack of
    language, 95, 98; t. localization, 99; t.
    logic, 70, 146, 180; t. meanings non-
    ontic, 90; t. origins forgettable, 116; t.
    others, 164–65; t. past, 49, 58; t. pre-
    knowing, 114; t. reason, 69, 70; t. re-
    flection, xlvii, 14; t. science, 8; t. self-
    criticism, xlv; t. sentence, 92; t. surface:
    128; t. un-captivation, 42; t. we en-
    worlded in history, 191
transcendental life: reductive givenness of, 5;
    self-dividing of, 24, 110; self-objectivation
    of, 148
transcendental subjectivity: as if existent, 74;
    becoming-for-itself, 80; being-in-itself,
    135, 147, 148; being-for-itself, 14, 113,
    135, 148; being-outside-itself, 113, 135,
    136; coming-to-itself, 135; infinite reflec-
    tivity of, 188; as new field, 42; non-
    worldly, xxxix–lx; not pregiven, 38;
    self-constitution into humanity, 106–07;
    and world-constitution, 58
transparency: 41, 48, 50, 89, 115, 117, 121,
    131, 134, 149, 155
truth(s): contradiction in, 117; for everyone,
    154; mundane and transcendental, 117;
    seeming, 101, 134; transcendental, 101,
    110, 117–18, 140; transcendental t., sys-
    tem of, 140; transcendental t. and appear-
    ance-truth, *see* appearance-truths
type(s): 11, 81, 82, 177, 181, 184–85
typical generality: 184
typicality: 177, 184–85; of totality, 184–85

un-humanization: 40, 76, 109, 120
unity in antithesis: lvi

Van Breda, Herman Leo: xxxiii, lxix, lxxiii, lxxviii, lxxxiii
Van Kerckhoven, Guy: lxviii, lxxiv, lxxvii, lxxxv, lxxxvii

wakefulness: 135, 190
waking life: 187
ways into phenomenology: 33; from logic, 34; from psychology, 34
wholeness: xlii, xliii, 46; egological, 63; structures of, 61, 64
world: xiv; as basis for all questions, 35; child of the w., 115, 199; as constituted, 163; as transcendentally constituted, 167; de-absolutizing of, 144; end-product of constitution, lvi, 22, 23, 45, 99, 138, 142; end-stratum of constitution, 144; existent w. an abstract stratum, 141; horizon of being, liii; infinite w., discovery of, 172; as infinite Idea, 175; in itself, 157; monadic

w. and natural w., 180; natural environing w., 82, 171; as nature, a construct, 189; pregivenness of, *see* pregivenness; a relative totality, 144; a relative universe, 141; riddle of, 173; structure of knownness and unknownness, 183; sum-total of ends in constitution, 142; totality of existents, 78, 128–29, 139, 143–44; transcendentally integrated, xxxviii; unity of immanence and transcendence, 158; universal unity of acceptedness, 157
world-belief: 10; and epoche, 41–42, transcendental fact, xxxviii
world-constituting life: 59, 65, 66, 69, 113, 179
world-constitution: lv, lvi, 4; beginning and end, 11; is unitary, 167; as on-going, 58, 62, 107, 108; proper theme of philosophy, 10, 72, 109
world-history: 129
world-horizon: 38, 181
world-time: 61, 128